Daniel Dorchester

The problem of religious progress

Daniel Dorchester

The problem of religious progress

ISBN/EAN: 9783337718978

Printed in Europe, USA, Canada, Australia, Japan

Cover: Foto ©Lupo / pixelio.de

More available books at **www.hansebooks.com**

OF

RELIGIOUS PROGRESS.

BY

DANIEL DORCHESTER, D.D.

———— ··◆·· ————

NEW YORK:
PHILLIPS & HUNT.
CINCINNATI:
WALDEN & STOWE.
1881.

CONTENTS.

—

CHAPTER III.

PHASES OF PROGRESS.

CHAPTER IV.

DELIVERANCE.

II. MORALS.

CHAPTER I.

TYPICAL PERIODS.

CHAPTER II.

THE PRESENT PERIOD.

CHAPTER III.

THE PRESENT PERIOD, (CONTINUED.)

III. SPIRITUAL VITALITY.

CHAPTER I.

TYPICAL PERIODS.

CHAPTER II.

THE NEW SPIRITUAL ERA.

IV. STATISTICAL EXHIBITS.

CHAPTER I.

STATISTICAL SCIENCE.

CHAPTER II.

RELIGIOUS PROGRESS AND STATUS.

PROTESTANTISM AND ROMANISM.

CHAPTER III.

RELIGIOUS PROGRESS AND STATUS IN THE UNITED STATES.

CHAPTER IV.

FOREIGN MISSIONS.

CHAPTER V.

THE WORLD-WIDE VIEW.

APPENDIX.

ECCLESIASTICAL STATISTICS.

THE UNITED STATES.

DIAGRAMS.

PROLOGUE.

PROLOGUE.

THE outward rite, the old abuse,
  The pious fraud transparent grown,
The good held captive in the use
      Of wrong alone—
These wait their doom, from that great law
  Which makes the past time serve to-day;
And fresher life the world shall draw
      From their decay.

O backward-looking son of time!
  The new is old, the old is new;
The cycle of a change sublime
      Still sweeping through.
So wisely taught the Indian seer;
  Destroying Seva, forming Brahm,
Who wake by turn Earth's love and fear,
      Are one, the same.

Idly as thou, in that old day
  Thou mournest, did thy sire repine;
So, in his time, thy child grown gray
      Shall sigh for thine.
But life shall on and upward go;
  The eternal step of Progress beats
To that great anthem, calm and slow,
      Which God repeats.

Take heart! The waster builds again.
  A charmed life old Goodness hath;
The tares may perish, but the grain
      Is not for death.
God works in all things; all obey
  His first propulsion from the night;
Wake thou and watch! the world is gray
      With morning light.

I, TOO, am weak, and faith is small,
And blindness happeneth unto all.

Yet, sometimes glimpses on my sight,
Through present wrong, the eternal right;
And, step by step, since time began,
I see the steady gain of man;

That all of good the past hath had
Remains to make our own time glad,—
Our common daily life divine,
And every land a Palestine! . . .

O friend! we need not rock nor sand,
Nor storied stream of Morning-Land;
The heavens are glassed in Merrimack,—
What more could Jordan render back?

We lack but open eye and ear
To find the Orient's marvels here;—
The still small voice in autumn's hush,
Yon maple wood the burning bush.

For still the new transcends the old,
In signs and tokens manifold;—
Slaves rise up men; the olive waves,
With roots deep set in battle graves!

Through the harsh noises of our day
A low, sweet prelude finds its way;
Through clouds of doubt and creeds of fear,
A light is breaking, calm and clear.

That song of Love, now low and far,
Ere long shall swell from star to star!
That light, the breaking day, which tips
The golden-spired Apocalypse! . . .

Flow on, sweet river, like the stream
Of John's Apocalyptic dream!
This maple ridge shall Horeb be,
Yon green-banked lake our Galilee!

Henceforth my heart shall sigh no more
For olden time and holier shore;
God's love and blessing, then and there,
Are now and here and every-where.—WHITTIER.

THE QUESTION OPENED.

THE

PROBLEM OF RELIGIOUS PROGRESS.

THE QUESTION OPENED.

APOSTLES of complaint and despondency
stand even in the pathway of progress. With
lugubrious faces turned toward the past, they mut-
ter dark predictions of approaching disaster. Not
a new phenomenon, these seers constitute an uninterrupted succession, under changing forms and
names. Pessimism, the latest designation of this
spirit, atheistic in origin, but broader in taint, has
intensely pervaded the atmosphere of our times.
We have had not only the pessimism of skeptics,
but also of Roman Catholics, of Ritualists, of
Premillennialists, and of disaffected and desponding
Evangelicals.

Criticism is the exhaustless heritage of Christianity. It has come both from within and without.
Especially has Protestantism been subjected to critical ordeals. "The Decline of Protestantism, and
its Causes," was the topic of an address to the citizens of New York, by Archbishop Hughes, about

thirty years ago, in which he asserted that "Protestantism had lost all central force and power over the masses of mankind." His uninspired auguries were caught up and echoed in High-Church circles; and in 1868 a bold volume—"Protestantism a Failure"—appeared, from the pen of Rev. F. C. Ewer, D. D., a very estimable and eminent ritualistic clergyman of the Protestant Episcopal Church. Three years later, a writer in the "Catholic World," in a somewhat elaborate article on the "Statistics of Protestantism in the United States," with an undiscriminating and unpardonable carelessness, drew a comparison between two abnormal periods—the one, of unnatural growth, under the Second Advent excitement, and the other, of declension, at the close of the civil war—and from this defective basis, evincing a meager growth, made a suppositious demonstration of the probable number of Protestant communicants in the year 1900; and triumphantly inferred that Protestantism is hopelessly falling, and must inevitably fall, behind the progress of the population. It is a fact, not to be omitted in this connection, that the 10,844,576 Protestant communicants, in the year 1900, according to the conjectural calculations of this Roman Catholic writer, are not much in excess, as will be shown in our future pages, of the present number; and twenty years yet remain before the close of the century.

Father Thomas S. Preston, an ex-Protestant, now

high in the counsels of Rome, as Vicar-General in the Diocese of New York, has lately renewed the charge, that Protestantism is a failure; and so says Père Hyacinthe, in a recent lecture on Deism, in Paris, declaring that "neither Deism nor Protestantism can be generally and permanently accepted by the French people," and that "a reformed Catholicism"—confessedly a hitherto unknown *ism*, and too uncertain a basis for theorizing—"is the only solution."

Besides Romanists and High-Churchmen, skeptical thinkers of various grades have represented Protestantism as having seen its best days, and as now rapidly losing its hold upon the world. Mr. Buckle, in his "History of Civilization," reiterated this view; and it has since been echoed in coarser and more vulgar forms. The advocacy of Protestantism has been represented as faint and apologetic—an indication of a loss of heart and internal demoralization. It is said that the scholars and thinkers are arrayed against its peculiar tenets; that they are rapidly extracting from it the best part of its social ethics, and gradually reducing it to the lowest terms—a kind of philosophic deism; that only Roman Catholics and a few "seared and shriveled relics of Protestantism" now attend church; and that, henceforth, the Bible, as an authoritative revelation, is to be discarded and laid upon the back shelf, as "a queer relic of an ancient faith,"

2

while the world moves on under the widening influence of modern ideas.

In an elaborate address, in 1868, Rev. William J. Potter,* of New Bedford, claimed to demonstrate that the Protestant sects in the United States are gaining very little, only five per cent., in ten years, (1850–1860,) upon the population.

In 1872 Rev. Henry W. Bellows, D.D.,† discoursed very eloquently upon the "Break between Modern Thought and Ancient Faith and Worship." Speaking of "the Church and its creed, on the one side, and the world and its practical faith on the other," he said: "An antagonism has arisen between them as of oil and water;" that "there are some millions of people in this country, not the least intelligent or useful citizens in all cases, who never enter a church door;" that "Church religion and general culture do not play any longer into each other's hands;" that "the professors in college, the physicians, the teachers, the scientists, the reformers, the politicians, the newspaper men, the reviewers, the authors, are seldom professing Christians, or even church-goers; and, if they do go to church, from motives of interest or example, they are free enough to confess, in private, that they do

* See First Annual Report of the Free Religious Association, Boston, 1868, p. 56.

† "Christianity and Modern Thought." American Unitarian Association.

not much believe what they hear." Dr. Bellows, nevertheless, expresses hope for the future of Christianity.

But a later and more serious complaint has come from Rev. Dr. Ewer, who, after a lapse of ten years, has recently renewed his bold indictment against Protestantism in several discourses* delivered in Newark, N. J., " at the request of leading Episcopal laymen in that city." He says that Protestantism is only " a miserable raft, its fragments floating apart like the flying rack of the heavens;" that " the poor remnants only of the great nations are clinging to its parted and broken logs, and earnest, thinking men are at their wits' end to know what is truth." He stoutly claims that " the solemn indictment against Protestantism, drawn up " by himself, in 1868, " in the fear of God, and in behalf of dying souls, and uttered in Christ's Church, Murray Hill, New York, was not met by argument, but only by a gale of holy malediction and impotent scorn;" that the volume passed through several editions, but has never been answered, and cannot be answered.

Dr. Ewer says: " To say nothing of the specifications in those eight discourses, what were two of the main counts in the indictment? First, that whereas, 250 years ago, the Protestant religious dogmas held captive to themselves great thoughtful peoples

* " Complete Preacher," June and July, 1878.

of the Germanic, the Swiss, and the Anglo-Saxon man, those dogmas had failed to retain the hold they once had, and have, to an overwhelming extent, lost at last the intellect of those peoples ; and that, while 250 years ago Protestantism held the masses as well as the intellect of those peoples, it has failed to hold and has lost those masses as well as the intellect ; that Protestantism, as a form of Christianity, stands to-day breast-deep in torrents of skepticism which itself hath let loose, which are deepening around it, and in which it is drowning; and that it stands there to-day aghast and incompetent. This was one count in the indictment. Gentlemen, you have seen that it has not been denied. A second count was that the fundamental religious premises of Protestantism were essentially anti-Christian, and must end, by inexorable logic, in infidel conclusions ; that if Calvin's and Luther's and Zwingli's premises were to be accepted, then Channing's conclusions were nearer right by logic than Cromwell's, and Theodore Parker's nearer right than Channing's, and Frothingham's and Adler's the rightest of all, and quite unanswerable by a Protestant ; that when the Calvinists burned Servetus at the stake they burned Calvin's own brainchild. It was claimed that if this logical aspect of Protestantism was correct, it ought to have shown itself finally in practical historical results. And the charge was made that what thus ought to have followed logically, had actually followed historically, and was patent to all in the comparatively empty churches and the wide-spread skepticism of thoughtful Germany, America, and Switzerland. This was another count." *

Dr. Ewer also calls "the Protestant movement" "a wide-spread destruction;" not an improver, but a deteriorater † of morals; "not a reformation, but a deformation, and a hideous destruction."

A writer in the "Atlantic Monthly," (October, 1878,) joins in this arraignment of the Churches. He says: "The disintegration of religion has proceeded rapidly. . . . The Church is now, for the most part, a depository of social rather than religious influences. Its chief force is no longer religious. There are still, of course, many religious people in the Churches who sincerely believe the old doctrines embodied in all the creeds. But these are every-where a small minority, and they are mournfully conscious that the old religious life and power have departed from the Church. . . . They are alarmed to find the atmosphere and tone of the Church becoming more and more secular and business-like. These people, who thus represent the better elements of a former state of things, are the real strength of the evangelical Protestant Churches, so far as religion is concerned, and their

---

* "Complete Preacher," June, 1878, p. 145.

† "Complete Preacher," July, 1878, pp. 223, 224.

character is one of the most wholesome and truly conservative forces of our national life. . . . But they are too few to regencrate the American Church, though their influence is highly valuable in resisting some of the evil tendencies of the age. Most of them are old, and they have few successors among the younger people. They have already done most of their work, and their number and strength diminish from year to year."

" The morality based upon the religion popularly professed has, to a fatal extent, broken down. Multitudes of men who are religious are not honest or trustworthy. They declare themselves fit for heaven, but they will not tell the truth, or deal justly with their neighbors. The money of widows and orphans placed under their control is not safer than in the hands of highwaymen. There is no article of food, medicine, or traffic, which can be profitably adulterated or injuriously manipulated, that is not, in most of the great centers of trade, thus corrupted and sold by prominent members of Christian Churches."

One of the latest of these gloomy utterances is that of Professor Goldwin Smith, who, in a thoughtful article, in the "Atlantic Monthly," for November, 1879, discoursed upon "The Prospect of a Moral Interregnum," consequent upon the supposed decadence of religious faith. He says:

" A collapse of religious belief, of the most complete and tremendous kind, is apparently now at hand. At the time of the Reformation the question was, after all, only about the form of Christianity; and even the skeptics of the last century, while they rejected Christ, remained firm theists; not only so, but they mechanically retained the main principles of Christian morality, as we see plainly in Rousseau's 'Vicaire,' 'Savoyard,' and Voltaire's 'Letters on the Quakers.' Very different is the crisis at which we have now arrived. No one who has watched the progress of discussion, and the indications of opinion in literature and in social intercourse, can doubt that, in the minds of those whose views are likely to become—and in an age when all thought is rapidly popularized sure to become— the views of society at large, belief in Christianity as a revealed and supernatural religion has given way. . . .

"All English literature, even that which is socially and politically most conservative, teems with evidences of a change of sentiment, the rapid strides of which astonish those who revisit England at short intervals. . . . There is perhaps an increase of church-building and church-going, but the crust of outward piety is hollow, and growing hollower every day."

From such assumed premises Mr. Smith proceeds to prognosticate the disastrous "effects of this revolution on morality."

Mr. James Anthony Froude, in the "North American Review," December, 1879, treats Protestantism as an exhausted factor: "Protestantism has failed. It is a hard saying. Protestantism, when it began, was a revolt against lies. It was a fierce declaration that men would no longer pretend to believe what in their hearts they did not and could not believe. In this sense Protestantism has not failed, and can never fail, as long as there is left an honest man upon the globe. But we cannot live upon negations; but we must have convictions of a positive sort, if our voyage through earthly existence is to be an honorable and successful one. And no Protestant community has ever succeeded in laying down a chart of human life with any definite sailing directions. In every corner of the world there is the same phenomenon of the decay of established religions. In Catholic countries as well as Protestant; nay, among Mohammedans, Jews, Buddhists, Brahmans, traditionary creeds are losing their hold. An intellectual revolution is sweeping over the world, breaking down established opinions, dissolving foundations on which historical faiths have been built up. Science, history, philosophy have contrived to create universal uncertainty." Nevertheless, he adds, "Christianity retains a powerful hold, especially over the Anglo-Saxon race."

Such are some of the allegations against Protestantism and the times.

THE PROBLEM.

THE PROBLEM.

IT is an important preliminary inquiry, What is comprised under the term Protestantism? and what does Protestantism claim?

In the foregoing arraignment we find two complex and widely divergent parties—on the one hand, Romanists and men of Romanizing tendencies; and on the other thinkers, who stand avowedly outside of Christianity, and those who, under the more indefinite name of "Liberal Christianity," maintain an attitude of criticism toward the generally accepted Protestant theology. And yet the latter portion of both of these classes are connected with denominations, which, in the broad sense of the term, are Protestant. In the course of modern progress, the term Protestant has undergone some modification in its common use, although it still stands, historically, as the name given to all bodies of Christians which have sprung up out of the Reformation—"the totality of the Churches which separated from the Romish communion." It also embraces those secondary protests against original Protestantism, such as Quakerism—a protest against its ordinances; Arminianism—a protest against its Calvinism; Methodism—a protest against its Cal-

vinism and its formalism; and " Liberal Christian
ity "—a protest against its Trinitarian and sacrificial
theology.   But these are only the subordinate divisions of the great Protestant body, now, as ever,
maintaining an unfaltering protest against the hierarchical prerogatives and exclusive functions of Romanism, which constituted the leading issues of the
Reformation.

In its broadest definition, then, and as the term
is used by Dr. Ewer and the Romanists, Protestantism embraces all avowedly Christian bodies outside of the Roman Catholic Church.   Jews and
Mormons, professedly rejecting Christianity, are excluded; and Universalists, Unitarians, Christians,
etc., are included.   The tendencies of modern religious thought, regarded by Dr. Ewer and others
as so baleful, and as logically and historically the
outgrowth of Protestantism, necessitates such an
inclusion of the " Liberal" Churches.   We accept
this definition, and shall adhere to it, so far as possible, in this volume ; but a narrower definition will
sometimes be necessary, restricting the term Protestantism to those Churches distinctively holding the
sacrificial and Trinitarian theology, which gave vital
impulse and moral unity to the Reformation, and
which even now identifies them with that period.
The reason for this is twofold: firstly, the scanty
statistics published in the " Year-books" of the
" Liberal" Churches, entirely omitting many items

furnished in the " Annual Minutes " of the Evangelical or Orthodox Churches, make it impossible to
carry out, at many points, on the broader definition, comparisons which are important in testing
the questions of progress, spiritual vitality, etc.;
and, secondly, because, in the foregoing indictments, eminent representatives of " Liberal " religion have sharply arraigned the " Evangelical "
Churches, and made heavy allegations of their decline, decrepitude, disintegration, and decay.

We have seriously pondered the foregoing
charges, scrupulously scrutinizing the tendencies
of the times, collating exact data, reviewing the
origin and progress of Protestantism, internally and
externally, and its relation to Christianity, as a
whole, in its entire history, and are fully convinced
that the foregoing indictment is both faulty and
false ; that it is predicated upon wrong assumptions
as to the genius and mission of Protestantism ; that
many of the assumed facts are only hasty and undiscriminating collections of the most meager data,
many well-attested facts and statistics being wholly
overlooked and ignored.

That part of the indictment which comes from
Romanists and Romanizing Ritualists implies that
the Christian religion has had a perfect ideal development in the Church on the earth ; that this development existed at some time in the past ; that
the aim of the modern Church should be to attain to

the ancient ideal ; and that there can be no future unfolding of any thing richer or deeper in the spirit, the import, or the power of Christianity, because the fullness of its meaning was exhausted long ago. It also supposes that Protestantism has claimed and still professes to be a finality—the perfect ideal of Christian life and experience, the last and perfect word of truth—an assumption not only false but impossible. Protestantism claims the holy Scriptures as the complete and final word of religious truth, though not of all truth, but that new and deeper discoveries of their meaning and power will be wrought out by the progressive studies and experience of the Church. An early representative of Protestantism, Rev. John Robinson, of Leyden, said: "I am confident that the Lord has more truth and light yet to break forth out of his holy word."

Protestantism has ever been conscious of imperfections and weaknesses, making necessary some kind of siftings, modifications, and restatements, that it may be purged from unreasonable and unscriptural features, from relics of Popery and mediæval civilization, to say nothing of the ages anterior; and that its life has been a growth, an evolution, in which, notwithstanding some painful deformities, it is steadily attaining, in its actual life and workings, fuller realizations of the ideal of Christianity presented in the holy Scriptures.

Protestantism has been doing its work under great disadvantages, under sudden and radical changes of conditions. As a reformation and revolt against old errors, it has had extremes, reactions, and other incidental evils. Doubts, disorders, and experiments are inevitable in such processes. The work of modification and restatement, gradually going on in connection with the advancement of general intelligence, has been a task of the most delicate and difficult character, sorely testing the highest wisdom, stability and piety of its adherents, and also its hold upon the confidence and respect of the masses. But this is not all. In its divorce from the State, in the United States, and in some European countries, it lost the advantage of prestige and influence over the popular mind, which the State afforded, and was cast upon fluctuating outward sources of voluntary support. Hence the natural inquiry, whether it could maintain its influence with the masses.

But another and still more important element has entered into the case—the Protestant religion considered as internal spiritual exercises between the individual and his God, with no priestly or hierarchical dependence. Under Protestantism, religion became purely a personal thing, passing out from under the exclusive control of the sacraments, and the arbitrary sway of assumed prerogatives, into irrepressible conflicts with individual lusts and

worldly influences. Instead of pompous rituals,
each soul was thrown upon its God and the deep
realities of its inner life. The scourge of the hierarchy disappeared, but the struggle with sense and
self went on. Still recognizing the validity of the
Church, as a divinely instituted body—a brotherhood and a guide—Protestantism pressed with powerful tenacity upon each individual the fact of his
personal responsibility; that he must bear the weight
of his own guilt to the foot of the cross; that he
must seek within himself and for himself access to
God, and, in the spirit of adoption begotten by the
Holy Ghost, find a satisfaction which will meet the
soul's deepest needs. Since its primitive days, except among small groups, Christianity had not existed under such conditions.

What was to be the effect of these new religious
conditions among large masses of people? It was
predicted that religion, wholly dependent upon the
fluctuations of individual affections, and the vacillations of individual wills, would be characterized
by inconstancy and alternations, until its influence
would be utterly wasted. In Europe, Protestantism
has been tested only under the latter conditions,
the voluntary spiritual action being supplemented
by the support of the State. Such, too, was the
situation of American Protestantism during the
colonial era; but after the Revolution the civil
bands were sundered, and it adjusted itself to whol-

ly voluntary conditions, externally and internally, and has undergone the trial of the transition, and the operation of the voluntary principle in its full measure.

There has been still another source of trial. These capricious and fluctuating voluntary sources of support have been tested in a country which everywhere yields to the supremacy of public opinion. We have passed out from under the tutelage of authority, and a new power, until late years little known, has risen up, exercising supreme sway—even the functions of empire. With vast, complicated, religious, moral, educational, social, and political interests, our young nation ventured upon its career under the supreme guidance of public opinion. Nothing is more irresponsible, or liable to be more capricious and destructive; and yet, in these unsteady hands are such great interests held.

How experimental and perilous, in the judgment of many, the task of Protestantism, under these new conditions! Those most sanguine of its success have expected vacillations, reactions, disorders, and even much decay. They are incidental and inevitable, necessary to her life and higher development.

Those who have written this terrible indictment against Protestantism do not correctly apprehend the case. No paralysis has come upon her, nor are there any indications of dissolution, as will be fully demonstrated, but the best symptoms of life and progress. The struggles of Protestantism are only the normal contests of the vital forces, expelling from the system disorders inherited from Rome, whose deadly taint has long disfigured and embarrassed her: and the evidences of decay, which some see, are only the devitalized elements, which vigorous life throws off, in its higher advances.

Opening wide our eyes, and wisely interpreting the signs of the times, in the light of the whole history of Christianity, we see indications, in the condition and progress of American Protestantism, which convey encouraging lessons. The past eighty years; at farthest, the past century; and, in some respects, the past thirty years, have been distinguished by a most rapid and marked development, in the actual life and workings of the Protestant Churches in the United States, of the true ideal of Christianity, which during long centuries was almost wholly lost out of the world. In no other period, if we except the brief period following the day of Pentecost—and possibly that should not be excepted—have the past eighty years been equaled, much less excelled.

Viewed in this light, every thing will be clear, although all is not perfect. Protestantism wears, for its motto the language of St. Paul, " Not as though I had already attained, or were already perfect; but I follow after, that I may apprehend that, for which I am apprehended in Christ Jesus."

To understand our times, and to meet the responsibilities, call for the clearest vision, the broadest analyses, the amplest resources, prepared hearts, and the best manhood. No hasty deductions by biased minds, from narrow generalizations and scanty data, can determine the situation. No personal ill-success, or ill-adjustment to our surroundings, or cramped routine perspective, should color the judgment and inspire evil prognostications. To the high mount of broad observation, then, we betake ourselves, to study the tendencies and prospects of the times.

One feature of our times is entirely new, and, therefore, experimental. Great and sacred questions are brought into the arena of public investigation. Never before were the people expected to have an independent opinion about such matters. The common soil of humanity * for the first time in all the ages is surveyed, plowed, and sown. The problem now pending is whether more of wheat or of tares will be harvested; whether, in the end, it will be productive of more of faith or of doubt, of genuine piety or ungodliness. In the United States, unlike the older countries, there are no conserving forces in the constitution of society, holding men to the old faiths—no old institutions, hereditary nobilities, State Churches, etc.; but every thing is new—communities, governments, and institutions,

* "Christianity and Modern Thought," p. 17.

and any number of new projects, trial schemes, and prophecies of newer and stranger things to come. All things stimulate to theorizing. The new is held at a high premium, and the old at a heavy depreciation. In such times men find it easy to break away from old morals and old faiths, and a supernatural system like Christianity undergoes searching examination. Every thing, however spiritual, is subjected to natural tests. The revolutionizing tendency of the times has invaded every department of thought and action. Thought is intense and bold. Principles, institutions, and usages, long sacred and venerable, are discarded and obsolete. In the midst of such tendencies, American Christianity has been called to experience a severer test than European Christianity, with its old institutions environing and sustaining it, but we shall see that her triumphs are purer and grander.

How is the conflict progressing, and what are the indications? This problem is our appointed task, and waits a solution—a solution, which we believe is radiant with hope and promise. Let us advance and see.

I. FAITH.

CHAPTER I.

THE BONDAGE.

Spiritual Despotism.
Papal Scholasticism.
Protestant Scholasticism.

I.—FAITH.

CHAPTER I.

BONDAGE.

IT is charged that Protestantism is a break with ancient faith and worship; that it discards anchors and moorings; that it is logically and historically the generator of skepticism; that the Protestantism of the present is very different from the Protestantism of the past; that its numerous modifications in doctrine and life indicate its rapid disintegrating tendencies; that it has become "a miserable raft," its fragments floating apart like the mere "flying rack of the heavens;" and that "poor remnants only of the great nations are clinging to its parted and broken logs."

That Protestantism was the leading factor in those great movements which burst the shackles for centuries restraining freedom of thought, and that it has quickened intellectual activity and enlarged its scope, can be regarded a reproach only by those who still loiter among the murky vapors of mediæval times. Even if it be true, as Dr. Ewer declares, that "it stands to-day breast-deep in torrents of skepticism," it is creditable to it to be able thus to stand; and, through the severe ordeals of external criticism and rigid self-introspection, to endure restatements and modifications, not only without loss of essential identity, but even with increased vitality and power.

In the midst of the scrutiny and conflicts of the centuries, Protestantism has strengthened itself, within and without; it has taken possession of "storm-driven outposts;" it has erected "Eddystone lights where surging waves of doubt are ever breaking;" it has established "last havens of stores and comfort for adventurous voyagers, bewildered in search of truth;" and has extended its lines to the ends of the earth. In future pages, the truth of these declarations will be demonstrated.

That Protestantism has been able to advance its position amid the stormiest seas of doubt and free inquiry, and grow larger, purer, and stronger, is its glory; but that it has "let loose" these "torrents of skepticism," because it broke away from the absolutism of Rome, and championed spiritual liberty, is too absurd a statement to come from a divine of high standing and culture. It is an oft-exploded complaint, that the Reformation produced the skepticism of the eighteenth century, by generating the revolution in philosophy, and, through that, the infidelity which accompanied it. Of that disastrous result, it was in no sense the cause. The Reformation and the philosophical revolution were both, in themselves, beneficent, necessary to the world's progress, and productive of irreligion only " as the cool bracing air may sometimes produce fever in a debilitated body, or warmth may hasten corruption in a corpse." The infecting malarial taint was spiritual despotism, intrinsically and eternally malignant.

The testimony of the centuries shows that, for the origin of skepticism and its fearful ascendency in the last century, the cause of causes was not liberty in any form, but an imbecile, corrupt, and imperious Church, obtruding itself between the world and God, and darkening the faith of the nations. The causes were " practical rather than speculative ; more moral than intellectual ; and less theological than ecclesiastical. The religious insurrection of the nations was political and social rather than metaphysical. The revolt was less from Christianity than from the Church ; or, at least, was from Christianity because of the (Romish) Church."*

Comparing the Protestantism of the present with that of the past, changes are, indeed, apparent in religious sentiment, in technical theology, and in the practice of enforcing religious belief. Theology is less scholastic and repulsive, has less of pagan adulteration, has been lubricated and broadened, and is the better for its siftings. Modern thought and

* " The Skeptical Era in Modern History," by Rev. T. M. Post, D.D., p. 257.

Protestant theology have been mutual benefactors and beneficiaries. Religious sentiment is less superstitious and more intelligent, is less actuated by fear and more by knowledge, lives less in damps and shadows and more in the light, and has become less a blind impulse and more a law written in the heart—at once a passion and a principle. Creeds are shorter, but broader, deeper, and stronger; have less of husk and more of kernel; are shedding the devitalized and retaining the vital. Stakes and fagots have disappeared; inquisitorial tortures have ceased; inquisitorial examinations are giving place to friendly utterance of mutual belief; and faith is no longer forced, but voluntary.

All this is as it should be—not the shame but the glory of Protestantism. But this gain has come through peculiar processes, both within and without —the fruit of discipline.

Protestantism had its origin at a time when tradition and the schoolmen, sustained by the terrors of the hierarchy, had dominated Europe for centuries. Two evils were rampant in the world of mind —the spirit of scholasticism, tenacious for dialectical forms, shaving truth with tools of iron logic, to the sacrifice of its simplicity and purity, and dishonoring it with human subtleties; and the spirit of dogmatism, which, with unrelenting authority, denied the freedom of personal convictions and enforced belief. †

Protestantism, a too apt pupil in the school of the centuries, inhaling the spirit of the age, started in its career hampered with these trammels. It could not, at once, purify the superincumbent air, nor lift itself wholly above the murky vapors. A revolt against the hierarchy, an advocate of freedom, and a champion of independence, early Protestantism, nevertheless, only feebly realized what liberty meant and what gross bondage it still retained. It brought out of Romanism the spirit of dogmatism, and the devotion to truth which fired its zeal against the falsities of the papacy was sometimes betrayed into a spirit of persecution. Husks of scholasticism were still retained, as seen in the rigidly drawn and extended theological formularies and systems. The iron logic of the reformers followed too closely in the dialectical lines of the schoolmen, cramping into systems of human devising, and perverting by human subtleties, truths which the Great Teacher and his apostles presented in simpler forms. With such a legacy of evil Protestantism began its work, and only by processes of severe purging could it be purified. These modifications have exposed it to the charge of change and disintegration, exciting alarm in some minds.

Are these allegations and apprehensions well founded?

Several lines of inquiry are necessary in bringing this subject fully before us.

How was Christian truth so brought into bondage that only through long, stern ordeals could it be delivered ?

Why did not original Protestantism wholly cast off these fetters ?

And, *What factors have providentially wrought with Protestantism for its deliverance?*

By pursuing these inquiries, we shall be able more intelligently to appreciate the present situation and tendencies. We shall find a true historic answer to the unfounded allegation that Protestantism is the generator of skepticism ; and shall also perceive that it has successfully pursued its course, and been developed, purified, extended, and strengthened, in spite of all infecting and antagonizing forces.

In the fifth century Christianity conquered paganism, and thenceforth paganism, in turn, enfeebled and burdened Christianity. " The rites of the Parthenon passed into the worship of the Church ; the subtleties of the academy into the creed. Similar trifles, just as subtle, interminable, and unprofitable, occupied the sharp intellects of the schoolmen. At length the time had come when the barren philosophy, which had worn so many shapes, mingled with so many creeds, had survived empires, religions, races, languages, was destined to fall. Driven from its ancient haunts, it had taken sanctuary in that Church which it at first had persecuted, and, like the daring fiends of the poet,

' Placed its seat next to the seat of God,
And with its darkness durst affront his light.' " *

The scholastic philosophy, based on the logic,
ethics, and physics of Aristotle, and the judgments
and decretals of the Church, and fostered by the
Church, dominated the realms of human thought
through the long, dark mediæval period. The
schoolmen, dialecticians, mostly theologians and
ecclesiastics, constructed out of the philosophy
of Aristotle an armory for the defense of the
papacy, whose formularies were traps, tricks, and
snares, involving the unwary in subtleties. Their
schemes of casuistry and intellectual legerdemain
bejuggled men out of common-sense beliefs and
into the acceptance of absurd dogmas uphold-
ing the papal Church. Around the intellect of
Europe, Romanism bound the chain of scholasticism, repressing the thought and faith of the
nations.

In the name of an infallible authority conferred
by Heaven, the Church applied the clamps of scholasticism to all science, usurped the prerogatives of
all truth, put all minds under censorship, and
burned men as quickly for new theses in physical
science, medicine, or astronomy, as in theology.
" Was a proposition in physics or metaphysics to
be determined? The schoolmen sent you, not to
analyze the thing; but they coerced it into the

* Macaulay.

categories and syllabus of the subtle Greek; they put it into the strait-waistcoat of some dialectic formula; they put it upon the rack and torture of syllogism and enthymeme; and, finally, bound it down and smothered it by the decrees of Councils and the bulls of Popes. Was the inquirer still unsatisfied? The ponderous names of a Duns Scotus, a Thomas Aquinas, or some Seraphic Doctor, or some Gregory or Innocent or Boniface, were made to thunder about his ears with the technical barbarisms of a scholastic jargon, till, overwhelmed and confounded, if not convinced, he was glad to be silent, especially as those barbarisms were no mere *bruta fulmina*, but behind them was brandished before his eyes the *ultima reason* of spiritual despots—the mightier logic of imprisonment, wheel, and fagot." *

Ages wore away under such processes, excluding scientific discovery and progress. It was a futile, fruitless toil, in an endless circle, "an endless round of sonorous nothings." Society "plodded its weary way over 'many a frozen, many a fiery Alp,' mid rivers of inky blackness, in endless mazes wandering, emulating, in its bootless and ceaseless toil, the fabled children of eternal night, till, at last, emerging from its dark sojourn, lo, it finds itself just where it started weary centuries ago."

* See "Skeptical Era in Modern History," by Rev. T. M. Post, D.D., p. 72.

Emancipation from such a bondage was a necessity, and, in due time, a certainty.

A quickening conjuncture of great events—the Revival of Letters, the Invention of Printing, the Discovery of America, the passage round the Cape of Good Hope, and the rapid development of the power of the municipalities and the burgher class, preceded and prepared the way for the Reformation of the sixteenth century. Out of these wide and deeply significant movements the Reformation sprung; and to their influence, stimulating mental activity, broadening the scope of human thought, and developing intellectual and moral independence, and not to the Reformation alone, are we to attribute the first advancement in philosophy, and in physical science, the rise of skepticism, etc. The seeds of these movements were widely sown, and germinated in the general quickening which started forth the Reformation. Each, springing from its peculiar conditions, had nevertheless points in common in their inception and earlier development, while the Reformation soon became the bold impulse and central figure, under whose leadership they went forth on their mission.

The Revival of Learning was the chief cause of the Reformation, but many causes contributed to the Revival. Feudalism declined; the State became consolidated; cities arose; new classes of free citizens came into existence; industrial and com-

mercial activities increased, producing material
prosperity; and with competence came leisure for
the adornment of life with the arts of peace. At
the same time there grew up a secular form of culture, as distinguished from the prevailing religious
and scholastic type. From 1348 to 1502, universities were founded in various parts of the
continent. Dante, Petrarch, and Boccaccio wrote,
extolling force and beauty, the manly courage of
severe contests, the delicate sentiments of love,
the fervor of devotion, the nobility of loyalty, the
ignominy of treason—stirring every natural and
moral feeling.

This humane culture awakened an interest in ancient poetry and in ancient conceptions of the world.
New desires for art and literature followed, and the
social life of the rising burgher class, and of the
noble families who had attained to wealth and
power, provided the taste, the leisure, and the
means for resuscitating the remains of ancient culture. First, Roman literature was explored anew;
then the Greek classics. Greece was visited, and
her "muses would have been brought to Italy if
they had not soon fled thither for refuge." Greek
scholars came to Italy before the capture of Con-
stantinople by the Turks, in 1453; but that great
event drove thither numerous Greek refugees, rich
in literary treasures, and the Halls of the Medici
received them as apostles. Convents brought forth

their resources; antiquity had a resurrection; and youth from Western Europe, Germany, and Hungary crossed the Alps to study the ancient classics.

This movement marked a new era in culture; the Church was to be no longer the sole instructor; a wider horizon was to open over the human intellect, and scholasticism was destined to wane. "The Fathers," hitherto for centuries read only in fragments, convenient for the use of the dialectician, were brought forth from their long obscurity; and the Scriptures, in the original tongue, once more served as the touchstone of truth. Printing facilitated the multiplication of books, and helped the spreading ferment. Little resistance was offered, for the new era, at first intent upon antiquities, projected no new theories. And yet, out of the antiquities with which Italy and even the Papal court were then captivated, important changes were to come. Through this channel were introduced into the West the Platonic, the Neoplatonic, the Epicurean, and Stoical philosophies, whose temporary mission, in the transitional period of philosophy then opening, was to supplant the Scholastic-Aristotelian method, and whose residuum, in the ages beyond, was a legacy of skepticism, harassing the faith of Protestantism.

This Revival of Learning was the instaurator of new ideas and movements.

In the midst of this period, Protestantism, the

4

most conspicuous of all modern movements, had its
birth, ushering in a new and better religious life,
but inheriting taints which only long and stern discipline could purge away.

"Side by side," says Ueberweg, "with this return of learned culture from scholasticism to the
early Roman and Greek literature stands, as its
analogue, the return of the religious consciousness
from the doctrines of the Catholic Church to the
letter of the Bible. . . . Acknowledging the authority of the holy Scriptures, and of the dogmas of the
Church in its earliest days, Protestantism rejected
the mediæval hierarchy and the scholastic tendency
to rationalize Christian dogmas. The individual
conscience found itself in conflict with the way of
salvation marked out by the Church. By this way
it was unable to attain to inward peace and reconciliation with God. . . . In the first heat of the conflict the Reformers regarded the head of the Catholic Church as Antichrist, and Aristotle, the chief
of the Catholic school philosophy, as a 'godless
bulwark of the Papists.' "

The logical tendency was to break with all philosophy, and adopt a simple, unquestioning faith.
But as Protestantism gained " fixed consistence,"
the necessity of some determinate order, in the new
ecclesiastical condition, pressed upon the attention
of the leaders. Melanchthon felt the need of some
kind of philosophy. He found the Epicureans too

atheistic ; the Stoics too fatalistic in theology and extravagant in ethics ; Plato and the Neoplatonists " either too indefinite or too heretical ; " while Aristotle, as a teacher of a unique method, met the needs of the young. Luther consented to the use of the text of Aristotle if uncumbered by scholastic comments. " There arose thus," says Ueberweg, " in the Protestant universities, a *new* Aristotelianism, which was distinguished from scholasticism by its simplicity and freedom from empty subtleties, but which, owing to the necessity of modifying the naturalistic elements in the Aristotelian philosophy, and especially in the Aristotelian psychology, so as to make them harmonize with the religious faith, soon became, in its measure, itself scholastic. The erection of a new independent philosophy, on the basis of the generalized Protestant principle," was, therefore, a necessity ; but its accomplishment was reserved for a later time and other hands.

In the mean time, burdened with limitations inconsistent with its fundamental principle, checking and falsifying its movements, Protestantism pursued its course, slowly and imperfectly developing and waiting the concurrent action of other factors, which should fully emancipate it from scholasticism and dogmatism, and invest it in simple forms, in closer harmony with the original ideal of pure Christianity. Those factors have wrought along the centuries, ostensibly a work of criticism, and sometimes of destruction, but, under Providence, developing those modifying tendencies in theological truth so conspicuous in our days.

What were these factors?

They comprise, in their fullest scope, the great movements of modern thought, some of which took their origin just anterior to Protestantism, others nearly simultaneously with it, and others still soon after Protestantism started upon its career. Their mission has been providential, under the wise over-rulings of " Him who is the Head over all things unto his Church," and who maketh the activities of human thought, and even human unbelief and wrath, to subserve his beneficent ends.

CHAPTER II.

LIBERATING FACTORS.

Modern Skepticism.
Physical Science.
Antitrinitarian Protestantism.
Modern Philosophy.

CHAPTER II.

LIBERATING FACTORS.

Modern Skepticism.

ANCIENT in its essence, and a residuum from antemediæval times, skepticism first appeared, in modern history, springing out of the bosom of Rome just prior to the origin of Protestantism.

A new philosophical movement was one of the first and most noticeable developments in the Revival of Learning, working simultaneously with its earliest beginnings, both as a factor and a product, and constituting the first division in modern philosophy—the period of transition* from the old scholastic method, of mediæval dependence upon the Church and Aristotle, to the beginning of the new method, of original and independent investigation, inaugurated by the bold genius of Descartes. It was an era of change, of transfer, of partial emancipation from the old, with, as yet, no fully developed system.

This movement had long been a felt necessity. As early as the eleventh century, and through the three following centuries, the spirit of freedom

* Ueberweg's " Division of the Historic Periods of Philosophy."

struggled in Italian minds, and champions of intellectual liberty appeared. At the beginning of the twelfth century "a numerous and powerful school of philosophers labored so persistently for freedom of thought and expression, that it was denounced by the Church as a school of Epicureans and Atheists." *

It has been already noticed that the Revival of Learning introduced the Platonic and the Neoplatonic philosophies into Italy. Averroës, a commentator upon Aristotle, in high repute, taught that "only the one universal reason common to the entire human race is immortal," "that the world-ordering divine mind is the active immortal reason," and denied "individual immortality." These doctrines prevailed in Northern Italy from early in the fourteenth to the middle of the fifteenth century, and in the school of Padua they were prominent tenets until the seventeenth century, though in different acceptations at different times. The heterodox elements in this belief were made prominent in some and toned down by others. In the fourteenth century Eckhart taught a mystical pantheism, and in the fifteenth century the antichristian and pantheistic system of Neoplatonism, which had been developed and systematized under the molding influence of Plotinus, Porphyry, and Julian,

* Prof. Vincenzo Botta, D.D. See Ueberweg's " Philosophy," ii,
p. 461.

prominent opponents of Christianity in the first
Christian centuries, became the favorite philosophy
of the cultured minds. Many made an easy passage
from Averroism to Pantheism.

Plethro, (1355-1442,) a "passionate Platonist;"
Bessarion, (1395-1472,) a moderate Platonist; and
Marcilius Ficinus, (1433-1499,) a meritorious trans-
lator of Plato, Plotinus, Porphyry, and other Neoplatonists, propounded theses which have been
characterized as "neither Christian nor Mohammedan, but Neoplatonic and heathen." With these
men there arose in Italy and elsewhere schools of
ideal Platonists, tending to Deism and Natural-
ism, and a class of Peripatetics, sliding into materialism and skepticism. Hallam says, "There
is strong ground for ascribing a rejection of Christianity to Plethro." Ficinus declared there was
no hope for religion except in the "bolstering
aid of the Platonic philosophy;" Pomponatius,
(died 1525,) that "Christianity was in a state of
obsolescence and decay," and that the immortality of the soul is doubtful on philosophic principles; and Machiavelli, (1464-1527,) that the highest political ends can be obtained without the aid
of the Church or of Christianity. "The Platonic
Academy in the gardens of the Medici," says
Hase,* "defended only a few of the religious ideas

* "Church History," p. 328. This academy was established
1440-1445.

peculiar to Christianity." " Infidelity and superstition were arrayed boldly in opposition to each
other." " To the Italian infidelity of this period
probably belongs the authorship of the book, ' The
Three Impostors,' (Moses, Jesus, and Mohammed,)
first mentioned in the sixteenth century ; " * also,
the " Dialogue Upon Religion," between " seven
learned freethinkers of Venice," by John Bodin,
(died 1597,) in which all religions are set forth
as " having the same merits and defects," and
" ideal deism " is commended as the " true religion." †

In the earlier stages of this movement, the new
views were sometimes accommodated to the Church
by attempted distinctions between philosophic and
theologic truth, and by a profession of submission to the Church. The Church condemned this
view of the twofold nature of truth, but the movement went quietly on so long as the Church was
not directly antagonized.

Thus the School of Humanists, enthusiastic worshipers of pagan antiquity, devoted to the revival
of classical study, became antagonistic to Christianity, and it was quite common for dignitaries of
the Church, in the circles of their friends, to avow
atheism. Even Pope Leo X. was credited with the
remark, regarded as credible by his contemporaries,
" It is not generally known how much we and ours

* Kurtz's " Church History," vol. ii, p. 159.   † Ibid.

have been profited by the fable of Christ." Opponents of Christian belief retained their positions, often of the highest rank, in the Church.

In this early movement in the quest of another philosophy, we see, in the Romish Church, the first outcroppings of European skepticism during the century before Protestantism arose. "The Reformation," says Professor Fisher, "is not responsible for the tendencies to skepticism and unbelief which have revealed themselves in modern society. These tendencies discovered themselves before Protestantism appeared. The *Renaissance* in Italy was skeptical in its spirit. This infidelity sprang up in the bosom of the Roman Catholic Church, partly as a reaction against the superstitious doctrines and practices which the Church countenanced, partly from the Epicurean lives of the ecclesiastics, and the worldliness which had corrupted the piety of the official guardians of religion."

Hallam,* speaking of those who called in question the "truths of natural and revealed religion," says, "The proofs of this before the middle of the sixteenth century are chiefly to be derived from Italy. . . . If we limit ourselves to those who directed their attacks against Christianity, it must be presumed that, in an age when the tribunals of justice visited even with the punishment of death the denial of any fundamental doctrine, few books

* Hallam's " Literature of the Middle Ages," vol. i, p. 288.

of an openly irreligious tendency would appear.   A short pamphlet by one Vallée cost him his life in 1574. . . . The list of men suspected of infidelity, if we could trust all private anecdotes of the time, would be by no means short."

Besides the Platonic and the Neoplatonic, other ancient philosophies were renewed in this transitional period.   Telsius (1508–1588) and other relatively independent investigators of nature, were considerably influenced by the doctrines of the natural philosophers of ancient Greece.   Stoicism was revived and developed by Lipsius, (1547–1606,) and Epicureanism by Gassendi, (1592–1655.)   Ueberweg says, " Ancient skepticism was revived, and, in part, in a peculiar manner further developed, by Michel de Montaigne," (born 1503,) and "more or less directed to the doctrines of Christianity."   Charron, (1541–1603,) and Sanchéz, (1562–1632,) a teacher of medicine and philosophy in France, "supported this tendency."   Le Vayer (1586–1672) applied the arguments of ancient skeptics to theology, and had successors among his pupils—Sorbiere, (1615–1670,) Foucher, (1644–1696,) Glanville, (died 1680,) Hernhaym, (died 1670,) Huet, (1633–1721,) and Bayle, (1647–1706,) the latter "breaking the pathway of a mere frivolous unbelief."   Ueberweg also says, " From its relation to the investigation of nature, in modern times, Gassendi's renewal of Epicureanism is of far greater historical importance than the renewal of any other ancient system;" and F. A. Lange says, "Gassendi is the one who may properly be styled the renewer, in modern times, of systematic materialism."

We have thus traced the lines of modern skepticism from its rise out of the revival of the ancient philosophies, through phases separate from the Reformation, however much it may have been emboldened, in its later stages, by the examples of the Reformers; and have reached a period, on the Continent, parallel with that of Herbert, (1581–1648,) Hobbes, (1588–1679,) Blount, (1654–1693,) and. Sir Thomas Brown, (1605–1682,) the earliest leaders in skeptical thought in England.

Such was the origin of one of the great factors destined to exert an extensive influence upon modern thought and upon theology. Let us now retrace our steps, and briefly notice the rise and early progress of

Physical science, another modifying factor.

The mental quickening commenced in the Revival of Learning soon extended to all the sciences. The superstitious scholastic methods, by which the schoolmen figured out with equal facility the population of Saturn, the number of feathers in the wings of the cherubim, and how many angels could stand on the point of a needle, could not meet the necessities of awakened thought in the new era. It must have more rational processes; but the true process was not at once reached. It first went backward to the old pagan philosophies. Dr. Ueberweg, whose competency none will question, shall tell the story.

"The modern mind, dissatisfied with scholasticism, not only went back to the classical literature of antechristian antiquity, and to the writings constituting the biblical Revelation, but, setting out from the sciences of antiquity, also directed its endeavors, more and more, to independent investigation of the realities of nature and mind, as also to the problem of moral self-determination, independently of external forms. In the fields of mathematics, mechanics, geography, and astronomy, the science and speculation of the ancients were first restored, and then, partly by gradual progress, and partly by rapid and bold discoveries, materially extended. With the assured results of investigation were connected manifold and largely turbulent attempts to establish on the basis of the new science new theological and philosophical conceptions, in which attempts were involved germs of later and more mature doctrines. Physical philosophy, in the transitional period, was more or less blended with a form of theosophy, which rested at first upon the foundation of Neoplatonism and the Cabala, but which gradually, and especially on the soil of Protestantism, attained a more independent character. A physical philosophy thus blended with theosophy, not yet freed from scholastic notions, nor contradicting the affirmations of ecclesiastical theology, and yet resting on the new basis of mathematical and astronomical studies, was maintained, about the middle of the fifteenth century, by Nicolaus Cusanus, (1401–1464,) in whom the mysticism of Eckhart (1260–1327) was renewed, and from whence, later, Giordano Bruno (1548–1600) derived the fundamental features of his own bolder and more independent doctrine. Physics, in its combination with theosophy, continued to be taught, and was further developed in the sixteenth century, and also in the seventeenth. Among its professors were Paracelsus, (1493–1541,) the physician; Cardanus, (1501–1576,) the mathematician and astrologer; Bernardinus Telesius, (1508–1588,) the founder of the Academia Cosentina, for the investigation of nature, and his followers, Franciscus Patritius, (1529–1597,) the Platonizing opponent of Aristotle; Andreas Cæsalpinus, (1519–1603,) the Averroistic Aristotelian; Nicolaus Turxellius, (1547–1606,) the opponent of the latter, and an independent German thinker; Carolus Borillus, (1470–1553,) a supporter of the Catholic Church, and a disciple of Nicholaus of Cusa, (1401–1464); Giordano Bruno, (1548–1600,) and Lucilio Vanini, (1585–1619,) the antiecclesiastical freethinkers; and Thomas Campanella, (1568–1639,) the Catholic opponent of Aristotle. The religious element prevailed with Schwenckfeldt and Valentin Weigl, Protestant theologians, and with Jacob Böhme, the theosophist, among whose followers have been H. Moore, John Pordage, Pierre Poivet, and, in more modern times, St. Martin, and whose principles were employed by Baader and by Shelling—by the latter on the occasion of his passing over from physical philosophy to theosophy. The themes of law and civil government were developed in an independent manner, without deference to Aristotelian or ecclesiastical authority, and in a form more adapted to the changed political conditions of modern times.*

Physical science, then, in its early modern stages, was hampered with the embarrassments incidental to the transitional period of modern philosophy— the newly revived ancient philosophy, the Cabala, the remaining influence of scholastic methods, and the ecclesiastical domination.   Beginning before the birth of Protestantism, in such an unnatural combination, it struggled through the fifteenth and sixteenth centuries into the seventeenth, when it received a new impulse under the independent method of original investigation promulgated by Descartes, and became another of the modifying factors in the progress of Protestantism.

* Ueberweg's " History of Philosophy," vol. ii, pp. 19, 20.

The Antitrinitarian theology, a residuum from the antemediæval age, restored with the Revival of Learning, has been another providential factor.

Antitrinitarianism has been incorrectly regarded by some as an offspring of Protestantism, because a protest against Protestant theology. While very many of those representing these opinions have been dissenters from the Trinitarian and sacrificial theology of Protestantism, yet it is not strictly true that Antitrinitarianism originated in the Churches of the Reformation. The rise of these ideas antedates the mediæval age. The Arian doctrines survived that dark period, and reappeared during the Revival of Learning. The same causes that produced the Reformation, modern skepticism, and the transition in philosophy and physical science, revived the Arian ideas of previous centuries—a part of the general resurrection of ancient knowledge.

Nor was this all. Before those great events took place which gave character to the Reformation, and determined its career, even in the midst of the Middle Ages, the efforts of the schoolmen to establish, by syllogistic gins, logical technics, and tenuous sophisms, the Trinity and other Church doctrines, invested them with absurdity, and awakened revulsions. The scholastic processes proved perilous. In the tenth century Arians appeared in the Diocese of Padua, a district of northern Italy. In the twelfth century Joachin, an Abbot of Flora,

5

taught that the union of the Father, Son, and
Holy Spirit was not a natural one, not one of essence, but wholly moral, like that of persons holding common opinions. In the thirteenth century
these views had many representatives. During the
revival of the Platonic and the Neoplatonic philosophies, prior to the Reformation, the Trinity came
under frequent discussion, in various speculative
forms, but cautiously, for fear of the Church. The
shocks occasioned by the collisions of thought, in
the convulsive moments of the Reformation,
brought to the surface the dissent which the scholastic methods had provoked.

"It was in Italy," says Professor Fisher, "among
the cultured class, in men of inquisitive and cultivated minds, that the Antitrinitarians appeared.
The peculiar tone of the *belles-lettres* culture that
followed upon the Revival of Learning was often
congenial with these opinions. There was a disposition to examine the foundations of religion, to call
in question the traditional doctrines of the Church,
and to sift the entire creed by the application of
reason to its contents. The writings of Servetus
(1509–1553) doubtless had much influence in diffusing Antitrinitarian opinions; but most of the conspicuous Unitarians who first appeared were of
Italian birth, generally exiles from their country on
account of their belief. After the publication of
the Antitrinitarian work of Servetus, in 1531, it is

said that not less than forty educated men in Vicenza and the neighborhood were united in a private association, all of whom held Unitarian opinions. The Unitarian doctrines were found in the Churches of Italian refugees at Geneva and at Zurich."

Hallam says:* "It is certain that many of the Italian reformers held Antitrinitarian opinions, chiefly of the Arian form. M'Crie suggests that these had been derived from Servetus; but it does not appear that they had any acquaintance. . . . It is much more probable that their tenets originated among themselves."

These views are confirmed by Mosheim, who says that "Socinian writers generally trace the origin of their sect to Italy;" and Kurtz also says, "Italy was the proper home of the rationalistic denial of the doctrine (of the Trinity;) it was the fruit of the half-pagan humanism which flourished then." Its advocates, compelled to flee, took refuge in Switzerland; but, being persecuted there, and banished, they went first to Germany, thence to Poland, Hungary, and the province of Transylvania, where princes or nobles protected them. Blandrata, Gentilis, Alciati, Grimbaldi, Claudius of Savoy, and Tellius, early disseminators of Antitrinitarian ideas, and some of them martyrs, and Lælius and Faustus Socinus, from whom the Socinian scheme took its name, were all from Italy—the fruitage of the Neopla-

* Hallam's "Literature of the Middle Ages," vol. i, p. 196.

tonic movement—and were all of them born between 1475 and 1540, and all but one prior to 1520.
The Socinii were descendants from an illustrious
family of Sienna.

Almost simultaneously with the first movements
of Luther, and doubtless mainly out of the general
quickening given by the Revival of Learning, there
arose in different parts of central and northern Europe various sects of Reformers, several classes of
whom received the designation of Anabaptists.   In
1521, within four years of Luther's bold theses on
the church door in Wittenberg, they were known
as distinct bodies, under fiery leaders, among whom
we find Antitrinitarian opinions.   The Antitrinitarian refugees from Italy and Switzerland, "some
of whom," says Hase, " in the name of the Scriptures or of intellectual freedom, claimed the right to
reject any ecclesiastical doctrine, and especially the
doctrine of the Trinity. as it had been taught by
the Church," indulging the hope of finding an asylum in countries possessing the Reformation," appeared at an early date in Switzerland, then in
Germany, and elsewhere.   They found sympathy
among the Anabaptists when they were repelled
by Luther and Melanchthon.   John Denck, (died
1528,) and Hitzer, (died 1529,) Anabaptist leaders,
learned and extensively read in polite literature,
and others, almost with the origin of the Reformation, avowed Antitrinitarian views.   These opinions

spread with this sect even to England, where they appeared "at the very dawn of the Reformation." * Poland and Transylvania became the centers from which they radiated, and the Catechism printed at the Socinian printing-office, in Racow, was a noted campaign document.

In England, in every period since the earliest dawn of the Reformation, Antitrinitarian ideas have been held by those who have shared the common protest against the Church of Rome. In the reign of Edward (1547–1553) these views excited the alarm of the authorities. Under the reign of Elizabeth and James I. (1558–1625) men suffered martyrdom on account of them. In the time of the Commonwealth, John Biddle, who had collected a body of worshipers holding these views, was banished by Cromwell, and subsequently returning, died in prison in 1662. Strong tendencies to Arianism existed among the English Presbyterians throughout the seventeenth century, and it was a bar to the effective union sought between them and the Independents near the close of the century. Prior to this time, divines of the Established Church—Chillingworth, Hales of Eaton, etc.—had thrown aside the system of Calvin, and exposed themselves to the charge of Socinianism, and, in the next period, Cudworth, Whichcote, Williams,

* Rev. Wm. Turner, A.M., "Unitarianism Exhibited." London, 1846, p. 157.

Tillotson, and Whitby, were added to the list.
Later, Clarke, Hoadley, Hare, Sykes, Law, Justin,
etc., not positively Antitrinitarians, expressed themselves in language admitting of Unitarian construction.   In the last decade of the seventeenth century an extensive controversy raged, developing
within the Establishment two parties — real and
nominal Trinitarians—in which Sherlock was pronounced almost a Tritheist, and South and Wallis
almost Sabellians.   Among the Presbyterians in
Scotland three eminent divines and professors in
the University of Glasgow belonged to this school
of thinkers.

Modern philosophy has been a modifying factor.

We have already noticed the first imperfect phases
of modern philosophy in its transitional period from
mediæval dependence on the authority of the Church
and of Aristotle.   Its establishment as an independent science, uncontrolled by any human authority,
occurred under Descartes about one hundred and
twenty-five years after Luther inaugurated the Reformation.   Indirectly the product of the Reformation, following the example of bold revolt against
authority, Ueberweg calls it " a new, independent
philosophy, on the basis of the generalized Protestant principle."   It was destined to be a great providential factor, modifying ancient philosophy, skepticism, physical science, and the formularies of

Trinitarian and Antitrinitarian Protestantism, and aiding their deliverance from the partial bondage to scholastic methods in which they were all still held.

A renovation more radical than any hitherto known suddenly consummated this transition, and Bacon and Descartes were the renovators—the systems of both products of the Reformation. While Bacon (1561–1626) is regarded as the forerunner of modern philosophy, and Thomas Campanello (1568–1639) as his echo, Descartes (1596–1650) is the acknowledged founder. Next, after him we find the pinnacles of philosophic development occupied by Spinoza, (1632–1677,) Locke, (1632–1704,) and Leibnitz, (1646–1713.)

Bacon, not so much an originator of a new method as an instaurator of a new era, resisted tradition in physical science, insisted upon independent inductive processes, and thus effectually broke from the authority and the scientific methods of the Church and the schoolmen, as Luther had broken from the authority of the hierarchy. But Bacon's task was only partly done. Descartes, following a few years later, inaugurated the new method, which characterizes modern from mediæval philosophy. Separating it from theology, he cast aside all assumptions and all human authority. It was a complete revolution, and bold and rapid movements followed in the realm of inquiry. "The most stupendous thought that was ever conceived by man, such as had never been dared by Socrates or the Academy, by Aristotle or the Stoics, took possession of Descartes, in his meditations, on a November night, on the banks of the Danube. His own mind separated itself from every thing besides; and, in the consciousness of its own freedom, stood over against all tradition, all received opinion, all knowledge, all existence except itself, thus asserting the principle of individuality as the key-note of all coming philosophy and political institutions. Nothing was to be received as truth by man which did not convince his own reason. Luther opened up a new world, in which every man was his own priest, his own intercessor; Descartes opened a new world, in which every man was his own philosopher, his own judge of truth." *

Luther preceded Descartes one hundred years, inaugurating the great revolt against despotism, and furnishing the inspiration for later and more advanced movements. Both were bold reformers—the one against the despotism of an absolute hierarchy, and the other against the despotism of scholasticism, products of the middle ages. And yet there are radical and practical differences between the two revolts. "The one was the method of continuity and gradual reform; the other of an instantaneous, complete, and thorough revolution. The principle of Luther waked up a superstitious

* Bancroft's " History of the United States," vol. ix, p. 500.

world, 'asleep in the lap of legends old,' but did not renounce all external authority. It used drags and anchors to check too rapid progress, and to secure its mooring. So it escaped premature conflicts. By the principle of Descartes, the individual man at once, and altogether, stood aloof from king, Church, universities, public opinion, traditional science—all external authority and all other beings— and, turning every intruder out of the inner temple of the mind, it kept guard at its portal, to bar the entry of every belief that had not first obtained a passport from himself." *

After his death, the philosophy of Descartes extensively spread. The Churches and schools of Holland were full of Cartesians, and the old scholastic philosophy became ridiculous. The Arminians and Coccijeans generally espoused his system, and modifications followed in all branches of inquiry.

By some persons, the spirit of free inquiry has been regarded as an unmitigated evil in its origin, and also in its entire influence and tendencies. Such, however, is not the testimony of history, nor will it be the verdict of the future. In its inception it sprung out of the roots of the great Reformation, and partook largely of its spirit and aims. The leading principles in both movements were germane; and, in their legitimate and unperverted operations, each seems to have been intended by Providence to

* Bancroft's " History of the United States," vol. ix, p. 500, etc.

supplement the other—the one a protest against hierarchical assumptions and intolerance, and the other against the not less rigid intolerance of mediæval scholasticism, in its theology, science, and general inquiry. As revolts against the enslavement of the religious and intellectual natures, their mission was one of universal emancipation. Each had its legitimate sphere.

Descartes, the powerful promoter of the purely rational system, from whose bold conception the radical method sprang, recognized an act of faith as lying at the basis of all the processes of the intellect, and proclaimed " God the first, the most certain, and the best of all truths." He comprehended that " if God is not, the most regular exercises of thought may deceive us, and that our reason affords us no guaranty." He confessed that all the force of his proofs " depends upon a belief which precedes them—that, without this belief, man is condemned to irremediable doubt." The spirit of free inquiry, therefore, in its inception, was not irreverent and reckless ; it did not disregard all limitations implied by faith in God ; but it was a revolt against the intellectual intolerance engendered amid the damps and darkness of the Middle Ages.

This is the mission upon which it was sent forth by " Him who is the head over all things unto his Church ; " to deliver his truth from the spirit of dogmatism ; to dissolve the rigid and perverted

forms into which it had been wrought by the iron
logic of the mediæval scholastics, and to restore it
to the more simple, practical, and vital forms in
which the great Teacher and his apostles originally
presented it. This is still its mission, and none the
less because it has been perverted in the interest of
unbelief. But, even as an opposing force, many incidental benefits have accrued to the cause of truth,
under the wise overrulings of Him who is its supreme source. The emancipation of mind from in
tolerance and old-time superstitions is now a rapid,
world-wide tendency, in which many forces, both
of faith and unbelief, either wittingly or unwitting-
ly, are participating.

In the history of Protestantism this new spirit has
been marked by hesitation, circumspection, moder-
ation, and gradual progress; but elsewhere it has
been reckless and defiant. In England and France
free thought became " speculative, skeptical, and
impassioned. This modern Prometheus, as it broke
its chains, started up with revenge against the ecclesiastical terrorism which for centuries had sequestered the rights of mind." Henceforth it every-
where actively assailed Christianity and invaded all
departments of science, politics, morals, and religion, proving the truth of the sentiment that " Error
is often the handmaid of Providence," rendering
two services to truth—intellectual and moral—com-
pelling clear definitions and testing offered proofs,

and also rousing languid natures into a passionate love for the truth which error threatens.

We have noticed the rise of the spirit of skepticism, in advance of the Reformation, out of the transitional movements produced by the Revival of Learning; and we have seen, on the continent of Europe, a succession of skeptical inquirers extending through a period of two hundred years, from the Platonic Academy in the gardens of the Medici, founded 1440–1445, to the first development of deism in England. The period of Herbert (1581–1648) and Hobbes, (1588–1679,) the first English deists, synchronizes with that of the French skeptics, Sanchez, (1563–1632,) Le Vayer, (1586–1662,) and Gassendi, (1592–1655.) Herbert and Hobbes traveled extensively and resided on the Continent, enjoying personal acquaintance with Gassendi, and other leading thinkers.

From the time of Locke, whose philosophy was "a middle term between Bacon's empiricism and Descartes' rationalism, on the one hand, and English deism and French materialism, on the other," English skepticism, adopting, in part, Locke's sensationalism, entered upon a new stage of development, under the leadership of Tolland, (died 1722,) the Earl of Shaftesbury, (died 1713,) Collins, (died 1729,) Woolston, (died 1733,) Mandeville, (died 1733,) Tindall, (died 1733,) Chubbs, (died 1747,) Lord Bolingbroke, (died 1751,) and David Hume, (died 1776)—the representatives of English deism, in the dark period, in the last century, to which we shall hereafter refer.

Under such powerful forces, the revolt against Christianity, in England and France, became wild, reckless, and ruinous to faith and morals. Many sacred truths were seriously periled, and their influence over many minds was destroyed. Such results, if not a necessity, were nevertheless a natural rebound from spiritual despotism and dogmatism. The scholastic philosophy, upheld by the hierarchy, and designed as a coat of mail to protect the Church, became a compress, preventing growth and stifling life. Disastrous consequences to Christianity could hardly fail to ensue, when a philosophy so subtle, so foul and tyrannical, but baptized and canonized as of God, should be exposed as "a barren, monstrous mockery." But is the party which tears away the mockery, or the one which made and upheld it, responsible for the unbelief which follows? Let not Protestants timidly distrust their own principles.

If the rebound from this hideous despotism was sometimes ruinous, it was not less necessary to the progress of humanity. "It is difficult for the human mind to stop in revolutions. When it begins to cast its false creeds and false gods overboard, it is apt also to throw away the true." It was spiritual despotism, paralyzing and darkening the intellect of the nations, that made mental emancipation wild, and mad with revenge for its long enslavement.

Protestantism, sharing in the same trammels, started upon its career. A new philosophy, a child of Protestantism, sprang up in her pathway, and carried into practical operation, in the realm of thought, the protest against human authority, which Protestantism had made against the Papacy. Its providential mission was to purify, although, sometimes, under a perverted spirit, it has been as by fire. Modern physical science and modern skepticism, both starting ahead of Protestantism, and antitrinitarian Protestantism starting quite as early as orthodox Protestantism, all in the same partial bondage to scholastic methods and the dogmatic spirit, have jointly shared in these modifying processes, and have mutually improved each other.

By such processes of development have these great modern forces come into being, taken their position, and started in the race, as working factors in the realm of mind. They have had points of unity and also of antagonism. Criticism, waste, and even destruction, have been inevitable; but, through them, pure truth and the best life of the race have been promoted. Which has best endured the purging, reaped the largest gains, and conferred the greatest blessings upon the world, the records of the centuries show.

CHAPTER III.

PHASES OF PROGRESS.

Threatening Aspects.
Safeguards.
Encouraging Indications.

CHAPTER III.

PHASES OF PROGRESS.

THERE is an impression in some quarters that serious changes are taking place in the religious thought of the world, that Protestant Christianity is losing its fundamental doctrines, and its hold upon the respect of cultivated minds, and that these things bode evil to the Churches, whatever their statistical exhibits may show.

Let us look at the worst aspects of the case, and see whether the symptoms are grounds of hope or alarm.

The first and most palpable indication is a drift of religious ideas. The present is called an age of infidelity outside of the Church, and of a decay of faith within. Changes are taking place in the accepted theology. Theological controversies are directed to new issues, or to old ones in modified forms. Some religious thinkers are changing their religious bases; some are rationalizing their beliefs, and adjusting them to new conditions of progress; others are toning up and growing more conservative; and others still are anxiously wondering whither we are tending.

6

Many are seeking relief from the embarrassments of close elaborated systems; the "liberal" are growing more "liberal," some, to be borne into seas where deadly calms reign, or others upon sunken rocks, or into engulfing quicksands of doubt and despair. Nevertheless, formulated creeds and books of discipline remain, and are likely to remain, to serve as buoys, pointing out deep water, and indicating the relative position of the fleet.

A considerable "drift of educated thought—in science, in art, and in philosophy—is away from Church life."* Some are "losing veneration for the Church and its ordinances," and no longer regard it as "a divine institution, in any peculiar sense," but only as "an association for education." It is popular to kick against dogmas. The old systems, which "supposed a logical connection in divine truth," "like a pyramid, tapering, point by point, to its very apex," and devolving upon its builders a kind of necessity to cramp Christian doctrine into forms harmonizing with preconceived ideals of theological symmetry, have fallen into disfavor, and, with many, into contempt, as relics of the old scholastic habit. The temper of the present age instinctively shuns every thing tending that way. Theodicies are put forth less elaborately and more modestly.

---

* The author acknowledges his indebtedness in this and in several of the following paragraphs, to Rev. Henry Ward Beecher's Sermons upon "Christianity Unchanged by Changes."

We find some men atheistically inclined, "not ignorant and malignant men," but men who "profess to have trained their minds to regular and scientific thought," who favor those views quietly and tentatively, and are "not active propagandists." Others, persons of mystical poetic natures, may be called moderate pantheists, whose god is "the sum of all the facts, attributes, and possibilities of all his creatures," but without personality, vague, mysterious, illusive.

Others are unsettled in regard to certain questions about the Bible—as to the extent of revelation —whether inspiration reached beyond the natural faculties of the writers; whether it was "an injection of thought;" whether it extended to every word of the original language; whether it was a special gift to the few men who penned the biblical books, or whether it has been bestowed upon other great religious teachers, in other lands and periods. There have been pressing inquiries in regard to the authority of the Scriptures; and how far, "in the last estate," doubtful points "come for audience and adjudication before the court of the reasonable moral consciousness, in an intelligent age." Rules and methods of biblical interpretation are undergoing modification.

Specific doctrines also have been subjected to close questionings. The trinity, depravity, redemption, the resurrection, penalty, the scope and im-

port of miracles, and other doctrines, have been
freshly and broadly discussed, the fields plowed and
replowed, subsoiled and drained.   In some circles,
the Christian ideas included in the words sin, re-
pentance, pardon, atonement, salvation, holiness,
etc., as long interpreted in religious thinking, are
radically opposed or explained away.   It is said,
and not without some basis in facts, that " thinkers
of great boldness and breadth," ministers and laymen, may be found in the "evangelical" Churches
of Scotland, in the Church of England, and in the
"orthodox" Churches in the United States, who
are turning aside from the old faiths.

Among many literary, scientific, and even business men there seems to exist a conviction that
there is a radical conflict between the current theologies and the natural sciences, while the attitude
of others is simply one of indifference to all theology, and even to religion.   A few years ago Mr.
Ruskin said that so utter was the infidelity of
Europe, no statesman would dare, in defending a
measure before Parliament or the *Corps Legislatif*,
to quote from the Bible in support of his position.
About the same time, at the annual meeting of the
Christian Evidence Society, in London, Lord Salis-
bury, the chairman, said, " The intense importance
of the prevalent unbelief pressed itself upon the
minds of thoughtful Christians, and acquired new
weight every day. . . . They were standing in one

of the most awful crises through which the intellect of Christendom had ever passed. They could point to many distinguished intellects from which all that belief had gone in which until now the highest minds coincided." Lord Shaftesbury, following him, said that "bishops, deans, men of science, the greatest minds in literature, avowed infidel principles." In the "Atlantic Monthly," for November, 1879, Professor Goldwin Smith also joined in this gloomy representation of our times, and discoursed upon "The Prospect of a Moral Interregnum," the result of the wide-spread infidelity of the present time. "Three fourths of the strongest and most original minds among the younger graduates of our American colleges" are claimed to hold "beliefs or unbeliefs diametrically opposed to the accepted faith of Christendom." Others, of less mental independence, are presumed to be unbelievers from fashion, or from pride of association; and others still are said to be simply in a condition of non-belief—a state of vacancy and indefiniteness—because they hardly know what to believe.

To complete the picture, "Lawyers, physicians, teachers, scientific men," says Rev. H. W. Beecher, "sit for various reasons under pulpit instruction, some because they feel a want of reverence and worship; some because their social relationships make it convenient for them; some because they are bringing up families, and they think it a good thing for their children to start in this way, and not blossom out into more perfect knowledge until their habits and characters are formed ; and some because it is respectable, fashionable, and profitable ; but, whatever the cause may be, our Churches are filled with men who are very much at sea in regard to their religious beliefs." *

In some localities, though in comparatively small circles, but active and many-seeming, a Babel of beliefs, new-fangled and old-fangled, loads the air. " Pre-existence of souls, regeneration by moral suasion, the religion of philanthropy, the ethics of expediency, the Bible to be judged by man's intuitions, inspiration reduced to genius, the gospel of physical strength, the gospel of aspiration, the eternity of matter, millenarianism, science the new Bible, the nineteenth century to sit in judgment on God's word and to *select* what it shall be pleased to believe, (the twentieth century of course to have the same privilege ;) why, these that I have named —and they are enough to dizzy one's brain—are only the first syllables of the clamor of the semi-infidel Church of the day." †

We cheerfully allow a considerable part of the foregoing statements, but these things excite in us no alarm.   Why?

* Discourse preached May 19, 1878. "Christian Union," p. 14.
† "The Light : Is it Waning?" p. 61. Congregational Publication Society, 1879.

1. The condition of things is not wholly nor even mainly the result of human depravity.

Many love darkness and hate the light, and carnal hearts resist the higher and purer truths. But this too common source of unbelief does not always nor even approximately account for the tendencies under consideration. A large portion of the world, in the Churches and out of them, is actuated by other motives. Many excellent persons, of high character and devout spirit, in these matters proceed thoughtfully, hesitatingly, and even regretfully, because of the perils attending both the surrender and the restatement of ideas. But they think they have gleams of new truths, or of new forms and relations of truth; and, probably, in some cases, they are more conscientious in saying what they do not believe than others in averring what they do believe. Such changes come not out of the baser elements of human nature, but largely out of higher aspirations. Bishop Butler said: "There is a middle ground between a full satisfaction of the truth of Christianity and a satisfaction to the contrary. The middle state of mind between these two consists of a serious apprehension that it may be true, joined with a doubt whether it is so." Such a state may co-exist with a simple love of the truth, and earnestness in seeking it. Such doubt is not criminal; it is one of the stages of progress in faith and knowledge. Faith becomes stronger from the investigations which honest doubt has prompted. Skepticism, in these milder forms, is only a suspense in the midst of investigation.

Some of the more moderate forms of the rationalistic spirit in our times, whether wise or unwise, have not been unfriendly, in intent, toward Christianity. They have simply attempted to discover elements of truth in the various systems of theology and mythology. The philosophy of Hegel was an elaborate attempt to identify the deductions of reason with the system of the Church. But how often, in such attempts, is faith surrendered at the outset, and reason accepted as supreme and final. A heavy discount must therefore be charged to even honest doubt, because of the unrest and peril which follow in its path. But we are learning that this is only one of many deductions, which the cause of Christianity is obliged to endure, in its attempts to save and utilize imperfect beings; that it can afford to endure very much of such loss; and that often, in the long stretch of events, large compensations come from these losses. The truth is strengthened and fortified by the stimulus they awakened.

2. Nor is the present situation an indication of the weakness of evangelical Protestantism.

It is rather an evidence of life, of activity, of mental inquiry and investigation — normal conditions of intelligent souls. Questions will arise, and there will be trouble in settling them. Rome says, "Come, cast yourself into my lap. I have settled every thing infallibly. My children have no doubts. Every thing with me has been thoroughly arranged, established, and vindicated for ages. No anxious changes are necessary. I have a tribunal that answers infallibly all inquiries. I give peace and rest." But God did not make man to live on any such basis, furnishing him with a "packed-up trunk of beliefs," to take with him all through the way of life. Nor does Rome meet the needs of her own children. Large numbers of thinkers in France to-day and elsewhere have broken radically from their traditional faith, and hold only a nominal relation with the Papal Church as *quasi* Catholics. We are made to be "thinkers with the divine Thinker," responsible for thinking and deciding. The spirit of inquiry and investigation may sometimes be bold, rash, irregular, discarding all responsibility. It may push sacred and well-established principles into temporary peril, with no just vindication for such conduct. But inquiry is the path of individual improvement, a normal state.

Considered as a whole, it should be regarded as the progressive movement of the world's best religious thought. Does it sometimes seem irregular and destructive? So is all progress, for it is the advance of living elements over the decayed. It is inevitable that sharp criticism, friendly, unfriendly, and even destructive, will arise to test truth. By such tests, piercing to the core, we get rid of old superstitions and husks destitute of vitality. Thus have physical science, medicine, and civil law been improved. What immense revolutions have taken place in all departments of knowledge!

Old ideas, sometimes, are inadequate to our needs. The old phraseology will not stand the test of the progress of philology, and, therefore, old formularies and technicalities must be modified. Any other course would logically carry us back to the phraseology and demonology of the Middle Ages. Some persons see only evil in such things, and think that evangelical ideas are dying out. But we see in them signs of the world's growth under the power of a divine impulse. Behind it are divine factors, and it will be sustained by the world's best consciousness. Its product will be a larger and deeper expression of the Divine will. During the past three centuries great factors have been oper-ating for the production of these results ; and Prot-estantism has been an influential participator, and also, by just right, a leading beneficiary.

3. Truth does not depend upon speculative con-ditions, nor upon purely intellectual apprehension. The heart-needs conserve and guard it.

We are little inclined to agree with those who think the power of Christianity, even with persons of the highest intellectual culture, depends upon its alliance with philosophical theories. " The Gospel of Christ is not the faint negative of the daguerreo-typist, which cannot be discerned by the usual vision, but must be held up to a certain light, under the direction of an adept operator. The Christian religion has never identified itself with any system of science, astronomical, intellectual, political, or natural." Liberal speculators in theology, and the champions of " advanced thought," forget these things, and are frequently betrayed into the old scholastic method of forcing the truth into meta-physical formulas—an offense to all just minds. How much wiser and truer the higher philosophy which aims to meet the deeper wants of the heart, than that which comes from intellectual restless-ness or morbid curiosity, or is hampered by precon-ceived logical conditions !

In this country, where liberalism in religion has been carried to the furthest limit, there seems little reason to fear that radical unbelief will be either extensive or permanent. " There are aberrations and vagaries without number, but they are, for the most part, ephemeral. The experiment of letting people think and preach what they like has not been so destructive as it was once thought it would be. . . . A practical adoption of the mild methods, which must after all be conceded to be in the true spirit of the Gospel, cannot, we think, with truth be said to have been unfavorable to its influence. It

is a fact of impressive significance that the minister*
who has borne liberalism in religion to lengths heretofore unknown in any public speaker professing
Christianity, has lately, in terminating his labors in
New York, deliberately announced his dissatisfaction with the results of his own teachings, whether
in himself or others." †

The human race cannot live in a state of unbelief. The soul needs faith and the benefit of faith,
and will demand " the bread of life."

Said Professor Austin A. Phelps, in " The Independent," a few years ago : " There was truth in
Robespierre's argument for the Being of God, that
'Atheism was an aristocratic belief.' It is true of
every variety of infidelity that, sooner or later, it
contracts itself within the circle of a few minds.
The masses of men never permanently embrace it.
The history of infidelity proves this. It has been
beaten so many times, in so many varieties, beneath
such adroit disguises, under such diversities of circumstances, with such accumulations of disadvan-
tage on the side of faith, popular opinion has so
often spurned it, respectable opinion has so often
become ashamed of it, that now we have settled
upon this as one of the axioms of Christian policy, that infidelity cannot become the permanent
belief of any people. The mania of suicide lurks in
its blood. Sooner or later a secret power in the

* Rev. O. B. Frothingham.   † " New York Evening Post."

popular instinct of faith will creep around it in a circle of fire, and it will act the scorpion in the fable. This we believe simply because the history of unbelief is a succession of such deaths. It is always braying in some new form, and is always gasping in some old form."

4. The present indications and tendencies of religious thought are not new, unusual, and exceptional experiences in the world's history, nor in the history of modern times.

We see but a tithe of these things as compared with Europe, in the opening half of the last century, when "the human mind, pushing its inquiries in all directions, approached and entered the domain of metaphysics in religion. The disclosure of ancient errors in natural science as well as the falsehoods of the Papacy, had cherished a rising habit of doubt, till incredulity was regarded a token of superior wisdom. . . . Theologians felt the influence, or yielded without consciousness. It was as if a mist had silently overspread the landscape; and neither tree nor hill, neither the house of God below nor the bright heaven above, was seen clearly. Not a land in Western Europe was exempt from that peculiar atmosphere, in which all forms of speculation glided into incredulity." *

"Never," said a writer in the "North British

* Bishop Burgess, of Maine, in "Pages from the Ecclesiastical History of New England."

Review," 'has century risen on England so void
of soul and faith as that which opened with Queen
Anne, (1702,) and reached its misty noon beneath
the second George (1732–1760)—a dewless night
succeeded by a sunless dawn. . . . The Puritans
were buried and the Methodists were not born. . . .
The world had the idle, discontented look of the
morning after some mad holiday." In 1729 the
heads of Oxford University complained of the
spread of open deism among the students, and
Cambridge struggled with the same evil. Isaac
Taylor says: "At the time when Wesley was acting
as moderator in the disputations at Lincoln College
(1729–1734) there was no philosophy abroad in the
world—there was no *thinking*—that was not atheistic in its tone and tendency."* The "Weekly Miscellany" (1732) said: " Freethinkers were formed
into clubs to propagate their sentiments, and atheism was scattered broadcast through the kingdom."
The pastoral letters of Bishop Gibson † show that
the most pernicious efforts were put forth to undermine religion. "Some set aside all Christian ordinances, the Christian ministry, and the Christian
Church ; others so allegorize Christ's miracles as to
take away their reality ; others display the utmost
zeal for natural religion, in opposition to revealed ;
and all, or most, pleading for liberty, run into the

* " Wesley and Methodism." Am. edition, p. 33.
† Quoted in Tyerman's " Life of Wesley," vol. i, p. 219.

wildest licentiousness. Reason is recommended as a good and sufficient guide in matters of religion and the Scriptures are believed only so far as they agree or disagree with the light of nature." A writer in " Blackwood's Magazine "* said, " Pope held his hereditary faith without the slightest appearance or pretense of any spiritual attachment to it." Sir John Barnard said, " It really seems to be the fashion for a man to declare himself of no religion." Montesquieu said, " There is no religion in England. If the subject is mentioned in society it excites nothing but laughter. Not more than four or five members of the House of Commons are regular attendants at Church." Bishop Butler said :† " It is come, I know not how, to be taken for granted, by many persons, that Christianity is not so much as a subject of inquiry ; but that it is now, at length, discovered to be fictitious. And, accordingly, they treat it as if, in the present age, this were an agreed point among all people of discernment, and nothing remained but to set it up as a principal subject of mirth and ridicule, as it were by way of reprisals for having so long interrupted the pleasures of the world."

The clergy were thoroughly infected by this tendency. Natural religion included most of their theology. The great doctrines of the Reformation

* About ten years ago.
† Preface to his "Analogy of Religion." 1736.

were banished from the universities and the pulpits. A large class of divines held to a refined system of ethics, having no connection with Christian motives and the vital principle of spiritual religion. Arianism and Socinianism were fashionable in the Established Church, and the prevailing creed of the most intelligent Dissenters. Among the Presbyterians the departures from orthodoxy were very grave. Three professors in the University of Glasgow were Antitrinitarians. An able school of Arian teachers arose among the Presbyterians, in Exeter,* about 1717. It spread through Devonshire and Cornwall to the metropolis, and established itself in Salter's Hall, in London, among the descendants of a Puritan ancestry. " Latitudinarianism spread widely through all religious bodies, and dogmatic teachings were almost excluded from the pulpit." †

Mr. Leckey says : ‡ " The doctrines of depravity, the vicarious atonement, the necessity of salvation, the new birth, faith, the action of the Divine Spirit in the believer's soul, during the greater part of the eighteenth century, were seldom heard from in the Church-of-England pulpits. The rationalistic tendencies of the Church rendered it little obnoxious to skeptics." Leslie Stephen says : § " Hume and Paley curiously agreed in recommending young

* " England in the Eighteenth Century," by Mr. Leckey, vol. ii p. 586.   † Ibid., p. 341.   ‡ Ibid., p. 593.
§ " History of English Thought in the Eighteenth Century."

men of freethinking tendencies to take orders;" and that " the skepticism of the upper classes was willing that the Church should survive, though faith might perish." Many of the clergy " taught but little that might not have been taught by Socrates or Confucius." " Dogmatic teaching had disappeared from the pulpits ;" " Christianity was reduced to the lowest terms," though some gave it "a *quasi* assent, because they felt it to be essential to society."

I have given but a partial exhibit of the facts, showing the dubious prospects of religious faith in England, in the first half of the last century. Many other dark shades might be added to the pictures. But this brief portrayal shows that the peculiar tendencies in religious thought, which we have recognized as existing in our day, are far more hopeful, and less radical, less widespread, and less influential, than in Great Britain a century and a half ago. This was recently admitted in the "Spectator," and yet, said the writer, "English unbelief melted away, and was succeeded by vehement forms of faith." Mr. Leckey also recognized this fact.

A similar condition of things existed in the United States in the last two decades of the last century, extending somewhat into the present century. The most radical and revolting forms of infidelity prevailed throughout the land. It especially infested the colleges and the legislative bodies.

7

The leading statesmen were Atheists or Deists. A writer in the "Index"* said: "All the great men who took part with Mr. Paine in laying the foundations of the government of the United States, with very few exceptions, held the same theological sentiments, although they did not publicly identify themselves with him in his attacks on the Church and its religion. And they would have completely revolutionized the sentiments of the American people but for the influence of George Whitefield and John Wesley." Chancellor Kent (1765–1847) said,† "In my younger days there were very few professional men that were not infidels; or at least they were so far inclined to infidelity that they could not be called believers in the truth of the Bible." Bishop Meade‡ vividly portrayed the prevalence of infidelity in Virginia at this time. Scarcely a young man of any literary culture believed in Christianity. As late as 1810, he said, "I can truly say that in every educated young man in Virginia whom I met I expected to find a skeptic, if not an avowed unbeliever." Said Rev. Lyman Beecher:§ "The boys who dressed flax in the barn read Tom Paine, and believed him." Yale College was pervaded with infidelity, and the dominant habit of thought

* May 13, 1870.
† Conversation with Governor Clinton, of New York.
‡ "Old Churches and Families of Virginia."   § "Autobiography."

was skeptical, when Dr. Dwight assumed the presidency in 1745, only four or five of the students being members of the Church. The members of the first Senior Class reciting to him were more familiarly known by the names of Diderot, D'Alembert, Voltaire, Rousseau, Robespierre, Danton, etc., which they had assumed, than by their own. To overcome the current infidelity taxed Dr. Dwight to the utmost, but he triumphed.* Princeton College was no better, and William and Mary's College was called a hot-bed of infidelity. Transylvania University, in Kentucky, founded by the Presbyterians, was wrested from them by infidels. At Bowdoin College, Me., in the early period of the presidency of Rev. Dr. Appleton, only one student was willing to avow himself a Christian. Dr. Appleton " stood in the current of destruction," with prayers, arguments, and pleadings, " long before he saw the tide turning." Mr. Parton, in his " Life of Aaron Burr," speaking of the infidelity of this period, says it was confidently predicted that Christianity could not survive two more generations.

Dr. Timothy Dwight's description of this period will remind us of many things we see and hear in our days:

" Striplings, scarcely fledged, suddenly found that the world had been involved in general darkness through the long succession of preceding ages, and

* See " Sketch of Dr. Dwight's Life," in vol. i of his works.

that the light of wisdom had just begun to dawn upon the human race. All the science, all the information, that had been acquired before the last thirty or forty years stood, in their view, for nothing. Experience they boldly proclaimed a plodding instructress, who taught in manners, morals, and government, nothing but Abecedarian lessons, fitted only for children. Religion they discovered, on the one hand, to be a vision of dotards and nurses; and, on the other, a system of fraud and trick, imposed by priestcraft, for base purposes, upon the ignorant multitude. Revelation was found to be without authority or evidence, and moral obligation a cobweb, which might indeed entangle flies, but by which creatures of stronger wing nobly disdain to be confined. The world, they concluded to have been probably eternal, and matter the only existence. Man, they determined, sprang, like a mushroom, out of the earth by a chemical process; and the power of thinking, choice, and motivity were merely the result of elective affinities. . . . From France, Germany, and Great Britain the dregs of infidelity were vomited upon us. From the 'System de la Nature' and the 'Philosophical Dictionary' down to the 'Political Justice' of Godwin and the 'Age of Reason,' the whole mass of pollution was emptied upon this country. The last two publications flowed in upon us as a deluge. An enormous edition of the 'Age of Reason' was published in France, and sent over to America, to be sold at a few pence per copy, and, where it could not be sold, to be given away." *

Rev. Dr. Baird said † of this period : "Wild and vague expectations were every-where entertained, especially among the young, of a new order of things about to commence, in which Christianity would be laid aside as an obsolete system." When Rev. Dr. Nathan Strong became pastor of the Congregational Church, in Hartford, Conn., in 1774, there were only fifteen male members in the Church, and the spirit of infidelity was already rife in all the larger towns. " The religion of Christ and its ministers were often the subjects of open ridicule and contempt, even on the part of those who were regarded as being entitled to the first standing in society." " Mr. Strong was not unfrequently attacked in public places by some of this class of persons, who, under the guise of a pleasant raillery, sought to inflict a wound upon his feelings, and to sink him and his office in the deference of the thoughtless bystanders." ‡

There was also a vast amount of what was called "heretical" sentiment in the Churches. The Universalist denomination was just starting ; the Chris-

---

* Dwight's "Travels," vol. iv, pp. 376, 379, 380.
† "Religion in America."
‡ "American Quarterly Register," Nov., 1840, p. 132.

tians had a small commencement, in 1801; the
Unitarian break did not come until 1815–1830, and
the Hicksite Friend movement until 1827.   All the
"orthodox" bodies were largely pervaded by the
leaven of Arian, Socinian, restoration, and no-fu-
ture-punishment ideas.   As we survey present indications, it is difficult to conceive the extent of
their prevalence at that time in the Churches of
"evangelical" Protestantism — an infection from
English and European sources, running back, as
we have seen, through Papal lines in Italy and the
gardens of the Medici, to ante-mediæval times,
though in part a revolt from High Calvinism.

A Congregational pastor, Rev. Dr. Huntington,
of Coventry, Conn., wrote the first book ever published in this country advocating the "death-and-
glory" doctrine, subsequently so conspicuous in
the teachings of Rev. Hosea Ballou.   And Rev.
Dr. Strong, of Hartford, Conn., in answering it, in
1796, deplored the extensive prevalence of those
sentiments in the "evangelical" Churches.   A Congregational pastor, Rev. Charles Chauncey, D.D.,
of Boston, and a Baptist minister, Rev. Elhanan
Winchester, of Philadelphia, wrote the first books
in favor of Restorationism published in America.

Boston Congregationalism, comprising nine
Churches, had become substantially Unitarian, and
only waited for a convenient time to take the
name.   Nine towns within ten miles of Boston had

no Congregational Church which remained true to orthodoxy. "In 1800," said Dr. Bradford,* "it was confidently believed there was not a strict Trinitarian clergyman [Congregational] in Boston." Rev. Dr. Eckley, at the "Old South," was variously regarded as a "High Arian," a "Semi-Arian," or a Socinian, and his Church, in the language of Dr. Lyman Beecher, "was shivering in the wind," and according to Dr. Bacon, "if an exception, might cease to be an exception" to the general Unitarian revolt. The most intense opposition to "evangelical" ideas pervaded the higher social and cultured classes, and dominated Boston. The little nucleus of devoted Trinitarians which organized the Park-street Church, in 1809, was called to endure an amount of opposition and obloquy unknown in more recent times, for the major sentiment of the city was overwhelmingly against them. When Rev. Dr. E. D. Griffin entered upon the pastorate of the Church, in 1811, his task called for a stout heart and a bold hand. The current of prevailing thought was so averse to evangelical religion, that to raise a voice in its defense was to hazard one's reputation among respectable people. "The finger of scorn was pointed at him, and he had to breast a tide of misrepresentation and calumny, of opposition and hatred, which would have overwhelmed him if he had not the spirituality of an apostle and the strength

* "Life of Dr. Mayhew."

of a giant." *   Attracted by reports of Dr. Griffin's genius and eloquence, gentlemen of culture and standing occasionally ventured into the church to hear his Sunday evening lectures, but in partial " disguise "—so unpopular was it to visit an evangelical church—sitting " in obscure corners, with caps drawn over their faces, and wrappers turned inside out." †

This condition of religious sentiment dominated Eastern Massachusetts, and more or less pervaded other localities throughout the State.   The orthodox historian of Massachusetts Congregationalism says, that of two hundred Congregational Churches, east of Worcester County, not more than two in five were under evangelical pastors.   In 1795, Socinian ideas, from reading Dr. Priestley's writings by members of the parish, drove Dr. Jonathan Edwards, 2d, from his Church, in New Haven, Connecticut, as similar notions had driven his father from Northampton forty years before.   The Bishops of the Methodist Episcopal Church, in their Pastoral Address, in 1816, deplored the prevalence of Arian and Socinian notions in their denomination.   No denomination was wholly exempt, so extensive had become the infection originally exhaled from the bosom of Rome, before the birth of Protestantism, and assailing her theology in every period of her history.

* "American Quarterly Register," 1840, p. 374.
† A Statement, by Rev. Nehemiah Adams, D.D.

During the period from 1800 to 1830 there were numerous schisms, secessions, and withdrawals from the evangelical Churches, which entered into the formation of the Unitarian, Universalist, Christian, and the Hicksite bodies, thus relieving the evangelical Churches of these heterogeneous elements. At this time, too, under the leadership of Rev. Hosea Ballou, Universalism took on its Arian type.

During the same period the infidels in Europe renewed their efforts to uphold their cause. Between 1817 and 1830 5,768,900 volumes of the works of Voltaire, Rousseau, and other infidel writers were circulated on the Continent.*

But if these dark periods had their bold doubters and deniers, they also had "hearts of faith and tongues of fire." God has never been without standard-bearers—the true "spiritual pontificate"—the heroic succession, whose lineage is divine. Under such leadership the spell of unbelief, in England and America, was broken, and the desolating hosts were turned back. Within the past thirty years they have rallied and assailed Christianity again, without and within; but this time they have been unable, even temporarily, to check the progress of the Churches. Our banners have uninterruptedly advanced, even more than in any previous period in the history of Christianity.

But more than this should be said. Already we

* "American Quarterly Register," August, 1830, p. 33.

discern indications that the skepticism of our times is staggering and receding. As English Deism, French Atheism, and the Old Rationalism of Germany, have been successively dismissed by thinking men, so also the mythical Rationalism of Strauss, Bauer, and the Tübingen critics, has run its course; Pantheism has lost its prestige; Materialism is encountering among its friends "significant shrugs of suspicion and dissent;" skeptical scientists are becoming weary in their long and fruitless waitings for the foundations of religious hope to be laid in irrefragable axioms; Spiritism has come to disgrace by the foulness of its tendencies, the monstrosity of its claims and the gigantic frauds of its *seances;* Ingersollism has damned itself with its terrible blasphemies; and Free Religion is only a respectable annual spectacular parade of many-shaded inquirers, rapidly decreasing in number.

Is it said that the evangelical Churches have lost their hold upon the intellect of the age? How, and wherein? When was it equally identified with the best, the most vigorous, and the most learned culture? It is a matter of clear demonstration * that the students in the colleges of the evangelical Churches in forty-eight years (1830 to 1878) increased twice as much, relatively, as the population of the country, and also that a half more, relatively, of the

---

* See Chapter on "Protestant Progress in the United States;" also "Table of Colleges" in the Appendix.

students in those colleges are professing Christians than forty years ago. The colleges of the evangelical Churches increased eight fold, and the population three and a half fold. These things indicate that evangelical Christianity is fully identified with the advanced educational movements of society, and entrenched in the highest institutions of culture.

The editor * of a leading religious journal, a man whose scholarship, culture, and breadth of Christian fellowship are conspicuous, recently said:

"It is one of the most familiar incidents in the reports of modern sermons delivered in 'liberal' pulpits, and in the pages of periodicals published under the patronage of the people who listen to such discourses, to find the assertion, in various forms, that what are termed evangelical views of revealed truth —such as those relating to sin and its retribution, to the triune personality of the Godhead, to the vicarious sufferings of Jesus Christ, and to the renewal of nature and character through faith in the Son of God—have become obsolete in the denominations which professedly hold them, and that it is only through disingenuousness that many ministers and members still remain in connection with Churches that hold to these doctrines as their creed. It is affirmed that they are rarely preached from the pulpit, that they are often disclaimed by ministers

* Rev. Bradford K. Peirce, D.D., in "Zion's Herald," Boston, Massachusetts, August, 1880.

of orthodox Churches, and that they are not accepted by the membership.

"Now, if these preachers and writers of 'liberal' views simply mean to say that there has been a great change in what may be called the philosophy of religion—in the development of a system of human discipline from the love rather than from the sovereignty of God—or if they affirm only that the necessary fruits of faith in a life of obedience and holy charities are more emphasized than they were when the early Protestants were insisting upon faith in contradistinction to the prevailing sacramental popery of the hour, or that the future retributions of sin are urged in less figurative and material forms, little objection would be made to the statement. But if it is meant that there is any serious weakening throughout the evangelical Churches on what is vital in these truths, we must say, the persons that hold these opinions have generalized too rapidly from very narrow premises. In large cities and considerable towns there may be found, over certain Churches of a special character, men of strong, original characteristics, of marked popular gifts, and usually of no inconsiderable self-conceit, who studiously shun the common modes of expressing and interpreting the doctrines of Revelation, and are disposed to give great prominence to the relative duties of life. These men can all be readily numbered on the fingers of one hand. And it is noticeable, in nearly every case, that when these men are called upon by ecclesiastical bodies or by the public press to define their position, they are ready to affirm that, in their own forms of expression, they hold all the vital doctrines of evangelical Protestantism. Even Mr. Beecher, far the most independent man of this description, and most disposed to tear in pieces formal creeds and traditional forms of religious expression, after one of his most abrupt and apparently positive renunciations of certain orthodox beliefs, hastens at his earliest opportunity in a succeeding discourse, in view of the public comments, to say that, with his own explanation of them, he still holds the evangelical as distinguished from the liberal interpretation of the divine nature and the New Testament plan of salvation.

"But outside of these well-known pulpits and a few periodicals, the great body of ministers and members in the orthodox Churches are entirely at rest in reference to their catechisms. Our theological seminaries, those which are not Arminian, while largely modifying the Calvinistic philosophy of previous centuries, have found no difficulty in expounding the Scriptures in the light of pronounced evangelical views. Modern destructive biblical criticism has had no perceptible influence in shaking the faith of those institutions in the authenticity and inspiration of the Holy Scriptures. In spite of the busy activity of this school of critics, there never was an hour when so many commentaries, written by accomplished Hebrew and Greek scholars, were published or so widely distributed. All that is valuable, that can stand sifting in this criticism, has been accepted, and a clearer and better interpretation of the Bible has been secured; but not one of the doctrines of the Nicene creed has been touched by this criticism, or any important excisions made in the received canon of Scripture.

"Take the great national Churches, more than keeping pace, as they do, with the growth of population—the Baptist, the Presbyterian, and the Methodist—and upon these millions of members scarcely any appreciable impression has been made by these modern liberal views. All over the land the old and impressive truths of Revelation, sanctioned by a Book in which the hearers have not the slightest distrust as to its divine origin and as accepted through the ages, are preached every Sabbath, and taught to susceptible childhood in the Sunday-schools. The Episcopal Church every-where utters its positive creed and sings its sublime evangelical anthems, as if a liberal discourse had never been preached or destructive criticism never laid its hand upon any sacred text. The Roman Church, with its millions of believers in its professed infallible truth, goes on year after year peremptorily affirming these articles of faith. There could be nothing more unsustained by the facts than these assertions that the evangelical views have become, or in any wise, as the signs of the times indicate, are liable to become, obsolete. The great revivals of religion, occurring in the centers of population and among multitudes liable to deteriorate morally, more than supply any loss that may happen from the lapse of certain professed evangelical teachers, or the deterioration of vital faith on the part of worldly members of wealthy Churches."

The foregoing facts show that the tendencies, in our times, to what has been styled " advanced thought," are not new ; that it is not new for men of education and literary taste to assail " evangelical " theology, or even Christianity itself; that the forces now assailing Christianity and sacrificial orthodoxy are less numerous, less dominant, and less influential than in the two previous periods of unbelief within the last one hundred and eighty years ; that skeptical thought repeats itself in varying forms and in intermitting waves ; and that out of each period of darkness and doubt Christianity has emerged to achieve greater conquests than before. The revival and wonderful progress of evangelical Protestantism in England since the first half of the last century, has become one of the palpable and incontrovertible facts of history, and its unparalleled growth, in this country, during the present century, is not less indisputable. In another place the facts of its progress will be fully demonstrated. Never before was there so much intellect and culture devoted to the vindication and propagation of evangelical religion as at the present time.

In and around Boston, eighty years ago, the liberal Churches, so called, immensely preponderated in influence, wealth, and number, over the evangelical Churches. It is difficult for us now to appreciate the situation then, when within a radius of ten miles around Boston there were twenty-three liberal Churches to eighteen evangelical, and in nine towns there were no Churches which, in the schism that soon followed, remained true to orthodoxy. Now, within the same limits, there are two hundred and fifty-seven evangelical Churches to eighty-one liberal Churches, the former gaining two hundred and thirty-nine and the latter fifty-eight. Morally and socially, the evangelical gain has been even greater. The "Harvard Advocate" recently stated a kindred fact. Inquiries extending through fourteen hundred graduates of Harvard College, within the last ten years, show only two skeptics, one an Atheist and the other an Agnostic, and never before were there so many evangelical Church members among the students of that institution. How different from the condition of the colleges in 1800!

CHAPTER IV.

DELIVERANCE.

Restatement.
Vindication.
Rejuvenation.
True Ideal.

8

CHAPTER IV.

DELIVERANCE.

THE purification of theology, under the modifying processes noticed in previous pages, has been sometimes mistaken for disintegration and decay. But the changes have chiefly related to surface forms rather than to central truths, to the husk rather than to the kernel; while some things once magnified are now minified, and others once in the background are now brought to the front. A purging process has been apparent in religious phraseology and never more so than at the present time. Great advances have been made in purifying and simplifying Christian doctrine and in developing fuller conceptions of the truth. Never, since the days of primitive Christianity, has the liberation from arbitrary systems been so complete; and never before has Christian truth stood upon conditions so favorable to the best and most enduring influence. We have learned that no setting of the truth in systems of human construction can save it or make it effective. Truth, in its purest and simplest forms, is its own best conservator and advocate.

Under Edwards, Hopkins, and the Andover and

New Haven theologians successively, Calvinism has undergone great modifications. The thought of the age, and especially the Arminian theology, have continually warred against it, producing a widespread revulsion. The doctrine of the imputation of Adam's guilt to his posterity; the old Calvinistic view of depravity, which represented unregenerate men as just as bad as they can be, and capable of acting only in the direction of evil; and the theory that regeneration is effected by irresistible grace effectually calling and saving men, are only faintly shadowed in any of the writings of this age; while the coarser and more offensive features of reprobation, infant damnation, etc., are rapidly dropping out of sight. Few American preachers—we doubt if one can be found—will allow Calvin's "Institutes" to be their theological standard. Calvinism, whether sublapsarian or supralapsarian, is now seldom uttered in pulpits. The religious consciousness recognizes it as effete, or as rapidly becoming so, notwithstanding an occasional quasi-ratification of the Westminster Catechism.

The doctrine of vicarious atonement, while firmly held as substitutional, is no longer preached as a ransom of war, or a commercial equivalent; and Christ is not often portrayed as a culprit, shrinking under the bolts of his Father's personal wrath, and sinking to the misery of the damned. Literal fire and brimstone, as the final portion of lost souls, is now generally discarded, although held by restorationists and evangelicals alike within the present century.* The doctrine of the Trinity no longer savors of Tritheism. The six creative periods are now interpreted by only a few scholars as six literal days. The theory of literal verbal inspiration has fewer advocates than formerly. Very considerable modification in the principles and methods of biblical interpretation have taken place. These are a few of the more noticeable changes.

But with these changes the central thoughts in all these doctrines remain. Striking to the core, we find them still cherished by the Churches. Take the great working doctrines of Christianity, strip off the husks, and state them in their simple forms: there is a personal Deity; God is a sovereign; he is a being of infinite perfections; he is the ultimate source of life and being; a mysterious Threeness, so distinct as to justify the use of three distinct names and the personal pronouns, is united in the oneness of the Godhead; the Bible is the divinely inspired book; it is so inspired as to be the authoritative rule of faith and practice; the soul is immaterial and immortal; man is accountable to God; he is so depraved and weak as to need a Saviour; he must be spiritually charged in order to rise into harmony with holiness; whatever education or

* See " Discourses on the Prophecies," by Rev. Elhanan Winchester, 1800, vol. ii, pp. 86, 131, 132.

culture may do, the Holy Spirit is the efficient agent in effecting this change; supreme Deity was embodied in the personage Christ Jesus; the death of Christ and his resurrection is the sole basis of pardon and ground of hope for sinners; the effects of faith in Christ are the love of God shed abroad in the heart and a new life; Christ will personally come the second time; he will raise the dead; there will be a day of future general judgment, and a state of fixedness of character involving endless retribution and reward in the future world.   These vital centers of the doctrines of Christianity are held, with little dissent, by all the denominations of evangelical Protestantism.   The exceptions are exceedingly rare among men capable of constructing a system, and there is no prospect of a change in these essential elements.   Christianity is losing nothing of its inherent original self—only that which human imperfection, subtlety, and folly have attached to it, trammeling and falsifying it.

Modern Philosophy and Science, either Directly or Indirectly, have Confirmed many of the Fundamental Tenets of Evangelical Theology.

The Kantian philosophy, rising little later than German rationalism, exerted an important and relatively ennobling influence upon rationalistic theology, and upon other currents of modern thought. "Immanuel Kant," says Kürtz, "saved philosophy from superficial self-sufficiency and quackery, and led it out upon the arena of a mental conflict unparalleled in power, energy, extent, and continuance. Kant's philosophy stood altogether outside of Christianity, and upon the same ground with theological rationalism. Nevertheless, by digging deep into this ground, it brought out much superior ore, of whose existence vulgar rationalism had no idea, and became, without wishing or knowing it, a schoolmaster to Christ in manifold ways. Kant demonstrated the impossibility of a knowledge of supersensuous things by means of the pure reason, but acknowledged the ideas of God, freedom, and immortality, as postulates of the practical reason, and as the principle of all religion whose contents are above the moral law."

Kant's philosophical writings are only a single example of the many contributions of modern philosophy to the cause of religious truth. They have modified the various forms of radical doubt, and the lines of true speculation are converging more and more to the lines of Christian truth.

When we closely analyze the situation we find little blank Atheism in the world, and whatever of Atheism and Pantheism does exist appears almost wholly in speculative forms, tentatively put forth, in connection with individual efforts, to explore the nature and mode of the Infinite. While Hartmann professedly holds atheistic opinions, his philosophy

sometimes leans toward Theism ; for he talks of the
" One Identical Subject," " One Absolute Subject."
In some form, though often imperfect and unsatisfactory to us, the existence of the Supreme Being
is recognized by skeptical, philosophical, and scientific writers.   We seem to be doubling the Cape of
Fear as to the effect of natural science upon speculative Theism, notwithstanding the God of scientific
Theism is a different being from the God of Christian Theism—often only the force, personal or im-
personal, behind all phenomena.   But this is a step
far in advance of the blank Atheism and the Atheistic theory of chance, so popular a hundred years
ago.

Heinholtz said, "If we direct our attention to the
progress of science, as a whole, we shall have to
judge of it by the measure in which the recognition
and knowledge of a *causative* connection, embracing
all phenomena, has advanced."   Kant said, " The
great whole would sink into the abyss of nothing, if
we did not admit something originally and independently external to this infinite contingent, and as
the *cause* of its origin." " Atheism," said Comté,
" is a consecration of ignoble metaphysical sophisms,
the last and least durable of all metaphysical
phases, ' inferior to the rudest philosophy of Theism,' and 'the natural adversary of the positive'
spirit." " I am no atheist," Comté protested warmly to a visitor, two years before his death ; "my at-

titude is that of belief: if not, I should have no right to treat of these matters. If you will have a theory of existence, an intelligent will is the best you can have."* Herbert Spencer, while professedly discarding the accepted idea of God, as the creator of all things or of any thing, and pushing back the first great cause as far as possible, like others of his kind, sometimes falls back upon anthropomorphic conceptions of deity, and speaks of the " Incomprehensible Existence," the " Unknown Cause," the " Inconceivable Greatness." " From the very necessity of thinking in relatives," he says, " the relative is inconceivable, except as related to *a real* non-relative."† Professor Tyndall said, " The idea of Creative Power is as necessary to the production of a single original form as to that of a multitude."‡ Professor John Fiske has said, " Provided we bear in mind the symbolic character of our words, we may say, ' God is a Spirit.' "§ And Mr. R. W. Emerson, after having long dwelt in the dreamy solitudes of Pantheism, has come to be, in the estimation of his intimate friend, Mr. Alcott, a Christian Theist.

The Bible, so sharply and extensively assailed by scientists during the last forty years, is rapidly emerging from the conflict, with multiplying attes-

* See review in " Christian Examiner," July, 1857, pp. 25–27.
† " First Principles," p. 96.   ‡ Belfast Address.
§ " Cosmic Philosophy," vol. ii, p. 449.

tation of victory. It has required a little time to mature the new developments of modern science; but since they have become more fully understood, they have been readily adjusted to the great cycle of truth, where God is the center, and all truth is in harmony with him. We are learning to read the old faiths in the light of modern thought. We seem to have reached the third of three * great epochs in the questions between science and the Bible. The first was the period of violent attacks upon the Bible from the scientific side, and of violent defense. This was followed by another period, of ingenious attempts to reconcile religion and science, attended with compromises and concessions on both sides. The third period, upon which we have now entered, is one in which the question is hardly asked whether religion and science can be reconciled, but rather, How are we to use the help of both in a rational interpretation of the universe?

The multiplication of theories of biblical inspiration show a deepening conviction of some peculiar inspiration, and consequently some peculiar value to be attached to the Bible; and the recent extensive attempts of students to compare it with other great religious books is a substantial concession to its high character. Professor Bowen †

* See "Old Faiths in a New Light." By Newman Smith. Charles Scribner & Sons. 1879.

† Professor Bowen's "Philosophical Lectures," p. 456.

quotes Hartmann as saying, "The germs of all revealed religion are to be found in the heated fancies of the mystics, these fancies being due to inspiration from the Unconscious;" and then adds, "The evidence adduced goes far enough only to confirm a text of Scripture, which he unconsciously labors to establish, that 'The prophecy came not in old time, by the will of man; but holy men of God spake as they were moved by the Holy Ghost.'"

Some of the specific doctrines of revelation have received ample confirmation from the best and strongest developments of modern thought. Kurtz said, Kant's "sharp criticism of pure reason, his deep knowledge of human weakness and depravity, revealed in his doctrine of the *radical evil*, his categorical imperative of the moral law, were all adapted to produce in profound minds a despair of themselves, and a want which Christianity alone could fully satisfy." But these confirmations are broader than mere individual opinions. "From a new quarter, namely, science itself, in the theory that is now held, and is likely to be more widely held, of the origin of man, the doctrine of universal sinfulness is assumed and believed, not as a dogma, but as a conceded universal fact. . . . Unexpectedly, from right out of the camp of science, comes a belief in the doctrine which underlies the whole truth of religion—the doctrine, namely, of the universal lost condition of man." *　The modern doctrine of the solidarity of the race corroborates this fundamental truth of the Bible.

As to the recognition of the divine in Christ, there has been a perceptible advance during this century. While some have gone down to purely humanitarian views, others have risen to higher conceptions. Leaving the Arian conception almost wholly, as a thing of the past and utterly unsatisfying, they have advanced to the Sabellian and the Logos theories, and some to the orthodox view. Renan could not resist the inclination to call Christ "divine," to speak of "his divinity" as "resplendent before our eyes," and to declare that "he is the center of the eternal religion of humanity;" while Schelling, after years of ranging between the idealistic and the realistic systems, near the close of life, declared that St. Paul's language, (Rom. xi, 36,) "For of him, [Christ,] and through him, and to him, are all things; to whom be glory forever, Amen," "is the foundation and last word of philosophy, . . . the key-note of the harmony between revelation and philosophy." Mr. Beecher has well said: "Henceforth, I think, in the endeavor of mankind to formulate a conception of God, no thinker and no theologian will ever be able to frame a distinct and efficient conception of the

---

* Sermon on "Christianity Changing yet Unchanged," by Rev. H. W. Beecher, p. 33.

divine nature without using the materials which were developed in the life and character of the Lord Jesus Christ."

Hon. W. E. Gladstone, M.P.,* has very forcibly and justly said, "You will hear much to the effect that the divisions among Christians render it impossible to say what Christianity is, and so destroy all certainty as to what is the true religion. But if the divisions among Christians are remarkable, not less so is their unity in the greatest doctrines that they hold. Well-nigh fifteen hundred years . . . have passed away, since the great controversies concerning the Deity and the person of the Redeemer were, after a long agony, determined. As before that time, in a manner less defined, but adequate for their day, so ever since that time, amid all chance and change, more, aye, many more, than ninety-nine in every hundred Christians have with one voice confessed the deity and incarnation of our Lord, as the cardinal and central truths of our religion. Surely there is some comfort here, some sense of brotherhood; some glory due to the past, some hope for the times that are to come."

As to the doctrine of immortality, the Church has abated nothing; but, in addition to all former proofs, the later interpretation of Scripture, and the latest revelations of physical and psychological science, have augmented the great volume of testi-

* Address at the Liverpool College, Dec., 1872, pp. 27, 28.

mony in its favor. The greatest names in modern philosophy, Bacon, Descartes, Leibnitz, Locke, Kant, Hamilton, and even Hartmann, are subscribed in its support. Mr. R. W. Emerson, at one time in grave doubt in respect to personal immortality, has recently expressed himself more clearly and confidently in its favor.

As to the doctrine of accountability to God, the multiplication of oaths and obligations, and their substitution, in modern society, in the place of former physical methods of binding men, show its increasing recognition. Kant's " categorical imperative of the moral law " has put this doctrine on an unshaken philosophical foundation of great weight with thinking men, and modern skepticism has virtually recognized it in her new styles of speech— talking of duty, obligation, and responsibility, of " the sacred obligation of truth," of responsibility for belief, of " the duty " of professing one's belief, and respecting the beliefs of others. Polite literature has recently come to abound in these allusions— though often we fear that they contain only half-truths. Such ideas were unknown, however, to classical antiquity, and to the skepticism of other days, as Isaac Taylor has clearly shown.

As to the doctrine of retribution, there have been some vacillations and transitions; but, on the whole, there is an increasing confidence. From 1815 to 1850 the form of belief held by Rev. Hosea Ballou,

and others of his class who departed from orthodoxy, was that all suffering on account of sin will end
with the close of this life: and that, at death, every
person will enter upon a state of holiness and happiness. Since 1850 this view has almost wholly
disappeared, and retribution is now almost universally recognized by the same class of "liberalists," as
running on indefinitely into the future world. In
respect to the endlessness of retribution, there
, has been, in some evangelical circles, a weakening of confidence, while others are more strongly
fortified than ever. Many of the ripest scholars
in the "liberal" bodies, particularly the Unitarian, have conceded that " by no just interpretation of the Scriptures can the final recovery of
all souls be made to appear," although they still
cherish the doctrine on philosophical hypotheses.
Others in those bodies have gone so far as to
declare that even the philosophical hypothesis of
such recovery is not sustained by natural theology
nor analogy, and is opposed by the weightiest
names in the realm of speculation. On the latter
point Professor F. H. Hedge, D.D., has cited Plato
and Leibnitz. *

We believe that, on the whole, the doctrine of
retribution has gained ground during this century
in the number of its advocates and the force of its

* See "Concessions of Liberalists to Orthodoxy," by Rev. D.
Dorchester, D.D. Boston : D. Lothrop & Co.

advocacy. The discourses and writings of Dr. Channing, W. G. Eliot, D.D., Orville Dewey, D.D., F. H. Hedge, D.D., E. H. Sears, D.D., Rev. J. C. Kimball, W. H. Rider, D.D., and many others, freely attest this position. The debates in the Universalist ministers' meetings in Boston, in November and December, 1877, abounded in very strong statements of the law of retribution.*

The comparative study of religions, sometimes conducted in a spirit hostile to Christianity, is making the absolute superiority of Christianity more manifest; and the religious element in the human soul is coming to be more definitely accepted, as not an accident, but an essential factor, of humanity. It is making it apparent that the soul has a Godward side, and that to discredit the religious instinct is to throw doubt on all the powers of the soul, and involve it in the blankest skepticism. The Christian conception of God and man is demonstrating its compatibility with a perfect religion and a perfect life; and the thorough study of the soul seems likely to lead to the acceptance of all the leading tenets of Christian theology, as the only adequate foundation—"the union of all antitheses, the solution of all problems, and the reconciliation of all opposites."

The ethics of Christianity were never so widely accepted in the current literature, the common be-

* See numbers of "The Universalist" during those months

lief, and actual life of the race. They are sifted into all departments of knowledge. New Testament morals are universally acceded and dominant, not because of civil or ecclesiastical authority, but from a rational conviction of their essential rightfulness. And the ethical theory that man has a religious nature, with religious needs, a conscious dependence upon the Divine Being, and a necessity for worship —in short, that in the constitution of man there is a foundation for religion—is now indicated by the greatest thinkers, as the result of careful scientific analysis. David Strauss, after years of wild and destructive criticism, in his last book declared that in both the fields of positive and natural theology there exist valid grounds for the deepest and purest piety, which, "under its twofold aspect of utter dependence and utter reliance, constitutes the inmost core of all the manifestations of religion."

While we may question whether such an answer can be given from his stand-point, we nevertheless rejoice to see so sturdy a critic acknowledge a sure ground of personal piety and spiritual consolation. It was the ground of Schleiermacher, in his great and successful contest with the Materialists and Pantheists, and on which we hope many may yet be led "into all truth."

These fundamental indications of the great ethical ideas of Christianity are establishing it more and

9

more firmly ; and no skepticism, no change of institutions, no revolution, nothing that has been developed by philosophy, from Descartes to Spencer and
Hartmann, can change the eternal fact inherent in
men's nature, of the necessity of utter dependence
and utter reliance upon God for true spiritual repose
and consolation.

Thus is Christianity being continually vindicated,
on some new basis, according to the changing phases
of knowledge and opinion, and more impregnably
established in candid minds.

*While the fundamental elements of Christianity
have been so fully attested and vindicated by the
best modern thought, and even by candid modern
skepticism, on the other hand, radical unbelief has
demonstrated its poverty and powerlessness for good.*

Some of the more courageous skeptics have attempted to push their theories to ultimate practical
results, in order to show that their systems are
capable of meeting the deeper needs of humanity.
But their efforts have only led to constrained or
implied confessions. A writer in the "Wesminster
Review," for October, 1872, set for himself the task
of estimating the capacity of the prevailing materialistic philosophy to console and elevate human
life. Its incentives and comforts to cultivated
minds were portrayed with feeble, vanishing touch-
es ; the necessities of the common heart of human-

ity were overlooked, and the article closed with seemingly conscious revulsion and disgust. On any purely materialistic basis life loses its noblest aims and ideals, self-sacrifice its significance and impulse, and virtue becomes an empty, unreal thing.

None more than the materialists believe in "the order of things," but they shrink from carrying their theories to the lowest terms. Thus reduced, the Systems of Schopenhauer and Hartmann would eclipse the universe. Their inevitable sociological bearings, so deteriorating and destructive in practical life, have opened many minds to their true character. Dr. Strauss, as we have noticed, lived long enough to see the unsatisfactory character of his form of unbelief, because it left great needs of the soul unmet, and to write his later work, " Ein Bekenntniss," (A Confession.) He did not wholly recant, but, rejecting the theories of Schopenhauer and Hartmann as contrary to the best consciousness of the race, this great critical iconoclast set forth the valid ground of the purest and deepest piety— " the innermost core of all the true manifestations of religion — utter dependence and utter reliance upon the Divine."

Thoreau, a gifted and beautiful writer, an ardent lover and worshiper of Nature, in one of his peculiar moods, complained of the failure of his pantheistic worship to satisfy the deeper needs of his con-

sciousness, and expressed the sadness of his inner
life in these lines:

> "Amid such boundless wealth without,
>   I only still am poor within;
> The birds have sung their summer out,
>   But still my spring does not begin."

With characteristic frankness, Mr. O. B. Frothingham, a leader in "Free Religious" doubt, said
of the system he had championed, "The new faith
cannot compete with the old in what are commonly called 'benevolent enterprises.' It would
not, probably, if it were as rich and capable as the
old faith is. Not because the Radicals are stingy,
as has been over and again asserted, but because
they cannot accept the principle on which these
exercises are conducted, and *no other principle is yet
in working order. No original work is yet possible.*
. . . The new methods of charity — reasonable,
scientific, practical — have not yet been devised.
. . . The new faith will exhibit its charity when it
finds an object which makes to it a commanding
appeal." *

More recently, in terminating his labors in New
York city, M. Frothingham "deliberately announced his dissatisfaction with his own teachings,
whether in himself or in others." †

---

* A Discourse on "The Living Faith," by O. B. Frothingham.
New York, 1871.

† "New York Evening Post," 1879.

Full of significance are also these lines of Matthew Arnold:

> "The sea of faith
> Was once, too, at the full, and round earth's shore
> Lay like the folds of a bright girdle furled.
> But now I only hear
> Its melancholy, long, withdrawing roar,
> Retreating to the breath
> Of the night-wind down the vast edges drear,
> And naked shingles of the world.
> Ah, love, let us be true
> To one another! for the world, which seems
> To lie before us like a land of dreams,
> So various, so beautiful, so new,
> Hath really neither joy, nor love, nor light,
> Nor certitude, nor peace, nor help for pain;
> And we are here, as on a darkling plain,
> Swept with confused alarms of struggle and flight,
> Where ignorance armies close by night."

On the other hand, the modifications in the statement of evangelical theology, we have noticed, have not been attended with a decay of faith or a decline of power, but the contrary.

We do not believe there has been any alarming decay of real faith, but that faith has extended her empire, even in the realm of the highest thought. Some lights have indeed been flickering, and others have gone out; but vastly more lamps are being lighted where they never before burned than have been extinguished where they have been burning. To change the figure, the apparent loss has been only a process of sifting more closely the wheat from the chaff, in which the kernels of religious truth have become cleaner and more precious.

With Mr. Beecher,* we say, " I do not believe that theology is ever going to pass away. I believe that to past theologies we owe a world of gratitude. They were efficient in bringing us up to the times that have gone by, and they were good enough for the periods in which they existed; but that there is no more light to break out of the word of God, or out of human experience, I do not believe. . . If we are losing our hold upon the older systems, or a part of them, it is only that we are preparing the way to build larger, deeper, and with more authority and power."

While we are shedding a few of our worn-out garments of technical expression, and rehabilitating ourselves, the Christian standards are advancing. Notwithstanding the gloomy mutterings of modern pessimism, faith in humanity, in God, in Christ's supreme divinity, and in the doctrinal and ethical system of Christianity, is increasing. Rightly interpreted, the present situation means that " Christianity has brought the world up to the point where some of the old forms and dogmatic terminology are no longer adequate to embody and express it." Such has been the " augmentation of

* Sermon in Plymouth Church, Brooklyn, N. Y., May 19, 1878, p. 19.

individual manhood," the "elevation of social relationships," the expansion and purification of philosophic thought, and the enlargement of the world's life.

While this rehabilitating process has been going on in the Protestant Churches, a similar process has been going on, not only in medicine, in statesmanship, and political economy, in education and general science, but also in the realm of skepticism. Infidelity has changed its dress and form. Even its spirit has been much altered, showing the modifying influence of Christianity. The defiant temper of the Diderots and Paines has disappeared. What naturalist now speculates like D'Holbach! What historian discourses like Volney! And what metaphysician dogmatizes like Helvetius! Infidelity has accommodated itself to Christian phraseology; has accepted, in the form of half-truths, fundamentals of the Christian system, and has become more rational and religious in its unbelief than a hundred years ago. However deceptive its attitude in these accommodated forms, the fact itself is a concession to the substantial truth of Christianity, a confession of the need of its faiths. Take a single specimen. By "a kind of an intellectual hypertrophy, it has developed a peculiar pantheism—call it eclecticism, spiritualism, free religion, or what not — which agrees in representing all things " as chaos, or temporary forms of God," and claims that all religions are more or less true—"phenomena, race drifts, or meteoric clouds"—shedding luster on our darkness, and affording gleams of light and hope. " Infidelity can now deny a personal God, and at the same time, as by a double consciousness, breathe out the devotional language of the Bible, in "spurious religiosity." It adorns itself with Christian sentiments, and the "words which belong of right to faith alone." " It talks of prayer, permeates literature with a self-conscious devoutness, breathes heavenly aspirations, wails languidly over the evils of the world, talks wonderfully of the All-Father, and even sings David's Psalms." *

What a prodigious power is this in Christianity, that " even its deadly foes and traducers borrow its speech and trade upon its capital. This borrowing and wearing in public view the insignia of the divine kingdom obscures somewhat the distinction between the body of faith and the body of unbelief, renders Christianity less conspicuous by reason of her very triumphs, and forsooth perils somewhat her hold upon undiscriminating minds." But it is her glory that, as a living power, she has so wrought upon her great enemy as, by constraint, to change it so far into her own image. A conviction of the substantial truth in Christianity has constrained to this result. The solid central beliefs of the Churches have compelled these things.

* " The Light ; Is it Waning ?"   Boston.   1879.

Amid all the changes that have been made, the aggregate of skeptical gain has been nothing. Not a single great concession has been made by Christianity to unbelief, not an evidence surrendered, not one sacred book has been given up ; while "the life of Jesus is still majestic and divine—the insoluble enigma to the cold critic, but attractive and comprehensible to the humble believer."

Looking at the positive side, "What has the Church been doing? Has the apologist made no advance? Is the map of Christendom now just what it was when the old independence bell broke with its first glad peal of liberty to both the hemispheres? We would not boast, but we must be grateful. God has been in the storm, and made it speed the ship of truth as in no equal period since the first Christian Pentecost. . . .

"The first great reply to Strauss was Neander's 'Life of Christ.' It was a constructive work, and not simply negative—the first of a long line of defensive writings of the foremost theologians of the century. It would take a good octavo to contain merely the titles of the works that the last forty years have produced in favor of the divine foundations of Christianity. The war has been carried into the enemy's camp, and the leading skeptical writers are more busied, just now, with defending their own ground than with advances upon the Church. . . . The recent apologetical literature of the Church is able, copious, and aggressive beyond example. There is no question that the most vigorous theologians of the present day are thoroughly orthodox, in whatever country we look for examination. Poor, skeptical Heidelberg, rich only in historical and natural associations, has lost her great number of theological students, because she has been giving them nothing but 'husks, that the swine did eat;' while evangelical Leipsic, Halle, and Berlin are thronged with busy seekers of 'the bread of life.' . . .

" The recent activity in missionary labor, in evangelistic work at home, in providing modest places of worship for the threadbare, despondent multitude, in humanitarian open-handedness, in paternal love, in care for the scriptural knowledge of the young, is a sure indication of the new voyage of evangelical Christianity from its old traditional moorings, out upon the broad sea of discovery and possession. The great forces of civilization are now Christian, and they are becoming more positively so every day." *

These purifying processes through which it is passing are restoring theology to the original type of Christian doctrine.

It is one of the clearest and most hopeful indications of the times that, under the progress of phil-

* Rev. J. F. Hurst, D.D., in the "Christian Advocate."

ological study and biblical interpretation, the true light is so breaking out of God's word; that Christian doctrines are outgrowing many of the old decayed formularies, casting off unwarranted appendages, assuming less dialectical and more simple forms, and that, under all these processes, the core of each remains, not only undecayed, but more vigorous and vital than ever—the best vindication of eternal truth. Church creeds, too, are shortening, are confined to root principles of the great doctrines, and stated in simpler forms. This is also a growing characteristic of modern doctrinal preaching and of the theological writings of our times. Simplicity and directness in the statement of religious truth— New Testament statements—are likely to command liberal premiums in the coming ages.

Truth is simple. The maturest thought embodies itself in the simplest forms; and the broadest analysis and most rigid synthesis fail of their ends unless they arrive at simple propositions. Systems of truth are well, if not hewn to suit the caprice of the builder. Dialectical knowledge may serve useful purposes, especially in detecting sophistry and subtleties; but dialectical arts savor of guile, and true men, loving truth and seeking only truth, have no use for them except for defensive warfare. Simplicity and directness characterized the inculcations of the great Teacher and his apostles. Apostolic Christianity was content with simple styles and forms, discarding the subtleties and elaborate methods of the schools.

Primitive Christianity was long without an elaborate authoritative creed. The so-called Apostles' Creed is supposed to have had its origin subsequent to the time of the apostles, taking form by slow accretions, and coming into its present shape in the third century. And yet this was the period of the greatest purity and power of the Church, when least shackled by dogmatic forms. Thus did the true philosophy and the ever-faithful friend of philosophy start upon their missions. But, in the course of time, both lost their simplicity and purity, and fell into a long and grievous bondage, from which they are now emerging.

Such is the emancipation which has been going on in Protestant theology, and the progressive recovery of the ideal of Christian truth, first shadowed forth in the apostolic Church, but long lost under the rubbish of Popery.

In a recent discourse Rev. Phillips Brooks very appropriately said : " I believe that religion, so far from being on its death-bed, is just ready to enter on a completer life than it has ever before had; and I believe that it must come by the results of religious inquiry, of which so many men are afraid, as we have learned so much about religion, knowledge has grown so wonderfully within our own short age. Now, to many men it seems that that growth of

knowledge has undermined the foundations of religious faith ; out of that knowledge must come
the grounds of a purer faith. It must come (it is
come) just as fast as knowledge brings us into con-
tact with the truth. What I believe we have a
right to look for as religious men is a great religious
revival which shall not be a despairing retreat upon
worn-out rituals, which once had life in them ; not
a great excitement of feeling ; but a devout search
after truth for the cause which gives to every truth
its meaning, and the triumphant acceptance of Him
as the glorious Lord, the example of our life, which
shall be as much more thorough and devout and
religious as it is intelligent over the best faith of
ages that have gone before us."

In Rome the traveler is assured, that however
violent the changes of temperature without, the
deep interior of St. Peter's preserves its uniform
medium. So is it with the spiritual life of the
Church. Unmoved by changes of outward condition, and slight variations in forms and terminology,
and feeding upon the covenants and promises, it
realizes a more profound entrance into that interior
heart of doctrine in which unity, simplicity, and
power dwell.

What, then, have been the effect of these modifications of doctrinal statements upon the moral influence, the spiritual vitality, and the growth of
Protestantism ? Have they been diminished or in-

creased? The answer given in subsequent chapters is full of encouragement.

The period of intellectual progress and activity in which these doctrinal modifications have been made has also been the period of the greatest spiritual activity. It has also been eminently characterized by practical beneficence, philanthropy, and the wide extension of Christian influence. Piety has become more intelligent, beautiful, and attractive, the sure foundation of a truer humanity and a more rational happiness.

II. MORALS.

CHAPTER I.

TYPICAL PERIODS.

II.—MORALS.

CHAPTER I.

TYPICAL PERIODS.

PERIOD I.—*The Period antedating the Reformation under Luther.*

This was a long, dark epoch, too hideous in corruption, brutality, and evil portents, to be easily exaggerated. Not the least noticeable was the immorality of the clergy—"a hissing and a reproach." "If," said an Italian bishop, "I were to enforce the canons against unchaste persons administering ecclesiastical rites, there would be no one left in the Church but the boys; and if I enforced the canons against bastards, they also must be excluded." The priests either married, although such unions were illegal, or maintained concubinage openly. The historians agree that the conduct of the monks and the clergy could hardly be worse than it was, and that the evil virus permeated society.

In an age like this, a new prerogative, for which the way had been preparing, still further augmented the already vast influence of the clergy. "Every individual pastor, in the tribunal of penitence, was

10

made the absolute inquisitor, judge, and dictator of every soul, male and female, belonging to his flock." "The decision of a single priest was pronounced final for the forgiveness of sins, and his solitary voice, uttered in secret, was pronounced as the voice of Christ himself, dispensing the prerogatives of the Most High." *

Out of the practical workings of the confessional arose schools of casuistry; and a decline in theoretical and practical ethics extended through the whole range of morals. "According to the Fathers of the Church and the rigid casuists in general, a lie was never to be uttered, a promise never to be broken. The precepts of revelation, notwithstanding their brevity and literalness, were held complete and literal. . . . But there had not been wanting those who, whatever course they might pursue in the confessional, found the convenience of an accommodating morality in the secular affairs of the Church. Oaths were broken, and engagements were entered into without faith, for the ends of the clergy, or for those whom they favored in the struggles of the world." †

Ingenious sophistries were resorted to for defending breaches of plain morality.

---

* "History of the Confessional." By Bishop Hopkins. Harper Brothers. 1850. P. 192.

† Hallam's "Literature of the Middle Ages." Harper Brothers. Vol. ii, p. 121.

Another source of demoralization grew out of the necessities occasioned by the immense extravagancies of the Papal Court, inspiring an avaricious ingenuity in the invention of new methods of extortion. Among these schemes, we find a system of indulgences—liberty to buy off the punishment of sin by pecuniary offerings—not fully invented at once, but gradually developed, and, at last, elaborately drawn out and "shaped by chancery rules," under which absolution from sin was made a matter of traffic. Scarcely a sin could be imagined but had its price.

"The doctrine and sale of indulgences were powerful incentives to evil among an ignorant people. True, according to the Church, indulgences could only benefit those who promised to amend their lives, and who kept their word. But what could be expected from a tenet invented solely with a view to the profit that might be derived from it? The venders of indulgences were naturally tempted, for the better sale of their merchandise, to present their wares to the people in the most attractive aspect. . . . All that the multitude saw in them was, that they permitted men to sin; and the merchants were not over eager to dissipate an evil so favorable to their sale.

"What disorders and crimes were committed in these dark ages when impunity was to be purchased by money? What had man to fear, when a small contribution toward building a church secured him from punishment in the world to come?" *

The priests were the first to yield to these corrupting influences. "The history of the age swarms with scandals;" and we would not cite them, but to exhibit the sad condition into which the Church had lapsed, and from which it emerged under Protestantism.

The fifteenth century opened amid turbulence, crime, lawlessness, and impurity. Profligacy and corruption pervaded the hierarchy, and the sacred offices of the Church were bartered and sold. Priestly avarice and arrogance wore an unblushing front, and deeds of darkness were performed by the highest dignitaries, and shamelessly avowed. The benefices were the carcasses around which the eagles gathered; and the question upon which ecclesiastical promotion turned was not, "Are you a fit man?" but, "Have you money?" "Scullions, pimps, hostlers, and even children," became Church dignitaries. The signature of the Pope had its price, and men ignorant, scandalous for vice, ambitious, cruel, and every way unfit, were promoted to bishoprics. An Englishman's *recipe* for the stomach of St. Peter and its complete reformation, quaintly given in the Council of Constance, was, "Take twenty-four cardinals, a hundred archbishops

* Merle D'Aubigné's "History of the Reformation under Luther." American Tract Society's Edition, vol. i, p. 61.

and prelates, an equal number from each nation, and as many creatures of the court as you can secure; plunge them into the Rhine, and let them remain for the space of three days. This will be effective for St. Peter's stomach, and will remove its entire corruption." "No Protestant doctor could have prescribed a harsher remedy."

At the Council of Constance (1414–1417) evidence was given, which no Roman Catholic can dispute, that the state of priestly morals was as low as the range of human nature could reach. The schism in the Church, and its two Popes—at Rome and Avignon—furnished occasion for severe utterances and plain dealing. The Bishop of Lodi, who had urged the Council to severity against Huss, in a funeral sermon of a Cardinal before the Council, rebuked the clergy as "so plunged in excess of luxury and brutal indulgence, that Diogenes, seeking a man among them, would only find beasts and swine." *

The well-known feelings of the Emperor in regard to the prevailing corruption, and the schismatic condition of the Church, secured freedom of speech, and the public discourses were the safety-valve through which the pent-up feelings of many found relief. One preacher declared that " almost the entire clergy were under the dominion of the devil."† "In the world falsehood is king; among

* L'Enfant, 339.   † Ibid., 494.

the clergy avarice is law. In the prelates are found only malice, iniquity, negligence, ignorance, vanity, pride, avarice, simony, lust, pomp, hypocrisy. At the court of the Pope there is no holiness. It is a diabolical court." Another said: "The clergy spend their money on buffoons, dancing girls, dogs, and birds, rather than in charity to the poor. They frequent taverns and brothels, and go from their concubines and prostitutes to mass without any scruple. It has passed into a proverb, that the priests have as many mistresses as domestics." The convents were not spared. "It is a shame," he says, "to speak of what is done in them; more a shame to do it. In all these abominations the Court of Rome sets the example, even in the place where it is assembled for the reformation of manners."

In the one hundred years between Huss and Luther some changes took place for the better in the civil and social condition of Europe. The labors of Wycliffe, Huss, etc., and the revival of learning, were exerting a beneficent influence. An invisible lever was lifting the century; the charm of lofty ecclesiastical claims was breaking; men's minds were disturbed on many subjects; the old unreasoning submission to authority was shaking off its deep slumber and awakening into inquiry. But these were only the first feeble motions of the mighty giant, starting up with fierce revenge against " the ecclesiastical terrorism which for centuries had sequestered the rights of mind." Men were weary of the establishments of former ages ; feudalism declined, royal power consolidated, and all Europe was ripening for a change in the relations of Church and State. Social life lost something of its coarseness and brutality. The invention of printing and the great maritime discoveries in the last half of the century quickened thought and gave an impulse to learning, but there was little moral improvement.

" Almost within hearing of the first motion of the press incalculable numbers of enthusiasts revived the exploded sect of the Flagellants of former centuries, and perambulated Europe, plying the whip upon their naked backs, and declaring that the whole of religion consisted in the use of the scourge. Others, more crazy still, pronounced the use of clothes to be evidence of an unconverted nature, and returned to the nakedness of our first parents, as proof of their restoration to a state of innocence. Mortality lost all its terrors in this earnest search for something more than the ordinary ministrations of the faith could bestow, and in France and England the hideous spectacles called the Dance of Death were frequent. . . . People danced the Dance of Death because life had lost its charm. Life had lost its security in the two most powerful nations of the time. England was shaken with contending factions, and France exhausted and hopeless of restoration. . . . A cardinal, bloated and bloody, dominated both London and Paris, and sent his commands from the palace at Winchester, which were obeyed by both nations." *

At the opening of the sixteenth century Alexander VI., (1492–1513,) "the most depraved and wicked of mankind," sat in the chair of St. Peter. No earthly ruler since the Roman Nero had equaled him in profligacy, and in the coarser vices of cruelty and oppression. Through his whole lifetime he was notoriously dissolute. In earlier life criminally connected with a Roman lady in Spain, he also seduced her daughters, and adopted one of them as his life-long mistress, having by her five children. Later, while occupying high ecclesiastical positions in Rome, he installed her in a house near St. Peter's, and shielded his amours under her pretended marriage to an intendant. Devoting himself to public duties and acts of piety by day and to lust by night, this infamous man easily, in an age of gross corruption, beguiled the Roman people. By heavy bribes procuring his elevation to the Papal chair, by outraging time-honored rights elevating his bastard sons over the old princely houses of Italy, he became at last a victim

* "The Eighteen Centuries," by Rev. James White.   Page 374. D. Appleton & Co.   1860.

of his own wickedness. After reveling in debauchery, venality, and blood, he was poisoned by the very dose with which he had connived to poison another. Julius II., a man of ferocious spirit, and Leo X., a patron of art, and of a polished licentiousness, followed in the Papal chair. Such was the head of the Church on the eve of the Reformation.

The condition of the clergy and the people of Europe was little different. The depravity of the Church followed its ramification every-where. The priests were proverbially ignorant, brutal, and drunken. The obligations of celibacy were unscrupulously eluded, and the disorders of the monasteries and convents were appalling. "In many places the people were delighted at seeing a priest keep a mistress, that the married women might be safe from his seductions." "In many places the priests paid the bishop a regular tax for the woman with whom he lived, and for each child he had by her. A German bishop said publicly one day, at a great entertainment, that in one year eleven thousand priests had presented themselves for that purpose. It is Erasmus who relates this."* How gross was the age which could tolerate such things!

The period of the Reformation was a vast crisis,

* Merle D'Aubigne's "History of the Reformation under Luther." American Tract Society's edition, vol. i, pp. 62, 63.

a ground-swell, heaving society from its bottom
depths, and stirring up much that was of evil report. Great tempests swept over Europe. There
were extreme movements and reactions, involving
much to be deprecated. In the midst of such
heavy throes, and out of such a low condition, the
new life of Protestantism emerged, taking into it
much of the moral imperfection of the age. Bancroft has said, " A man can as little move without
the weight of the superincumbent atmosphere as
escape altogether the opinions of the age in which
he sees the light." With the Reformation there
was destruction, and with the advance recession. It
was no small task for the· Reformation to raise itself out of a slough so foul and so universal, and
maintain at once a clean front, a clear head, and a
secure footing. It is not strange, therefore, that
we find Luther and his followers, while reacting
against the papal doctrine of works, in their advocacy of faith as the only ground of justification,
" running perilously near the abyss of Antinomian-
ism," if they did not even topple into it, as seems
evident from some of Luther's utterances recently
quoted by Sir William Hamilton, S. Baring Gould,
and Rev. Dr. F. C. Ewer. The legitimate fruit of
this extreme was dissolute manners. For a time,
with advanced purity, there was much impurity, and
with wisdom, folly and madness. Hence we find
Luther saying that " for one devil of Popery ex-

pelled, seven worse devils entered" into some of his followers. Bucer said that some, "in their revolt from the tyranny of the Pope and the Bishops," "gave themselves up freely to their caprices and all their carnal passions."

The Reformation did not at once produce a complete improvement in manners. Rev. Dr. Ewer, in his recent effort to prove the failure of Protestantism,[*] cites the capital convictions of Nuremburg in three centuries, as evidence that morals declined after the Reformation under Luther began. He says, "There were condemned to death, in Nuremburg, for incest, highway robbery, murder, infanticide, unnatural crimes, etc., in the fifteenth century, before the Reformation, 41; in the sixteenth century, after the Reformation, 190; in the seventeenth century, after the Reformation, 270." But what do these statistics prove save an increased attention to the promotion of moral order by the enforcement of law? Before the Reformation, under the unchallenged dominion of the Papacy, crime was committed with such impunity that it could hardly be called crime. Even indulgences to murder were granted by the Church for sums ranging from twenty dollars to fifty dollars. The increase in the number of convictions, then, is evidence of progress in the administration of laws, either long in disuse or

* " The Complete Preacher," July, 1878, p. 224.

newly enacted, and the elevation of the standard of order.

And now, after three hundred years have passed, who can fail to see a great improvement in morals, and also a marvelous difference between those countries which have remained Roman Catholic and those which have been Protestant? Who can fail to observe the rapid advancement of Protestant over Papal nations in useful arts, commerce, literature, education, civil rights, social privileges, moral sense, and political influence? Trying the case by any reasonable standard of existing facts, it will be obvious that the system which lives by indulgences and the confessional does not advance and elevate nations, but depresses, degrades, and impoverishes them.

Progress has been made amid conflicts, by varying stages, through ebbs and flows, eddies, rapids, and even stagnant lagoons. Advance movements in society are seldom by straight lines or in uniform rates, free from retarding frictions; but rather uneven, irregular, sometimes oscillatory, with frequent recessions and reactions. Keeping these things in mind, let us pass over the intervening period, and pause amid the scenes which preceded the Wesleyan Reformation in England.

PERIOD II.—*England from* 1660 *to* 1750.

The English Reformation had passed; Protestantism had triumphed and securely intrenched itself; Puritanism and other forms of dissent, as sub-protests, championing a still purer faith and life, arose and exerted their influence.

The rigid *regimen* of Cromwell was followed by a terrible rebound. The great soldier and his Puritan supporters came to be regarded as " lank-haired gentlemen," with " sour-faced hypocrisies," " speaking through the nose," " debarring from social meetings, from merry-making at Christmas, and junketing at fairs," and " forswearing all innocent enjoyments." After " years of weary restraint and formalism," on the restoration of Charles II., the accumulated tide burst all barriers. " A flood of dancing and revelry and utter abandonment to happiness burst over the whole country. . . . Never, since the old times of the Feasts of Fools and the gaudy procession of the Carnival, had there been such a riotous jubilee as inaugurated the Restoration. The reaction against Puritanism carried the nation almost beyond Christianity, and landed it in heathenism again." *

Through nearly one hundred years this reaction extended. The first half of the eighteenth century was the darkest period, morally, since the birth of

* White's " Eighteen Christian Centuries," p. 472.

English Protestantism ; and yet, with all its terrible gloom, it was many degrees brighter than either England or the Continent two centuries before. Scrutinizing the picture, we shall be able to appreciate the struggling stages through which the better life of the race has passed in reaching its present condition.

In the higher classes of English society, the taint left by Charles II. and his licentious court still festered; and in the lower, laziness and dishonesty were universal. Extravagance was the order of the day, and "scarcely a family kept within its income." In 1723 Lady Mary Montagu wrote, " Honor, virtue, and reputation, which we used to hear of in the nursery, are as much laid aside as crumpled ribbons." The masses entertained themselves with brutal amusements, instigating bloody quarrels, and engendering savage dispositions. " The essayists, in their matchless prose; Pope, in verse no less terse and vigorous; and Hogarth, on canvas, attacked, with all the weapons of satire and ridicule, the vicious tendencies, which struck them chiefly as instances of folly and bad taste."* But art and culture failed to regenerate society; and the spirit nourished by these savage sports found vent in tumults, uproars, manslaughters, etc., which more recent records of crime fail to parallel. The picture is a dark one.

* Julia Wedgewood.

Lecky says:* "The impunity with which outrages were committed in the ill-lit and ill-guarded
streets of London during the first half of the eighteenth century can now hardly be realized.   In
1712 a club of young men of the higher classes,
who assumed the name of Mohawks, were accustomed nightly to rally out drunk into the streets to
hunt the passers-by, and to subject them, in mere
wantonness, to the most atrocious outrages.   One
of their favorite amusements, called 'tipping the
lion,' was to squeeze the nose of their victim flat
upon his face, and to bore out his eyes with their
fingers.   Among them were the 'sweaters,' who
formed a circle around their prisoner, and pricked
him with their swords till he sank exhausted on the
ground; the 'dancing masters,' so called from their
skill in making men caper by thrusting swords into
their legs; the 'tumblers,' whose favorite amusement was to set women on their heads, and commit
various indecencies and barbarities on the limbs
that were exposed.   Maid-servants, as they opened
their masters' doors, were waylaid, beaten, and their
faces cut.   Matrons, inclosed in barrels, were rolled
down the steep and stony incline of Snow Hill.
Watchmen were unmercifully beaten and their noses
slit.   Country gentlemen went to the theater, as if
in a time of war, accompanied by their armed re-
tainers.   A bishop's son was said to be one of the

* "England in the Eighteenth Century," vol. i. p. 522, etc.

gang, and a baronet was among those who were arrested."

Said the Bishop of Lichfield, in 1724: "The Lord's day is become the devil's market day. . . . Sin, in general, is grown so hardened and rampant, as that immoralities are defended, yea, justified, on principle." Smollett said, in 1730, "Thieves and robbers are now become more desperate and savage than they had ever appeared since mankind were civilized." "All men agree," thus begins the "Proposal for a National Reformation of Manners," in 1734, "that atheism and profaneness never got such a high ascendant as at this day. A thick gloominess hath overspread the horizon, and our light looks like the evening of the world." The mayor and aldermen of London, in 1744, drew up an address to the king, in which they stated that "Divers confederacies of great numbers of evil-disposed persons armed with bludgeons, pistols, cutlasses, and other dangerous weapons, infest not only the private lanes and passages, but likewise the public streets and places of usual concourse, and commit most daring outrages."

Tyerman, after portraying the usual condition of London, says of this period, "The country was an apt imitator of the vices of the town," and that "the dark picture might easily be enlarged, not from posterior writings, or even from the religious publications of the period, but from periodicals.

magazines, and newspapers, which had no temptation to represent the customs, manners, usages, and vices of the age in a worse aspect than was warranted by facts."

A fearful passion for gambling reached its climax under the first two Georges. Swift says, Lord Oxford denounced it as "the bane of the English nobility." The Duke of Devonshire and Lord Chesterfield were bewitched by it. It "reigned supreme" "at Bath, the center of English fashion;" and the passion was quite as strong among fashionable ladies as among fashionable gentlemen.

And yet gambling was only *one* of many mammoth evils of that time. We will not pause to speak of the "Fleet marriages"—the strangest scandals of English life. But drunkenness was one of the distinguishing vices, the consumption of distilled spirits increasing from 2,000,000 gallons in 1684, to 11,000,000, in 1750, besides the milder drinks. Physicians declared gin-drinking was a new and terrible source of mortality, of murders, and robbery. "The evil acquired such fearful dimensions," says Lecky, "that even the unreforming Parliament of Walpole perceived the necessity of taking strong measures to arrest it." No efforts, however, availed for some years. Violent riots followed the first attempts, and the evil still increased. Crime and immorality of every description became more terrible. "The London physicians," says Lecky, "stated, in 1750,

11

that there were in and about the metropolis no less than 14,000 cases of illness, most of them beyond the reach of medicines, directly attributable to gin." Fielding said that "gin was the principal sustenance of 100,000 people in the metropolis," and he predicted that "should the drinking of this poison be continued at its present height, during the next twenty years, there will, by that time, be very few of the common people left to drink it." Bishop Benson, in a letter written from London a little later, said : " There is not only no safety in living in this town, but scarcely any in the country now, robbery and murder are grown so frequent. Our people are now becoming, what they never before were, cruel and inhuman. Those accursed spirituous liquors, which, to the shame of our government, are so easily to be had, and in such quantities drank, have changed the very nature of our people ; and, they will, if continued to be drank, destroy the very race of people themselves."

The political corruption in England in the first half of the eighteenth century was one of the most serious blemishes of that age. Capitalists and corporations descended into the political arena, and carried measures by sheer corruption. Lavish sums were spent by the East India Company among members of Parliament, and in the elections corruption was universal. Brokers stock-jobbed elections on the Exchange. One writer said, " Boroughs are rated in the Royal Exchange like stocks or tallies; the price of a vote is as well known as of an acre of land, and it is no secret who are the moneyed men, and generally the best customers."[*]

Lecky said: "He [Walpole] governed by an assembly which was saturated with corruption; and he fully acquiesced in its conditions, and resisted every attempt to improve it. He appears to have cordially accepted the maxim that government must be carried on by corruption or by force, and he deliberately made the former the basis of his rule. He bribed George II. by obtaining for him a civil list exceeding by more than £100,000 a year that of his father. He bribed the queen by securing for her a jointure of £100,000 a year, when his rival, Sir Spencer Compton, could only venture to promise £60,000. He bribed the dissenting ministers to silence by the *regium donum*, for the benefit of their widows. He employed the vast patronage of the Crown uniformly and steadily with the single view of sustaining his position; and there can be no doubt that a large proportion of the immense expenditure of secret-service money during his administration was devoted to the direct purchase of members of Parliament."[†]

---

[*] Somers' "Tracts," vol. xiii, quoted by Lecky.

[†] Lecky's "England in the Eighteenth Century," vol. i, pp. 395, 396, etc.

But Mr. Lecky says that " Bribery, whether in the elections or in Parliament, was no new thing" under Walpole.   He quotes from Davenant and De Foe to show its prevalence at the close of the seventeenth and the beginning of the eighteenth centuries ; that men made it their business to buy and sell seats in Parliament ; that the market price was one thousand guineas ; that "bribery, buying of votes, freedoms, and freeholds" were "open and barefaced;" and that in 1716 the Earl of Dorset said, "A great number of persons have no other livelihood than of being employed in bribing."

He further says, that if corruption did not begin with Walpole it did not end with him.   His expenditure of secret-service money did not equal that of Bute, and "it is to Bute, and not to Walpole, that we owe the most gigantic and wasteful of all forms of bribery.   In 1754 Sir John Barnard, with a view to the approaching elections, actually moved the repeal of the oath against bribery, in the interest of public morals, on the ground that it was merely the occasion of general perjury. ... Very few statesmen of the eighteenth century had less natural tendency to corruption than George Grenville.   His private character was unimpeachable. ... The expenditure of secret-service money during his administration was unusually low, yet, such was the condition of the legislature by which he governed, that he appears to have found it necessary to offer direct money bribes to members of the House of Lords. If Walpole was guilty of corruption, it may be fairly urged that it was scarcely possible to manage Parliament without it." [*] He also says [†] that " supporters of the government in Parliament frequently received, at the close of the session, from £500 to £1,000 for their services ;" and that " it is certain that the consentient opinion of contemporaries accused the ministers of gross and wholesale corruption."

An English gentleman, [‡] before the Unitarian Conference, at Saratoga, September, 1878, speaking of the political corruption in England, said : " There had been no political parties in England until the time of William of Orange, and then things began to grow corrupt, and reached their height in the times of Walpole, when they were more corrupt than in our own day."

Fashionable life and sentiment were coarse and foul. The writings of De Foe, Swift, Fielding, and Smollett fully illustrate this, and the two Georges did not improve the condition. According to Lord Hervey and others, " each king lived publicly with mistresses, and the immorality of their courts was accompanied by none of that refinement and grace which has often cast a softening veil over evil."

[*] " Lecky," i, pp. 398, 399.   [†] Ibid., p. 403.
[‡] Dorman B. Eaton, Esq.

Speaking of the queen of George II., Lecky says:
" Living herself a life of unsullied virtue, discharg-
ing, under circumstances of peculiar difficulty, the
duties of a wife with most exemplary patience and
diligence, exercising her great influence in Church
and in State with singular wisdom, patriotism, and
benevolence, she passed through life jesting on the
vices of her husband and of his ministers with the
coarseness of a trooper, receiving from her husband
the earliest and fullest account of every new love
affair in which he was engaged, and prepared to
welcome each new mistress, provided only she
could herself keep the first place in his judgment
and in his confidence."

On her death-bed, says Lord Hervey, "Caroline
advised the king to marry again. Upon which his
sobs began to rise and his tears to fall with double
vehemence. While in the midst of this passion,
wiping his eyes, and sobbing between every word,
with much ado, he got out this answer: 'No, I
shall have these mistresses.' To which the queen
made no other reply than, 'O, my God, that will
make no difference!'"

Doubtless there were " party libels " of the time,
imputing great iniquities to objects of personal
dislike; and discrimination should be made between
the "place-hunters" at St. James' and other per-
formers in the greater scenes of life and the great
body of English and Scotch gentry. The latter

should not be involved in the condemnation of the former. Many examples of morality and religion, of pure and noble champions of truth remained; but the more active currents of society were thoroughly tainted.

A writer in "Blackwood's Magazine," about ten years ago, said:

"Walpole served his country and the devil together, and laughed at the very idea of goodness. Chesterfield, in devotion to one of the most blessed of natural pieties, did not blush to encourage his young son in shameless wickedness. Pope babbled loudly of the vice for which his weak frame incapacitated him. . . . It was the age when delicate young women of the best blood and best manners in the land talked with a coarseness which editors of the nineteenth century can represent only by asterisks; and in which the most polished and dainty verse, Pope's most melodious, correctest couplets, were interspersed with lines which would damn for ever and ever any modern poetaster. Personal satire—poor instrument of vengeance, which stings without wounding—had such sway as it never had before in England; but that sense of public honor which prevents open outrage upon decency was not in existence. The public liked the wicked story, and liked the scourge that came after, and laughed, not in its sleeve, but loudly, at blasphemy and indecency and profanity. Even the sentiment of cleanness, purity, and honor was lost to the generation."

Turning to the Churches, we find no amelioration of the dark picture, for those who should have been reformers needed themselves to be reformed. The dissenting Churches, which felt themselves to be the bulwarks of truth and morals, lamented that many of their own ministers were immoral, negligent, and inefficient, while their communicants partook largely of the prevailing corruption. Of many of the clergy of the Established Church what shall we say? One familiar with the facts shall bear testimony.

" The foulest sins were made sinless by intemperate zeal for the Pretender, and the fairest virtues besmeared in those who showed a friendly feeling for Dissenters. A man might be drunken and quarrelsome all the week, but if on Sunday he bowed at the altar and cursed King William he was esteemed a saint. He might cheat every body and pay nobody, but if he drank health to the royal orphan, hated King George, and abhorred the Whigs, his want of probity was a peccadillo scarcely worth noticing. On the other hand, a man might be learned, diligent, devout, and useful, but if he opposed the Pretender and Popery, or if he thought the Dissenters should not be damned, he was at once set down as heterodox, and, according to his importance, became a target for the shafts of High-Church

malice. . . . The court of England was corrupt to
its very core, and the people were too faithful imi-
tators of the bad example. Popery was intriguing,
Dissenters were declining, and the Church was full
of fiery and drunken feuds." *

Another English writer † says : " In a great many
instances the clergy were negligent and immoral ;
often grossly so. The populace of the large towns
were ignorant and profligate ; and the inhabitants
of the villages added to ignorance and profligacy
brutish and barbarous manners. A more striking
instance of the rapid deterioration of religious light
and influence in a country scarcely occurs than in
our own, from the Restoration to the rise of Methodism. It affected not only the Church, but the
dissenting sects in no ordinary degree."

Such is the dark picture of English morals two
hundred years after the birth of Protestantism.
Even in its worst aspects it is many degrees brighter
than the moral condition of either England or the
Continent when the Lutheran Reformation commenced, for some new alleviating lights irradiate
the page. But a comparison of the lights and
shadows of the present with those of England one
hundred and fifty years ago, will show stupendous
progress.

In the midst of such a state of morals the great

---

* Tyerman's " Life of Wesley," vol. i, p. 65.
† Rev. Richard Watson.

religious revival under the Wesleys and Whitefield
had its origin, spreading out into a broad evangelical movement among Churchmen and Dissenters,
permeating the British Isles with elements of new
life, and elevating the moral tone of society.   While
Luther gave special prominence to the doctrine of
justification by faith, Wesleyanism laid its emphasis
upon holiness of heart and life, and thus became
not only a revival, but also a reformation in morals.
The story shall be told by one who will not be suspected of partiality.

Mr. Lecky says: " From about the middle of
the eighteenth century a reforming spirit was once
more abroad, and a steady movement of moral as-
cent may be detected.   The influence of Pitt in
politics, and the influence of Wesley and his followers in religion, were the earliest and most important
agencies in effecting it. . . . The tone of thought
and feeling was changed. . . . The standard of
political honor was perceptibly raised.   It was felt
that enthusiasm, disinterestedness, and self-sacrifice
had their place in politics ; and, although there was
afterward, for short periods, extreme corruption,
public opinion never acquiesced in it again." *

Again he says : † " Although the career of the
elder Pitt, and the splendid victories by land and
sea that were won during his ministry, form un-

* " England in the Eighteenth Century," vol. ii, pp. 562, 563.
† Ibid., p. 567, etc.

questionably the most dazzling episodes in the reign of George II., they must yield, I think, in real importance, to that religious revolution which shortly before had been begun in England by the preaching of the Wesleys and of Whitefield. The creation of a large, powerful, and active sect, extending over both hemispheres, and numbering many millions of souls, was but one of its consequences. It also exercised a profound and lasting influence upon the spirit of the Established Church, upon the amount and distribution of the moral forces of the nation, and even upon the course of its political history."

Among the ulterior advantages of the Wesleyan Reformation Mr. Lecky cites its influence in preserving the English nation from the French revolutionizing tendencies which were felt by many classes in England at the close of the century. He says: " England, on the whole, escaped the contagion. Many causes conspired to save her, but among them a prominent place must, I believe, be given to the new and vehement religious enthusiasm which was at that very time passing through the middle and lower classes of the people, which had enlisted in its service a large proportion of the wilder and more impetuous reformers, and which recoiled with horror from the antichristian tenets that were associated with the Revolution in France."

Mr. Lecky's testimony is luminous and valuable. After speaking of the divergent tendencies in English society and the growing inequalities in the conditions of the rich and the poor, in connection with the increase of capital and the great manufacturing interests, the evils and the dangers incident to such a condition of things, the growing distrusts, alienations, etc., between the higher and the lower classes, not yet duly estimated by political economists, he proceeds to say :

" The true greatness and welfare of nations depend mainly on the amount of moral force that is generated within them. Society can never continue in a state of tolerable security when there is no other bond of cohesion than a mere money tie ; and it is idle to expect the different classes of the community to join in the self-sacrifice and enthusiasm of patriotism, if all unselfish motives are excluded from their several relations. Every change of conditions which widens the chasm and impairs the sympathy between rich and poor cannot fail, however beneficial may be its effects, to bring with it grave dangers to the State. It is incontestable that the immense increase of manufacturing population has had this tendency ; and it is, therefore, I conceive, peculiarly fortunate that it should have been preceded by a great religious revival, which opened a new spring of moral and religious energy among the poor, and at the same time gave a powerful impulse to the philanthropy of the rich." *

In the more recent periods English morals have never fallen to so low a condition.

PERIOD III.—*The United States from* 1700 *to* 1800.

Passing over to the American Continent, we find a manifest decline in morals during the one hundred years following the landing of the Pilgrims. The influence of the licentious and debauched court of Charles II. had been felt among all English-speaking people, at home and abroad, and new classes of immigrants, not actuated, like the first settlers, by high religious motives, but by secular aims, and many of them paupers and criminals from workhouses and jails, had been infused into the colonial population. The corruption of manners, working downward through English society during the reigns of William III., Queen Anne, and the first two Georges, extended to American shores, changing the moral aspects of the people. In the first third of the eighteenth century this deterioration was very plain. The drinking habits, hitherto very moderate, were increased, though not as bad as at the close of the century. West India rum had been introduced in trade with those islands, and the manufacture of rum was commenced in New En-

* "England in the Eighteenth Century," vol. ii, pp. 691-694.

gland in 1730, reducing the price and leading to its
more general use.   In the forty years preceding the
Edwardean revival intoxicating drinks had come
into common use, and there was much hard drinking; but darker days were to come.

"It is easy to praise the fathers of New England," said Theodore Parker; "easier to praise
them for virtues they did not possess than to discriminate and fairly judge those remarkable men.
. . . Let me mention a fact or two.   It is recorded
in the probate office that, in 1678, at the funeral of
Mrs. Mary Norton, widow of the celebrated John
Norton, one of the ministers of the First Church in
Boston, fifty-one gallons and a half of the best Ma-
laga wine were consumed by the 'mourners;' in
1685, at the funeral of Rev. Thomas Cobbett, minister of Ipswich, there were consumed one barrel of
wine and two barrels of cider, and, 'as it was cold,'
there were 'some spice and ginger for the cider.'
You may easily judge of the drunkenness and riot
on occasions less solemn than the funeral of an old
and beloved minister.   Towns provided intoxicating
drink at the funeral of their paupers.   In Salem, in
1728, at the funeral of a pauper, a gallon of wine and
another of cider are charged as 'incidentals;' the
next year, six gallons of wine on a similar occasion.
In Lynn, in 1711, the town furnished 'half a barrel
of cider for the widow Dispaw's funeral.'   Affairs had come to such a pass that, in 1742, the

General Court forbid the use of wine and rum at funerals." *

Among the Scotch-Irish Presbyterians, who settled at Londonderry, N. H., about 1719, drinking habits became quite as bad as in other localities. In allusion to their inflexible adherence to their creed, and their social irregularities on festive occasions, it was commonly said, " The Derry Presbyterians never gave up a *pint* of doctrine or a *pint* of rum." The " Derry Festival," introduced and kept up for many years, was " a sort of Protestant carnival "—" a wild, drinking, horse-racing, frolicking, merry-making, at which strong drink abounded." Those who good-naturedly wrestled and joked together in the morning, not unfrequently closed the day with a fight. William Stack, in describing his ancestors, the first settlers of Amoskeag Falls, says:

> " Of the goodly men of old Derryfield
> It was often said that their only care,
> And their only wish, and only prayer,
> For the present world, and the world to come,
> Was a string of eels and a jug of rum."

In the inland town of Northampton, said Edwards, " there was far more degeneracy among the young than ever before." " Licentiousness, for some years, greatly prevailed among the youth." " The Sabbath was extensively profaned, and the

* " Speeches, Addresses, and Occasional Sermons." By Theodore Parker. Pp. 341–397. Boston: Horace B. Fuller, publisher. 1871.

decorum of the sanctuary not unfrequently disturbed." This was a fair sample of many New England towns at this time ; while the average morality of Virginia, Maryland, and some other sections, was even lower, not having so many conserving elements as New England.

The clergy, in the Virginia Colony, following the style of those in England, were morally low, and the people lower still. Bishop Meade said: "As to the unworthy hireling clergy of the Colony, there was no ecclesiastical discipline to correct or punish their irregularities and vices." In the Province of Maryland, in the latter part of the seventeenth century, "The Lord's day was generally profaned, religion was despised, and all notorious vices were committed, so that it had become a Sodom of uncleanness and a pest-house of iniquity." * "The clergy were remarkable for their laxity of morals and scandalous behavior." In the forty years following the formal establishment of the Episcopal Church as the State Church in Maryland, in 1692, there was no moral improvement, but rather a steady decline, as letters to the Bishop of London, quoted by Dr. Hawks, fully show.

It was at this time, simultaneously with the origin of the Wesleyan movement in England, though of briefer duration, and less radical in character,

* "Letter to the Archbishop of Canterbury," quoted by Dr. Hawks.

that the ten years of Edwardean and Whitefieldian revivals began, (1735-1745.) They were an incalculable blessing to the Colonial Churches and communities, checking for a time the spread of immorality. But there speedily followed a long and troublous period, (1750-1800,) and its distracting events—the French and Indian wars; the conflicting agitations preceding the Revolutionary War; the war itself, with the usual depraving influences; the depressing financial condition afterward; the sharp conflicts on questions of civil polity attending the organization of the Federal Government; the general infusion of European skepticism and manners; and the spread of New England rum. A detailed statement of American manners in the last quarter of the eighteenth century will exhibit a condition of immorality, having no later parallel on our shores.

The Revolutionary War had not progressed far before the faithful ministers of the Presbyterian Church, in their Synod, deplored the spread of "gross immoralities," "increasing to a fearful degree." In 1779 they lamented "the degeneracy of manners," and "the prevalence of vice and immorality that obtain throughout the land." A sentiment of insubordination grew up out of the infusion of French ideas, which declared "moral obligation to be a shackle imposed by bigotry and priestcraft," revolution a right and duty, and au

12

thority usurpation. The revolutionizing spirit, serviceable in the war, was so thoroughly diffused among the people that it threatened new trouble. Men had vaunted about rights until many felt that any government was an imposition. Demagogues multiplied, poisoning the minds of the masses, engendering the spirit of domestic scuffle, instigating local rebellions, discontent, and heart-burnings. A relaxation of moral principle, and licentiousness of sentiment and conduct, followed in the footsteps of liberty—the offspring of her profane alliance with French infidelity. In not a few even of the New England towns desecration of the Sabbath, lewdness, neglect of the sanctuary, profanity, and low cavils at the Bible were common, and "the last vestiges of Puritan morals seemed well-nigh irrecoverably effaced."

This corruption extended into civil and literary circles. The newspapers partook of the general demoralization. Jefferson wrote: "Nothing can now be believed which is seen in a newspaper. Truth itself becomes suspicious by being put into that polluted vehicle. The real extent of this state of misapprehension is known only to those who are in a condition to confront facts within their knowledge with the lies of the day." Rev. Theodore Parker said: "The general character of the press since the end of the last century has decidedly improved, as any one may convince himself of by comparing the newspapers of that period with the present."

It was an era of bad feeling, and a political bitterness was indulged, unknown to the partisan strifes of our day. The debates on the adoption of the Federal Constitution were of the most exasperating character. The Jacobin intrigues inflamed the public feelings, and political bitterness was the bane of Washington's administration. With our exalted views of Washington, it is impossible for us to conceive how he was assailed, maligned, and abused by the press, and also in public and private circles. The acts of his administration were tortured, and the grossest and most insidious misrepresentations made "in such exaggerated and indecent terms," said Washington himself, "as could scarcely be applied to Nero, or a notorious defaulter, or even to a common pickpocket." In this dark period (1796) a gentleman of the highest character wrote to Washington : "Our affairs seem to lead to some crisis, some revolution ; something that I cannot foresee or conjecture. I am more uneasy than during the war. . . . We are going and doing wrong, and therefore I look forward to evils and calamities. . . . We are wofully and wickedly misled. Private rage for property suppresses public considerations, and personal rather than national interests have become the great objects of attention." Washington replied, " Your sentiments that we are drawing rapidly to a crisis accord with mine. What the event will be is beyond my foresight." Rev. Theodore Parker said: " Political servility and political rancor are certainly bad enough and base enough at this day; but not long ago they were baser and worse. To show this, I need only appeal to the memories of men before me, who recollect the beginning of the present century. Political controversies are conducted with less bitterness than before; honesty is more esteemed; private worth more respected. The Federal party, composed of men who certainly were an honor to their age, supported Aaron Burr for the office of Vice-President of the United States, a man whose character, both public and private, was notoriously marked with the deepest infamy. Political parties are not very Puritanical in their virtues this day, but I think no party would now, for a moment, accept such a man as Mr. Burr for such a post."

Dueling was then not a sectional, but a national, vice. The whole land was red with the blood of duelists, and filled with the lamentations of widows and orphans. It was a common crime of men high in office, and a duelist was elected, by a large majority, Vice-President of the Union, even coming within a narrow chance of the presidential chair.

Profanity terribly abounded, and was not then regarded as ungentlemanly. The stocks, the pillory, and the whipping-post were common. Slavery existed in all the States.

Intemperance was an alarming evil. The manufacture of New England rum commenced in 1730, increasing the home consumption of this fiery stimulant; but the milder liquors, beer and wine, continued in general use, until the war of the Revolution cut off foreign commerce, and gave an impulse to the distillation of rum, when this most vitiating of all beverages became universal. Furnished freely to the soldiers in the army, at the close of the war, they went forth with vitiated appetites, increasing the demand for distilled spirits throughout the land. In the forty years following the Revolution, drunkenness fearfully increased, until, in the language of a European traveler in the United States at that time, it became "the most striking characteristic of the American people."

Intemperance had not then the weight of public sentiment to struggle against, which has since been raised up. To get drunk did not then injure a man's reputation or influence. Members of Churches, the highest Church officials, deacons and ministers, drank immoderately, without seriously compromising their positions. Said Rev. Leonard Woods, D.D.: "I remember when I could reckon up among my acquaintances forty ministers who were intemperate." Another gentleman, living in those times, subsequently said in a Boston newspaper, "A great

many deacons in New England died drunkards. I
have a list of one hundred and twenty-three intemperate deacons in Massachusetts, forty-three of
whom became sots."

The following sketch will afford a picture of the
moral condition of some portions of the country in
this period. The party referred to flourished about
1780–1790, in Orange County and Smith's Cove,
New York. They organized for the purpose of destroying Christianity and civil government, and the
portrayal is by one who personally knew the facts
and the parties.

"They claimed the right to indulge in lascivious-
ness, and to recreate themselves as their propensi-
ties and appetites should dictate. Those who composed this association," says the writer, "were my
neighbors; some of them were my school-mates. I
knew them well, both before and after they became
members. I marked their conduct, and saw and
knew their ends. Their number was about twenty
men and seven females. . . . Of these, some were
shot; some hung; some drowned; two destroyed
themselves by intemperance, one of whom was eaten
by dogs, and the other by hogs; one committed
suicide; one fell from his horse and was killed; and
one was struck with an ax and bled to death. . . .
Joshua Miller was a teacher of infidelity, and was
shot off a stolen horse by Colonel J. Woodhull.
N. Miller, his brother, was shot off a log while he

was playing at cards on first-day morning, by Zebed June, in a scouting party for robbers. Benjamin Kelley was shot off his horse by a boy, the son of the murdered, for the murder of one Clarke; he lay above ground until the crows picked his bones. J. Smith committed suicide by stabbing himself while he was imprisoned for crime. W. Smith was shot by B. Thorpe and others, for robbery. S. T. betrayed his own confidential friend for five dollars; his friend was hung, and himself afterward was shot by D. Lancaster; said to be an accident. I heard the report of the gun and saw the blood. J. A. was shot by Michael Coleman, for robbing Abimel Young, in the very act. J. V. was shot by a company of militia. J. D., in one of his drunken fits, lay out, and was chilled to death. J. B. was hanged for stealing a horse. T. M. was shot by a Continental guard, for not coming to when hailed by the guard. C. S. was hung for the murder of Major Nathaniel Strong. J. Smith and J. Vervellon were hung for robbing John Sackett. B. K. was hung for stealing clothes. One other individual, hung for murder. N. B. was drowned, after he and J. B. had been confined for stealing a large ox sent to General Washington, as a present, by a friend. W. T. and W. H. were drowned. C. C. hung himself. T. F., Jun., was shot by order of a court-martial for desertion. A. S. was struck with an ax, and bled to death. F. S. fell from his horse, and was killed. W. Clark drank himself to death; he was eaten by the hogs before his bones were found, and they were known by his clothing. He was once a member of respectable standing in the Presbyterian Church. While he remained with them, and regarded their rules and regulations, he was exemplary, industrious, sober, and respectable; and not until he became an infidel did he become a vagabond. His bones, clothing, and jug were found in a corn field belonging to John Coffee, and they were buried without a coffin. J. A., Sen., died in the woods, his rum-jug by his side. He was not found until a dog brought home one of his legs, which was identified by the stocking. His bones had been picked by animals. J. H., the last I shall mention in connection with that gang, died in a drunken fit. . . .

" The conduct of the females who associated with this gang was such as to illustrate its practical effects upon them. I shall only say that not one of them could or would pretend to know who were the fathers of their offspring. Perhaps hell itself could not produce more disgusting objects than were some of them." *

Numerous localities, at that time, presented similar moral phases. Virginia, Pennsylvania, and New

---

* " Practical Infidelity Portrayed." By Alva Cunningham. 12mo. New York City. 1836. Pp. 42–46. These facts, and other similar facts, are supported by numerous affidavits of respectable men.

Jersey could produce many parallel cases. Societies, or clubs of *Illuminati*, existed in Virginia, in affiliation with those of France. The infidelity of the age far exceeded any thing before or since known in America, and was of the grossest kind. The above portrayal shows this, and also the gross character of the habits in other respects. In some other incidental matters, also, it exhibits the low social and moral condition.

The Rev. Devereux Jarratt gave a dark picture of society in Virginia near the close of the last century, and Bishop Meade's sketches of the "Old Churches and Families of Virginia" deepen the shades. Of a portion of Kentucky, Peter Cartwright, speaking of the year 1793, said, "It was called 'Rogues' Harbor,' because 'law could not be executed.' The most abandoned and ferocious lawlessness prevailed. It was a desperate state of society. Refugees from justice, murderers, horse-thieves, highway robbers, and counterfeiters settled there, and 'actually formed a majority.' The better elements of society, called 'Regulators,' organized and attempted, by arms, to put down the 'Rogues,' but were defeated."

As late as 1803, according to Rev. Joseph Badger, Cleveland, Ohio, had no church, and "infidelity and Sabbath profanation were general." A gentleman visiting Western New York in 1798 said: "Religion has not got west of the Genesee River.

Some towns are hot-beds of infidelity." Of many other sections of the country it was said, "There was scarcely a vestige of the Christian religion."

Rev. Dr. I. N. Tarbox says: "A sentence from the 'Andover (Mass.) Manual' opens another subject of great significance, as showing the real condition of the Churches in the last century. We are told, as a part of the history of that Church, that 'the chief causes of discipline for a hundred and twenty-five years were fornication and drunkenness.' And the writer adds: 'He who investigates the records of this or any other Church for the same period will be astonished at the prevalence of these vices, as compared with the present time.'" *

The Pastoral Letter issued in 1798 by the General Assembly of the Presbyterian Church was full of alarm and expostulation: "When formidable innovations and convulsions in Europe threaten destruction to morals and religion; when scenes of devastation and bloodshed, unexampled in the history of modern nations, have convulsed the world; and when our own country is threatened with similar calamities, insensibility in us would be stupidity; silence would be criminal. . . . We desire to direct your awakened attention toward that bursting storm, which threatens to sweep before it the

---

* "Historical Sketch of the Congregational Churches of Massachusetts from 1776 to 1876." Minutes of the General Association for 1877, p. 33.

religious principles, institutions, and morals of our people. We are filled with deep concern and awful dread, while we announce it as our conviction that the eternal God has a controversy with our nation, and is about to visit us in his sore displeasure. . . . We perceive with pain and fearful apprehension a general dereliction of religious principle and practice among our fellow-citizens ; a great departure from the faith and simple purity of manners for which our fathers were remarkable ; a visible and prevailing impiety and contempt for the laws and institutions of religion ; and an abounding infidelity, which, in many instances, tends to atheism itself." In this alarming condition of things, they say: "A dissolution of religious society seems to be threatened by the supineness and inattention of many ministers and professors of Christianity." "Formality and deadness, not to say hypocrisy, a contempt for vital godliness and the spirit of fervent piety, a desertion of the ordinances, or a cold and unprofitable attendance upon them, visibly pervaded every part of the Church." "The profligacy and corruption of public morals have advanced with a progress proportioned to our declension in religion. Profaneness, pride, luxury, injustice, intemperance, lewdness, and every species of debauchery and loose indulgence, greatly abound."

The means for combating these evils were then small. In large sections of the land the people

either were not supplied with gospel preaching or
the supply was very scanty. There were no tracts,
and very few religious books and Bibles. The age
of tract and Bible societies had not dawned. During the colonial history no Bibles except Eliot's Indian Bible were allowed by the mother country to
be printed. They were, therefore, scarce and expen-
sive, and during the Revolutionary War a few were
imported, with great difficulty, from Scotland and
Holland. The first American edition of the holy
Scriptures was published in 1781, by Robert Aiken,
of Philadelphia. So meager were the means of
resistance against the evils of that period.

CHAPTER II.

THE PRESENT PERIOD.

SPECIFIC TENDENCIES.

The Sabbath.
Slavery and Barbarism.
Unchastity and Divorce.
Impure Literature.
Crime.

CHAPTER II.

THE PRESENT PERIOD.

THE review of the preceding periods has prepared us to judge more intelligently the moral
condition of our own times. The task, however, is
still attended with difficulties; for to judge our times
is much like judging ourselves. Future judges may
modify our best conclusions. To compare the
moral condition of the same people in two different
periods requires much careful discrimination. So
many diverse elements, currents, ebbs, and flows
enter into the life of any people, and especially of a
young nation like ours—an asylum for all nations—
and in times so stimulating, intense, and revolutionizing in the realm of ideas, that there is a liability to
error in any conclusion that may be reached. With
many first appearances, or fancies and prepossessions,
instead of a definite basis of facts, determine conclusions. It is not strange, therefore, that on a question so complicated as this a considerable diversity
of views should exist; and it would be wonderful if
a being so much inclined to fault-finding as man
should fail to sometimes indulge in that peculiar
luxury.

For ourselves, we may say that the careful study
of the period under consideration, notwithstanding
its serious currents of evil, some of them increasing
and others new, has resulted in the comforting conviction that a very great and substantial improvement has taken place in the average moral purity of
American society and of the American Churches.

It should, however, be kept continually in mind
that the world abounds in evil; that under the extraordinary light and intelligence of the age unusual hardness and impiety are to be expected in
those resisting; that an age so intensely active will
be likely to be characterized by a corresponding
activity and intensity in evil; and that rank and
monstrous developments of evil will justify the prediction, "Evil men and seducers will wax worse
and worse," even while the average moral condition
may be radically improving.

The progress of society is not wholly in straight
lines or by uniform rates. Currents have their eddies, flows their ebbs. The best advancement of
the world has sometimes seemed oscillatory or receding. Beating against the wind is a frequent
method of moral navigation. Human Progress,
said Theodore Parker, is much like the flight of
wild fowl. The leaders continually change; the old
fall to the rear, and new ones come to the front,
soon to give place to others. But the whole flock
is advancing. So with the flock of virtues and

vices. The actual progress of communities can be determined only with due discrimination in regard to things phenomenal, temporary, and collateral.

In such a spirit we inspect the facts of our national life, indicative of the moral condition and progress during this century.

The great revival of religion which spread through almost the whole land from 1800 to 1803, inaugurated an era of better moral and religious life. The dark and gloomy spell of evil under which the country had struggled in the two preceding decades was in a good measure broken; the Churches were invested with new power; the tone of public morals improved; and new currents were introduced, destined, in due time, to work out beneficent results. Such intelligent observers as Rev. Drs. Heman Humphry, E. D. Griffin, Nathan Bangs, Elijah Hedding, Lyman Beecher, and Hons. Reuben H. Walworth, John Cotton Smith, and John Quincy Adams, all familiar with those times, bore ample and decisive testimony to this change. But the testimony of facts must be cited.

The Sabbath.

The disregard of the Sabbath in the last two decades of the last century, so serious in all the older communities, and total in many of the new settlements, still continued a flagrant offense against morals after the present century opened. In large

13

portions of the West and South-west the only recognition of the Sabbath was a general devotion to
pleasure, gaming, and visiting. The home missionaries and itinerant preachers who first visited Western New York, Ohio, Michigan, and the regions
farther south and south-west, encountered a condition of morals calling for stern courage and heroism. They found Sunday a day of amusement,
spent in horse-racing and dissipation. The stores
were kept open, and " the only distinguishing feature of the day was an excess of wickedness." This
state of things existed in those sections for several
decades.

Bishop Meade represented the condition of things
in Eastern Virginia as but little better. At the
time of his consecration to the ministry, in 1811, at
Williamsburgh, Va., the seat of William and Mary's
College, and, therefore, presumed to be the most
cultivated part of that State, (Bishop Madison of
that diocese, president of the college, residing
there,) the disregard of the Sabbath was almost total. " On our way to the old church," he said,
" the Bishop and myself met a company of students
with guns on their shoulders and dogs at their sides,
attracted by the frosty morning, which was favorable to the chase, and at the same time one of the
citizens was filling his ice-house. On arriving at
the church we found it in a wretched condition,
with broken windows and a gloomy, comfortless as-

pect. The congregation consisted of two ladies and fifteen gentlemen, nearly all of whom were relatives or acquaintances." * He also describes a similar condition of things in Richmond, and elsewhere in Virginia.

In staid Connecticut Sabbath desecration was so serious that the " Society for the Reformation of Morals," organized in 1812, under the leadership of Rev. Lyman Beecher, in addition to intemperance, gave special prominence to Sabbath-breaking as one of the evils from which they hoped to deliver the State.

After 1810, mails were carried on the Sabbath on all the routes in the United States, and the post-offices were kept open. This practice continued more than twenty years, notwithstanding numerous remonstrances. All the religious bodies repeatedly protested, and memorialized Congress on the subject, from 1812 until after 1830, but with little effect. Matters grew worse instead of better ; for whereas the law of 1810 required only those post-offices where the mails arrived on Sunday to be kept open, and that only for an hour, in 1825 a more lax law was enacted, requiring that all post-offices, at which mails arrived on the Sabbath, should be kept open during the *whole* of the day.

---

* "Old Churches, Ministers, and Families of Virginia." By Bishop William Meade. Vol. i, pp. 29, 30, etc. Philadelphia : J. B. Lippincott & Co. 1857.

Public military honors were paid to General La-
fayette, in 1824, on the Lord's day. At its next
session, the General Association of Massachusetts
expressed grave apprehensions on account of " the
growing indifference to the sanctity of the day," and
the " repeated violations of it." In 1827 a crowd
of opposers violently interfered and prevented Rev.
Gardner Spring, D.D., and other influential gentlemen, from holding a meeting in City Hall, New
York, for promoting the better observance of the
Sabbath.

In March, 1830, Hon. Richard M. Johnston, Post-
master General, outraged the moral sentiments of
the nation, in an official reply to memorials asking
for the repeal of the laws requiring the post-offices
to be kept open the whole of Sunday. Respecting
that report it was said: " Satan never accomplished
a greater victory over the Sabbath, through any
agency, in any country, than was accomplished by
this report, if we except the abolition of the Sabbath, in France, during the reign of infidelity."

In 1834, by a general repealing clause, all the
Sabbath observance laws in New York city disappeared, and in their place was found a law *prohibiting religious* meetings in the Park and other public
places, unless held by a licensed minister of the
Gospel, and with the written permission of the
mayor or aldermen. Some years later the only
law bearing on the Sabbath, in New York, was a

prohibition against the firing of a gun on Sunday, and the sale of intoxicating drinks, the latter of which was supposed to be superseded by a law of the State.

In 1840 the "come-outer" wing of radical abolitionists assailed the Sabbath, and denounced it in conventions, lectures, newspapers, etc., exerting a very pernicious influence against the sacred day, through several years.

In 1842 the American and Foreign Sabbath Union was formed. Under the leadership of Rev. Justin Edwards, D.D., its agent, a redoubtable champion of reform, a broad and influential movement was inaugurated, enlisting leading statesmen, and influential gentlemen, in all sections of the land, and securing favorable action by the State Legislatures. In 1844 a National Convention was held in Baltimore, attended by upward of seventeen hundred delegates, from eleven different States, at which Hon. John Quincy Adams presided. Through several years much attention was devoted to the discontinuance of railroad trains and steamboats on Sundays; and Hon. E. C. Delavan, of Albany, printed, and gratuitously circulated among the stockholders and travelers of the New York Central road one hundred thousand copies of Dr. Edwards' "Sabbath Manual," to prepare the way for the cars to cease running on Sunday. After eight years of arduous labors, traveling more than forty-eight thousand miles, in twenty-five different States, addressing men through the pulpit and the press, Dr. Edwards summed up the glorious results of his labors in these lines:

"Railroad directors, in an increasing number of cases, have confined the running of their cars to six days in the week; locks on canals are not opened; and official business is not transacted on the Sabbath. Stages and steamboats in many cases have ceased to run; and more than eighty thousand miles of Sabbath-breaking mails have been stopped. . . .

"About forty railroad companies have stopped the running of their cars on that day, on about four thousand miles of roads. The communities through which they pass, and whose right to the stillness and the quiet of the day had for years been grossly violated, by the screaming and rumbling of cars in time of public worship. are now free from the nuisance, and are permitted to enjoy their rights and privileges without molestation."

The year 1850 was the period of the best general observance of the Sabbath that had then been known for one hundred years. About that time, however, a very large new element was introduced into American society, destined to seriously modify our habits and life. The great European immigration set upon our shores about 1848, and came in rapidly swelling waves in the following years, bringing Sabbath ideas and habits radically different from ours. A decline in Sabbath observance was soon apparent.

To resist these encroachments upon public morality, in 1854, Christian men came together and organized the New York Sabbath Committee, the record of whose labors is worthy of more extended notice than we can here devote to it.

In 1856 the Sabbath desecration in New York city was described as presenting a fearful picture. Steamboats arrived and departed, and railway trains bore an immense freight of passengers into neighboring towns, to return at night with half-intoxicated crowds; dance-houses emitted mingled noises of music, dancing, and swearing; red-curtained grog-shops stood open in the larger avenues; the public gardens were full of target-shooters, gamblers, and drinkers; many branches of business continued in full blast; shops, foundries, and machine factories continued their work; engine companies and processions paraded the streets; academies of music and theaters were open for " sacred " performances; and, in short, " the Sabbath became the vilest day of the seven."

No such picture could then be drawn of any other Northern Atlantic city. Boston was bad enough; but the Sabbath was a quiet day. Its wickedness was not noisy and demonstrative, nor in the majority. But there was a growing laxity in the observance of the Lord's day.

The New York Committee attributed the growing desecration of the Sabbath to the following
causes: Selfishness and worldliness, the preoccupa-
tion and neglect of Christian men, the multiplication
of lines of travel into the interior of the country,
European travel, the immense immigration from
Europe, and, above all, the desire for recreation.

In 1859 a New York newspaper said: "It appears that there are 7,779 places where liquors are
sold in the city, of which only 72 have license from
the Excise Commissioners, and that 5,186 houses
continue their business on Sunday, in violation of
State and city statutes; and it is estimated that at
least the sum of $1,348,360 is expended in the grog-
shops on the fifty-two Sundays of the year. It further appears that of the 27,845 commitments to
prison in 1857, no less a proportion than 23,817 of
these, or about 6 out of every 7, were of persons of
'intemperate habits;' of whom, again, sixty per
cent. were mere youths and young men between
ten and thirty years of age. Lastly, another set of
statistics shows that, taking seventy-six successive
Sundays, the criminal arrests were 9,713, while for
the same number of Tuesdays there were but 7,861
—a difference of twenty-five per cent.—traceable to
the Sunday grog-shops."

Foreign immigration exerted an influence almost
incalculable in promoting Sabbath desecration. At
the date of which we now speak, more than one

half of the population of New York city were either foreign-born or their immediate offspring, and with European ideas of the Sabbath. Few of the cities of Ireland had a larger Irish population, and few cities of Germany a larger German population, than New York, and it was particularly the Germans who took the lead in Sabbath profanation, transplanting to our country, not the German Sabbath of Germany itself, but of the most irreligious and atheistic portion of that people. In this new soil it reached an enormity of development that would have astonished the natives at home. The great mass of the children, released from the imperative necessity of receiving a good theoretical religious education, which in Germany is rigidly enforced upon all, in this land grow up to live absolutely without any recognition of God or his sacred laws; many of their newspapers openly denying the sacredness of the Bible, and even the existence of God. To them Sunday was a day to eat, drink, and be merry. It was early seen that every year an increasing portion of the American people were adopting these customs, so that this element, instead of being absorbed into our native element, was absorbing a portion of the native element.

We have spoken of New York city because these agencies were there most conspicuously working at that time, and, through the hot-bed fermentations of city life, earliest ripened there into the natural fruit. But the same seed was scattered all over the continent. The cities of the West partook of the same type, those of the East were infected, and the fruitage was destined to be seen every-where.

At one time, reviewing the work of the Sabbath Committee, Dr. Gardner Spring said :

"They have not labored in vain. They have suppressed the vociferous cries of the Sunday news-boys, . . . in defiance of the most violent ribaldry and abuse. They have suppressed the Sunday pageant of the Fire Department, so that it has fallen into disuse under the weight of its own folly. They have rectified the abuses of the Sabbath in Central Park. They have suppressed the Sunday liquor traffic to a great extent, . . . and driven it into corners. They have suppressed the Sunday theaters and beer-gardens, and the Sunday concerts, etc. . . . They have carried the reform into our canals, our steamboats, our flouring and salt establishments, and our fisheries."

Since that time the wave has receded ; but, after all, Sabbath desecration is the exception rather than the general practice. But few, relatively, of the railroad trains run. Nearly all the engines lie still. Business is almost entirely hushed. But few stores, libraries, and museums are opened. With almost no attempts, by legal prosecutions, to enforce the observance of the day, its very general *voluntary* observance, becomingly and sacredly, by such large masses of people is clear evidence of the elevated moral sentiment that dominates the land, speaking more loudly of real virtue than the constrained observance secured by rigorous civil penalties under the regimen of our Puritan fathers.

It must be confessed that theoretical changes have been working in many minds, the views of good men of the highest rank, religiously and morally, having undergone some modifications. The Puritan Sabbath has come to be regarded as an extreme toward the Talmudical Sabbath of the Pharisees, incumbered with vestments not scriptural, nor even Mosaic, and far removed from the spirit and character of the Christian Sabbath. The tendency is toward a Christian ideal of the sacred day. Many, however, have gone to the extreme of laxity.

Each age requires for its peculiar necessities a restatement of familiar truths and principles ; for they are assailed from new quarters and by new arguments. The Christian Church is adjusting lines of discussion which will fully meet these demands, and is freshly presenting and arguing fundamental principles, which will effectually vindicate the eternal sanctity of the Sabbath. It is demonstrating that the essential sanctions and obligations of the Jewish Sabbath are transferred to the Christian Sunday ; that the evidences for the necessity of a day of rest are inwrought in man's physical, intellectual, and religious nature ; and that the laws requiring Sab-

bath observance are compatible with the most perfect personal freedom—"the law of rest of all being necessary to the liberty of rest of each."

Slavery.

At the beginning of this century slavery existed
throughout all the world.   Hungary numbered nine
millions of slaves, and the Russian, Austrian, and
Prussian peasantry were mostly slaves, or serfs in
a low condition.   For some years after this century
opened an Englishman might sell his wife into
servitude.   Slavery existed in Scotland down to the
very last year of the eighteenth century.   The col-
liers and salters were slaves bound to service for
life, and were bought and sold with the works at
which they labored.   During the first seven years
of this century English ships conveyed annually
over the Atlantic forty thousand Africans, one half
of whom perished at sea or soon after landing.
Twenty-six acts of the British Parliament expressed
approval of the traffic, and it required twenty
years of agitation to suppress it, and twenty-six
more to procure emancipation.   The whip was freely
used in the English West Indies, and even the flogging of women was practiced till eight years after
the Battle of Waterloo.   In 1833 emancipation
was decreed, and six hundred thousand slaves were
liberated by the expenditure of twenty millions
sterling.

In the United States the evil was not so easily disposed of. Here it wrought with incalculable mischief and demoralization in all ranks of society, North and South. Considered in all its phases, the institution of slavery did more to corrupt and deteriorate American manners than any other single cause. It was a fountain of glaring injustice, bloody barbarism, the grossest licentiousness, the darkest ignorance, the most perfidious sophistry; in short, "the sum of all villainies." It extended its corrupt sway even to the best circles of society in the North, and made eminent instructors in law and piety pleaders and apologists for the rankest injustice. The hallucinating power of our Western cotton rivaled the hempen hasheesh of the East, and made

> "Or fools or knaves of all who ate it."

> "The preacher eats, and straight appears
>   His Bible in a new translation;
> Its angels negro overseers,
>   And heaven itself a snug plantation.

> "The noisiest Democrat, with ease
>   It turns to slavery's parish beadle;
> The shrewdest statesman eats, and sees
>   Due southward point the polar needle.

> "The judge partakes, and sits ere long
>   Upon his bench a railing blackguard;
> Decides off-hand that right is wrong,
>   And reads the ten commandments backward."

The legislation of the country on the slavery question was of the most corrupt and deteriorating

character: whether we look at the local legislation
of the several States, delivering over the blacks
more and more completely, soul and body, to the
most abject and debasing servitude, shutting out
the means of enlightenment and amelioration allowed in earlier periods; or the legislation of Congress, violating grave ordinances which had been
declared final and unalterable, compromising and
then violating compromises, bartering sacred human rights for the broth of office, entering into war
with Mexico for the purpose of extending the area
of slavery, turning the whole North into a hunting-
ground for slaves, and outraging the most palpable
principles of law and justice in their arrest and re-
committal to slavery. Each and all these acts, from
the great Missouri Compromise, through all the pro-
slavery constructions placed upon the Constitution,
to the infamous Kansas perfidy and crime, were
not only destructive of good morals, but also positively barbarous and brutalizing in tendency—the
abundant seed-sowing of the more recent outrages
and atrocities in the Southern States. The pro-
slavery theories, in their politico-moral bearings;
the Scripture vindication of slavery, in its religious
bearing; the humiliating bondage of large ecclesiastical bodies to the slave power; the loose sexual
relations of the whites with the slaves; the almost
entire absence of ethical inculcations in connection
with the scanty religious instruction imparted to

the slaves, leaving them wholly undeveloped in moral ideas, and immoral in habits while ardent in religious sentiment; and the brutal severity practiced to hold in subjection the rapidly multiplying serfs—were productive of an untold amount of moral impurity and deterioration.

The statistics of homicides and other atrocious crimes in the South show that the pernicious pro-slavery seed-sowing of the century has produced a fearful harvest. According to the last census, in North Carolina there was one violent death to every twenty-two thousand of population; in South Carolina, one to nineteen thousand; in Georgia, one to ten thousand; in Alabama, one to ten thousand; in Florida, one to four thousand; in Mississippi, one to nine thousand; in Louisiana, one to six thousand; in Arkansas, one to six thousand three hundred; in Texas, one to two thousand five hundred. The ratio in the nine States is one in seven thousand three hundred; and, even excluding Texas, which shows such a horrible record, the proportion is one to nine thousand six hundred. At this rate the homicides in the whole United States should have exceeded forty thousand, or nearly twenty times as many as actually occurred. It may put these figures in a somewhat clearer light if we call attention to the fact that the homicides in Florida exceeded by two those in all the New England States; that Louisiana exceeded those for the two most populous

States—New York and Pennsylvania—combined; and that Texas alone records more than half as many murders as all the States that were loyal during the war.

" If statistics are good for any thing, these figures prove conclusively that a state of society existed in the South, previous to the passage of the Ku-Klux bill, which demanded interference. In a great section of the country, comprising fourteen States, with a population of thirteen millions, life was so insecure that one in every ten thousand met death by premeditated violence in one year, and a large proportion of these, in at least twelve of the States, was traceable directly to an *organization* which aimed at political power through murder and robbery."

Statistics recently collected in Kentucky, covering the period of about five years, (1874–1879,) in several counties, present a most appalling showing of high crimes and the laxity of law.

When will the barbarism engendered by slavery pass away? " How long, O Lord, how long?"

But, thank God, this most prolific of all the sources of our demoralization, the institution of slavery, is dead—the greatest moral triumph of the nineteenth century; the triumph of the higher virtues of the American people. And in due time the desolating effects of slavery must disappear.

Chastity and Divorce.

The French infidelity, so prevalent in America at the close of the last and the beginning of the present century, exerted a baleful influence upon social and domestic relations. Numerous facts might be cited, if the details were not so indelicate, showing the prevalence of the grossest licentiousness, in large sections of the country, and of unchastity, in slightly milder forms, in even the better communities. Shocking examples of indiscriminate sexual relations between parents and children, continuing for years without civil interference, not in the festering centers of the population, but in the sparser communities, might be cited, on the authority of regularly drawn and duly attested affidavits. Data now exist showing that rural towns in Massachusetts and Connecticut, of more than average thrift, rank, and intelligence, favored with the ministrations of some of the most eminent and faithful divines, were not exempt from this evil, that enforced marriages were frequent, and that the Churches, much more frequently than in our days, were under the necessity of administering discipline for crimes against chastity.

In large sections of the land newly settled, and either without Churches, ministers, and magistrates, or only scantily supplied, there was little or no civil or ecclesiastical recognition of matrimony, and men

14

and women assumed family relations without marriage forms. These cases were very numerous.
Some of our most eminent civilians were the fruits
of the low habits prevailing in the beginning of this
century.

In the older portions of the land "runaways"
from matrimonial relations were frequent. The
stringency of the divorce laws gave little hope of
relief from unhappy unions. The comparative se-
clusion of local communities, then not penetrated
by railroads and telegraphs, and unvisited by ubiquitous reporters, gave abundant opportunity for
concealment and remarriage, even though removed
but a short distance from a former residence. The
newspapers of that time abounded in advertisements of " runaway wives." A gentleman writing
in 1815 said : " I cut out of all the newspapers we
received the advertisements of all the ' runaway
wives,' and pasted them on a slip of paper, close
under each other. At the end of a month the slip
reached from the ceiling to the floor of a room more
than ten feet high, and contained one hundred and
twenty-three advertisements. We did not receive,
at most, more than one-twentieth part of all the
newspapers in the United States." Many, it is to
be presumed, were not advertised, and we have no
statistics of the runaway husbands.

About 1824–1826 Robert Owen and Fanny
Wright nearly simultaneously commenced their rad-

ical socialistic efforts, lecturing in all parts of the country, and inculcating the most disorganizing theories. It was a national excitement somewhat like that of a religious revival or a political campaign. The movement organized eleven communistic societies within a few years, and scattered broadcast sentiments unfavorable to the dignity and permanence of the marriage relation.

More recently, chiefly during the last forty years, a series of legislative acts, in numerous States, have removed the stringent restrictions upon divorce, and the separations of husbands and wives have become so numerous as to awaken much concern.

" Beginning with Connecticut, we find Benjamin Trumbull, in 1785, mourning that 439 divorces had taken place in Connecticut within a century, and that all but 50 had occurred in the last 50 years. About twenty years later, when the corrupt influence of French infidelity had reached its height, President Dwight was alarmed that there was one divorce to every hundred marriages. The evil, however, seems nearly checked in increase until 1843, when ' habitual intemperance ' and ' intolerable cruelty ' were added to the two existing causes for divorce. Even then the increase was small. But in 1849 several causes were added, including the notorious ' omnibus clause,' making *nine* in all, and jurisdiction was taken from the Legislature and given to the courts. That year divorces numbered

94; the next year, 129; and in 1864, 426. Then for 15 years they averaged 446 annually, varying less from year to year than the reported births or marriages, or deaths. During this period the ratio of divorces to marriages was 1 to 10.4. The repeal of the 'omnibus clause,' in 1878, reduced the divorces of the next year to 316. Another slight change in the law for the better was secured a year ago.

"Vermont grants divorces for six causes. There were 94 divorces granted in 1860, and from the close of the war they increased to 197 in 1878, with the ratio to marriages of 1 to 14. That year an amendment to the laws resulted in a reduction of divorces in the year following to 126.

"Rhode Island grants about 180 annually, and her ratio is 1 to 13.

"New Hampshire prints no statistics either of divorce or marriage, but it has been found that there were 159 divorces in the entire State in 1870; 240 in 1875, and 241 in 1878. Three counties, that had only 18 in 1840 and 21 in 1850, granted 40 in 1860, and 96 in 1878. There are fourteen causes for divorce, but no more inclusive, probably, than those of most other States.

"I do not know that the divorces of Maine have ever been reported. I have secured an examination of the county records in that State giving the divorces of the 16 counties of the State for the year

1878. In these 16 counties there were 478 divorces in that year. It is also found that in the five counties giving the number for 1880, there was an increase of more than one third in the latter year, from 166 to 223. Penobscot County granted 84 divorces last year.

"And now take Massachusetts, which I have reserved to the last, because she is the heart of New England, and for the facilities she affords for studying this whole problem. This State, following closely English law, granted divorce for only two causes until 1860. That year there were 243 divorces, or 1 to 51 marriages. Then, by a series of acts passed, chiefly in 1860, '67, '73, and '77, the causes for absolute divorce became *nine*, copying a Connecticut vice just as Connecticut began to forsake it. In 1866 there were 392 divorces; in 1870, 449; and in 1878, 600. The ratio to marriages, 1 to 51 in 1860, became 1 to 21.4 in 1878. It is probable that in Massachusetts the increase still goes on.

"If now we sum up for New England, there were in the year of grace 1878 in Maine 478 divorces; in New Hampshire, 241; in Vermont, 197; in Massachusetts, 600; in Connecticut, 401; and in Rhode Island, 196; making a total of 2,113, and a larger ratio in proportion to the population than in France in the days of the Revolution. In France the ratio of *separation* to marriages, latterly, is about 1 to 150;

in Belgium, of *divorce* to marriages, 1 to 270, with a few separations; and in England, of *petitions* for both divorce and separation, 1 to 300. On the basis of population by the present census there was one divorce to every 819 inhabitants in Maine; one to about 820 in Penobscot County, the seat of a theological seminary; one to every 1,443 in New Hampshire; one to every 1,687 in Vermont; one to every 2,973 in Massachusetts; one to every 1,553 in Connecticut; and one to every 1,411 in Rhode Island. But no State is likely to have a larger divorce rate than Massachusetts, unless the laws and discussion speedily check the evil.

" But the Catholic marriages are, in four States, 27 per cent. of the whole. Assuming what is very nearly true, that there are no divorces among these, the ratio of divorces to marriages among Protestants is 1 to 11.7 for the four States together : it being 1 to 15 in Massachusetts, 1 to 13 in Vermont, 1 to 9 in Rhode Island, and 1 in less than 8 in Connecticut.

" But what of divorce in the West? Has not this practice, in going West with the New Englander, run into greater extremes? Few States, if any, west of Ohio, collect statistics of divorce. In Ohio the ratio for many years averaged 1 to 25, and now it is about 1 to 18. Indiana has changed her laws for the better, while Illinois has, it is said, adopted better forms of procedure. No city has had a worse reputation in divorce than Chicago. Yet the records of Cook County, with a population of about 600,000, for the five years, 1875–79, show a ratio of divorce suits *begun* to *marriage licenses taken out* of 1 to 9.4. But for the year 1875 it was found that one fifth of the petitions heard were denied. Making this allowance— and the more strict practice of later years fully justified it—the ratio becomes 1 to 12. Chicago is not as bad as Hartford or New Haven." *

The last report † of Hon. Carroll D. Wright, Chief of the Bureau of Statistics of Labor in Massachusetts, contains a very succinct *resumé* of the legislation of that State in reference to divorce, since 1780. The divorce law of 1786 recognized only two causes for divorce—*adultery* and *impotency*. Seven other causes have since been added—*sentence to imprisonment at hard labor for five years or more, desertion for three consecutive years*, separation without consent, refusal to cohabit and union for three years with a religious sect or society holding the relation of husband and wife unlawful, extreme cruelty, gross and confirmed habits of intoxication, abusive treatment and neglect to provide. Under these general causes there have been other sub-

---

* Monday Lecture delivered by Rev. Samuel W. Dike, of Royalton, Vt., in Tremont Temple, Boston, Mass., January 24, 1881, and published in full in the " Boston Traveler," January 25, 1881. Mr. Dike is a high authority in the matter of divorce statistics.

† January 7, 1880, pp. 199–235.

causes or specifications, for which complete or partial separations have been granted. The statistics
in this volume, gathered from the records of the
Massachusetts courts, covering a period of nineteen
years, (1860–79,) show forty-four causes or specifications in which the courts have granted 7,233 divorces, of which the following is a condensed summary, under eight general heads :

Desertion	3,013	Cruel and abusive treatment 223
Adultery	2,949	Neglect to provide 154
Intoxication	452	Imprisonment.... 50
Extreme cruelty	375	Impotency................. 17

"It will be observed," says Mr. Wright, "that
but 3,016 of these 7,233 divorces were granted for
causes that would have been valid even so late as
half a century ago. 'Desertion' was not admitted as a cause for divorce at all until 1838, and not
until after the passage of the law of 1857 could it
be used to any considerable extent. 'Intoxication' and 'cruel and abusive treatment' came in
with the revision of the laws of 1860. 'Extreme
cruelty' and 'neglect to provide' did not until
1857 become causes for which decrees of full divorce
could be entered. Practically, therefore, more than
half of the whole number of divorces to which our
tables refer were granted for causes that have come
into legal existence within twenty-five years. . . .

"Of 1,169 divorces granted to wives in the whole
period, on account of 'intoxication,' 'extreme cru-

elty,' 'cruel and abusive treatment,' and 'neglect to provide,' 985, or more than 84 per cent., were decreed within the last half dozen years. It would hardly do to assume that husbands have given so much greater cause of late than ever before for complaint in the directions indicated by these several legal specifications. The explanation lies in the fact that certain material modifications of law took place in 1870 and 1873."

Simultaneously with this increase of divorces there has been another serious fact, the decrease of the number of marriages. In Massachusetts, in 19 years, the average ratio was 1 divorce to about 36 marriages; during the past 3 years, it was 1 to 23 marriages; in Vermont, in 7 years, there were 730 divorces to 15,710 marriages, or 1 to 21; in Ohio, in 1866, 1,169 divorces to 30,479 marriages, or 1 to 27; in Connecticut, in 8 years, 2,910 divorces to 33,227 marriages, or 1 to 11; in Rhode Island, 1 to 14.

Several considerations claim attention—

1. The increase of divorces during the past thirty years is an ominous symptom; and, in even the most liberal view of the question, can but awaken concern for the permanence of social order and the stability of public virtue.

2. The comparison of the number of divorces with the number of marriages annually is not satisfactory; for the number of marriages varies with the prosperity of the country and other causes. The

financial embarrassments following 1873 have diminished the number of the marriages, while they have not reduced the number of the divorces; and the larger facilities for obtaining divorces, granted in 1870 and 1873, is another cause not to be overlooked in such an investigation.

3. Loose legislation in regard to the matrimonial relation is an evidence of a change in the type of morals and a modification of the moral standard.

4. Some divorces, now granted, are for causes which do not imply serious immorality, or for immoralities not new, and probably not so numerous or so serious as in former times. Hence, the mere fact of an increase of divorces does not imply an increase of wickedness.

5. The divorces in our days, morally considered, count against the runaways from matrimony and the illegalized assumptions of marriage relations, quite extensive under the deleterious influences of French infidelity, less than one hundred years ago. The elopements and runaways now are few in comparison with those of that period, less even than twenty-five years ago. Now, combining the runaways and divorces, we find no such condition of things as existed when one twentieth part of the newspapers, in a single month, contained one hundred and twenty-three advertisements of runaway wives.

We have only to go back a few centuries to find

the family a very different thing from what it is to-day, with all the present evils. Out of what low conditions, before the Reformation, has it gradually risen into the dignity and purity with which we find it invested! It is not long since wives were exposed for sale in England.* A gentleman in this country in 1815, having access to not a very large number of English sources of information, found in a single year thirty-nine instances of wives exposed to public sale, like cattle at Smithfield. In hotly contested elections, in places where a freeman's daughter conferred the right to vote by marriage,† it was common for the same woman to marry several men. The ceremony over, the parties went into the church-yard, shook hands over an open grave, saying, " now death do us part," and away went the man to vote with his new qualification, and the woman to qualify another husband at another church.

How have laws and customs pertaining to mar-

---

* The following is an extract from an English publication : "Shrop-shire.—The town of Ludlow lately witnessed one of those scenes *to which custom has attached the character of lawful transactions in the minds of the lower classes.* A well-looking woman, wife of John Hall, to whom she had been married only one month, was brought by him in a halter, and sold by auction in the market for two and sixpence, with the addition of sixpence for the rope with which she was led. In this sale the customary market fees were charged— toll, one penny; pitching, three pence."—*New Monthly Magazine.* for Sept., 1814.

† The qualifications for voting differed at different places. Bristol, England, is here referred to. See " Espriella," by Southey.

riage been purified and improved! how much honor
and influence is now accorded to woman! how has
the sacredness and sweetness of home-life been developed throughout Christendom! This home sanctuary still has its evils, but less numerous and inveterate than those which cursed the family before
Protestantism arose.

Numerous socialistic communities, organized in
this country on an antimarriage basis, have nearly
all disappeared; and those remaining have abandoned the system of promiscuous sexual relations.
The recent change in the Oneida Community has
received much attention, and is clearly the effect
of the advancing moral sentiment of the nation.

Impure Literature.

The immorality of much of our current literature
and its pernicious influence, deserves more attention than we can give it in the present limits. The
number of trashy and sensational papers published
in New York city alone has been stated * to be
twenty-five, with an aggregate circulation of three
hundred and thirty-six thousand copies weekly.
Add to this vast number a reasonable estimate of
the circulation of other papers of the same class, in
other cities, and multiply the total by the average
number of readers, say three or five to each copy
of a paper, and we have an audience of several mill-

* "National Quarterly Review," July, 1879.

ions, chiefly boys and girls, young men and young women, to whom these papers minister intellectual food—with many, their only nutriment. These papers have been classified as bad, worse, worst.

"The first class do not contain that which is obscene or profane to any considerable extent, but are full of highly sensational stories. The titles of some of them, selected at random, indicate their character: 'Dashing Dolores, or Chincapin Dick on the Border,' 'Spider and Stump, the Plagues of the Village,' 'The Boy Pedestrian, or, Walking for a Life,' etc. The staple characteristic of these stories is the narrative of adventures. There is no real portrayal of character, no picturesque description, no pure sentiment—nothing but the recital of thrilling, blood-curdling adventure after adventure. Other stories in these papers recite in appropriate slang the tricks and practical jokes played by daring youngsters upon their parents and guardians. The distinction between the two lower classes of papers is a question simply of more or less. They have sensational stories, dealing largely with the relations of the sexes, together with illustrations of current events of a sensational character, portraits of burglars, murderers, and other criminals, and pictures of crime. In their reports of crime, especially those against purity, they enter into the minutest details, and they are spiced not infrequently with accounts of the doings in saloons and dance-halls. The effect upon the reader, the 'Review' writer observes, is as if he were put into constant companionship with criminals. Crime is not only made familiar to him, it is glorified, and his imagination is stimulated until he is ready to imitate the adventures which have been painted for him in such brilliant colors." *

The fruits of such reading were justly described by the writer already referred to:

"The completed product, then, brought forth as the result of these publications, is a foul-mouthed bully, a cheat, a thief, a desperado, a libertine. Instead of a clean-minded, high-toned, honorable young man, not afraid of work, and knowing that whatever is of value in this world is gained by work—a young man of courage, in which the moral element is greater than the physical, a young man respecting the law and other men's rights, a young man worthy of the love of a good woman—we should have one who, when the fictitious gloss, the stage-tinsel, the mock-heroic glamor, had been rubbed off, would be found preferring to live by his wits rather than his labor; rotten at heart, and hence foul in speech; as likely as not a betrayer of innocence; a pest and a plague in society." †

It is seriously feared that our public libraries foster rather than restrain the cravings for the sen-

* Editorial in "Boston Journal," Aug. 2, 1879.
† "National Quarterly Review," July, 1879.

sational thus awakened. "The gravity of this question was confessed in a recent congress of librarians,
and the ratio of sensational fiction in the various
libraries, (in some Sunday-school libraries,) is admitted to be ominously large, in spite of all that
has been done to diminish it. The nature of the
difficulty is illustrated by the fact that the Hartford
librarian recently reported that one boy had taken
out one hundred and two story books in six months,
and one girl one hundred and twelve novels in the
same time."

This is a great and subtle evil. A New York
judge, recently interviewed, traced a great deal of
the current crime to the influence of the flashy and
sensational story papers. But, besides, there are
the dime novels, cheap song books, *et id omne genus*,
turned out by the ton, and equally unhealthy to
morals. Nor should we fail to specify the perni-
ciously illustrated weeklies.

While fully accepting these facts, and in no sense
depreciating their importance, we must not forget
that the Christian public are fully aroused to resist
this evil. It is being assailed by the pulpit, the
press, the schools, and the public lectures, and organized movements have been formed against it.
An immense work has been accomplished by that
ever-to-be-honored champion of reform, Mr. Anthony Comstock, in protecting society against this
malignant foe, and a better sentiment is becoming

apparent—of itself, we may hope, to prove a salutary safeguard.

But great as is this evil, it is only a slight blem-
ish upon the vast mass of the general literature of
our times, the character of which, as compared
with previous centuries, has immeasurably improved. Where do our times furnish novels of the
vicious character of those of Smollett, Fielding, and
their company? And yet such books were read by
all classes in their day, in the higher as well as the
lower ranks of English society. Where are our
poets who babble loudly of vice " in dainty verse,"
as did Pope, Moore, Byron, etc.? A writer in
"Blackwood's" recently said: "Pope's most melodious, correctest couplets were interspersed with
lines which would damn for ever and ever any
modern poetaster."

Another said: " It is now necessary to prepare
expurgated editions of Shakspeare and of Dryden
if we would introduce them into our families.
Coming down almost to our own days, compare the
works of Lord Byron and of Tom Moore with the
works of Tennyson and of Longfellow. Here is
the title of one of De Foe's most popular works, so
much of it as decency will allow us to quote:
' Fortunes and Misfortunes of Moll Flanders, who
was born in Newgate, and during a Life of Continued Variety for Threescore Year, besides her
Childhood, was Twelve Year a Harlot, Five Times

a Wife, whereof once to her own Brother, Twelve Year a Thief, Eight Year a transported Felon to Virginia, at last grew Rich, lived Honest, and died a Penitent.' Such a book, reaching the widest circulation of any book of its time, reveals the state of public morals.'' *

Crime.

The subject of crime should not be overlooked in these inquiries, for the study of morals cannot be dissociated from the study of crime. Moralists and legislators mutually influence each other. Under advancing conditions of society the moral lapses of one generation become the criminal offenses of another, and deeds once praiseworthy become punishable. In the progress of an ever-expanding civilization, religious beliefs, theories of ethics, science, the growth of commerce and trade, and whatever affects the moral tone of society, exert an influence upon criminal legislation.

Many complain of the recent growth of great evils, but we believe that great crimes are relatively less, both in this country and in Europe, than before the present century, and that piety and morality are higher than ever before, except in the earlier periods of a few of the American colonies, when, of course, the condition was anomalous, and would not fairly admit of such a comparison.

* Editorial in the "Christian Advocate," New York City, November 30, 1876.

The difficulty in the way of comparing the crime
of the past with that of the present is the want of
sufficient exact *data*.   No single individual has had
the needed amount of personal observation, at once
comprehensive and minute, and the public statistics
of previous periods are too scattering and imperfect
to form a definite basis for calculation.   The
amount and character of crime against society, as
recognized by the police, may be assumed as a
pretty good standard of the public morality; but
even that is confessedly imperfect, and mostly limited to quite recent dates.   Perfect statistics of
criminal jurisprudence, for any given State or city,
or for the whole country, through the successive
decades of a century, cannot now be obtained, and,
even if they could be, some abatements and modifications, suggested by collateral facts, would be
found necessary.   During the past twenty or thirty
years considerable improvement has been made in
collecting and arranging criminal data, some of
which will be introduced in this discussion.

But it is too palpable to be disguised, nor are we
disposed to do so, that great crimes have been
shockingly frequent since the close of the late civil
war.   The large cities have become centers of
crime, where it multiplies, and often claims. impunity.   Lechery riots and putrefies, groggeries
keep open on Sunday in the face of worthless officials, filthy performances draw crowded audiences

to theaters, and elaborately furnished gambling hells flourish unnoticed. The larger cities are babels of manifold crimes, in crowding regiments, besieging and threatening the very existence of law and order.

Grave charges have been made, with too much truth, we fear, against the official guardians of law and order, in our larger cities, as the aiders and abettors of crime. The report of the Legislative Committee in New York, in 1875, appointed to investigate the conduct of the officials of New York city, gave a startling picture of the demoralization of the police, the offices of the District Attorney, the Coroner, and the Sheriff, the Prisons, and the Reformatories. Even the detective force, under Captain I——, was described as a band of skillful and treacherous robbers, who, when in lack of subjects, robbed and betrayed each other, to keep their hands in." We cannot pause to give even a tithe of the deplorable facts developed by this committee, nor need we speak in detail of similar things elsewhere.

Nor in the larger cities only. The rural communities, also, have furnished cases of daring atrocity. Crimes against life and property have seemed to move in waves, sometimes for a few months, coming with shocking frequency. The newspapers have freely discoursed of " The Reign of Violence," " The Era of Blood," " The Carnival of Crime," and sounded notes of alarm. An editor, not given to sensationalism,* said, " The problem revealed in such developments of the murderous propensity is certainly one calculated to justify the profoundest anxiety of every thoughtful citizen, not only because the evil has reached alarming proportions, but because the mere fact of prevalence begets a sort of social influenza, which becomes a distinct and additional source of crime."

The editor of one of our largest religious newspapers has thus summed up these complaints against the crimes of our times :

" To bring the whole case before us, let us catalogue the crimes, charges, criminations and recriminations, and the conflicting convictions concerning public affairs. So much has been poured into the public ear that disheartened men are not a few. Many charges have been urged on both sides with a view to make them public convictions. We will emphasize them, then analyze them. It is trumpeted abroad that distrust, the forerunner of destruction, fills the very air; that virtue herself veils her face, lest an idolatrous multitude should brand her as a hypocrite ; that even integrity weeps at the bar of the public judgment, waiting for a vindication by events. It is said that every place of public trust is polluted; that thieves in the public treasury consort with criminals in the halls of jus-

* The " Boston Journal."

tice; that creatures, wearing the badges of honorable and ancient orders, fawn about the steps of
power that they may barter the secrets of friend-
ship for the booty of conspirators; that the slime
of corruption has reached the most holy place, till
avenging angels seem to guard the very approaches
to the mercy-seat. But what is worse than all else,
the very efforts at reform are alleged to be conceived in sin and born in iniquity. Partisans seek
not criminals, but victims. If any scrap of honor
remains in public life it attracts assault.

"Liars and informers and thieves can fatten at
the public expense, to secure room for greater
crimes. Language can do but poor justice to the
case when men who have plundered the treasury
are the sole protectors of the government they
failed to bankrupt and overthrow. If these things
be true, it is no wonder that the air is full of accusa-
tions. In the last year we have seen thirty-seven
investigating committees appointed apparently to
slander political antagonists whose demerit is, at
the worst, only equal to that of their persecutors.
We have nearly three hundred indictments for
offenses that were fatal to honor. Over seventy
have pleaded guilty to crimes that involve the hon-
or of a vast net-work of officers.

"The case is summed up in a few terribly dark
characters. Public integrity is said to be lost in the
sewer where politicians are spawned; so that all

turpitudes in public servants are accounted for, if not justified, by the use of the single term '*politi-cian.*' Public trust, that at once partakes of the honor of the citizen and the fidelity of the father, rests as lightly on the political conscience as the passing shadow of a summer cloud. Office is said to mean opportunity for spoils. Justice is called a cat-o'-nine-tails with the stock end in the hand of the great criminals, while the small rogues and helpless victims dance at its business end. Faith in eternal verities is said to stumble over its own deserted altars, strangled by the profligacy of its own priests. Private fortunes are thought to be in perpetual peril from the treachery of personal friends as well as from the assaults of organized bands of plunderers." *

Astounding cases of defalcation, forgery, and other offenses against trust and honor, involving in heavy crime men of highest respectability, of lofty religious profession, pillars of Churches, and conspicuous in Christian and charitable labors, have been the most pa.nful and staggering to public confidence of all the recent developments. While setting their hands to deeds for which they now lie in penitentiaries, they were " repeating every Sabbath the prayers of the Church ; singing songs hallowed by the voices of martyrs; giving freely of stolen goods to Christian benevolences; and seemingly

* " Christian Advocate," New York city, Nov. 30, 1876.

delighting in deeds of charity more than in hoard-
ing gold. So tortuous, serpentine, and idiotic, under
the wiles of evil, have consciences become." Faith-
less officials have lived in splendid mansions, driven
fast horses, and traveled in foreign lands, on the
money of poor people, putting industry and economy at a discount.

The effect of these oft-repeated defalcations has
been fearfully cumulative. Sermons, homilies,
scathing editorials, public and social indignations,
have multiplied, inculcating virtue, protesting
against venality, and warning of the consequences
of dishonesty. Then straightway one supposed to
be incorruptible takes a hand in the unequal game,
and surprises the public with a fresh example of
perfidy and ruin. Within a brief period a single
New England city has furnished a half-dozen illustrations of defaulters in high social and religious
positions.

No theory fully accounts for the recent increase
of crime. Sometimes it is said to be owing to the
infusion of a large immoral foreign population into
the country; but the next moment we hear of some
horrid atrocity by a native American of education
and good social standing. Then we talk of the
cities as the peculiar abodes of crime; but the next
day a quiet rural district furnishes a case which for
savagery matches anything perpetrated in the vilest
haunts of the large centers. It is impossible to go

to the deepest root of homicidal crime, for it involves "some of the most occult and difficult problems of mental and moral psychology." Malignant ulcers, horrid deformities, and infectious distempers have always afflicted the highest civilizations, and probably will continue to do so.

We have given the alleged demoralization so much prominence and emphasis that we may do full justice to many palpable facts, and lest we should seem to unduly eulogize the present age. But a broad and discriminating analysis of these unfavorable aspects of our times, in the light of previous times, will throw a clearing light upon the page, and show that the indications are not doleful but hopeful ; that some are temporary reactions under temporary causes ; that others are eddying circles in the stream of progress ; others, first, and probably transient, out-puttings of new and immature stages of civilization ; and that, whatever shadows here and there may darken the picture, its average light and beauty are immeasurably greater than in former days.

There are many weighty considerations which shed an alleviating light upon the situation.

First of all, it must be borne in mind that a large part of the increase of crime is apparent rather than real. It is not simply that more crimes are committed, but more are reported. " We read about defalcations and rascalities, but we forget that we skim the whole creation every morning and put the results in our coffee. Years ago a crime had to be of unusual proportions to make its way into an adjoining State. Only the giant crimes could cross the continent. But now we see and know every thing."

"The ubiquitous reporter," says the editor of the "Boston Journal," (July 11, 1879,) "is responsible for the gloomy showing. His note-book and pencil are every-where, and the telegraph is the ready agent for transmitting news to all parts of the world. The scope of the press has vastly broadened of late years, and its facilities for collecting news are immensely multiplied. We have had the curiosity to look back over some early files of 'The Journal,' in order to show by comparison the change which has taken place. Selecting an issue of the paper at random, in July, 1850, we find that out of thirty-two columns contained in the paper precisely one third of a column is taken up with telegraph news, and two thirds of a column with local news, half of the latter space being devoted to an account of tenement-house life on Fort Hill. Of actual news, gathered by reporters and by telegraph, the paper contained hardly more than half a column. 'The Journal' of that day was not less enterprising than its contemporaries; but journalistic ideas and ideals were altogether different. The newspaper reader then was content with the narrow

horizon which his paper supplied him, and troubled
himself very little about matters which went on at
a distance.   The newspaper editor presented news
as it happened to come, and when it came, and was
not given to making special exertions for procuring
it.   How different this is from the journalism of to-
day, with its net-work of agencies, embracing the
most insignificant places and the most remote quarters of the world; with its complex facilities and
mighty rivalries; with its special correspondents
here, there, and every-where—scouring the deserts
of Central Asia, exploring Africa, watching the military movements in Zululand, and even going out in
quest of a way to the North Pole—we hardly need
say.   The editor of thirty years ago would have
stood aghast at the expenditures for news collecting
necessary to a journal of to-day.   But we may note,
in passing, that in the scanty space devoted to
news in the issue of July, 1850, to which we refer,
we find mention of nine crimes."

What proportion of crime is apparent and what
is actual cannot be satisfactorily answered.   Our
bureaus of statistics are preparing materials which
may at some time assist us.   Unquestionably, more
crimes are now committed than twenty or thirty
years ago.   But during this period great changes
have taken place in the composition of our population.

It must be evident to all that as society develops

life becomes more rapid and intense, and the liability to break down under overstrain increases, with those naturally frail or ill-balanced; but such failures do not indicate a general deterioration of morals. An over-wrought civilization will exhibit some painful features. The high nervous tension characteristic of our times easily slips into some form of derangement or aberration, or enfeebles self-control, and makes men easy victims of temptation and passion, to which in a truly normal condition they would not have succumbed. "I believe," said an English writer, "it may hold true that any period of great mental activity in a nation will be prolific of crime. The Greeks were sad knaves; that is to say, there were sad knaves among them; and so, God knows, there are in England, at the present day of free trade and swift intercommunication, stimulating mental activity into rapid, perhaps morbid, action. The knavery of the Italian republics was enormous—hidden from us, however, to some extent by their astounding ruffianism. Macchiavelli, Guicciardini, and a host of other writers, show how deeply the depravity of actual life had corroded all moral principles. The theory of the Italians was worthy of their practice, and their practice of their theory. Yet what marvels of intellect they were—intellect in all its branches!"

Another effect of advanced civilization is that the higher the taste is cultivated the fewer pictures do we see which challenge admiration. A nearer inspection of the Fénelons, Madame Guyons, Augustines, etc., would present points of criticism to us which did not arrest attention in their age; and future ages may exalt into first-class saints some of the average saints of to-day.

In talking of the enormous wickedness of large cities, sufficient allowance is not made for the palpable fact that large aggregates of population necessarily concentrate and intensify large aggregates of evil. In the year 1800 the population of London did not vary much from the present population of New York city; but the amount of crime and the criminal population of London at that time far exceeded these elements in New York at the present time. Colquhoun's " Police of London " furnished ample statistics of London crime eighty years ago. The number of offenses designated as " *high* crimes," in a single year, was 10,880;* and the number of

---

* *Later statistics of the police and crime of London :* In 1831 the population comprised within the metropolitan police district of London was 1,468,442, and the number of police was 3,341. In 1878 the population was 4,534,040, ("British Almanac and Companion," 1880, p. 131,) and the police numbered 10,477. The ratio of increase was nearly the same in both.

The Chief Commissioner's Report for 1878 ("British Almanac and Companion," 1880, p. 273) shows :

Arrests 83,746
Summarily convicted or held for trial.................... 57,038
Subsequently discharged after trial...................... 817
                                                      ———
Total convicted.......... 56,221

persons living by "different sorts of villainy regularly carried on" was 119,500, or one for every nine inhabitants. These figures were the results of "long experience and minute inquiries" by Mr. Colquhoun, and "did not include every kind of fraud and dishonesty practiced." We do not believe our national metropolis, with all its corruptions, can produce such a record. But the forces of good are relatively more numerous, active, and powerful in large populations than in smaller. Virtue also aggregates and concentrates in large populations. What powerful centers of moral, reformatory, and religious agencies, of world-wide influence, are New York and London, and how vastly more so, too, relatively, than eighty or a hundred years ago.

The past fifteen years have compared favorably with other *post-bellum* periods. Wars are the prolific causes of moral deterioration, deadening and brutalizing the finer sensibilities, cheapening the estimate of human life, and introducing an era of fictitious prosperity, greed, and extravagance. But, as compared with other periods and people, we hardly know what luxury means, as might be demonstrated by scraps gathered from the ancient

Of this number 16,227 were cases of drunkenness, leaving 39,994 cases of more serious offenses, in a police district containing 4,534,040 inhabitants, or one for 113 inhabitants. But, according to Mr. Colquhoun, as cited above, in 1800, with a population of 958,863, there were 10,880 "high crimes," or one for 89 inhabitants. This is an indication of progress.

and modern world. Roman luxury squandered in a single dinner amounts equal to many modern fortunes ; Roman youths of seventeen summers needed from three to five millions of dollars " to make them even ; " vast Roman estates often changed hands for the merest trifle, to gratify pride or appetite ; Roman freedmen purchased three hundred thousand dollar estates from desperate debauchees, for one hundred dollars ready money; Mark Anthony squandered three quarters of a billion of the public money; in Roman thoroughfares tables were publicly spread with money for the purchase of votes ; in the Roman baths· thousands of men and women were abandoned, without shame, *en masse*, to the lowest crimes. These are a few citations showing the demoralization following successful Roman wars.

Coming nearer to our own times, we look at England after the Restoration, and find Hobbes publicly teaching that the will of the king is the ground of right and wrong, and the standard of morals, under such doctrine, the lowest, perhaps, of any court since the days of the Cæsars. Even " the Restored Church was powerless, because it had driven out the Puritans to make room for itself. Saved by the sinners of that age from the saints, it could do little or nothing to correct the evils that flooded the land." * His fifteen illegitimate children en-

* See editorial in "Christian Advocate," New York city, Nov. 30, 1876, from which some of these citations are made.

dowed and ennobled by Parliament, the king abandoned himself to his score of vile mistresses. Squandering upon his sons public money raised for a war against Holland, he was still in want; and, in spite of his plundering of the treasury, was destitute of linen, his unpaid grooms having carried it off for their pay.

The typical periods of a previous chapter furnish ample facts, which may be cited, showing our more favorable condition, even in this *post-bellum* period.

The recent period of financial straits, depressing business, closing up large manufacturing and mechanical establishments, and throwing out of employment several hundred thousand men, in all parts of the country, has been one of the most productive causes of crime. Great crimes often spring, not so much from vicious purposes, as from downright idleness. The unemployed have not far to go before they tumble into dangerous pitfalls, or are drawn into fatal allurements. It is easy enough for vice to come from having nothing to do.

It is to be feared that the sensational and detailed accounts of crime, which some journals publish, awaken a morbid emulation among the criminally disposed, and suggest acts which might not otherwise be thought of. Thus a murderer becomes an object of interest as soon as he is arrested. Ladies weep in the court room when he is tried; and when he is condemned heaven and earth are moved to save him from the gallows. Leniency in sentences and flagrant abuse of the pardoning power have diminished the restraint upon crime. The laws are right, but a maudlin sentimentalism has interfered with their execution. Take away the fear of punishment, and the criminal classes become rampant.

There has also been too much disposition to speak of successful crime as "smartness." Great swindlers have been exalted above ordinary pilferers and pickpockets. The perverted popular moral sense has honorably discriminated in favor of Wall-street gamblers over the denizens of the gambling "hells."

Our greatest and meanest criminals have been the "game" men to the people, "chiefs" of the "rings," "sachems" of Tammany. Their very effrontery has been a species of heroism. Such things indicate low commercial morality, and have exerted a deteriorating influence. But this spell has been broken, and we are doing better. A better moral sentiment aroused the people; the "sachem" was compelled to succumb to the majesty of law; and now no position, however sacred, shields from arrest and conviction.

The influence of the large foreign immigration during the past thirty years, infusing lower and antagonistic moral elements into our population, has been several times incidentally alluded to, as a cause of much of the moral decline which has been apparent. This new and heterogeneous element has been a large one, sufficient to impart a changed aspect to American society. Between 1850 and 1880 eight millions of foreigners, a number nearly equal to one third of the total increase of our population during that period, were added to our people. Their immediate offspring, partaking fully of the same ideas and habits, have swelled the number to nearly one half of our total increase. So large an addition of people of loose moral culture has been a severe strain upon our morals. Their drinking habits have given a new impulse to the use of alcoholic liquors, and their holiday-Sabbath habits have exerted an evil influence on our communities, relaxing the sanctity of the Lord's day. French and German Communists have become a serious element of trouble, and may yet tax our virtue and wisdom more severely. The people of foreign extraction in New England, constituting twenty per cent. of the population in 1870, furnished seventy-five per cent. of New England crime—probably also true of other sections of the country. This is the testimony of United States official statistics.

And yet it is idle to say that our greatest crimes are committed by escaped criminals from Europe. We must confess that people of our own nursing commit a large share of the flagrant offenses; that maelstroms of vice in our midst are ready

16

to engulf newly arrived immigrants ; that we have done comparatively little to throw around these new-comers saving moral influences ; and that we have allowed multitudes of children from Ireland, Germany, and Italy, of parents too poor or depraved to care for them, to become waifs, to grow up without any purposes higher than brutal indulgence, and to swell the terrible aggregate of our criminal classes. And, further, it must be acknowledged that our rural population furnishes a considerable per cent. of our gross criminals. The excitements and variety of city life attract young men from the country, to become victims of evil, and rapidly descend the terrible gradations of crime.

But it is also a very noticeable and encouraging fact, that large portions of our foreign population have very greatly improved in morals and intelligence since they came among us. Even those representing the Roman Catholic Church have changed for the better by inhaling the atmosphere of Protestant society ; and hence American Romanism exhibits a higher moral type than European Romanism. Italian and Spanish Romanism could not exist in the United States. Among these signs of moral elevation may be mentioned the purchase of houses, farms, and lands, in all portions of the country, by industrious and economical foreigners, and the enrollment of one hundred thousand Irishmen in total abstinence societies.

May it not be said that we have endured the heavy strain upon our moral forces from so large and sudden a foreign increment quite as well as could be expected, and that the improving indications now warrant the hope that, after another score of years, with due effort by those already arousing and concentrating for the work, we may see a still higher moral development?

The latest statistics indicate a decrease in crime in the largest cities. In Boston, where a half-dozen years ago murders were so frequent, there has been but one murder for about a year and a half. The report of the Police Justices for 1880, in New York city, contains encouraging facts. While the city population has increased over seventy thousand in the last five years, crime has diminished more than twenty-five per cent. This improvement is attributable to the growing temperance sentiment, the discouragement of willful pauperism by systematic charities, the enforced attendance upon schools, the punishment of truancy by the civil authorities, the relative decrease in the foreign-born population since 1870, the widely extending mission work among the most degraded population, and the increase of the practical activities of the Churches. And yet a sufficient amount of crime remains, in startling and destructive forms, to tax all the virtues and efforts of the better portion of society for higher progress.

A common misconception often leads to hasty and improper conclusions in regard to the prevalence of crime. Statistics of crime are often accepted, without the needful discrimination in regard to the progress of criminal legislation, which is constantly increasing the number of offenses cognizable by law. The figures themselves, accepted without discrimination, show an apparent increase of crime, when much of the increase is affected by legislation. "Civilization has raised many things formerly considered perhaps as immoral, and as offenses against moral law, into well-defined crimes, and subject to punishment as such. The result is, we are constantly increasing the work of criminal courts, by giving prosecuting officers new fields to canvass, and by adding to the list of offenses defined as crimes. The number of sentences is thus increased comparatively."* "The number of offenses designated as crimes by the criminal code of Massachusetts largely exceeds that of other States; for instance, the statutes of Massachusetts comprehended, in 1860, one hundred and fifty-eight offenses punishable as crimes, while the code of Virginia for the same year recognized but one hundred and eight, or fifty less. The same is true, to a greater or less extent, of nearly if not quite all the other States." †

* "Eleventh Annual Report, Bureau of Statistics of Labor, State of Massachusetts," Jan., 1880, p. 193.   † Ibid., p. 178.

This tendency of civilization, by legislative enactments to increase the list of offenses recognized as crimes, must be kept distinctly before our minds, when the present is compared with the past.

In earlier times many serious offenses against individual, social, and public welfare were hardly elevated into the dignity of crimes. In large circles of men killing was no murder, taking no robbery, the violation of a woman no rape, in the modern sense. Further on, robber chieftains were tolerated even by governments which enacted laws for the suppression of robbery and violence. From these lower conditions the law of improvement can be traced, restricted to no class or race, but wide as the range of history. It is seen in the progress of language, and the progressive significance of words, as well as in statutory legislation.

The times are not very remote when brave lawbreakers not only believed themselves good men and true, but even had the sympathy of large numbers of their fellow-countrymen. In the history of criminal legislation in England, says the " Encyclopædia Britannica," " we find the ideas of the primitive tribesmen steadily resisting the advance of civilization, retreating very slowly from position to position, and rarely yielding one without a long and desperate struggle." " The crime of forcible entry hardly ceased to be common before the eighteenth century. When valor was the greatest or only vir-

tue, one clan took land by force from another."
"Long after this half-savage condition of society
it remained a maxim of the English law, that there
was no legal possession of land without actual
seisin." " As late as the reign of William IV. the
fiction of a forcible entry continued to be one of the
chief implements of the conveyancer's art."

"The modern security of life and property of
every description represents the triumphs of new
ideas over old. . . . Fraud has never increased
with the increase of trade and civilization. It infected commerce at the very beginning, and existed during the darkness of the Middle Ages in
every form then possible. It may, and it sometimes
does, assume new shapes, as society groups itself
anew, as occupations and the relations of man to
man are changed. . . . With infinite difficulty has
civilized mankind so far gained the victory over
its own primitive nature as to concur, with some
approach to unanimity, in reprobation of the forger-
monk, the brigand-knight, and the man who
regarded a woman as a chattel and a tempting
object for appropriation."

" It is most necessary to bear in mind the contrast between the habits and ideas of one period
and of another, if we wish to estimate correctly the
position of the criminal in modern society, or the
alleged uniformity of human actions to be discovered by statistics. There is, no doubt, some

truth in the statement that in a modern civilized country—Great Britain, for example—the statistics of one year bear a strong resemblance to the statistics of another in many particulars. But a little reflection leads to the conclusion that there is nothing at all marvelous in such coincidences, and that they do not prove human nature to be unalterable, or circumstances to be unchangeable. They only show, what might have been predicted beforehand, that human beings of the same race, remaining in circumstances approximately the same, continue to act upon nearly the same motives and to display nearly the same weaknesses. The statistics of a quarter of a century, of half a century, even of a whole century, (if we could have them complete for so long a period,) could tell us but little of those subtle changes in human organization which have come to pass in the lapse of ages, and the sum of which has rendered life in Britain, in the nineteenth century, so different as it is from life in the sixth. . . . If, for instance, we look at the statistics of homicide and suicide in England during any ten recent years, we perceive that the figures of any one year very little exceed or fall below the general average. Yet no inference could be more erroneous than that homicide has always borne the same proportion to population in England as at present ; for in the reign of Edward III. there were, in proportion to population, at least sixteen cases of homicide to every one which occurs in our own time." *

We have no statistics of crime in Great Britain prior to 1840, but the following tables, collated from English sources,† show a great improvement since that time :

THE HIGHER CLASS OF CRIMINAL CONVICTIONS.

Average for three years.‡	England and Wales.	Scotland.	Ireland.	United Kingdom.
1840–1842	23,980	2,907	10,118	37,005
1850–1852	21,140	3,150	13,979	38,269
1860–1862	13,753	2,508	3,348	19,609
1870–1872	11,920	2,281	2,623	16,824
1876–1878	12,203	2,111	2,312	16,626

The following table will indicate the relative progress, by showing *the number of inhabitants for one criminal conviction*, in the given periods :

Average for three years.	England and Wales.	Scotland.	Ireland.	United Kingdom.
1840–1842	664	902	810	722
1850–1852	854	919	466	713
1860–1862	1,463	1,222	1,729	1,477
1870–1872	1,909	1,476	2,057	1,873
1876–1878	2,111	1,682	2,309	2,011

The above tables show that the number of criminal convictions, from 1840 to 1878, decreased, in

---

* "Encyclopædia Britannica." Ninth Edition. Vol. vi. Article, "Crime."

† These statistics are taken from the "Financial Reform Almanac," London, 1880 ; Whitaker's "London Almanac," 1880 ; and the "Encyclopædia Britannica." Ninth edition.

‡ The average for these years in each period is taken, because in some single years the number is exceptionally large or small. This gives a more just basis for comparison.

England and Wales, from 23,980 to 12,203 ; in Scotland, from 2,907 to 2,111 ; in Ireland, from 10,118
to 2,312 ; and in the United Kingdom, from 37,005
to 16,626. But during all this time the population,
except in Ireland, was increasing. Comparing with
the population, we find that in England and Wales,
instead of one conviction for high crimes for 664
inhabitants from 1840 to 1842, there was only one
for 2,111 inhabitants from 1876 to 1878.* In Scotland it had decreased from one for 902 inhabitants
to one for 1,682 inhabitants ; in Ireland, from one
for 810 to one for 2,309 inhabitants ; and in the
United Kingdom, from one for 722 inhabitants to
one for 2,011. The ratio of improvement in England and Wales was 3.18 fold ; in Scotland, 1.86
fold ; in Ireland, 2.85 fold ; in the United Kingdom,
2.78 fold. These statistics fully justify the statement in Whitaker's " London Almanac " for 1880,
page 203, that " the criminal element is happily on
the decrease, and will be further diminished as the
lower classes become better educated."

But popular education promotes general morality.
The wide-spread conviction that the increase of
education will lead to a decrease of crime and pauperism is susceptible of at least partial demonstration from the following statistics of England and
Wales, which show an encouraging decrease of the

* Calculated for 1877 on the basis of population given in the
London Almanacs for 1880.

pauper population since 1850, and vast increase in attendance upon the public schools.

PAUPERS OF ALL CLASSES IN ENGLAND AND WALES RECEIVING AID "IN-DOORS" AND "OUT-OF-DOORS." *

Average yearly, from 1850–1852, 871,953, or one for 20.6 inhabitants.

Average yearly, from 1860–1862, 895,869, or one for 22.4 inhabitants.

Average yearly, from 1870–1872, 1,046,327, or one for 21.7 inhabitants.

Average yearly, from 1876–1878, 773,548, or one for 31.7 inhabitants.

Here is evidence of an actual decrease of nearly 100,000 paupers since 1850, while the population increased about 6,500,000.† Instead of about 5 paupers in every 100 persons there are only about 3.

Similar progress has been made in the education of the masses. The progress of popular education in Europe and America is one of the brightest indications of the times. Especially does it appear in an interesting light in connection with the diminution of high crimes in England. At the opening of this century the number of schools, public and private, in all England, numbered only 3,363. "In 1818 it was found that one half of the children were growing up without an education. A few years after it was noticed that of all the persons who came to be married, one third of the men and

---

* See the "Financial Reform Almanac," London, 1880.

† According to recent calculations by the Registrar-General.

one half of the women could not sign the register. In the manufacturing districts it was still worse." In 1850 the schools in England, of all kinds, had increased to 45,000; but these were almost wholly paid schools. In England and Wales the government schools, in 1850, numbered only 1,844, but they increased to 14,875 in 1878, and the annual grants for their support increased from £431,594 in 1868 to £1,415,333 in 1877. The average attendance in these schools, in 1850, was 197,578; in 1860, 751,325; in 1870, 1,255,083; in 1876, 2,007,732. Although the adult population is yet little affected by this recent progress in school provision and attendance, nevertheless a vast improvement is perceptible among the adult generation, as is proved by the constantly growing number of those able to sign their names to the marriage registers. In the quinquennial period, 1841–1845, in England and Wales 32.6 per cent. of the men and 48.9 per cent. of the women who were married signed the register with their marks, being unable to write. From 1871 to 1875 only 18.5 per cent. of the men and 25.2 per cent. of women married were of this class. The Registrar-General, in his thirty-eighth annual report, in 1877, gave the hopeful calculation that, " if instruction increases in future years at the same arithmetical rate as it has done in the years from 1841 to 1875, then all the men will be able to write in thirty-eight years, and all the women in thirty-one years." And in reference to Ireland, Mr. Robert Mackenzie says: * " How broad and deep the foundations of a prosperous future have been laid may be read in the fact that in 1875 there were 1,012,000 Irish children attending the national schools, representing an educational condition unsurpassed in Europe." The removal of Ireland's social and civil disabilities must in due time follow.

The statistics of crime in the United States are, for the most part, fragmentary, covering periods of such brief duration, or gathered and arranged in plans so diverse, as not to afford a satisfactory basis for a just comparison. But great improvement is being made. The statistics of crime in Massachusetts, recently published,† are the best specimens of this advance. They show a great increase of crime after the close of the civil war. The sentences for crime went up from 17,276, in 1865, to 46,132 in 1873, when it reached its maximum, since which time it declined to 28,149, in 1879. These figures for 1879 show that the bulk of crime, as indicated by sentences, has increased 70.4 per cent. since 1860, while the population has increased 50.4 per cent., or 20 per cent. more than the increase of the population. But, examining these statistics, we find that out of 28,149, the total sentences in 1879,

* " The Nineteenth Century," Franklin Square Library, pp. 22, 28.

† Report of Hon. Carroll D. Wright, chief of the Bureau of Statistics of Labor in Mass., January, 1880.

direct rum crimes occasioned 16,871 ; minor crimes, 10,662 ; and felonies and aggravated crimes but 616. The latter class furnished 505 in 1860. While the population, from 1860 to 1879, increased 50.4 per cent., general crime, eliminating all direct rum-crimes, increased but 20.1 per cent. The liquor offenses have fluctuated according to the raids of executive officers, in obedience to the prevailing sentiments of the administration or the require-ments of existing laws. But the prosecution of high crimes depends upon steady, settled princi-ples of government. The whole number of sen-tences for the crimes of murder and manslaughter for the twenty years was 110, an average of five and a half per year. These crimes have not kept pace with the population. The same is true of the whole body of high crimes. While they have " in-creased in a deplorable degree," they have not kept pace with the population, this class of sen-tences increasing 39.5 per cent., and the popula-tion 50.4.

The foregoing conclusions are ably demonstrated by Hon. Carroll D. Wright, in his last " Report of the Bureau of the Statistics of Labor to the Legis-lature of Massachusetts," (January, 1880.) He pro-ceeds further to show the prison population of the State of Massachusetts, in the last twenty years, in-creased 47.7 per cent., or 2.7 per cent. less than the whole population, and adds : " This analysis would be quite crude without understanding the effects of legislation upon criminal statistics. It should not for a moment be supposed, because the tables show a decided increase in the number of sentences for any year, that more crime existed during that year : as, for instance, that, because drunkenness, as represented by sentences, reached an increase of 276.4 per cent. in 1873 over the number for 1860, that much more drunkenness occurred in 1873 than in 1860. The cause is to be found either in legislation or public sentiment, which caused a more vigilant prosecution of offenders."

The care of orphans is receiving, both in England and America, increased attention, not only as a philanthropic measure, but also as a wise provision of political economy—a means of reducing the amount of crime. From orphanage and pauperism come crime. Statistics show that a large part of the criminals were first destitute orphans, driven to crime by want and neglect. Delinquent and destitute children become petty thieves or beggars, and thus ripen into a harvest of crime. The recent multiplication of institutions for orphans and the destitute has improved morals and public security ; and the future will, doubtless, bring still greater benefits.

CHAPTER III.

THE PRESENT PERIOD.

(CONTINUED.)

Intemperance.

Dueling.

English Morals.

New England Morals.

Immigration.

Irreverence, etc.

Pauperism.

The Economic View.

Longevity.

Sanitary Science.

Philanthropic Agencies.

Penal Inflictions.

Criticisms and Testimonies.

CHAPTER III.

THE PRESENT PERIOD.—(CONTINUED.)

Intemperance.

THE vice of intemperance, so conspicuous during the closing quarter of the last century, wrought with increasing malignity, until it reached its culmination in the year 1825. The average annual consumption of distilled spirits and wine, but chiefly distilled liquors, (no account being made of beer, ale, etc.,) in 1790, was two and a half gallons per capita ; in 1810 it had increased to four and a half gallons ; * in 1823 to seven and a half gallons † for distilled spirits alone ; and in 1830, after four years of vigorous temperance work,‡ it was six gallons, or a half a gill daily for every inhabitant of all ages and conditions. At the latter date there were 400,000 confirmed drunkards in the land, " not including those in some stage of progress toward the fixed habit," or one for every thirty inhabitants.

* Statistics prepared by Hon. Samuel Dexter, LL.D. See "Report of the Massachusetts Society for the Suppression of Intemperance," 1814.

† " Boston Recorder."

‡ The American Temperance Society was organized in January, 1826.

A writer in the old " American Cyclopedia," published in 1830,* gives the following account of the drinking customs of this early period, in the light of which we cannot fail to see the great moral progress that has since been made :

" The men now upon the stage remember, from their childhood till within the last ten years, to have seen distilled spirits, in some form, a universal provision for the table, at the principal repast, throughout this country. The richer sort drank French and Spanish brandy ; the poorer, West India, and the poorest, New England, rum. In the Southern States whisky was the favorite liquor ; and the somewhat less common articles of foreign and domestic gin, apple brandy, and peach brandy, made a variety which recommended itself to the variety of individual tastes. Commonly at meals, and at other times by laborers, particularly in the middle of the forenoon and afternoon, these substances were taken, simply diluted with more or less water. On other occasions they made a part of more or less artificial compounds, in which fruit of various kinds, eggs, spices, herbs, and sugar, were the leading ingredients.

" A fashion at the South was to take a glass of whisky, flavored with mint, soon after waking ; and so conducive to health was this nostrum esteemed, that no sex and scarcely any age were deemed ex-

* Article, " Temperance Societies."

empt from its application. At eleven o'clock, while
mixtures under various peculiar names—sling, tod-
dy, flip, etc.—solicited the appetite at the bar of
the common tippling-shop, the offices of the professional men and the counting-room dismissed
their occupants for a half hour to regale themselves
at a neighbor's or a coffee-house with punch, hot
or iced, according to the season ; and females and
valetudinarians courted an appetite with medicated
rum, disguised under the chaste names of *Huxam's
Tincture* or *Stoughton's Elixir*.

"The dinner hour arrived, according to the different customs of different districts of the country,
whisky and water, curiously flavored with apples,
or brandy and water, introduced the feast ; whisky,
or brandy and water, helped it through ; and whisky
or brandy, without water, often secured its safe di-
gestion, not again to be used in any more formal
manner than for the relief of occasional thirst, or for
the entertainment of a friend, until the last appeal
should be made to them to secure a sound night's
sleep. Rum, seasoned with cherries, protected
against the cold ; rum, made astringent with peach-
nuts, concluded the repast at the confectioner's ;
rum, made nutritious with milk, prepared for the
maternal office ; and, under the Greek name of par-
egoric, rum, doubly poisoned with opium, quieted
the infant's cries.

"No doubt there were numbers who did not use

ardent spirits, but it was not because they were not perpetually in their way. They were an established article of diet, almost as much as bread ; and with very many they were in much more frequent use. The friend who did not testify his welcome with them, and the master who did not provide bountifully of them for his servants, were held niggardly ; and there was no social meeting, not even of the most formal or sacred kind, where it was considered indecorous, scarcely any where it was not thought necessary, to produce them. The consequence was, that what the great majority used without scruple large numbers indulged in without restraint. Sots were common of both sexes, various ages, and all conditions ; and, though no statistics of the vice were yet embodied, it was quite plain that it was constantly making large numbers bankrupt in property, character, and prospects, and inflicting upon the community a vast amount of physical and moral ill in their worst forms."

Such is the description, by an able writer living in those times, of the social drinking customs in the period when intemperance reached its culmination in America. In England the evil was not less rampant. It infested all circles, and became especially a social vice. It was deemed indispensable that visitors should evince their appreciation of the hospitality they received by becoming intoxicated. The host claimed it as his due that every guest should drink until he could drink no longer. "The supreme crowning evidence that an entertainment had been successful was not given till the guests dropped, one by one, from their chairs to slumber peacefully on the floor till the servants removed them." The worst phases of society, in our day, in either country, fail to parallel the general habits then.

From 1808 to 1815 a few beginnings were made, in various localities in the United States, in the direction of reform, with meager results. The organization of the American Temperance Society, in 1826, inaugurated more thorough, energetic, and far-reaching efforts, and, for thirty years, the Temperance Reformation was one of the most mighty and extensive movements in the nation. The moral renovation was incalculable. The average annual consumption of distilled and fermented spirits, beer and ale excepted, declined from seven and a half gallons in 1823, to two and a half gallons in 1850.

Intemperance was, however, still a great evil, of immense power and sway, and its desolations were fearful. In the State of Massachusetts, in the year 1849, of 2,598 paupers, 1,467, or 56 per cent., and of 8,760 committed for crime, 3,341, or more than 38 per cent., resulted from intemperance. In the city of New York, in the same year, there were 4,425 licensed houses, 750 selling without license, and 3,896 selling on the Sabbath. In a single quarter 1,600 persons were arrested for drunkenness, 1,485 for intoxication and disorderly conduct, 744 for vagrancy, 1,214 for assault and battery, and 1,006 for disorderly conduct, besides more serious crimes. In Philadelphia, in 1849, there were admitted to the alms-house 5,119, of whom 2,323 were intoxicated when received; and in the mayor's court 5,987 persons were under arrest for drunkenness and disorderly conduct, and only 324 for other crimes. In the State of New York, in 1849, 36,610 persons were committed for crimes perpetrated under the influence of intoxicating liquors, and 69,260 were in the poor-houses from intemperance.

Between 1850 and 1855 "The Maine Law" was enacted in about a dozen States. For a time it was faithfully executed, with splendid results. Large numbers of towns, chiefly rural, were almost wholly rid of the evil of intemperance. So clear and beneficial was the influence in Massachusetts, that Governor Briggs, only a short time after the adoption of the law, declared that it had already been worth one hundred millions of dollars to that State alone. This was the period of the best temperance habits in the United States.

After that time a great abatement in temperance efforts was apparent, seemingly under the false conviction that the battle had been fought, and that the enactment of stringent laws, entirely prohibiting the sale of liquors as a beverage, had put a final stop to the evil of intemperance. But " while men slept,

the enemy sowed tares;" and a reverse movement
has since taken place in the sentiment of total
abstinence, and also of prohibition. Many, once
fully committed to these principles, have abandoned
them as extreme and impracticable; and the consumption of the milder alcoholic beverages has increased and spread into circles from which they
were once excluded. The use of distilled liquors,
however, declined from 1870 to 1879, as will be seen
in the table below; but the figures for 1880 indicate an increase again. The following table, prepared with extraordinary labor and care, is believed
to be thoroughly reliable, and will, in part, indicate
the progress made:

CONSUMPTION* OF FOREIGN WINES AND FOREIGN† AND DOMES-
TIC DISTILLED SPIRITS OF ALL KINDS IN THE UNITED STATES.

Year.	Gallons Consumed.	Average for each Inhabitant.
1810 ‡	33,278,505	$4\frac{3}{8}$ gallons.
1823 §	75,000,000	$7\frac{1}{2}$ "
1830 ‖	77,196,120	6 "
1850 ‡	57,428,989	$2\frac{1}{2}$ "
1870 ‡	89,558,489	$2\frac{1}{3}$ "
1878 ‡	58,800,754	..
1879 ‡	50,865,207 ¶	..
1880	74,895,180	$1\frac{1}{2}$ "

* Exports and re-exports deducted.
† American wines are not included, because no reliable statistics can be ob-
tained. Appleton's "Cyclopedia" estimates that 20,000,000 gallons are made an-
nually; but this is too high, and only an estimate.
‡ Carefully collated from United States official documents, and closely revised.
For years ending June 30.
§ On the authority of the "Puritan Recorder" for that year.
‖ On the authority of the old "American Cyclopedia."
¶ Since 1870 the quantity of wine imported has decreased more than one half;
and the quantity of American distilled liquors exported has increased.

CONSUMPTION OF BEER, ALE, ETC.

Year.	Gallons Consumed.	Average for each Inhabitant.
1850 *	36,678,444	1⅗ gallons.
1870 *	189,430,195	nearly 5 "
1878 *	273,989,588	..
1879	344,622,378	..
1880	414,190,350	8¼ '

NOTE.—No account is made of the adulteration of liquors, for there are no statistics of the quantities.

The foregoing table shows that the quantity of distilled spirits and foreign wines consumed in the United States has considerably decreased—from seven and a half gallons *per capita* in 1823, to six gallons in 1830, to two and a half gallons in 1850, to two and one third gallons in 1870, and one and one half gallons in 1880. But the quantity consumed in 1880 increased greatly over the quantity in 1878 and 1879.

On the other hand, the consumption of beer, ale, etc., has vastly increased—from one and three fifths gallons *per capita* in 1850, to five gallons in 1870, and eight and a quarter gallons in 1880, or nearly seven gallons increase for every inhabitant. There has also been a great increase in the quantity of native wine manufactured and consumed, while the foreign wines imported have very much decreased.

It should be said that distilled liquors are extensively adulterated and expanded, and that such

* Carefully collated from United States official documents, and closely revised. For years ending June 30.

liquors do not enter into any computations. This is not, however, a recent evil, nor is it probably relatively more extensive than thirty or forty years ago. The Washingtonian speakers, from 1840 to 1845, who went forth to tell their stories of inebriation and ruin, often complained of the vile compounds with which they had been deceived and injured; and we find Addison, in the " Spectator," mentioning the vile concoctions manufactured in his day, by a fraternity of chemical operators, in dens under the streets of London.

A recent editorial in the " Boston Journal" said: " A distinguished Englishman, now in this city, expressed himself most warmly in regard to the sobriety of our people. He declares that during his stay in the United States he has seen but four drunken men. He says that, as a rule, the people do not drink, and, to him, it is a matter of profound surprise that wherever he has been he has found that the use of strong liquors is abandoned. It may be true that his lines have led him among a better class of people, for drunkenness prevails to some extent among the lower classes, but in a far less degree than was observable years ago. Intemperance is no longer tolerated in good society. It is no longer tolerated in business circles. A young man knows that he stands no chance of success in life if he is addicted to the use of strong drinks, and, what is a still stronger provocative of temperance, the youth of our country know that life is sacrificed by the use of spirits, and that length of days and a vigorous old age are not boons which can be expected by those who violate the laws of health. This great change has been brought about by that enlightened public sentiment which prevails, and this feeling is increasing."

The aspect of most rural towns in respect to temperance is encouraging. Not a tithe of intemperance exists as compared with fifty years and more ago. Maine retains her famous law, and a high authority * says there is not an open bar in the whole State. In 1832 there was one for every 225 persons. The Maine Law is so far sustained that a more stringent amendment was made in 1877, without a dissenting vote in the Legislature.

Our adopted fellow-citizens, who in large numbers have come among us, settling chiefly in large centers of population, have given a more unfavorable aspect to society in respect to drunkenness. But even this class is coming to learn the necessity and value of abstinence, and is organizing for the promotion of this virtue. They are already enrolled in large numbers as abstainers from alcoholic liquors. The Catholic Total Abstinence Union held its ninth session at Detroit in September, 1879, at which delegates were present representing over 500

---

* Address of Ex-Governor Dingley, at Winthrop, Maine, December 6, 1877 ; and letter from Hon. Neal Dow, February 12, 1878.

Catholic Temperance Societies, and a membership of nearly 100,000.

The decline in the consumption of the more fiery drinks is a fact attested by the daily observation of men whose personal knowledge extends back thirty or forty or fifty years. The great reformatory movements from 1872 to 1876, under the "Crusaders," the "Woman's Christian Temperance Union," Dr. Reynolds, Francis Murphy, and Mr. Moody, introducing a more positive religious element into this department of effort, greatly improved many localities, and placed the virtue of temperance on purely moral grounds.

But a reaction has followed, carrying back to their cups many reformed men; and the general introduction of beer into common life, within a few years, is leading many young men and women downward in intemperance. There is reason to believe that the free use of beer, which was advocated on moral grounds, as a means of decreasing drunkenness, is likely to prove the means of more extended intemperance and ruin, as it did in England after the enactment of the celebrated "Beer Act" some years ago. Sufficient time has not yet elapsed to determine what the results will be; but the indications are regarded by many as ominous of evil.

In the British Isles intemperance is still an evil of enormous dimensions. It is estimated that the

people of Great Britain and Ireland expend annually from one hundred to one hundred and twenty
millions sterling on intoxicating liquors.   " For
upward of a generation," says Mr. Mackenzie,[*]
" nobly persistent and self-denying efforts have been
put forth by associations of men impressed with the
magnitude of these evils, to direct adequate attention to the subject. After many years of discour-
aging toil they are now rewarded with a measure of
success."   Recently it was publicly stated that there
are now no less than 4,000,000 of total abstainers in
Great Britain.[†]   Within a few years, in addition to
the moral-suasion measures long used in this reform,
other supplementary means have been resorted to
for the purpose of guarding, strengthening, and establishing reformed men, and keeping the young
away from the temptation of strong drink.   They
have especially provided for working men,[‡] who
have hitherto had but few places of resort but the
public houses where liquors are sold.   The first
movement was made in Dundee, where a coffee-
house was established for working men twenty-five
years ago.   In Leeds, in 1867, the first " British
Workman's Public House" was opened.   A company with this designation was organized, in 1875,

---

* "The Nineteenth Century," Franklin Square Library, p. 25,
note.

† " The British Almanac and Companion," p. 30.   1880.

‡ See article on Temperance Refreshment House Movement in
the " British Almanac and Companion."   1880.   Pp. 38–58.

in Liverpool, with a capital of $100,000, which has now thirty-five of these houses open, with accommodations for 10,000 persons. In Manchester the Coffee Tavern Gompany was started in 1877. It has eight houses opened to the public, with an average weekly attendance of 65,000 persons. In numerous other towns and cities similar houses have been founded.

Dueling.

Dueling, a custom of former ages introduced into England by the Normans, has had a luxurious growth among Anglo-Saxon populations on both sides of the Atlantic. Before the opening of this century it became a capital offense, in England and the United States alike, to kill in a duel; but public sentiment was so tolerant of dueling that juries would not ordinarily convict the offenders, and they were seldom arrested. Far into the present century it was frequently practiced by men in high and low stations alike. In England, Fox, Pitt, Castlereagh, Lord Hervey, Canning, the Duke of York, Daniel O'Connell, the Duke of Richmond, Wellington, and others, all fought duels—the latter as late as 1829, and others as late as 1850. In the United States, De Witt Clinton and John Swartwout, in 1802; Hamilton and Burr, in 1804; Benton and Lucas; Jackson and Dickinson; Clay and Randolph, in 1826; Cilley and Graves, in 1838; and others later, are a few of the more notable examples. Dueling was a national sin, and no bar to the highest civil position in the gift of the nation. Since 1850 it has nearly disappeared in both countries—a clear indication of moral progress.

In England the reform is attributed largely to Prince Albert. He induced the Duke of Wellington and the heads of the service to use their influence to discredit and discourage the odious practice. But there were other and wider influences at work, in the general progress of the times, which were the effectual agencies under which the improvement came. M'Carthy says:* " Nothing can testify more strikingly to the rapid growth of genuine civilization, in Queen Victoria's reign, than the utter discontinuance of the dueling system. When the queen came to the throne, and for years after, it was still in full force. . . . At the present hour a duel in England would seem as absurd and barbarous an anachronism as an ordeal by touch or a witch-burning. Many years have passed since a duel was last talked of in Parliament, and then it was only the subject of a reprobation that had some work to do to keep its countenance while administering the proper rebuke. But it was not the influence of any one man, or even any class of men, that brought about in so short a time this striking change in the tone of public feeling and morality.

* "A History of Our Own Times," by Justin M'Carthy. Harper & Brothers. 1880. Pp. 106, 107.

The change was partly the growth of education and of civilization, of the strengthening and broadening influence of the press, the platform, the cheap book, the pulpit, and the less restricted intercourse of classes."

English Morals.

At the beginning of the century England, in manning her navy, supplemented her system of voluntary enlistment by the barbarous methods of the press-gang. Any seaman who could be stolen from the merchant service was carried on board of a ship-of-war and compelled to fight. A band of men lurked in the sea-ports armed with this terrible power to seize any returning sailor.

Military and naval discipline was maintained by the use of the lash, the doctor standing by to see how much the victim could bear. The torture was often changed, at short intervals, until five hundred lashes were inflicted ; or, if unable to bear so much, he was taken down, carried to the hospital, and recruited, then brought back to receive the balance of his punishment. When the attempt was made, after the battle of Waterloo, to limit such punishments to one hundred lashes, it failed through the opposition of Lord Palmerston, and there was no reform until after 1846, when, a sailor dying under the lash, the number of lashes was limited to fifty ; and twenty years later the House of Commons decreed that flogging, in the time of peace, should be wholly abolished. The new army bill proposes to entirely abolish flogging in the national service.

Women and children worked in coal-pits, dragging little wagons by a chain fastened round the waist, and crawling like beasts, on hands and feet, in the darkness of the mine. Children of six years were habitually employed, their hours of labor extending to fourteen and sixteen daily. They were often mutilated and sometimes killed with impunity by their brutalized associates. There being no elevating machinery, women carried the coal to the surface, climbing long wooden stairs, with baskets on their backs. Little boys and girls of five and six swept chimneys. Being built narrower than now, only a child could crawl into them, often driven by blows to the horrid work. Sometimes they were burned by the hot chimney, sometimes stuck fast in the narrow flue, and extricated with difficulty, and occasionally taken out dead. Parliament refused to interfere, and not until 1840 was this practice suppressed. Children of six were often put to work in factories. The hours of labor ranging from thirteen to fifteen daily, the children often fell asleep at their work, and received injuries by falling against the machinery, or were beaten by the overseer to keep them awake. They were stunted in size, pallid, emaciated, scrofulous, and consumptive. Recent laws in England and America have alleviated their condition. After

1833 no child could be employed in England under nine years of age, and those under thirteen were limited to forty-eight hours a week. Ten years later the hours of labor were further reduced for all classes of operatives. And numerous other alleviations from exacting toil have since been made. These things, related by Mr. Mackenzie, in his sketch of the English people, were also in some measure true of the United States.

Of English morals, at the opening of this century, and the improvement since that time, the same writer* says: "Profane swearing was the constant practice of gentlemen. They swore at each other, because an oath added emphasis to their assertions. They swore at inferiors because their commands would not otherwise receive prompt obedience. The chaplain cursed the sailors, because it made them listen more attentively to his admonitions. Ladies swore orally and in their letters. Lord Braxfield offered to a lady at whom he swore, because she played badly at whist, the sufficient apology that he had mistaken her for his wife. Erskine, the model of a forensic orator, swore at the bar. Lord Thurlow swore upon the bench. The king swore incessantly. When his majesty desired to express approval of the weather, of a handsome horse, of a dinner which he had enjoyed, this "first gentleman in Europe" supported his

* "The Nineteenth Century," Franklin Square Library, p. 18.

18

royal asseveration by a profane oath. Society clothed itself with cursing as with a garment.

" Books of the grossest indecency were exhibited for sale side by side with Bibles and prayer books. Indecent songs were sold, without restraint, on the streets of London, and sung at social gatherings by the wives of respectable tradesmen, without sense of impropriety.

" Many causes have conspired to bring about the remarkable improvement which has taken place in the moral tone of British society. Among these the influences exerted upon public morals by the pure domestic life of Queen Victoria and Prince Albert fills no inconsiderable place. The intellectual ability recognized in the queen and her husband, and their manifest devotion to the public good, added largely to the authority which their high station conferred upon them, and disposed the nation to be guided by their example. The queen and prince lived conspicuously blameless lives in the earnest and effective discharge of the family and public duties which their position imposed. Their example confirmed and powerfully re-enforced the influences which at that time ushered in a higher moral tone than had distinguished previous reigns."

New England Morals.

Much has been said about the decline of morals in New England. It should not be overlooked that this section of the country has undergone a great change in its population. It has been a great emigrating region—a feeder of the West. First, Western New York was peopled from New England; then the large Western Reserve region in Ohio; then all other portions of the West received large accessions, continually depleting the original stock of New England. Hon. John Sherman, at the New England Dinner in New York city,* said: "We have in the West more people of New England ancestry than you have in all New England, with New York thrown in." Confining our calculations to the nativity of those living in 1870, we find that the United States Census for that year shows 801,301 inhabitants born in New England, a number equal to one third of her population born, and then residing, in New England, who were living in other sections of the Union. Within forty years not less than one half of all born in New England have gone forth to other States. While this depletion has been going on, carrying with it the best elements of New England life, the vacant places have been filled by a very different class of people. The same census shows 638,001 persons,

* December 22, 1878.

or nearly one fifth of the whole population of New England, born in foreign lands, 421,850 more, both of whose parents were foreign-born, and 84,957 more, one of whose parents was foreign-born; total 1,144,809, or one third of the whole population, either foreign-born, or one or both of whose parents were from foreign lands. From 1850 to 1870 the actual increase of the native-born inhabitants of this section was 327,956, and of the foreign-born 431,752; but probably full one third of the native-born increase was from foreign parentage, and hence foreign in ideas, habits, etc., which, deducted from the former number and added to the latter, gives 541,080 increase of the foreign element to 218,682 of the native in the last two decades. Such changes, extending to one third of the population, and so extensively engrafting a different class of habits and customs, clearly accounts for a very considerable part of the modification that has been apparent in the character of New England society. But while New England has suffered from this loss, other sections of the country have been immensely benefited.

Reverence, etc.

Is it said that the feeling of reverence has greatly declined during the present century? that fundamental truths have lost their sanctity, and the spirit of veneration is exhaling? True; and this is what

has been repeatedly said during previous centuries.
Nor is it altogether an evil omen. Moral ideas, as
well as scientific theories, are undergoing a sifting—
a process attended with gain as well as peril. We
are, indeed, outgrowing that excessive reverence
which, in the past, has been unreasonable and akin
to superstition. We are casting off our superstitions; but the next generations may discover that
we have retained many of them. We are accustomed to characterize one of the past stages of
society as "the pagan," and another as "the elfic;"
and only those who live after us can characterize
the stage in which we live.

As society advances in intelligence reverence becomes more intelligent and rational. We have a
more rational reverence than our ancestors. Con-
sidering the natural law of rebound to extremes,
are we not doing quite well? Do we not exhibit a
good degree of morally conserving power?

Are we told that "moral questions are becoming
unsettled, and the moral judgments, whether of individuals, or of the Church, or public opinion, have
lost much, and with many have lost all their
weight?" It has been well replied that these
things "result from two excellent features of the
times—the exposure of old fallacies and the cultivation of mental independence." Revolutions in
thought know no limits. Every thing must be
tested—the false sifted out, the husk separated from

the kernel. The domain of morals must endure these siftings, and modifications of moral ideas are inevitable.

This spirit is wide spread. " The *débris* of old maxims, notions, and institutions strews the land, as the shells of the seventeen-year *cicadæ* strew the woods of New Jersey. Their time was out, and they had to go; the world had no more room nor tolerance for them. But they leave us necessarily the knack of questioning and the habit of demolition—of looking on old things as candidates for the hammer and the fire. And this, of course, develops a spirit that is proud of not leaning on antiquated supports, and is only too ready to call any thing antiquated that is not new."

And here is our danger. " This spirit not only insists upon testing afresh all things that are clearly doubtful, which is the sacred duty of every generation; but it discards that most wholesome principle which accepts provisionally what has hitherto been believed, and throws the burden of proof on whoever assails it. Now, the irreverent mind of the age, so much of it as there may be, holds under indictment whatever has come down to us from a former generation, because it has come down."

But this is no new tendency. This spirit pervaded Great Britain on the eve of the Wesleyan reformation. Rev. Dr. Timothy Dwight described the same condition of things in this country in the time of the general prevalence of French infidelity here, at the close of the last century, which the rising tide of evangelical Christianity, after the great revival of 1799 to 1800, very considerable suppressed. It is one of the alternate waves of modern progress.

But is it said that "public opinion was once, and to a very influential degree, a unit in this country," on moral questions? and that "there was no reason to doubt what the judgment of society would be upon an unfaithful wife, or a defaulting officer, or a perjured witness, or an evil doer in the ministry?"

When and where? Only in New England, in the very earliest colonial times. In the Middle and Southern colonies it was never so, except in a few localities. Certainly the last quarter of the last century did not exhibit such moral superiority, when men notoriously dissolute and gross held the highest positions in public life, and a perfidious intriguer, debauchee, and duelist was an almost successful candidate for the presidency of the United States. Such a man could not be a candidate for the presidency to-day. Disreputable conduct in the Christian ministry was not as thoroughly and as easily subjected to discipline then as now. Many who held high positions in the ministry and in the State then would not be tolerated in those positions now. We believe the moral judgment of society is clearer, more uniform and emphatic to-day, than

ever before for one hundred years. Christianity
has evidently made great moral progress. The
apostolic Church was probably purer in morals than
that which preceded it. But it appears, however,
from the apostolic epistles, that, even in the days
of the apostles, false and pernicious doctrines and
corrupt practices existed in the Church. St. Paul's
remarks concerning the Lord's Supper show this.
We read, in 1 Cor. xi, 21, " For in eating every one
taketh before other his own supper: and one is
hungry, and another is drunken." Is there a Church
in Christendom that needs such a rebuke? Again,
we read: " It is reported commonly that there is fornication among you, and such fornication as is not
so much as named among the Gentiles, that one
should have his father's wife." St. Paul is speaking not of those without, but of persons tolerated
in the Corinthian Church, who were guilty of practices which would expel them from any Church in
these days. He interposed to elevate the standard.

A clear evidence of a high-toned morality, rising
above the corruptions of the times, is the current
dissatisfaction with the evils which have been afflict-
ing us, the impatient demand for the purification
of society, the sharp indictment of public evils, their
fearless exposure and scathing criticism. We are
ferreting out corruption and applying caustic remedies. These are indications of moral sensitiveness,
vitality, and recuperative power, Criticism and

self-introspection are auspicious omens—the diagnosis, which precedes the prescription. Vigorous remedies are closely following the analysis. Everywhere the call is for official honor, fidelity, pure laws and equitable civil service. Reform is the watch word in most circles—the talismanic word in political and ecclesiastical life. We are finding our reckonings and mending our course. Beating against the wind is sometimes better than sailing before it. The moral sentiments of society are mighty and cumulative. The action of the two great political parties, in nominating Generals Garfield and Hancock, both morally unobjectionable men, as candidates for the Presidency, is a concession, by politicians, to the moral sentiment of the country.

Pauperism.

Pauperism, though less obviously, yet more reliably, than crime, indicates the standard of public morality. Most cases of publicly recognized pauperism are intimately related to criminality and viciousness of character as their cause, though the criminal cause of poverty is often found in a different person from the individual sufferer. Pauperism generally increases and diminishes with the decline and advance of public morals. If this is a correct conclusion, a reference to the statistics of pauperism, in almost every parish in the nation, will afford the most gratifying refutation of the late lamentations over the "moral declension" of the country. Without adducing statistics, we are *sure* that no well-informed person will question the general accuracy of the assumption that pauperism has greatly diminished during the century.

In regard to both crime and pauperism, a distinction should be made between persons educated among us and those whose characters were formed under influences antagonistic to the influences which prevail among ourselves. A Protestant of foreign birth may be presumed to have a character not wholly different from that of an American. The the religious element is the most considerable one, though we must still claim for our free institutions an influence for good, a tendency to engender a rational patriotism, a self-respect, and a general moral sentiment, which cannot be looked for under a despotic government. If, then, in this reckoning, we confine ourselves either to native Americans, or to Protestants and persons of Protestant parentage, the result will show a very much larger relative diminution of crime and pauperism. Removing all foreigners and their children, or all Romanists and their children, from our penitentiaries and eleemosynary institutions, the remnant will be very small compared with the mass of our Protestant population. Take out the emigrant paupers, and you will find that the masses have advanced astonishingly in this respect since the Revolution.

It must be remembered that many of the fathers of New England owned the bodies of their laborers and domestics, and that this condition of things, in a modified form, in large sections, extended into this century. The condition of workingmen has improved relatively to the wealth of the land ever since. Wages of every kind bear a higher proportion to the things needed for comfort and convenience than ever before for two hundred years. Said Theodore Parker :

" If you go back one hundred years I think you will find that, in proportion to the population and wealth of this town or this State, there was considerably more suffering from native poverty then than now. Now public charity is more extended and more complete, works in a wiser mode, and with far more beneficial effects, and pains are now taken to uproot the causes of poverty—pains which our fathers never thought of."

Rev. Timothy Dwight, D.D., writing in 1815, estimated the paupers in the towns of New England outside of cities at one for three hundred inhabitants, a ratio far exceeding the present.

Another minister,* referring to the condition of things at the time of his settlement, in 1810, at North Coventry, Conn., a fair sample of many inland towns, at that time, said :

* Rev. George A. Calhoun, D.D., sermon on the fortieth anniversary of his settlement, 1850.

"There were only four floors with carpets on them, but four houses painted white, and not more than ten four-wheeled vehicles. Even whitewash on the walls of rooms was very seldom used. Nor was the difference in the times merely. Real poverty was the cause. Even in the condition in which they did live, there were few who had money at interest compared with those who were in debt, and those whose farms were mortgaged. Property was constantly changing hands by the foreclosure of mortgages and insolvency. But the expense of living then, as compared with now, was very small. What, then, was the reason for this depression in worldly circumstances? Their gains were consumed, and they were oppressed, by the use of intoxicating drinks." "At least one man in every score became a drunkard, and not a few women were addicted to habits of intemperance." "There was probably not one in five hundred who did not believe that the use of intoxicating drinks, as a beverage, was absolutely needful."

The Economic View.

A writer in the "Fortnightly Review," (June, 1880,) said: "We are at length beginning to read history in the light of Economic causes. These causes, silent, simple, potent, and pervading, have been always, and must be always, at work in all sorts of societies, in all ages, from the most rude to the most artificial." He then directs attention "to the following epitome of the evidence relating to the progress of the population of England, and in England and Wales since the close of the eleventh century," and to certain inferences therefrom, which throw much light on the question of moral progress.

" The researches which have been undertaken and the discussions which have occurred regarding the population of England, and of England and Wales, at various periods antecedent to the first actual census of 1801, justify us in accepting the following results as near the truth: About the year 1100 (Henry I.) the total population of England was certainly not more than 2,000,000 of persons, if so many. After the lapse of three centuries it had become (including Wales) 2,750,000 in 1400, (Henry IV.) The lapse of another century raised it to somewhat less than 3,500,000 in 1500, (Henry VII.) At the close of the reign of Elizabeth, in 1600, the population was 4,500,000. In 1700, under William III., it was 5,500,000. In 1801 the first census gave the population of England and Wales at 9,250,000, and in 1880 it is computed officially that the total has risen to quite 25,000,000.

" From these figures we deduce the following very striking variations of progression, always remembering that soil, climate and seasons, and national character, have remained essentially the same, and

that there has not been any foreign invasion : In
the three centuries (1100–1400) the increase was
700,000, or 233,000 in each, equal to about 10 per
cent. in each hundred years.   In the single century
(1400–1500) the increase was 700,000, or 25 per cent.
In the next single century (1500–1600) the increase
was 1,110,000, or 30 per cent., and it was the same
total increase, equal to 25 per cent., in the hundred years 1600–1700.   But in the following century (1700–1800) the increase was more than
3,500,000, equal to say 64 per cent. ; and in the
eighty years (1800–1880) the increase has been the
vast total of nearly 16,000,000, equal to 172 per
cent.   The percentages of increase have been, therefore, (stated in general terms,) for each of the seven
periods of one hundred years, as now described, 10,
10, 10, 25, 30, 25, 64, and for the last eighty years
172 per cent., and, if emigration be allowed for, this
last percentage would be largely increased.

" We find in this statement a foundation of solid
evidence regarding the progress of this country in
the resources and appliances of civilization ; that is
to say, in the growth of capital and skill and science.   In a country by nature temperate and fertile, a population which increases slowly means
(apart from circumstances of a very special kind
not easily overlooked) a country the people of
which are deficient in the wealth and knowledge
whereby reasonable food, clothing, and shelter can

be provided, and diseases and epidemics averted or cured. Devastating invasions or domestic wars, for example, the Turkish inroads in the East of Europe, or the Thirty-years' War in Germany, may, when they occur, reduce the population of a fertile region to a low ebb for a considerable time. But in the case of England during the four hundred years from 1100 to 1500, there were no sweeping calamities of this nature to account for the fact that the population grew only at the rate of 10 per cent. in each of the first three, and at the rate of only 25 per cent. in the last of the four centuries indicated. Nor can it be said that the government of the country during these four centuries was ill-suited to the times, or more corrupt or oppressive than the governments of other parts of Western Europe. On the contrary, the English kings and English statesmen of the period in question were considerably better and wiser, on the whole, than their foreign contemporaries. The small number of people and their tardy increase can be attributed only to the circumstance that capital accumulated so slowly that each generation had the greatest physical difficulty in maintaining as many offspring as would just replace it, sometimes with a trifling surplus and sometimes with a deficiency. And this incessant conflict with nature for mere life necessitated dense ignorance, the rudest and hardest labor, the diseases and epidemics which follow close upon

hunger, cold, and exposure, and the sweeping destruction of infant and advanced life."

Longevity and Sanitary Science.

Another class of facts throws light upon this
question ; we refer to the average extent of human
life. Vice, whether it results in squalid poverty or
in sensual luxury, is always unfriendly to health and
longevity, while viciousness of character is both directly and indirectly destructive of human life.
These propositions are so obvious as not to need
proof or illustration. It is ascertained that the average measure of human life, in this country, has
been steadily increasing during this century, and is
now considerably longer than in any other country.
The proximate agencies that have produced this
result are thrift, temperance, parental care, and self-
control—all proofs of public and private virtuous-
ness of character. This is one of the most reliable
tests of our real moral *status ;* and it must be granted that the conclusion to which it leads is highly
satisfactory, although much remains to be done.

Sanitary science, a department of study almost
unknown until recent times, is every-where receiving attention and working out beneficent results.
There are few people whose sanitary condition is
not better than that of their fathers. Progress is
quite perceptible in Great Britain, France, Germany,
and the United States. Especially marked is the

economy of life among the young, on whose immature strength evil sanitary conditions press most
heavily. The influence of sanitary legislation traces
its benign and enduring record in the higher physical conditions of city populations, in comparative
exemption from epidemic diseases, and the increased
duration of human life. At the beginning of the
century the deaths in London exceeded the births,
and the growth of the metropolis depended upon
immigration from the provinces. In England and
Wales, in 1710, the annual death-rate was 28 in every 1,000 persons; in 1837 it had fallen to 24.7; in
1876, according to Mr. Mackenzie,* it was 21; while
in Hungary it was 37.2; in Austria, 29.4; in Italy,
28.7; in Prussia, 25.4; in France, 22.7. A great
improvement has been effected; but " the waste of
human life is still discreditably great."

TABLE OF THE AVERAGE ANNUAL RATES OF MORTALITY IN
THREE ENGLISH CITIES.

Periods.	Number of years.	LONDON. In 1,000 persons.	LIVERPOOL. In 1,000.	MANCHESTER. In 1,000.
1865–66....	2	25.5	40.2	33.5
1867–70....	4	23.8	31.1	31.8
1871–74....	4	22.8	30.1	30.2
1875–78....	4	22.9	27.8	28.6

In 1840–44, with 16,367 inhabitants to the square
mile, in London, the average annual mortality was
24.5 persons in 1,000; in 1874–78, with 28,602 inhabitants to the square mile, the rate was 22.9. Rela-

* " The Nineteenth Century," Franklin Square Library, p. 26,
note.

tively, the rate of mortality, figured according to density, should have been 26.2. Here is a saving of 12,178 lives annually in London, from 1874 to 1878, as compared with the death-rate and density in 1840 to 1844. This improvement the Registrar-General attributes, in part, to the extensive sewerage introduced, measuring 1,300 miles.*

Philanthropic Agencies.

One of the noblest traits of the century is the development of organized voluntary effort to relieve the suffering and raise the fallen. Near the beginning of this century the humane spirit of Christianity was seen struggling for a wider dominion. It came forth slowly, for a long period of hatred, personal bitterness, and bloodshed had preceded, and left its spirit lurking in all departments of society. But after the great European war which ended in the defeat of Napoleon at Waterloo, a spirit of toleration, tenderness, and forbearance began to prevail, and men's minds were directed to the work of helping the helpless, protecting the unprotected, providing for the needy, and alleviating suffering. Charities, many of them before unknown, sprang up and multiplied. Hospitals, infirmaries, dispensatories, asylums, homes for the aged, lodging-houses, institutions for the blind, the deaf and dumb, the idiotic, and for drunkards, have been

* See " The British Almanac and Companion," 1880, p. 121

established every-where, and number their inmates
by hundreds of thousands. Children without guardians have been snatched by merciful hands from the
perils which surrounded them, and committed to
institutions for education and training. Fallen
women are gathered into institutions devoted to
their moral recovery. Criminals whose terms of
punishment have expired are provided with employment. A vast machinery of charities, with a spirit
of noble devotedness, is spreading its net-work of
kindly influences in all our cities and towns. Five
hundred * charitable societies in London expend
$5,000,000 annually; and in New York city about
$4,000,000 annually are expended. In the United
States 43 institutions care for 5,743 deaf and dumb
annually; 30 institutions for the blind minister
to 2,179 pupils annually; 11 idiot asylums minister to 1,781 idiotic and imbecile persons. The first
two classes of these institutions show a property
of $10,000,000, and the three classes an annual ex-
penditure of $2,250,000, for persons heretofore left
to be trodden down and passed by with indifference.
Not to specify other humane and philanthropic institutions, it may be said that nearly all institutions
and organizations for these unfortunates have had
their origin since the battle of Waterloo. This disposition to raise the fallen, to befriend the friend-

---

* Low's "Hand-Book to the Charities of London," 1879–1880,
shows one thousand charitable institutions in that city.

less, is now one of the governing influences of the world, whose dominion is widening every year, and winning to its support a growing public sentiment.

Penal Inflictions.

Within one hundred years the criminal laws of even the most enlightened countries were atrociously savage, and administered in a relentless spirit.   Hon. Edmund Burke said he could obtain the consent of the House of Commons to any bill imposing punishment by death.   English law recognized two hundred and twenty-three capital crimes —not wholly a legacy of the Dark Ages, for one hundred and fifty-six of them bore no remoter date than the reigns of the Georges.   " If a man injured Westminster bridge he was hanged.   If he appeared disguised on a public road he was hanged.   If he cut down young trees, if he shot rabbits, if he stole property valued at five shillings, if he stole any thing at all from a bleach-field, if he wrote a threatening letter to extort money, if he returned prematurely from transportation—for any of these offenses he was prematurely hanged. . . .   Men who were not old when the battle of Waterloo was fought were familiar with the nameless atrocities which it had been customary to inflict upon traitors.   Within their recollection men who resisted the government were cut in pieces by the executioner, and their dishonored heads were exposed on Temple Bar to the derision or pity of passers-by. It seemed, indeed, as if society were reluctant to abandon these horrid practices. So late as 1820, when Thistlewood and his companions were executed for a poor, blundering conspiracy which they were supposed to have formed, the executioner first hanged and then beheaded the unfortunate men. The prison accommodations provided by the State were well calculated to reconcile criminals even to the gloomiest of all methods of deliverance. It was in 1773 that John Howard began his noble and faithful researches among the prisons of England, but many years passed before remedies were found for the evils which he revealed. In Howard's time the jailer received no salary : nay, he often paid a considerable sum for the situation which he filled. He was remunerated by fees extracted at his own pleasure, and often by brutal violence, from the wretches who had fallen into his power. It was his privilege to sell their food to the prisoners, and to supply, at an extortionate price, the straw which served them for beds, unless they were content to sleep on the damp floor." *

The penal codes and usages of all civilized countries retained too long the barbarism of the less-enlightened ages. But a marked modification in statutes and prisons has been apparent in the last sixty years. The more sanguinary penalties of

† Mackenzie's "Nineteenth Century." Harper & Brothers.

other ages have been left behind, and the retribution which savors of vengeance has been eliminated.
Penal justice is administered with reference to what
is required for the safety and well-being of society—
not exact retribution—so much suffering for so much
crime—but the principle of self-defense, security,
and reformation.

Criticisms and Testimonies.

It has been well said, "It takes but little length
of line to touch the bottom" of such criticisms on
current morals as appeared in the October "Atlantic" last year. But many good people inconsider-
ately indorse such criticisms, notwithstanding "they
come not much short of violating the ninth com-
mandment." There is much carping and unjust
depreciation of our times, a whining tone of distrust, and an exaggerated confession, often both un-
intelligent and unmanly. A sensational press pa-
rades, in exaggerated and highly colored forms, the
disgusting details of pollution, and many eagerly
catch them up, depreciate the present, and pro-
nounce lofty eulogiums upon the past. Many are
notoriously incapable of appreciating the virtues of
the age in which they live, but have a keen scent
for corruption, a horrid relish for scandal, look with
a fixed, contracted gaze upon the ulcers which af-
flict their fellows, and presume that every body else
but themselves has ulcers.

If we search the records of the past for contemporaneous recognitions of a golden age, we shall fail to find them. In the course of our review we have found men of each generation dwelling upon the degeneracy of their age, and the preachers thundering against its unprecedented vices. " The present always lies bare to the gaze, with all its deformities and hideousness in view, while the enchantment of distance hangs over the past."

But, thank God, there are not wanting those of high intelligence, of accurate observation, of close scrutiny, who have studied the moral condition of our times in the light of preceding ages, who hail the multiplying indications of the brightening days.

Theodore Parker said: " It is very plain that the people of New England are advancing in wealth, intelligence, and morality ; but in this general march there are little apparent pauses, slight waverings from side to side; some virtues seem to straggle from the troop; some to lag behind, for it is not always the same virtue that leads the van. . . . It is probable that the morals of New England in general, and of Boston in special, declined somewhat from 1775 to 1790. There were peculiar but well-known causes, which no longer exist, to work the result. . . . To estimate the moral growth or decline of this town we must not take either period as a standard. But take the history of Boston, from 1650 to 1700, from 1700 to 1750, and thence to 1800, and you will see a gradual but decided progress in morality in each of these periods. From 1800 to 1849 this progress is indisputable and well marked. Let us look at this a little in detail.

"It is generally conceded that the moral character of trade has improved a good deal within fifty or sixty years. It was formerly a common saying that, 'If a Yankee merchant were to sell salt water at high tide, he would cheat in the measure.' The saying was founded on the conduct of American traders abroad, in the West Indies and elsewhere. Now things have been changed for the better. I have been told by competent authority that two of the most eminent merchants of Boston, fifty or sixty years ago, who conducted each a large business, and left very large fortunes, were notoriously guilty of such dishonesty in trade as would now drive any man from the Exchange. The facility with which notes are now collected by the banks, compared with the former method of collection, is itself a proof of the increase of practical honesty; the law for settling the affairs of a bankrupt tells the same thing. Now this change has not come from any special effort; and consequently it indicates the general moral progress of the community."

After speaking of the improvement of the moral tone of the press, he says: "Yet a publicity is now-adays given to certain things which were formerly kept more closely from the public eye and ear.

This circumstance produces an apparent increase of wrong-doing, while it is only an increase of publicity thereof. . . . There has been a great change for the better in the matter of intemperance in drinking. . . . Probably there is not a respectable man who would not be ashamed to be seen drunk, in ever so private a manner, or who would willingly get a friend or a guest in that condition to-day. Go back a few years, and it brought no public reproach, and, I fear, no private shame. A few years further back, it was not a rare thing, on great occasions, for the fathers of the town to reel and stagger from their intemperance."

Another eminent gentleman said: "The present age is not pre-eminently a bad one. On the contrary, I believe the present age to be the purest and best the world has ever seen. It is not an age of gross licentiousness, either in life or literature, as some former ages have been. The student of literature meets few 'terrible temptations.' Writers like Tom Paine would be to-day turned out of the synagogues of skeptics."

The late Hon. Rufus Choate is said to have maintained that there had been a decided growth in political and personal morality since the early days of the Union, and two Massachusetts gentlemen with whom he was conversing, as well qualified as any to judge of such matters, concurred in his views.

The editor of a leading secular daily* said: "If we look back over the history of England, even in modern times, we shall easily note several distinct periods when the moral tone of the nation was low, politics were corrupt, and every thing apparently tending to ruin. And yet a few years in each instance enabled the people to outgrow these deleterious influences, until finally the age of Victoria may be considered, on the whole, decidedly superior in all moral elements to that of any former sovereign. Nor have we any reason to doubt that the unfavorable peculiarities of the present times, in the United States, are ephemeral, and must yet yield to the inherent moral vigor of the Nation."

A short time before his death, Hon. Charles Sumner was asked: "And what do you think, Mr. Sumner, of our country—are we going to destruction?" "No, no," cried Mr. Sumner, emphatically; "I believe in the Republic. I believe in the future of our country." "But think of all the lawlessness, the anarchy, and corruption every-where prevailing. We are treading in the footsteps of France. What can save us from falling as she has done?" "It is true," he answered, sadly, "these terrible disclosures in New York, in Washington, in Kansas, in Louisiana, are enough to make us tremble. The worst feature of it is the apathy of the people. When corruption is discovered the judgment of the

* "The Boston Journal," 1875.

people should strike like the thunderbolt." After
a pause his face brightened, and he concluded:
" But it does not matter. Our people have immense recuperative power. I believe in their recuperative energy. I believe in the Republic."

One of the most vigorously edited of our secular
dailies,* noted for its independent criticisms, said:
" Let the 'Atlantic' essayists, and Professors Shedd
and Schopenhauer, and the millenarians, tell us of
the night. Let them put out the storm signals,
and fix the buoys, and ring the fog-bells. We may
have to slow up for a while ; we may have to beat
against winds just now dead ahead, and currents
drifting strong toward a lee shore ; but God lives
as well as the devil, and this pessimistic tack will
bring us, in the next wearing of the ship, well ahead
in the open sea."

The stringent morals of the Puritans are often
referred to. Rev. Washington Gladden said : † " I
should like to explore the period of the Reformation and the days of the earlier Puritanism, and
show you, by typical cases, how far inferior to our
own the moral standards and practices of those
days were. We should find them, indeed, vastly
higher and purer than those we have encountered
in the earlier days of the Church, for progress is
the law of God's kingdom in the world ; but there

* "The Springfield Republican," 1879.
† Thanksgiving Discourse, Springfield, Mass., Nov. 28, 1878.

would be proofs enough that none of the former days were better than these.

"The kingdoms of this world are becoming the kingdoms of the Lord and of his Christ. It is his power that is doing all this mighty work. It is the influence of his Gospel, more than all other causes combined, that has purified our jurisprudence—that has revealed to men the great doctrines of rights, and taught them how to secure and maintain their rights ; that has lifted the family out of the pagan degradations and the mediæval corruptions ; that has gradually purified the sentiments and the ethical ideas of society, so that all our institutions are pervaded by its spirit, and all our civilization shines with the Light that lighteth every man that cometh into the world."

A leading religious editor * said : "The world never saw such extensive business organizations as at the present time. When one man, like a Stewart, can combine the abilities of several hundred men, and reap the margins on all their work, we cannot doubt general confidence.

"Take the single branch of business known as *banking.* How it depends upon letters of credit, and on dispatches, and on statements ! Think of the millions that daily pass through the channels of exchange, and how seldom a penny rolls out into any by-way. It hardly amounts to the one hun-

* "Christian Advocate," Nov. 30, 1876.

dred thousandth part of one per cent. Take the
25,000 men in American banks that have it in their
power to steal : see how seldom they do it. The
cases will not average more than one every two
weeks, or one in a thousand a year. A leading
banker said not long ago, ' I would be willing to
take the men up from the street as we meet them,
and put them in charge of the vault, saying, " This
vault is open, you watch it for an hour," and not
one in a hundred would disappoint the confidence.'
We are not all abandoned. Honesty is not one of
the lost arts.

" Take another class of community now much
abused by certain secular papers. There are now
more than 80,000 ministers in the United States.
Make an estimate of the percentage of failures in
morals. There is not an average of one a month in
the entire land. One in 6,500 is not a bad showing
for a year. Would to God there were none at all !
But we are far ahead of the infant Church, where
the failures were one in twelve. . . . We have great
reason to hope, for we are going in the right direction. Slavery is not defended, but dead. Alcohol
is no longer imbibed in the pulpit, but denounced.
Corruption is not concealed and apologized for, but
denied and condemned ; the cry against it is demanded by the public conscience. The Churches
were never more vigorous in their evangelizing
work. The credit of the nation has been so estab-

lished that its paper has advanced from thirty-five to ninety cents on the dollar. The losses on disbursements by corruption and fraud were never so small in the entire history of the country as at present.

"In the time of Van Buren the loss was $21 15 on every $1,000. Now it is only twenty-six cents. In the days of Buchanan, United States bonds bearing six per cent. interest, issued to pay current expenses of the government, which exceeded the revenues by over $75,000,000, were hawked about the country, and sold with great difficulty at seventeen per cent. discount. Now four and a half per cent. bonds sell at par. Surely capital, which is the most sensitive nerve in the world, does not indicate much distrust. . . . We are bad enough, but we are better than ever in the past. God has not a surplus of earthly governments that do as well by the masses of the people as our government does. We may confidently expect him to use us as long as we are fit for use ; then he will do the next best thing with us."

Said another eminent preacher and writer: "All the great ideals of civilized life of to-day are baptized in the spirit of the Gospel. Ideals are the engines that draw men up to higher planes of being. It is from ideals that aspirations spring, and it is by them that development is produced ; although they may be but little flickering lights, they are like the north star that guides men, and that enables them to find their way on the trackless sea by its constant bright-↲ness. The ideals of the family, the ideals of active men in commercial relations, the ideals of the patriot, the ideals of the whole civilization of our time, are essentially Christian. Honor, truth, purity, self-denial, love, intelligence, and general manliness, are all largely inspired and shaped by the Spirit of Christ. . . . The steady shining of the Spirit of Christ through the ages has imbued laws and formed customs. In the procedure that is most universally approved among civilizations there is an element of Christianity that has entered into it ; so that, besides conceptional Christianity and the Christianity of the record of the Book, there is a concrete Christianity, which consists of the equity, purity, justice, love, and generosity that are inculcated by the customs, public sentiments, laws, and institutions of human society." *

Moral self-poise is one of the best tests of true progress. The masses of the world have not yet reached a perfect equilibrium, as occasional occurrences remind us ; but how much greater the self-control of the human race than one hundred years ago ! Arbitrary enactments and standing armies are now little better than mockeries ; for men with elevated ideas need no overawing forces to restrain or compel them. Popular outbreaks against law

* Rev. Henry Ward Beecher. 1878.

and government, once so frequent, are now comparatively rare, seldom disastrous, and are usually quieted
by personal moral influence rather than by force.
International difficulties, once decided wholly by
the sword, are coming to be settled chiefly by
diplomacy. International conferences seem destined
to supplant sanguinary encounters. In pending
elections the sharpest partisan agitations, enlisting
however much of acrimony, and sometimes exciting
painful apprehensions for the future peace and stability of governments, quietly subside with the
verdict of the people—the most ardent demagogues
promptly bowing to the popular will. Men are
learning, more than ever before, that they can disagree and yet live happily together. France has
at last come, may we not believe, after many unsuc-
cessful experiments, to a condition in which its
excitable elements are susceptible of that self-control essential to republican government. One hundred years ago, or even fifty or thirty years ago, it
was not possible. England and America have also
improved in this regard. Many far-off lands, Australia, some Polynesian isles, Southern and Western
Africa, portions of South America, and Mexico, only
a little time ago dominated by savagery or an intol-
erant priesthood, are learning the great moral lesson of self-government. Thus, under the tutelage
of Christianity, God is fulfilling the ancient prediction, "*I will write my laws in your hearts,*" etc.

III. SPIRITUAL VITALITY.

CHAPTER I.

TYPICAL PERIODS.

* The Eve of the Lutheran Reformation.
  The Eve of the Wesleyan Reformation.
  The Eve of the Edwardean Revival.
  The Eve of the Revival of 1800-1803.

20

III.—SPIRITUAL VITALITY.

CHAPTER I.

TYPICAL PERIODS.

SPIRITUAL Christianity had almost disappeared when Protestantism arose. The spirit
of ecclesiasticism was dominant, and the Roman
hierarchy, assuming all control of spiritual functions,
raised its imperious head between the individual
and his God. Imposing forms and elaborate cere-
monials supplanted spiritual life. Piety retired to
cloisters, which, indeed, developed some conspicuous examples, but disfigured by morbid introspec-
tion, abnormal ecstasy, physical flagellation, and
antinomian quietism. Pining to dwell

> " In dark monastic cells,
> By vows and grates confined,"

these illustrious religionists, whose devotion the
Church of Rome has proudly cited as evidences of
her high spiritual capabilities, overlooked the prime
obligation of true saintship—

> " Freely to all ourselves we give,
> Constrained by Jesus' love to live
> The servants of mankind."

In such a period Luther appeared, protesting against the exclusive functions of the Romish priesthood, and proclaiming every man his own priest. The theory of the priesthood of believers, as an issue with the hierarchy, was fought out in the great Reformation of the sixteenth century ; but it was only imperfectly realized in the practical life of the Reformation Churches. We recognize it, in an excessive and fanatical form, among the Anabaptists in Germany, who claimed immediate and even prophetic inspiration, and, a little later, among the early Quakers. It had a better but yet imperfect development among the Puritans.

Absorbed in the outward battle of great principles, the Reformation, in its earlier stages, did not exhibit much spirituality, except in some of its best leaders, in whose hearts the most radical truths were combined with intense religious devotion. Nor did early Protestantism exhibit much missionary and soul-saving power. The subject of spiritual regeneration did not receive the distinctive prominence which it had in the primitive Church.

Before the death of Luther all Northern Europe had broken away from the Papacy, and the Reformation was established by law. Great religious wars occurred, extending through three generations, during which the spirituality of Protestantism was extinguished and its aggressive power lost. It became political, and contented itself with maintaining itself within its own limits.

From Luther to Wesley few revivals occurred, except at long intervals, among the Presbyterians in Scotland, the Moravians, and in some of the earliest Churches of the Massachusetts Colony. One hundred and fifty years ago spiritual death and formalism pervaded the Protestant Churches of Europe and America. No aggressive impulse, no lay activities, no outgoing desire for the salvation of the world, marked the period. The New England Churches had a few feeble missions among the Indians; English Protestantism had one society that reached beyond the British Isles—the "Society for the Propagation of the Gospel in Foreign Parts," organized in 1701 for the benefit of English colonists on foreign shores, not for heathen populations; and on the Continent of Europe a missionary afflatus had just come upon the Moravians, under which they went forth to sublime achievements.

It will now be necessary to sketch the progress of Protestantism more in detail, and examine closely the changing phases of its history. As we do so we shall notice at considerable length the period of spiritual decadence in England and America one hundred and fifty years ago, from which, in the former country, it emerged into a gradual development for more than a century; and, in the latter, it partially and temporarily emerged, but was followed by another period of decline, from which it has since risen into grander life and progress than ever before.

It should be kept in mind that Protestantism never claimed perfection. Exceedingly immature at first, and ever a growth, it started upon its career with great disadvantages, heavily encumbered with relics of popery and mediæval life, beclouding its vision, depressing its spirituality, dividing its counsels, and holding its laity in partial bondage. The English Reformation, embarrassed with state patronage, imperfectly restored the primitive idea of Christianity as " the kingdom of God within." Typical examples of spirituality under the English Reformation, Churchmen and Puritans, bright and worthy of their times, fall below more recent standards. Pure and noble men they were, in advance of the next preceding centuries, and some of them ahead of their own age ; but the spiritual influence of the movement was confined to narrow circles.

Southey says : " Among the educated classes too little care was taken to imbue them early with this better faith ; and too little exertion used for awakening them from the pursuits and vanities of this world to a salutary and healthful contemplation of that which is to come. And there was the heavier evil that the greater part of the nation were totally uneducated—Christians no further than the mere ceremony of baptism—being for the most part in a state of heathen, or worse than heathen, ignorance. In truth, they had never been converted; for, at first, one idolatry had been substituted for another —in this they had followed the fashion of their lords—and when the Romish idolatry was expelled, the change on their part was still a matter of necessary submission. They were left as ignorant of real Christianity as they were found."

With such a view of the English Reformation it is not surprising that it was subject to alternations and reactions, and that the rigorous dispensation of the Puritan Cromwell should be followed by the lax and dissolute reign of Charles II. Churchmen and Nonconformists alike bear concurrent testimony respecting the low condition of religion from the time of Charles II. to the middle of the eighteenth century. The reaction against Puritanism, following the restoration of the Stuarts, left a universal blight upon the nation. A total irreligion and lifeless formality spread every-where. A haughty dislike repelled the spiritualities of religion. Archbishop Leighton complained that the Church was " a fair carcass without a spirit."

The pathetic lamentation of Bishop Burnet,* in 1713, on the state of the Church, has often been quoted : " I am now," he says, " in the seventieth year of my age, and, as I cannot speak long in the world in any sort, so I cannot hope for a more

* " Pastoral Care."

solemn occasion than this of speaking with all due
freedom, both to the present and to the succeeding
ages. Therefore I lay hold on it to give a free
vent to those sad thoughts that lie in my mind,
both day and night, and are the subject of many
secret musings. I cannot look on without the
deepest concern when I see the imminent ruin
hanging over this Church, and, by consequence,
over the whole Reformation. The outward state
of things is black enough, God knows, but that
which heightens my fears rises chiefly from the inward state into which we are unhappily fallen."
Referring to the condition of the clergy, he says :
" Our ember-weeks are the burden and grief of my
life. The much greater part of those who come to
be ordained are ignorant to a degree not to be apprehended by those who are not obliged to know
it. The easiest part of knowledge is that to which
they are the greatest strangers. Those who have
read some few books yet never seem to have read
the Scriptures. Many cannot give a tolerable account even of the Catechism itself, how short and
plain soever. This does often tear my heart. The
case is not much better in many, who, having got
into orders, come for institution, and cannot make
it appear that they have read the Scriptures or any
one good book since they were ordained, so that
the small measure. of knowledge upon which they
got into holy orders not being improved, is in a

way to be quite lost ; and then they think it a great hardship if they are told they must know the Scriptures and the body of divinity better before they can be trusted with the care of souls."

Watts declared that there was "a general decay of vital religion in the hearts and lives of men ;" that this condition extended " to Dissenters as well as Churchmen ;" that it was " a matter of mournful observation among all who lay the cause of God to heart ;" and he called upon " every one to use all possible efforts for the recovery of dying religion in the world."* Another writer asserts that " the Spirit of God had so far departed from the nation that hereby almost all vital religion is lost out of the world." † The " Weekly Miscellany" (1732) said : " The people are engulfed in voluptuousness and business, and a zeal for godliness looks as odd upon a man as would the antiquated dress of a great-grandfather."

In Scotland, under the early visits of Whitefield, the Churches were somewhat quickened, but the work was limited in extent and power by divisions and dissensions, and was followed by a deeper moral slumber, called " the midnight of the Church." The infidelity of the times had infected the ministry, and only tame " moral sermons," after the style of Blair, were preached, and convivial cir-

* Preface to his " Humble Attempt," etc.
† Harrison's " Sermons on the Holy Spirit."

cles were more attractive than pulpits to the clergy. Dr. Hamilton said : " To deliver a Gospel sermon, or to preach to the consciences of dying sinners, was as completely beyond their power as to speak in the language of angels. . . . The congregations rarely amounted to a tenth of the parishioners, and one half of this small number were generally, during the half-hour soporific harangue, fast asleep. They were free from hypocrisy ; they had no more religion in private than in public."

A writer in "Blackwood's Magazine" said of that period that it was "singularly devoid, not only of religion, but of all spirituality of mind, or reference to things unseen. . . . It was one of the moments in which the world had fallen out of thought of God. Other ages may have been as wicked, but we doubt whether any age had learned so entirely to forget its connection with higher things, or the fact that a soul which did not die—an immortal being akin to other spheres—was within its clay. The good men were inoperative, the bad men were dauntless; the vast crowd between the two, which forms the bulk of humanity, felt no stimulus toward religion, and drowsed in comfortable content."

Lecky says: "A great skeptic described the nation as ' settled into the most cool indifference with regard to religious matters that is to be found in any nation in the world.' "

Leland,* an eminent Dissenter, said : " It cannot escape the notice of the most superficial observer that an habitual neglect of public worship is becoming general among us, beyond the example of former times." " People of fashion," said Archbishop Secker,† " especially of that sex which ascribes to itself the most knowledge, have merely thrown off all observance of the Lord's day, . . . and if, to avoid scandal, they sometimes vouchsafe their attendance on divine worship in the country, they seldom or never do it in town." Cabinet councils and cabinet dinners were constantly held on that day.‡ Sunday card-parties, during the greater part of the eighteenth century, were fashionable entertainments in the best circles. §

Bishop Butler said : " The general decay of religion in this nation, which is now observed by every one, has been for some time the complaint of all serious persons." " The influence of it is more and more wearing out of the minds of men, even of those who do not pretend to enter into speculations upon the subject ; but the number of those who do, and who profess themselves unbelievers, increases, and with their numbers their zeal."

* Leland's " View of the Deistical Writers," ii, 442,
† Secker's Sermons, works i, 114, 115.
‡ Stanhope's " History of England," vii, p. 320.
§ " Rambler," 30, etc.

Addison said: " There is less appearance of religion in England than in any neighboring state or kingdom."

Crossing the Atlantic, we find the Churches of the American Colonies not much better. The Virginia Colony was never noted for either its morality or piety, and the tendency was downward rather than upward. In Maryland, under the numerous civil and ecclesiastical distractions which prevailed through the seventeenth century, things were even worse. The Lord's day was generally profaned, religion despised, and the clergy were scandalous in behavior. In the New York Colony the Dutch Church, dependent upon the mother Church in Amsterdam, performed its work under serious embarrassments; and the Episcopal Church, sustained by the civil power, partook of the prevailing laxity in English manners at home.

The Presbyterians, commencing under the indefatigable labors of the spiritual and apostolical Makenzie (1684) and Mackie, (1692,) spread through New York, New Jersey, Pennsylvania, Delaware, and the Eastern Shore of Maryland. But the pioneers passed away, (1708, 1716,) and a change came over the Churches. Being in close affiliation with the Presbyterian Churches of Scotland and Ireland, and receiving their ministers from those countries, they partook of the same spirit that was working such deteriorating results in the Churches of the

British Isles. The primitive zeal of Makenzie and his compeers declined, "revivals of religion were nowhere heard of, and an orthodox creed and a decent external conduct were the only points on which inquiry was made when persons were admitted to the communion."

And no more was required of the ministers, except intellectual and scholastic qualifications. Vital piety almost deserted the Church. The substance of preaching was a "dead orthodoxy," which laid no emphasis on human sinfulness or regeneration. "Some of the preachers," says Dr. Gillett,* "whom Tennent rebuked, were unquestionably 'Pharisee preachers.' Among them, too, were bitter opponents of the 'revival' which subsequently occurred, 'if not of evangelical religion.'" A change of heart not being required of members or preachers, unconverted men became pastors. Some of them, subsequently awakened under Whitefield's preaching, mourned over themselves as "soul-deceivers and soul-murderers."

Puritan New England was not exempt from the general decline. The early Churches were noted for piety, and during the first thirty years after the landing of the Pilgrims deep spirituality prevailed— almost continual showers of refreshing. Subsequently spirituality declined, and at the close of the century there were many lamentations over

* "History of the Presbyterian Church."

the low state of religion. The eighteenth century opened with no improvement. In 1702 Increase Mather said : " Look into our pulpits and see if there is such a glory as there once was. Look into the civil state. Does Christ reign there as he once did ? How many churches, how many towns, there are in New England over which we may sigh and say the glory is gone." Dr. Trumbull described the condition of Connecticut in similar terms. In 1707 the downward tendency, attributable, in part, to the adoption of the Half-way Covenant forty-five years before, was accelerated by the action of Rev. Solomon Stoddard, of Northampton, a man of larger public influence than any other in western New England, whose subversive practice of admitting unconverted persons to the Lord's supper, at first feebly resisted, became current in many Churches. The Half-way Covenant had admitted the impenitent, if baptized in infancy, to Church fellowship, so far as to allow them to become voters, but not to partake of the Lord's supper. It was the wooden horse within the walls of Troy. Henceforth they were admitted to full fellowship in the Church if correct in faith and not scandalous in life. From this time justification, regeneration, and the cognate doctrines were discarded, or preached in new and accommodated forms. Piety being no longer a condition of membership, nor of ministerial ordination, zeal was at a discount, and refined moralizing and speculation constituted the staple matter of pulpit discourses.

Spasmodic efforts, like the convulsive twitchings of dying muscles, were occasionally put forth to arrest the decline. In 1725 Cotton Mather, in behalf of the convention of ministers, petitioned the Legislature that, " in view of the great and visible decline of piety," a Synod might be called to remedy the unhappy condition, but without avail. Two fatal epidemics, carrying off from one tenth to one seventh of the people in some localities, produced temporary alarm, but did not essentially change the religious condition.

The evil tendencies working down through English society from the coronation of Charles II., unbinding the safeguards of virtue and faith, and promoting skepticism, frivolity, and profligacy, were only too contagious among the children of the Pilgrims, the Covenanters, and the Cavaliers. The religious enthusiasm of the fathers had passed away, and devotion, self-sacrifice, and sanctity of life had subsided into staleness of thought and stagnancy of feeling in all the colonies. The Churches were valleys of dry bones.

In such a condition of the Churches in Great Britain and the American Colonies the memorable religious movements known as the Wesleyan Reformation in England, and " the Great Awakening " in this country, commenced. Simultaneous and

unique, but unconnected, these remarkable quick-
enings bore the divine impress.

The Wesleyan movement, beginning in the individual longings of the Wesleys and Whitefield after
spiritual life and purity, became at once a revival
and a reformation. It emphasized spiritual life,
spiritual power, holiness of heart and life, and the
priesthood of believers. The latter, one of the
leading theses of the Reformation, but imperfectly
carried out in the actual life of the Reformation
Churches, except the Moravians, developed into a
distinguishing feature of the Wesleyan movement.
All converts, male and female, were joyful witnesses
for Christ, and went forth to active labor for their
new Master. Wesleyanism was characterized by
intense vitality. Social services, the favorite privileges of the people, were almost as prominent as the
preaching of the Word, and large numbers of lay
preachers and exhorters went forth into neglected
by-ways.

This movement gave a broad impulse to English
Christianity. Wesley, forming societies, and Whitefield forming none—the former Arminian and the
latter Calvinistic, but one in impulse and purpose—
awakened the spiritual life of the national Church
and also of the dissenting bodies. English Protestantism became a live, aggressive, regenerating force.
Under the influence of Whitefield and the Countess
of Huntingdon, Calvinistic Nonconformity rose, as

from the dead, with an energy increasing ever since ; while, in co-operation with Wesley, a powerful evangelical party arose in the Establishment, and new measures of gospel propagandism were inaugurated, which have kept British Christianity alive and extended its activities into far-off lands " sitting in darkness and the shadow of death." Chiefly out of this spiritual quickening came forth those great Christian enterprises through which British piety has spread its influence around the globe. "The British Bible Society, most of the British Missionary Societies, Tract Societies, the Sunday-schools, religious periodicals, negro emancipation, etc., all arose, directly or indirectly, from this impulse." *

Isaac Taylor said the Established Church owes to the Wesleyan movement, " in great part, the modern revival of its energies ; " and, " by the new life it has diffused on all sides, it has preserved from extinction and has reanimated the languishing Nonconformity of the last century, which, just at the time of the Methodist revival, was rapidly in course to be found nowhere but in books." Also Mr. Leckey says of the Wesleyan movement that " it incalculably increased the efficiency of almost every religious body ; " † that " it has been more or less felt in every Protestant community speaking the

---

* Mr. Lecky's " England in the Eighteenth Century," vol. ii, p. 674. † Ibid., p. 682.

21

322 PROBLEM OF RELIGIOUS PROGRESS.

English tongue;" * and that Wesley "has had a wider constructive influence in the sphere of practical religion than any other man who has appeared since the sixteenth century." † Dean Stanley has uttered similar tributes to Wesley.

At the time when the Wesleys and Whitefield were pressing into higher spiritual life in England, across the Atlantic, in the Massachusetts Colony, in the retired town of Northampton, the ablest young minister of the age, a descendant of a London clergyman in the days of Elizabeth, was striking massive blows against the foundations of false hope on which, in stupid lethargy, the Churches were reposing. Jonathan Edwards, born in the same year with John Wesley, was a fellow-champion with him of spiritual religion, evangelical theology, and advanced spiritual movements. He proclaimed with powerful cogency man's lost condition, Christ's death the only ground of justification, and the necessity of regenerating grace. His bugle-call awakened the slumbering Churches, and aroused them to higher spirituality. In Central and Western Massachusetts and in Connecticut a large number of towns were quickened, and the dormant Churches of New Jersey also felt the pulsations of the new life. The Edwardean revival attracted much attention; but the visit and labors of Whitefield extended

* Mr. Lecky's "England in the Eighteenth Century," vol. ii, p. 690. † Ibid., p. 687.

the circle of its influence, and made it the great religious event of the period.

In the Middle States the way had been providentially preparing. In 1718 Rev. William Tennent, a clergyman of rare scholarship and deep piety, emigrated from Ireland, and about 1729 established at Neshaming, not far from Philadelphia, the famous "Log College" as a training school for ministers—the first Presbyterian school in America. Here, at a time when a cold and formal religion called only for intellectually drilled ministers, candidates for the sacred office received both intellectual and spiritual culture, and a body of young preachers was raised up who warmly welcomed the coming of Whitefield. Under his flaming ministrations the influence of Edwards' revival was suplemented and extended, saving the languishing Churches of the Middle States from extinction. The Tennents, father and three sons—John, Gilbert, and William, 2d—Finlay, Robinson, and Davenport, all educated at the "Log College," were leaders in this movement.

The Presbyterian Churches assumed an attitude of aggressiveness and power; faithful men were enthused and enlisted in active labor; Nassau Hall received its birth and baptism; and Whitefield's preaching and the reading of his published sermons introduced Presbyterianism into Virginia. Much of "the stock from which the Baptists in Virginia, and those farther south and south-west, sprung was also Whitefieldian." In New England, Wheelock, the founder of Dartmouth College, and the instructor of many Indian youth who became missionaries to their red brethren, lighted his torch in this flame. Brainerd was fired from the same altar, and, under the last sermon of Whitefield, Benjamin Randall, the founder of the Free-Will Baptists, was awakened.

The result of the revivals, not to speak of other gains, was the addition of from 20,000 to 30,000 members to the Churches. But more serious errors and irregularities accompanied these movements than have characterized the revivals of later times, leaving ample occasion for criticism, even by the friends, in cooler moments of review. The Churches of the Middle and New England States were divided. A stout resistance to the extreme measures of the revivalists, and a growing spirit of dissent—the incipient stages of the later Arian and Socinian development—sharply arrayed parties against each other. The revival, therefore, with all its great and never-to-be-depreciated advantages, was not an unmixed blessing, but left behind a residuum of evil, to harrass the Churches, and bring again coldness and death.

There speedily followed a long period of spiritual decline, extending through a half century, occasioned by new and continually multiplying troubles: the French and Indian wars, the political agitations ushering in the Revolution, the sanguinary scenes and deep trials of that severe contest, the pecuniary embarrassments following it, the agitations connected with the organization of the Federal Government, the local rebellions in several of the States, the infusion of English Deism through the British officers aiding in the French and Indian wars, and the spread of French infidelity, during and after the struggle for independence.

The disbanded armies poisoned every community with skepticism and immorality. On the borders, lawless Indians and renegade white men kept the settlers in perpetual alarm. In large sections there was no other vestige of the Christian Sabbath than a faint observance of the day as a time of rest for the aged and a play-day for the young. The intrigues of infidel politicians thickened around the best statesmen; and, without Divine interposition and the steady moral courage of Washington, the newly emancipated people would have relapsed into anarchy.

The Half-way Covenant was a prolific source of evil to the Congregational Churches of New England. "In the light of it," says Rev. Dr. Tarbox,* "we can easily understand why the Churches of Massachusetts were in a very unhealthy condition

---

* Historical Survey of the Congregational Churches of Massachusetts, 1776–1876. "Minutes of the General Association of Massachusetts, 1877," p. 42.

one hundred years ago. They had not, it is true, lost all their power as Churches of Christ, but they were greatly shorn of their strength. From 1745 on to the close of the century there was a woeful absence of those special breathings of the Holy Spirit which we call revivals of religion. The Churches were built up as to numbers, but largely with earthly materials, and the standard of Christian conduct came to be very low.

"We talk of the good old times, but all through the last century there were strifes and contentions in many of these Churches, such as were far below the Christian standards of the present day. We refer to these things not to dishonor our fathers, but rather to honor the Gospel of Jesus Christ, in its power to overcome evil, and make the world better from generation to generation.

"The drinking habits of all classes, ministers included, hung like a dead weight upon the Churches. Ordinations were scenes of festivity, copious drinking having a large share in this festivity, and an ordination ball often ended the occasion. Not very far from the period of the Revolution several councils were held in one of the towns of Massachusetts, where the people were trying to be rid of a minister, who was often the worse for liquor, even in the pulpit, and once, at least, at the communion table; but some of the neighboring ministers stood by him, and the people had to endure him till his death."

Such was the condition of the Churches in the older communities. The younger settlements were even worse. Rev. David Rice, who went to Kentucky in 1783, said,* "I scarcely found one man, and but few women, who supported a creditable profession of religion. Some were grossly ignorant of the first principles of religion; some were given to quarreling and fighting; some, to intemperance; and perhaps most of them were totally ignorant of the forms of religion in their own houses." And yet "many of them procured certificates of having been in full communion and good standing in the Churches from which they had emigrated."

The religious outlook was dismal indeed. Spirituality was at a low ebb. The revival idea nearly died out of the actual life of the Churches. Many of them, decimated by the war, and sunken in apathy, dragged a miserable existence. From 1745 to 1797 † only few and comparatively small revivals of religion occurred: in 1764 and 1770, under the

---

* "Memoirs of Rev. David Rice, of Kentucky."

† "Long before the death of Whitefield, in 1770, extensive revivals in America had ceased. And, except one in Stockbridge, and some other parts of Berkshire County, Massachusetts, about the year 1772; and one in the north quarter of Lyme, Connecticut, about the year 1780; and in several towns in Litchfield County, Connecticut, about the year 1783, I know of none which occurred afterward, till the time of which I am to speak, (1797–1803.)"—Rev. E. D. Griffin, D.D., Letter on Revivals to Rev. William B. Sprague, D.D. (See Sprague's "Lectures on Revivals." Albany, 1832. Appendix, p. 151.)

labors of Dr. Laddie, in New York city; in 1767, a small revival, with only ten or twelve converts, in Norfolk, Connecticut; in 1778, at Vance's Fort, Pennsylvania; in 1781–1787, in the region of Cross Creek, Upper Buffalo, Lebanon, and Cross Roads, Pennsylvania; in 1772 and 1784, at Elizabeth, and in 1790, at Hanover, New Jersey; in 1764, 1785, and 1791, under Dr. Buel's labors, at Easthampton, Long Island; in 1788–89, in the upper regions of Georgia; in 1795, under the labors of Dr. Griffin, at New Hartford, Connecticut, and again in 1799; in 1781 and 1788, in Dartmouth College, but not again for seventeen years; in Yale College, in 1783, but not again until after 1800, the undergraduate membership of the College Church dwindling to four or five; and in 1757, 1762, and 1773, in Princeton College, and not again until 1813, during which time, according to Dr. Ashbel Green, there were only two or three students who professed religion, and only four or five who scrupled to use profane language. These were almost all the revivals for fifty years. William and Mary's College was "a hot-bed of infidelity," and Harvard College of Arian and Socinian sentiments.

Writing of this period, one pastor said, " Prior to this year (1799) there never was any extensive revival of religion in this town ;" another mentioned a small revival in 1767, and another in 1783, and nothing more until 1799; another said, " I cannot learn from any of the first settlers that there had been any remarkable revivals in this town, until June, 1799;" and Rev. Ebenezer Porter, of Washington, Connecticut, in 1803, wrote, "Though this Church has enjoyed a preached Gospel with very little interruption since its formation, a period of sixty-four years, nothing that could be properly termed a revival of religion had ever taken place until the present." In describing the condition of things in Lenox, Massachusetts, a pastor wrote: "The situation of this Church calls for the earnest prayers of all who have any heart to pray. The number of its members is not much greater than it has been at any time for twenty-five years, and almost all of them are burdened under the infirmities of years. Not a single young person has been received into it for sixteen years." And another, in Canton, Connecticut, said, "Religion has gradually declined among us, the doctrines of Christ grow more and more unpopular, family prayer and all the duties of the Gospel are less regarded, ungodliness prevails, and modern infidelity has made alarming progress among us. It seems as though the Sabbath would be lost, and every appearance of religion vanish, yea, that our Zion must die without any helper, and that infidels will laugh at her dying groans." We might multiply these testimonies, for these were not the exceptional utterances of men of melancholy temperament, but the frequent and almost universal expression of the best minds of that day.

The General Assembly of the Presbyterian Church, embracing men of high character, broad culture, and superior intelligence, in its Pastoral Letter, in 1798, said : " A dissolution of religious society seems to be threatened by the supineness and inattention of many ministers and professors of Christianity." " The statements of the Assembly," says Rev. Dr. Gillett, " grave and startling as they were, were by no means exaggerated. The prospect for religious progress or improvement was almost cheerless. By public men in high station infidelity was boldly avowed. In some places society, taking its tone from them, seemed hopelessly surrendered to the impious and the blasphemer."

The last two decades of the eighteenth century were the darkest period, spiritually and morally, in the history of American Christianity—so dark and ominous of evil that it was a fruitful topic of discourse, of correspondence, of profound inquiry and consultation ; and numerous fasts were appointed by the ecclesiastical bodies—annual fasts, quarterly fasts, monthly fasts, and weekly fasts—and, in some localities widely separated, a half hour at sundown on Saturday night, and a half hour at sunrise on Sunday morning, were devoted to special prayer for the divine blessing on the land.

CHAPTER II.

THE NEW SPIRITUAL ERA.

New Life.
The New Life Organizing.
The New Life Aggressive.
New Lay-Activities.
City Missions.
Home Missions.
Young Men's Christian Associations.
Foreign Missions.
Pecuniary Benevolence.
Imperfections.
Type of Religious Character.
The Outlook.

CHAPTER II.

THE NEW SPIRITUAL ERA.

IN the midst of the low spiritual condition described at the close of the preceding chapter the great religious awakening, known as "the revival of 1800," performed its beneficent work. From 1795 to 1797 a few isolated revivals occurred in western Massachusetts and Connecticut, but in the autumn of 1799 the Holy Spirit was more powerfully poured out in Eastern Tennessee and Kentucky. The flame of revival rapidly spread, crossing the Blue Ridge into Virginia and North Carolina, extending southward and northward throughout almost the entire land. It continued, with varying force, from 1799 to 1803, but most deeply marked the years 1800 and 1801, and inaugurated a new era of deeper spirituality in the American Churches.

Rev. Dr. Tyler said : * "Within the period of five or six years, commencing with 1797, it has been stated that not less than one hundred and fifty Churches in New England were visited with 'times of refreshing from the presence of the Lord.'"

* "New England Revivals." By Rev. Bennett Tyler, D.D.

Rev. Ebenezer Porter, D.D., said: "The day dawned which was to succeed a night of more than sixty years. As in the valley of Ezekiel's vision, there was a great shaking. Dry bones, animated by the breath of the Almighty, stood up new-born believers. The children of Zion beheld with overflowing souls, and with thankful hearts acknowledged, 'This is the finger of God.' The work was stamped conspicuously with the impress of its divine Author, and its joyful effects evinced no other than the agency of Omnipotence." Rev. E. D. Griffin, D.D., said: "I could stand in my door, at New Hartford, Litchfield Co., Conn., and number fifty or sixty contiguous congregations laid down in one field of divine wonders, and as many more in various parts of New England."

Since that time American revivals have been frequent and extensive, attracting the attention of European divines as remarkable phases in the history of the Christian Church. Rev. Dr. Gardner Spring said: "From the year 1800 down to the year 1825 there was an uninterrupted series of these celestial visitations spreading over different parts of the land. During the whole of those twenty-five years there was scarcely a time in which we could not point to some village, some city, some seminary, and say, 'Behold what God hath wrought.'" Rev. Dr. Heman Humphrey said: "It was the opening of a new revival epoch, which has lasted now more than half a century, with but short and partial interruptions. . . . Taken altogether, the revival period, at the close of the last century and the beginning of the present, furnishes ample materials for a long and glorious chapter in the history of redemption."

Between 1825 and 1845 these spiritual visitations were very powerful ; from 1848 to 1857 was a period of reaction and spiritual decline, following the widely extended, but abnormal, Millerite excitement ; but since the great revival of 1857 and 1858, the revival seasons, except during the civil war, have been more frequent and continuous, and the declensions less disastrous. Numerous local Churches have enjoyed a well-nigh uninterrupted revival condition for many years, few weeks passing without conversions. In later years, too, there has been less excitement, and less of the peculiar physical phenomena which characterized the early revivals in Scotland among the Presbyterians, in England under the Wesleys, in America under Whitefield and Edwards, and in Tennessee and Kentucky at the beginning of this century. A more deliberate and intelligent action of the religious sensibilities is everywhere apparent. And the fruits of this new life have been an increase of nearly ten millions of communicants in the Evangelical Churches from 1800 to 1880—a gain without a parallel in religious history.

As one of the effects, though, in an important

sense, a cause, of these great revival movements, and an unmistakable evidence of the deepening spiritual vitality of the American Churches, we have the every-where patent fact of a more general and intelligent acknowledgment of the Holy Spirit's influences as the efficient agent in all spiritual work.   During the last one hundred and fifty years this doctrine has come to a fuller recognition than ever before for eighteen centuries, and Christian men are accustomed to labor in humble reliance upon this divine agent for spiritual success.   The supernatural influence of the Holy Spirit in awakening sinners, in begetting and sustaining Christian experience—the vital and vitalizing power in true piety—has come into very distinctive prominence in the religious literature also of this period. As a consequence, there has been a deeper awakening of the religious consciousness, a wider exploration of the field of religious experience, a development of a more joyful and victorious type of piety, and a spirit of heroic effort in keeping with our best ideals of pure Christianity.

New wine must have new bottles; new life develops new organizations.   The old methods of religious work no longer sufficed.   The vigorous converts of the new era became conspicuous as organizers and standard-bearers of great advance movements.   Under the hay-stacks on the banks of the Hoosac, Mills, Hall, and Richards, three devoted

young students of Williams' College, all fruits of
the revival of 1800, "prayed into existence the em-
bryo of foreign missions," and soon after, at Andover, enkindled the hearts of Newell, Nott, and
Judson with the same flame. Dr. Justin Edwards,
one of the wisest and most influential organizers
of moral and religious enterprises, and the most
effective champion of the temperance and Sabbath
reforms this country ever knew; and Jeremiah
Evarts, Esq., devoted to religious literature, missions, temperance, Sunday-school and tract movements, and numerous others—were also fruits of
that revival. Home Missionary, Foreign Missionary, Bible, Tract, and Sunday-school Societies
sprang up sporadically in the new religious soil.

Rev. Heman Humphrey, D.D., writing about
1850, alluding to the far-reaching results of the revival of 1800, said:

"The glorious cause of religion and philanthropy
has advanced, till it would require a space not
afforded in these sketches so much as to name the
Christian and humane societies which have sprung
up all over our land within the last forty years.
Exactly how much we at home and the world
abroad are indebted for these organizations, so rich
in blessings, to the revivals of 1800, it is impossible
to say, though much every way. . . . It cannot be
denied that modern missions sprang out of these
revivals. The immediate connection between them,

22

as cause and effect, was remarkably clear in the organization of the first societies, which have since accomplished so much; and the impulse which they gave to the Churches to extend the blessings which they were diffusing, by forming the later affiliated societies, of like aims and character, is scarcely less obvious."

The religious quickening in England, under the Wesleys and Whitefield, was followed, at the close of the last and the beginning of the present century, by the organization of numerous societies for Christian and beneficent purposes. Foreign and Home Missionary, Bible, Tract, Sunday-school, Educational, Peace, African Amelioration, Seamen's, Prison Discipline, and Philanthropic, Societies were organized, with extended ramifications, mostly between 1780 and 1830, with additions and enlargements since the latter date. Their pecuniary receipts are among the most wonderful examples of modern munificence, and the fruitage of Bible, tract, and mission work is marvelous.

The same tendency followed the religious quickening in America. During the present century American Christianity has fully attested its deep vitality by its wonderful self-organizing power. The numerous local societies for missions, home and foreign, tracts, Bibles, Sunday-schools, temperance, education, the Sabbath, seamen, etc., which came into existence during the first two decades of this century, were subsequently combined * into large national organizations, with countless auxiliaries covering the entire land. Each successive decade has developed new organizations, and extended more widely the old, comprising all conceivable forms of benevolence and beneficence, and enlisting an army of Christian workers, outnumbering the largest armies of ancient or modern times. The last quarter of a century has witnessed no decline in these agencies, but rather a vast increase in their number, resources, workers, and the scope of their operations, beyond any previous period, even several times greater than in the previous half century. Besides the purely Christian organizations directly connected with the Churches, there are numerous philanthropic, social, civil, educational, and reformatory societies, indirectly or directly growing out of the impelling life-flow of Christianity. Thus has the new life attested its divinity—quickening, enlightening, humanizing, reforming, and saving men. "The poor have the gospel preached unto them."

This new life has also been wonderfully aggressive and expansive, following closely the large populations spreading over our broad national domain with enlightening and saving influences. Pioneer preachers, colporteurs, and Sunday-school agents, stepping closely in the footprints of pioneer settlers, hailing the cabin builder with religious salutations,

* Mostly from 1820 to 1830.

calling him to an extemporized worship on his half-hewn log, and including his home in a plan for future religious visitation, in the spirit of zealous propagandism, founded Churches, Sunday-schools, Church seminaries and colleges, and made the wilderness, less than three generations ago a vast moral waste of howling savages, to bud and blossom with the institutions of Christian civilization. In the region beyond the western line of New York, Pennsylvania, Virginia, North Carolina, and Georgia, which, in the year 1800, had but few scattering Protestant Churches, there were, according to the Census of 1870, 37,855 Protestant Church organizations, or two thirds of all the Protestant Churches in the United States—the abundant harvest of zealous pioneer seed-sowing. And what a multitude of cognate religious institutions accompany these Churches, comprising an amount of Christian life scarcely paralleled in any other land—the results of seventy years' labors, fully testing the spiritual vitality of the American Churches.

A great change has taken place in the spiritual activities of the Churches. Formerly, prayer-meetings, except in the occasional revival seasons, were rare, and only a very few persons were allowed or expected to participate in them. All through the last century, and for some time into the present, this custom prevailed. The gifts of the laity were not exercised, and their voices were seldom heard in exhortation or supplication. Rev. Mr. Fisk,* of New Braintree, Mass., had been pastor of that Church eleven years before he heard the first word of prayer from one of his members. And when the little band of zealous evangelicals went off from the Old South Church, Boston, in 1808, to organize the Park-street Church,† as a breakwater against the incoming tide of Arianism, they met several times for consultation before any one of even these redoubtable champions of orthodoxy had sufficient courage to open his lips in vocal prayer. Women never prayed or spoke in any religious services.

"The only religious meetings of the week were on the Sabbath. There was no evening lecture, no altar for social prayer, no intercessions in concert for the coming of the kingdom, no schools for the religious education of the young, no religious weekly periodicals, discoursing earnestly of the signs of the times, the demands of the age, the great questions of faith and practice, or giving tidings of the refreshing visits of the Spirit abroad, and thus quickening the sympathies and animating the activities of Christians at home."‡ There were no associations for printing and scattering Bibles, tracts, etc.

* See his " Half-Century Discourse."
† " Memorial Volume."
‡ Deacon Samuel Willis, Judge Samuel Hubbard, and Peter Hobart, Jun., in the " Memorial Volume of the Park-street Church, Boston," p. 130.

During the present century marked progress has
been made in the practical working of the principle
of the universal priesthood of believers; and numerous modifications have been made in the usages and
politics of all the religious denominations, bringing
into prominence and activity Christian men and
women in great moral and spiritual enterprises.
True Christianity, claiming the whole world for its
field, is, in its nature, irrepressible and aggressive.
Almost within the period of a generation social
religious services have not only come to be regarded
as indispensable, but increasingly prominent, often
gathering the largest audiences of the Sabbath.
These meetings are for the most part lively and
spiritual—a great advance upon those of other days
—the few old-time prayers and exhortations having
given place to "a cloud of witnesses" for Christ.
Large numbers of Christian laymen and women are
engaged in religious work in our cities and destitute localities throughout the country.   Religious
services in halls, depots, groves, public squares,
popular watering-places, etc., are held by Young
Men's Christian Associations, and tons of religious
tracts are annually distributed.   The prisons, alms-
houses, and reformatory institutions, are visited,
and Sunday-schools are sustained in them, by lay
workers.   Sunday-schools, conducted by laymen,
become *nuclei* of Churches; systematic religious
visitation is maintained in large centers by pious

women; praying-bands, of young men and older men, conduct series of religious services; and systems of colportage are carried on, by unordained men, through which large quantities of tracts and religious volumes are scattered in the land.

An order of deaconesses, or class of devout women engaged in religious labors, has been recognized in the Protestant Episcopal Church, and the late Triennial Convention authorized the appointment of lay-preachers. The Methodist Episcopal Church has 12,475 local preachers, and all branches of Methodism in the world about eighty thousand.

City missions, almost entirely the work of the present century, are conducted by lay agencies. The Boston City Mission Society (Orthodox Congregational) was founded in 1816; the New York City Mission and Tract Society in 1827; a few others, and but very few, were elsewhere organized at this early period.*

In the great revival of 1830–1832, particularly in connection with the religious labors of Harlan Page and others in New York city, a new interest was awakened in personal efforts for the salvation of individuals, and in city evangelization. But the work slowly progressed, and it is worthy of special notice, that since the year 1850 city mission work throughout the United States has received a much greater

* See "Church Almanac," 1879, p. 27.

impulse, and the amount of money and labor expended has increased beyond all calculation. At the present time no cities are without these agencies, and they are chiefly in the hands of evangelical Protestantism.

"The utilization of lay help," says Charles Mackeson, "to supplement the work of the clergy, is a modern improvement of no slight importance; and, in the Diocese of London alone, has brought into the field 2,788 unpaid laborers, 121 of whom hold the Bishop's license to conduct services for the poor. All these centralized and consolidated agencies may be fairly reckoned as not the least important elements in the progress of religion and philanthropy in London; and not one of them can be said to be superfluous in a condition of society which, unlike that of the continental city, or even of the English provincial town, has led to an almost complete separation of classes, until between the east and west of London, there is literally 'a great gulf fixed;' and it is to bridge over the chasm that the efforts of all who wish well to the race must be directed." *

The Annual Reports of the Boston City Missionary Society, (Orthodox Congregational,) probably the most thoroughly organized, intelligent, and spiritual body of laborers in the United States, furnish the most gratifying exhibits.

* "British Almanac and Companion," 1880, p. 134-5.

Summary for Forty Years, (1840–1880* inclusive.)

Number of religious visits made............................... 1,275,607
" " religious visits made to the sick.............. 182,568
" " tracts distributed............................ 6,960,728
" " Bibles distributed............................ 8,252
" " Testaments distributed........................ 10,516
" " prayer-meetings held.......................... 55,651
" " persons hopefully converted................... 2,169
" " times, pecuniary aid to families.............. 175,437
" " garments given away........................... 176,304
Amount of money received and given to the poor........ $141,461
Amount of money received for the Society.............. $376,099

The following table will show how much more has been done by this society, in the ten years, (1869–1879,) than in ten years prior to 1850 (1841–1850)— a growth similar to that of all city mission societies:

	1841–1850.	1869–1879.
Religious visits made.....................	70,014	404,702
Religious visits to the sick..............	4,792	65,914
Tracts distributed.......................	2,121,251	1,252,641
Bibles distributed.......................	1,448	2,169
Testaments distributed...................	779	4,166
Prayer-meetings held.....................	3,492	17,239
Persons hopefully converted..............	270	771
Pecuniary aid to families, number of times.	7,518	70,365
Garments given away......................	1,300	73,089
Money received and given to the poor.....	$4,666	$66,311
Money received for the Society...........	$39,443	$138,093

These figures show an increase of from five to sevenfold in the labors and beneficence of the latter period over the former.

In the city of New York† the total number of the

* Year ending December 31, 1880.
† See Document No. 20, of N. Y. City Mission Society, 1881.

city missionaries is reckoned at 266, who make 800,000 visits each year. Besides these are hundreds of tract visitors and poor visitors, and other voluntary agents of various Churches and societies, who are continually going about and doing good. There are 118 Protestant missions in this city, where Sabbath-schools, preaching, and other religious and moral services, for adults, or children, or both, are regularly carried on. The latest Census gives 356 Protestant Sabbath-schools, with 88,237 scholars on roll, and an average attendance of 56,187. And of Roman Catholics, Jews, etc., there are 62 Sabbath-schools, having 27,589 scholars on roll, and an average attendance of 81,274. Forty-five Protestant missions are permanently established in suitable commodious chapels, with the Christian ministry and ordinances, and others are rapidly approaching this condition.

The largest of these societies is the New York City Mission, now and for many years under the able superintendence of Mr. Lewis E. Jackson. It has in its employ forty missionaries, who make nearly eighty thousand visits and calls annually, carrying help, sympathy, comfort, and Christian influence to twenty thousand families outside of parochial care. The following are the

RESULTS OF THE YEAR ENDING DECEMBER 31, 1880.

Mission Chapels...................................... 5
Missionaries.. 4c
Missionary visits.............................. 45,910

Missionary calls made and received 33,789
Volunteer visitors and helpers 186
Bibles and Testaments given 760
Books loaned and given 3,079
Children led to Sabbath-schools........................ 1,888
Children led to day-schools............................ 137
Persons induced to join Bible classes 593
Persons persuaded to attend churches and missions........ 4,277
Temperance pledges................................... 1,308
Religious meetings 4,266
Persons restored to Church fellowship 46
Persons united with Churches 261
Three organized Churches.   Whole number received, 1,707,
    present number.................................. 1,012
Four Mission Sabbath-schools, with 2,000 children taught
    during the year.   Average attendance.............. 1,500
Aggregate attendance upon religious services during the year 250,000
1,932 families and 5,581 persons aided ; cash distributed $3,268 95
Tracts distributed................................... 700,000

Results of Fifty-four Years, (1826-1880.*)

Years of missionary labor 1,256
Missionary visits.............................. 2,421,994
Tracts distributed............................. 51,476,740
Bibles and Testaments given to the destitute........ 90,027
Books loaned and given 174,787
Children gathered into Sabbath-schools............ 114,842
Children gathered into day-schools........ 23,667
Persons gathered into Bible classes................ 15,723
Persons induced to attend church.. 257,652
Temperance pledges obtained........ 56,809
Religious meetings held......................... 126,366
Converts united with Evangelical Churches.......... 13,911
Amount expended (fifty-four years)...............$1,217,194 85

The following figures, prepared by Mr. Lewis E. Jackson, show the character of the mission-field in

* Chiefly since 1835.

New York city. Other large cities are rapidly approximating similar exhibits.

POPULATION.—The population of the city of New York, according to the United States' Census of 1880, is 1,206,577.

SEXES.—Of the population of the city, 590,762 are males, and 615,815 are females.

TRANSIENT POPULATION.—The transient or floating population may be estimated as follows: in any one day, on an average, we may suppose, there are of immigrants, temporarily stopping in the city, 5,000; of seamen and boatmen, 5,000; of visitors at hotels, 10,000; of visitors at boarding and lodging-houses, 10,000; or in all say 30,000.

NATIVITIES.—727,743 persons were born in the United States; and 478,834 persons are from foreign countries of forty different nationalities.

CHURCHES AND ACCOMMODATIONS.—There are 489 churches, chapels, and missions of all kinds, with accommodations for 375,000 persons.

PROTESTANT CHURCHES AND ACCOMMODATIONS.—There are 396 Protestant places of worship, with accommodations for 275,000.

PROTESTANT CHURCHES AND COMMUNICANTS.—There are 278 regularly incorporated Protestant Churches, with an average membership of 300, which would give a total of 83,400 communicants.

SABBATH-SCHOOLS AND ATTENDANCE.—There are 418 Sabbath-schools of all denominations, with an attendance of 115,826 pupils.

PROTESTANT SABBATH-SCHOOLS.—There are 356 Protestant Sabbath-schools, with an attendance of 88,237 pupils.

YOUNG MEN AND YOUNG WOMEN.—The number of males between the ages of 15 and 30 years, is 145,749. The number of females between the ages of 15 and 30 years, is 172,777. Probably 30,000 of the latter are servants.

CHILDREN BETWEEN FIVE AND FOURTEEN.—The number of children in the city between the ages of five and fourteen is 204,275. The number from five to eighteen years of age is 270,496.

PUBLIC INSTRUCTION.—In the schools under the Board of Education there is an average attendance of 130,076.

PRIVATE SCHOOLS, ETC.—In parochial schools, industrial schools, private schools, colleges, etc., there must be 35,000 more.

WHOLE NUMBER AT SCHOOL.—In the public schools and private schools, etc., there are probably 165,076 regularly in attendance. The number of pupils who attend these schools for a longer or shorter period is over 250,000.

STREET CHILDREN.—Children growing up without any instruction are variously estimated, but may be set down at about 10,000.

City mission organizations are now universal in all American cities, and all of them the growth of the last sixty years.

The general home missionary work of the country has enlisted a large amount of lay and clerical talent, and developed astonishing results. The unparalleled increase of our population since 1790 has created extraordinary demands upon the Christian activity of the American Churches. With an average yearly gain in population more than three times as large as in any European country, new villages and cities springing up as by magic, and the inhabitants spreading over an immense territorial area, it has been incumbent upon the Churches to furnish the new communities with religious watch-care and instruction. Large masses of ignorant and unevangelized people from other lands—Papists and Rationalists from Europe, and heathen from Asia—have crowded to our shores, and the utmost diligence and sterling virtue have been required to preserve the land from misrule and ruin. How have these moral and religious necessities been met? Has the spiritual vitality of the Churches been sufficient for these demands?

The great revivals of religion extending through
the nation at the opening of the nineteenth century,
followed by successive waves of spiritual impulse in
the subsequent decades, prepared the Churches to
appreciate the necessities of the situation, and inspired them with the requisite spirit of self-sacrific-
ing labor.   Home Missionary Societies, the immediate fruits of the new revival era, sprang up, multiplying auxiliaries and laborers, and spreading
through thousands of localities.   In reviewing the
century we cannot fail to recognize the profound
significance of those providential movements which
turned back the dark tide of infidelity spreading
over the land at the close of the last century, and
prepared the way, in the American Churches, by
which the nation has been religiously permeated
and strengthened to endure so well the severe strain
from the large exotic and heterogeneous masses absorbed in its population.

The full record of the labors of these Home Missionary Societies, about twenty-five in number, not
including City Societies, would fill many pages with
most significant statistics and evidences of immense spiritual force.   Their toils and triumphs
cannot be matched in either ancient or modern
times.

The following partial aggregates, taken from official reports, of Home Missionary Societies, combine
such data as can be obtained for a single year, (1879:)

Ministers, licentiates, colporteurs, and teachers employed
by eighteen societies................................... 9,033
Localities supplied, reported by eight societies........... 9,365
Conversions and additions to the Churches reported by
nine societies.......................... 26,918
Churches organized in one year reported by five socie-
ties.. 332
Sunday-schools organized in one year reported by four so-
cieties. 4,621
Sunday-school scholars reported by ten societies 548,569
Time spent in labor, by missionaries, in one year, reported
by seven societies, equal to ....(years) 1,906
Religious visits in one year reported by missionaries of five
societies.. 920,202
Prayer-meetings held by missionaries of three societies in
one year 17,131

The system of colportage, inaugurated by the
American Tract Society in 1841, has been another
important lay agency, exhibiting, in a practical form,
the vital religious force of the Churches. In 1850
their number had increased to 508, and their labors
were extended to the German, Irish, French, Welsh,
Norwegian, and Spanish populations, both Protestant and Papal, in all portions of the land, but especially throughout the Mississippi Valley. They
went forth from house to house, selling religious
books wherever practicable, bestowing them gratuitously among the poor, accompanying their visits
with religious conversation and prayer, holding religious meetings, forming Sunday-schools, promoting temperance, and in many other ways advancing
the kingdom of God.

The following partial summaries of the Home
Missionary and Colportage work, full of instructive
significance, will be pondered with pleasure and
profit:

RELIGIOUS VISITS.

By missionaries of the Baptist Home Missionary Society in forty years, (1840–1880)	1,667,813
By agents or colporteurs of Baptist Publication Society in fifty-six years, (1824–1880)	664,580
By colporteurs of American Tract Society in thirty-nine years, (1841–1880)	12,360,647
By colporteurs of American Bible Society in fourteen years, (1866–1880)	6,826,894
By colporteurs of Presbyterian Board of Publication in twenty-five years, (1855–1880)	2,469,573
Total visits	23,989,507

PRAYER-MEETINGS HELD.

By missionaries of Baptist Home Missionary Society in forty years, (1840–1880)	385,141
By colporteurs of the Baptist Board of Publication in twenty-six years, (1854–1880)	53,086
By colporteurs of the American Tract Society in thirty-nine years, (1841–1880)	412,109
Total by agents of three Boards	850,336

ADDITIONS TO CHURCHES BY PROFESSION OF FAITH.

By missionaries of American Home Missionary Society in fifty-four years, (1826–1880)	291,770
By missionaries of Presbyterian Home Missionary Board in eleven years, (1870–1880)	82,719
By missionaries of American Baptist Home Missionary Society in forty-eight years, (1832–1880)	84,081
Total additions by agents of three Boards	458,570

RELIGIOUS VOLUMES GIVEN AWAY.

By colporteurs of Presbyterian Board of Publication in
twenty-six years, (1854–1880) 940,483
By agents and colporteurs of American Baptist Publication Board in fifty-six years, (1824–1880)........... 92,139
By colporteurs of American Tract Society in thirty-nine
years, (1841–1880)................................. 2,942,485
By colporteurs of American Bible Society in fourteen
years, (1866–1880,) (Bibles and Testaments)........ 941,685

Total by agents of four Boards......(volumes) 4,916,792

PAGES OF RELIGIOUS TRACTS GIVEN AWAY.

By agents and colporteurs of Baptist Publication Board
in fifty-six years 6,937,445
By colporteurs of Presbyterian Board of Publication in
twenty-six years................................... 63,687,107

Total pages of tracts by two Boards.......... 70,624,552

Other Boards have gratuitously distributed large
quantities of tracts, but we are unable to tabulate
them. The American Tract Society has published,
from the beginning, 2,852,129,263 pages of tracts,
besides 5,860,260,893 pages of religious books—
leaves of the tree of life, "for the healing of the
nations."

YEARS OF LABOR PERFORMED.

By missionaries of American Home Missionary Society in
fifty-four years.................................... 34,423
By missionaries of Baptist Home Missionary Society in forty-
eight years, (incomplete)......................... 5,297
By missionaries of Presbyterian Board of Home Missions in
eleven years...................................... 9,453
By colporteurs of Presbyterian Board of Publication in thirty
years... 1,153

23

By agents and colporteurs of Baptist Board of Publication
in forty years, (incomplete) 719
By colporteurs of American Tract Society in thirty-nine
years.. 5,313

Total by agents of six Boards...........(years) 56,358

These are only partial exhibits of the spiritual activities of the American Churches during the last half century. If the full statistics could be gathered they would thrill and amaze us. What we have here gathered are highly significant, and indicate religious activities of incalculable proportions, almost wholly unknown until within the last eighty years. They are unmistakable evidences of the deep spiritual vitality of the modern Churches, and their ardent aggressive force.

Young Men's Christian Associations, also, have become active factors in the evangelization of the masses. Wholly the products of the last third of a century, they have come to number 2,113 Associations in the whole world. Australia has 13; Austria, 1; Belgium, 15; France, 65; Germany, 293; Great Britain and Ireland, 295; Holland, 406; India, 2; Italy, 6; Japan, 2; Madagascar, 1; North America, 792; Sandwich Islands, 1; South America, 3; Spain, 8; Switzerland, 204; and Syria, 4. In our own country, in 1880, 506 out of the 792 Associations report 62,514 members; 96 Associations exist in colleges, with a membership of 4,268; 58 own buildings and property amounting to $2,400,350:

at 72 points they perform work among railroad men; 97 daily and 137 weekly prayer-meetings are held; 105 open-air meetings are held; 46 hold Sunday-schools; 125 hold cottage prayer-meetings; 400 hold meetings in jails, hospitals, etc.; 73 provide situations for 8,473 persons; 61 sustain educational classes; 120 hold Bible classes for young men; 146 own libraries valued at $145,555, etc.*

In some of the large cities the members of these Associations number from 2,000 to 4,000. In five years one Association distributed eleven tons of religious tracts. The non-professional character of these lay-workers gives them access to some who would reject the professional visitations of the clergy. They prosecute evangelistic labors, literally fulfilling the command, "Go out into the highways and hedges, and compel them to come in." In the larger cities they go into saloons, billiard parlors, concert halls, "to the very borders of hell," to rescue their fellow-men from ruin. They visit hotels, boarding-houses, and workshops to find out strangers coming into the city, to invite them to the Association rooms, and shield them from the snares which surround unsophisticated youth.

Young Women's Christian Associations are also

* See "Year Book of Young Men's Christian Associations" for 1880, by International Committee, New York city.

performing a similar work; and the Woman's Christian Temperance Union, starting in 1873, and now numbering 1,572 auxiliaries and 31,630 members, is a distinctively religious movement, reporting last year 15,085 prayer-meetings held in seven States,* besides other phases of practical effort.

In addition to these recently developed forms of Christian activity, so numerous and potential in the home field, and wholly unlike any religious effort in former times, numerous Foreign Missionary Societies have been organized in Europe and America, all but seven within the present century, and forty within the last fifty years, sustaining in the foreign field 6,696 ordained missionaries and 33,856 assistants, ministering to at least one million communicants in mission Churches, and three millions of adherents who have renounced paganism.† Such are the inroads made into the empire of pagan darkness within the last century, and mostly within the last eighty years. Never, since the apostles' age, has the Christian Church so deeply felt her obligation to convert the world as during the last thirty years.

And yet, with all these new and manifold activities every-where bearing ample fruits of Christian beneficence, we are told that the spiritual vitality of American Protestantism has sadly declined.

* Report for 1880.
† See Table XXXVIII (Appendix) for fuller statistics.

Such is the blindness of those who, having eyes, see not.

The progress of pecuniary benevolence in the Churches is another evidence of advancing spirituality. It shows the overmastering power of Christian love in the human heart, breaking down its selfishness, and drawing it out in practical offerings for the good of others. It is a crucial test of real religious progress.

It is not possible for us now to appreciate the stern contest with covetousness which the founders of the Foreign and Home Missionary organizations fought in the first twenty-five years of this century. The standard of giving was very low, while the number of the givers was much smaller relatively. The fathers tell tales of penuriousness in those days which now seem scarcely probable. Dr. Harris' magnificent prize essay on " Mammon," published in 1836, since followed by numerous other valuable books and tracts on systematic giving, and floods of sermons and homilies on the same subject, have exerted a powerful influence for pecuniary liberality. A change for good is very perceptible, but the battle is not fully fought.

We have collected and tabulated summaries of the receipts of the Foreign and Home Missionary Boards of the evangelical Churches of the United States. Arranged in a table, they constitute an instructive object lesson.

AMOUNTS RAISED FOR FOREIGN AND HOME MISSIONS, (1810–1880.)

Inclusive.	Foreign Missions.*	Home Missions.†
1810–1819..........	$206,210	......
1820–1829..........	745,718	$233,826
1830–1839..........	2,885,839	2,342,712
1840–1849..........	5,078,922	3,062,354
1850–1859..........	8,427,284	8,080,109
1860–1869..........	13,074,129	21,015,719‡
1870–1880	24,861,482 §	31,272,154 §
Additional..........	2,349,362 ‖	6,269,927 ‖
Total	$57,628,946	$72,276,801

We look with great satisfaction upon these grand aggregates—for Foreign Missions, $57,628,946 ; for Home Missions, $72,276,801, raised for these two leading benevolences. For Foreign Missions almost nothing was raised in America until since 1810, and only two or three Home Missionary Boards were organized until after 1800, and even those were very small, and the scope of their operations was narrow. There was some unorganized home-missionary work prior to 1800, but there has been vastly more of this kind of work since 1800, which is wholly unrepresented in the above table. All

* Including $3,580,775, by the Woman's Missionary Boards.

† Including the Seamen's Friend Society, the American Sunday-School Union, Young Men's Christian Associations, and Freedmen's Aid Societies, all of which do home-missionary work ; but not including City Missions, because only a few of the statistics of the latter can be obtained with full satisfaction.

‡ Including money expended by the Christian Commission as the agent largely of the Young Men's Christian Associations.

§ Eleven years.

‖ Sums reported in the aggregate, but not by periods.

the Sunday-school Boards and the Religious Publication Boards do much home-mission work which is not included in our figures. The American Tract Society and the denominational Tract Societies are all engaged in it almost wholly, but the foregoing table does not comprise them. The figures given, therefore, show $129,905,747 raised in the United States in seven decades for two charities almost unknown on this continent until this century.

The table shows that of the whole amount (omitting the "additional," which cannot be divided into periods) collected during the seven decades for these two charities, $106,730,877, or eighty-eight per cent., was raised during the last thirty years—the period over which many people croak so dolefully. In these thirty years American Protestantism has raised more money for purely missionary purposes than the Protestants of all Christendom raised in the previous three centuries, for the same objects.

It is an encouraging fact that during the last decade, in which we have suffered so much and so long from financial embarrassments, these two grand charities of American Protestantism have not declined, but have averaged $5,103,057 yearly, which is more than three times as much as the yearly average from 1850 to 1859. These facts show the abiding devotion of Christian people to these two great causes, in times of financial stringency and reverse.

Taking these two benevolences as a fair index of the benevolent spirit of the Churches, and we find that the pecuniary liberality has increased at a rate a little more than from 16 to 51, or little more than threefold. But the aggregate wealth of the United States increased, from 1850 to 1870, from $7,135,780,228 to $30,068,518,507, or four-and-one-fifth fold. The increase in giving, if this is a fair test, has not quite kept pace with the increase of the national wealth. And yet it is undoubtedly true that the increase in pecuniary benevolence has *more nearly* corresponded with the advance in national wealth than at any former period. During the same period the value of the Church property of the denominations represented in the above tables, (the Evangelical Protestant Churches,) as given by the United States Census, increased from $71,275,909 in 1850 to $271,477,391 in 1870, nearly fivefold ; and we do not doubt that the money invested in collegiate and academic institutions during the same time has increased still more. These things show that the Christian people are advancing well in the right direction ; and we should be stimulated to greater progress.

In this almost infinite number of wayside laborers, is it strange that some are not profound thinkers, mature Christians, or discreet actors? Are they not deepening, maturing, and learning wisdom, as others have done, by the old process of experience? Some may have erred in carrying the principle of the priesthood of believers to an extreme, discarding the Christian ministry as a divinely instituted order of the Church; some local communities have suffered from religious decline; some Churches have died out, from change of population, unwisdom, possibly from more culpable causes; some are in a transitional condition, occasioning anxiety in regard to the results; some sad cases of collapse and ruin have occurred in men occupying high religious positions; some futile attempts at reform have gone upon record; some abuses still survive all denunciations; some outbursts of religious enthusiasm have left individuals and communities almost barren of spiritual fruitage; and the spirit of worldliness is often dominant in the Churches—a fatal impediment to progress.

All these things, and many more still, exist with mischievous tendencies. They are imperfections incidental to human agents. Some wonder there are not more of them; while others wonder that Christianity can endure so much imperfection and still stand and work so powerfully. It is because of its inherent conserving power, and its immense vitality. The healthy body can throw off great quantities of devitalized matter, resist malaria, heal wounds, and grow strong under heavy strains.

Winters, tornadoes, storms, and devastating currents do not stop the course of nature.

Is it said, "There is much rootless piety," an "incessant cultivation of sentiment," a "reckless popularization" of sacred things, and "floods of namby-pamby talk?" Be it so. But how slight are these blemishes on the great mass of true piety; and how much less offensive than the whine, the nasal twang, the cant, the rant, the abnormal ecstasy, the jerking, the selfish exclusiveness, the superstition, and the torpid inactivity, which characterized much of the piety of other days. Religion is less sanctimonious, has less of "holy tone," but is not less genuine and worthy of respect, but more so, on that account. There is relatively more "well-rooted" piety, more intelligent religious affection, more faithful testimony for Christ.

Is it still insisted that much of the work done is routine work; that "sentiment substitutes pleasant songs and pensive looks for self-denial and arduous service;" and that an antinomian spirit often seeks "to rectify a dishonest ledger by a prayer, or gild a malignant temper by a holy tone, so that to too many modern religionists the words of Hood may be applied, without caricature—

> ' Rogue that I am, I cheat, I lie, I steal ;
> But who can say I am not pious ? "

There is a measure of truth in all these allegation. But why are these things so?

"It is because there is so much genuine religious activity, and so many new and taking methods of work and worship. The penumbra is child of the light. The evil is real; its growth is alarming; not, however, as threatening the existence or perpetuity of the Church of Christ, but as portending grievous falls for many true believers, and the stumbling of many sinners, who, when they fall, will not rise again." *

Nor should it be overlooked that the common soil of humanity was never before so widely plowed by the Church. In large circles, among large masses, it is being plowed and sowed for the first time on purely voluntary conditions. No hierarchy nor civil power interposes to exert a steadying or sustaining influence in times of fluctuation or decline; nor does an overshadowing formalism throw its concealing mantle over irregularities and defects. But we have a type of piety incalculably higher in true elements of personal godliness than has been furnished by any other age, or under hierarchical or State conditions.

Is it said that the influence of religion is less marked than formerly? When religion has conquered its position, and become an established working force, it cannot be expected to produce such a sensation as when it first enters the field; yet

---

* See book entitled, " The Light : Is it Waning ?" Boston, 1879, pp. 81, 82, etc.

it does not follow that there is any real declension or loss of power. There have been times of much physical demonstration, and brief periods of exceptional spasmodic fervor, but such phenomena do not measure Christianity. Paroxysms may attract attention, but do not indicate normal progress. Genuine religious progress is indicated by moral renovations. In numberless instances, even within the last twenty years, or the last ten years, under many American preachers, gospel truth has exhibited a potency not excelled in any other days, reaching and transforming large numbers of the most abandoned persons, and proving as all-controlling in the life, as when Peter preached, and the disciples had " all things in common."

It is often declared that the contrast between the Church and the world is less perceptible than formerly, and therefore the Church has degenerated. Christianity has largely transformed Christendom—morally, intellectually, and socially—and, therefore, it cannot look as bright on the new background as on the old. Her very success has dimmed the relief. Christianity has " softened and shaded the world to her own likeness." How different is American society now from eighty years ago, and from the Roman world when Christianity entered it ; and yet the distinguishing characteristics of Church members are the same as in the days of the apostles. They bear the same marks of attachment to

Christ, and the same evidences of genuine experience are exhibited.

Rev. Orville Dewey, D. D., says: " When irreligious skeptics, learned or worldly wise, tell us that religion is to die out, we can't think much of it. There is a foolish talk, I sometimes hear, about faith's having been greater in the dark Middle Ages than it is now; credulity it should be called. Faith, true faith, deepens as thought, reasoning, feeling, the heart's great searching, goes deeper. It is so to-day. As knowledge grows, as culture advances, there are more and more men whose souls are fraught full with a swelling and undying sense of religion; who seek after God, after the living God, and feel that all the interest of life is gone if that great all-hallowing Presence is gone from the world. No; religions may die out of the world, but not religion. Forms, usages, false ideas of religion, have changed and will change, but not the central reality." *

Rev. Dr. Henry W. Bellows has said of the widely diffused and operative influence of Christianity in our times, " Christianity is happily quite as much in the world as in the visible Church. Its leaven is working, never so powerfully as now, in politics, literature, life. . . . A great part of the piety once expended in emotion, and profession, and dogmatic belief has gone into practical action. It has passed

* " Unitarian Review," January, 1877, pp. 66.

out of the sanctuary into the workshop; is no longer exclusively in the religious organ, but in the general organism; is not to be seen in the shape of pure leaven, but in the lightness and wholesomeness of the leaf. Religious faith, which takes form in gorgeous cathedrals, gay festivals, and splendid rituals, may indicate the exclusive predominance for an age of certain powerful religious ideas, but by no means indicate the prevalence of equality, justice, truth, self-respect, or private worth. Protestantism buries its Christian ideas in secret places, in private hearts and consciences, and they come up in domestic, social, and political rights and graces. Roman Catholicism places hers in golden chalices, and under embroidered cloths upon the altar, to be worshiped; and they remain, not without influence, but essentially barren and powerless for the advancement of society.

"We cannot admit, therefore, that the Christian religion, or Protestant Christianity, so far as it is the Christian religion, is declining, or waning in influence, or demands any new forces, or has failed to accomplish the expectations of its Founder, or the reasonable hopes of his faithful disciples. We cannot concede that the doubt or question of certain theological ideas long associated with Christianity, which now prevails, is any discredit to the truth or reality of the Gospel. We seem to see the faith of Jesus of Nazareth every day emerging from the cerements in which it has been buried, like Lazarus in his tomb." *

The multiplication of schools, books, newspapers, and, especially, religious literature, and the loud demand for universal illumination, prove that the mind of Christendom is rising, and going forth, on a scale and with an impulse never before witnessed. How mighty and cumulative the moral and spiritual forces exhibited in our day! Never before was the moral consciousness of the Churches so quickened, or their exertions, at home and abroad, so amazing, or so fruitful. Islands have been born as in a day. New nations have come suddenly to the light, embraced the faith, maintained their own preachers, builded their own churches, and furnished martyrs for Christ. In a single year, one missionary society received eighteen thousand seekers after the truth; another baptized nine thousand converts, six thousand in one day; and another received six thousand to membership. A hundred thousand pariahs are numbered among the followers of Christ. Forty thousand savages are Christianized in Fiji. Five hundred thousand spiritual converts praise God in mission churches. Four hundred thousand pupils study the divine word in mission schools. Polygamy, the suttee, and widow celibacy, are doomed all over Hindustan. Schools and colleges are rising; and scores of presses are printing millions of pages

* "Unitarian Review," May, 1876, pp. 466–7.

a year in the heathen world. Christian civilization has permeated heathen society, and called forth apostles of truth out of the bosom of paganism; and the Church of Christ has seized the strongholds of the enemy, and established a base line of operations throughout the heathen world. Forward, is the motto, all along the vast lines of Christ's militant host. It is an era of sublime progress, answering the long-repeated prayer, "Thy kingdom come."

A century and a half ago the outlook for Christianity was dreary enough. The science, the philosophy, the culture of the age, were all against it; little spirituality, only as a feeble dying flame, was left; and its aggressive power was reduced to a minimum. Since then, it has reached its greatest known maximum. We have seen, that from the days of the Apostles down to near the middle of the last century, if we except some remarkable examples among the Moravians, the world has known nothing of such spiritual activities as have been since developed, chiefly within the last eighty years, and many of them within thirty years. Piety has come out from the cloisters and gone forth among the masses, in imitation of "Him who went about doing good." Never was the life of Jesus more fully illustrated, in the average lives of Christians, than in the United States, during the last quarter of a century. Never was there a more intelligent spirituality.

The habit of some minds of investing every thing in the past with a halo of glory, is inconsiderate and superficial. No judicial mind will do this. Previous ages do not furnish parallels of what this age has witnessed. What then is the significance of such extraordinary and augmenting religious activity, if it be not a deep and deepening religious vitality? Such tangible evidences of extraordinary spiritual vitality, and the wonderful increase of more than nine and a half millions of communicants, in eighty years, in the evangelical Churches in the United States, far outrunning relatively the growth of the population, are two cognate facts, mutually supplementing each other, as irrefragable crucial tests. Such remarkable religious phenomena must have for their cause a powerful underlying religious force. No other inference is philosophical.

Christ reigning over a territory hitherto unrivaled in its extent; great benevolences awakened and sustained by a deeper religious devotion; rapidly multiplying home, city, and foreign mission stations, the outcome of an intelligent consecration; magnificent departments of Christian labor, many of them heretofore unknown, and none of them ever before so numerous, so vast, or so restlessly active ; the great heart of the Church, pulsating with an unequaled velocity; the fires of evangelism burning with unwonted brightness on multiplied altars; and a religious literature such as has characterized no other

24

age, replete with life and power, eminently practical, intensely fervid, and richly evangelical, ema-
nating from her presses: all conspire to show, more
than ever before, that God has a living Church
within the Churches, towering amid them all in its
mightiness, the strength, the support, and central
life of all; and that an increasing number of true
believers are "walking with him in white"—a grand
constellation of light and purity—a bright Milky
Way from earth to heaven.

IV. STATISTICAL EXHIBITS.

——•——

CHAPTER I.

STATISTICAL SCIENCE.

Preliminary Observations.

IV.—STATISTICAL EXHIBITS.

CHAPTER I.

STATISTICAL SCIENCE.

IT is the habit of some persons to discard religious statistics, and to complain that an undue importance is attached to them. " Of what consequence," they ask, " is it that three new churches are built every day, so long as the ideas they are supposed to represent are fast dying out?" " Some denominations are so infatuated with their numerical growth and preponderance, that they are in danger of losing sight of those higher, and deeper, and more potent elements and forces which Christianity represents." " Give us the Gospel with its moral and spiritual forces, and we care not who holds the book of numbers."

No mathematics, certainly, are cunning enough to fully calculate the work of Christianity, and sum up its effects as it goes through the world, moderating its coldness, calling forth countless forms of life, activity, and beauty, purifying its fountains, and filling it with verdure and fragrance and music. And yet it is also true that there are no phenomena which may not be approximately enumerated, and the more distinct and positive they are, the more definitely may they be numbered and aggregated.

"For those who do not believe in the permanency and the importance of the Church," says one of the most cultured religious editors, "as an external institution, it is well enough to talk contentedly about the indirect influence of literature and the leavening effected by opinions as they percolate through society in secret ways. But if the Church is a lasting and indispensable agency we must be seeing to it, not merely that the community is liberalized, but that Church institutions are organized and ideas crystallized in organic forms. . . . Christianity, from the days of the apostles, has been a propagandism of Christ's truth by means of Church organizations. The spirit of Christianity alone is not a Church ; and without a Church it degenerates and loses itself in vague aspirations." He, therefore, calls upon his brethren to strive to disseminate their principles, and "show at the end of each year a plain and positive gain in numbers, faith, and influence." *

In previous pages, we have carefully examined the question of religious progress in its intellectual, moral, social, and spiritual aspects. It is, therefore, fitting that attention now be directed to the more concrete numerical forms in which the progress and

* "Liberal Christian," 1871.

results of Christianity may be traced in the world. Positive ideas assume a clear, distinct, differentiated form ; and the positive elements in a religion determine its character, durability, influence, power, and destiny. It is the positive elements which a man receives, and not what he rejects, that assimilate and organize themselves into his fibers and faculties, and reveal themselves in concrete forms in his life. This is the law of growth in spiritual, social, and ecclesiastical life. Ecclesiastical success is the development of religious principles in organic forms, according to laws of religious growth.

" Influential Churches and sects are never built up. Men cannot put their heads and hands together and manufacture a religion. They cannot create permanent and potential organizations ; for the creative, organizing force is behind and above the human will, in ideas and sentiments which at best they can but perceive and lay hold of, and flows down into the spirit of man through faith, taking possession of intellect and imagination, making men the keys through which its ideal harmonies are poured into history. Denominations are not designed and constructed by human carpentry ; a great truth takes possession of a multitude of men through their faith in it, binds them into a body, becomes the informing spirit of their organization, and puts forth its power through all available channels of influence. A religion is the crystallization of a great idea, a spiritual force, in the history of the race." *

Viewed in such a light, ecclesiastical statistics, like moral, social, commercial, and political statistics, have a distinct significance. Their importance has been enhanced by the recent studies of exact science. Comté and Buckle gave an impulse to statistical inquiries, and they are now becoming "a specialty" in Europe and in America. " Statisticians rank as a class of *savants*, with important organizations or ' societies,' in the principal cities of Europe, and the results of their researches are highly appreciated by the governments.

" Difficult as statistics must be—liable to the greatest errors, in results, by the smallest errors of fact or number—they have nevertheless attained the truest proof of scientific character, namely, that the statisticians can *predict*. Science is the ascertainment of laws ; the knowledge of laws enables us to foretell results. This is the test of a scientific theory—the distinction of truth from speculation. And this the statisticians can now claim in a remarkable manner. They can tell the averages of births and deaths for a given year in a given population, how many suicides, how many misdirected letters, etc. And they can thus predict without denying the moral freedom of man, for freedom itself, rightly defined, is compatible with law."

* Editor of the " Liberal Christian."

European journals have lately published the results of the extensive researches of M. Bertillon, of Brussels, so distinguished in this department of inquiry. Elaborately investigating questions of social, domestic, and physical ethics, by the statistical classification and analysis of concrete facts, he has demonstrated that marriage is favorable to longevity and morality, and that married people are less liable to suicide, assassination, theft, and insanity; thus showing, by the aid of figures, a scientific basis of morals, and attesting the truth of Christian morality.

Modern science measures material forces, subjecting even the more subtle elements — steam, gas, heat, light, the winds, and the atmosphere—to accurate registration. We have noticed the great progress made in collecting and classifying statistics representing moral and social phenomena, in making generalizations and deductions from such bases, and determining questions of moral and social progress. Nor is the realm of spiritual religion so hidden and intangible that it is impossible to measure the forces which move and dominate it; for it has its exact phenomena, its numerical representations, its distinctly cut channels, its streams of varying depth and velocity, registering water-marks all along their pathways. The United States Census, the Annual Year Books and Minutes of the American Churches, and the Annual Reports of the various organizations connected with them, combine with increasing care and exactness, from year to year, carefully collected data, reliably representing the changing phases of our religious life, and enabling us to determine questions of religious progress. No department of statistical inquiry requires more care and discrimination, closer attention to incidental and collateral facts, or the application of severer crucial tests. But, with due attention, impartial, broad analysis and rigid synthesis, reliable conclusions may be reached, definitely determining the religious status.

The most noticeable objective feature of apostolic Christianity was its aggressive impulse, indicating a powerful latent force. The facts are so familiar as to need little repetition. The Pentecost registered three thousand converts; the close of the first century, five hundred thousand; the close of the third century, five million. The conversion of Constantine soon followed, and Christianity ceased to work from a purely moral and spiritual impulse, its spread being henceforth dependent upon the civil power.

The reformation under Luther, at first partly ecclesiastical and partly spiritual, soon became of a more mixed character in the great political revolutions it inaugurated; and one hundred and fifty years ago Protestantism had lost its aggressive spiritual force. The Wesleyan movement, starting in 1739, and closing the century with four hundred and fifty preachers and one hundred and twenty thousand communicants, in England, inspired new life into British and American Protestantism; but its influence was not much felt in the United States until near the close of the century. Some persons, not properly informed in regard to this matter, consider the progress of Protestantism since that time as small and feeble, both in Europe and America, dragging slowly behind the growth of the population.

The statistics of this progress presented to the public have been for the most part fragmentary, lacking completeness, only partially covering given periods, or failing in some way to cover such points as are necessary to justify clear and legitimate deductions. It is to be regretted that for some of the earlier periods in the history of Protestantism no exact statistics are now obtainable; and it must be confessed that, for even the more recent periods, we have only partial statistics of Protestantism in Great Britain and the continent of Europe, and must content ourselves with incomplete or approximate statistics and, in some cases, mere estimates. But the estimates are such as have been made by those who have intelligently studied the question, and are worthy of high consideration.

For the United States, however, within this century, our statistics are as nearly exact as can reason-

ably be expected, and have been derived almost
entirely from official sources—the Year Books and
Annual Minutes of the various denominations, and
the United States Census.   They are the results of
some years of extensive, painstaking study, involving much correspondence and numerous consultations with representative men of the Churches.
Careful discrimination, also, has been exercised;
collateral facts and modifying circumstances have
been duly considered; and periods selected, for
comparison, as free as possible from abnormal influences.

As to the *relative* progress of Christianity, compared with the total population of the world in former centuries, it is impossible to calculate.   No trustworthy estimates of the total population of the earth,
until within the present century, can be found.
Malté Brun (d. 1826) estimated the whole number
to be six hundred and forty-two million, and M.
Adrien Balbi, (d. 1848) at seven hundred and thirty-
seven millions.   About 1850 it was commonly reckoned at one billion.   But it is probable that all these
estimates were defective, little better than guesses.
Sufficient data did not then exist, had not been, and
could not be, collected, for a satisfactory basis of
calculation.

" Owing to the progress of the science of statistics," says Professor Schem, " the population of the
globe can now be estimated with a degree of proba-

bility with which, as we see in the light of modern science, estimates made in former times have no claim whatever. All of the countries of Europe, with the exception of Turkey, most of the countries of America, and the European colonies, with a number of independent States in other large divisions of the globe, from time to time, take an official census, which establishes the actual population with a certainty, which, it seems, leaves hardly any room for considerable improvement. . . . In the countries in which no official census has as yet been taken, the researches in regard to the number of the inhabitants made by learned travelers give us at least figures vastly superior, in point of trustworthiness, to those found in geographical works of an earlier date. The famous geographical establishment of Perthes, in Gotha, Germany, has for several years been publishing a periodical specially devoted to the most recent information relating to the area of all the divisions and States of the globe, where the results of the entire literature of the world relating to this subject are carefully garnered. and where every figure can be traced to the source, official or inofficial, from which it has been derived."

"The greater accuracy obtained for the statistics of populations has, of course, enabled us to estimate more correctly the population professing the various creeds. Most of the states include in the census questions one in regard to the religious profession. Where this is not done, as in the United States, in England, and Scotland, most of the religious denominations publish annual accounts of adult membership, of number of Churches and ministers, and other facts from which inferences as to the total population, which more or less is influenced and controlled by the doctrinal tenets of a particular religious denomination, may be made. It is interesting to observe, in the religious statistics of those States which include the religious profession of the inhabitants in the official census, the small number of persons who avow themselves as atheists. Thus, in Prussia, which, by friends as well as by foes, is sometimes looked upon as the El Dorado of atheists and opponents to the belief in a personal God, avowed atheists can only be looked for in the column of "persons of unknown religions," who number 4,495, and free religions, of whom there were 2,531. Thus no more than about seven thousand in a total population of 24,600,000 made a statement that might cause them to be looked upon as atheists. In France 81,951 persons were returned as "without religion" or "religion unknown," in a total population of 36,000,000. In the Dominion of Canada, according to the official census of 1871, of a total population of 3,486,000 only twenty persons claimed to be atheists, 409 deists, and 5,144 to have no religion. Facts like these indicate that, however large the number of persons may be who are indifferent in religious matters, or have discarded a belief in a personal God and in Christianity, the population of the Christian countries continues to be almost a unit in its outward connection with Christianity. This includes the Christian character, more or less explicit, of laws, of customs, of literature, and of education. Thus the countries of Europe, of America, and Australia may be looked upon as representatives of the Christian religion and of Christian civilization to as high a degree as at any former period of their history." *

With these preliminary observations, we proceed to notice the progress of Christianity since the dawn of the Reformation of the sixteenth century.

In doing this we have rigidly discarded transient newspaper statistics, because liable to many inaccuracies from misprint and otherwise, and have closely adhered to official documents and standard authorities. Even these have been scrutinized and compared, and personal conferences and letters have drawn from authors and compilers necessary attestations and explanations. Many items of statistics which have passed current have been thrown aside, as unworthy of confidence.

Nevertheless, notwithstanding entire accuracy has been laboriously sought for, we dare not affirm that we have always succeeded in attaining it: but the

---

" Methodist Quarterly Review," Jan., 1876, pp. 154, 155.

figures given are believed to be close approxima-
tions, sufficiently correct to enable us to make intelligent comparisons of religious progress.   They are
the best available exhibits.   The variety of forms
in which different religious bodies prepare their statistics has occasioned much trouble, and prevents
entire uniformity in tabulating.   But every year
brings some improvement, and before another decade shall pass away the ecclesiastical statistics will
furnish materials for more exact study.   When those
who have the care of ecclesiastical year-books and
registries come more distinctly to realize that every
unit figure represents an immortal soul, they will
be more careful in their work, and the distrust of
Church statistics will give way to confidence.

CHAPTER II.

RELIGIOUS PROGRESS AND STATUS.

PROTESTANTISM AND ROMANISM.

In Europe.
In South America.
In Mexico.
In the British Dominion.
In Portions of the U. S. formerly Papal.

25

CHAPTER II.

RELIGIOUS PROGRESS AND STATUS.

PROTESTANTISM AND ROMANISM.

STATISTICIANS are nearly agreed that in the year 1500 Europe had a population of about 100,000,000,* all Roman Catholic, except the major portions of Russia, Turkey, Greece, and the Ionian Isles, in which the Mohammedan and Greek religions prevailed. In Central and Western Europe there were few who did not hold at least nominal relations to the Church of Rome. The Waldenses, the Hussites, a remnant of the Lollards, and a small number of Jews—all combined, scarcely enough to count at all against the overwhelming odds of the Papacy—were the only exceptions. Eighty millions may be accepted as an approximate estimate of the Papal population in Europe and in the whole world, at the opening of the century which introduced the Lutheran Reformation.

Passing over the intervening periods, for which no definite basis for comparison exists, and coming to our own times, we find the population of Europe divided in respect to religions, as follows:

* Seaman's "Progress of Nations," p. 551.

Roman Catholic population * 149,000,000
Protestant population 74,000,000
Greek Church population 75,000,000
Jews 4,500,000
Mohammedans 6,600,000

Romanism, starting on a basis of about eighty millions in the year 1500, has gained in Europe sixty-nine millions, while Protestantism, starting soon after, from unity, has gained seventy-four millions of adherents in the same territory.

During three hundred and eighty years the population of Europe increased threefold;† but Romanism did not double her population, and Protestantism had all of hers to gain, and in the face of powerful opposition.

Hereafter we shall notice another aspect of Protestant progress, in this period, of much greater significance.

Within the last twenty-five years Protestantism has made large inroads into the Roman Catholic countries of Europe, laying the foundations for numerous Churches and communicants before another generation shall pass away. How different is the condition of Romanism in France, Italy, Austria, and Spain, from thirty years ago, not to go further

* These figures, by Professor Schem, nearly correspond with those in Hubner's Statistical Tables, and also with those given in the "Catholic Family Almanac," for 1876. See also "Encyclopædia Britannica," article "Europe," p. 713.

† According to Bem and Wagner, in 1874, the population of Europe was 309,178,300.

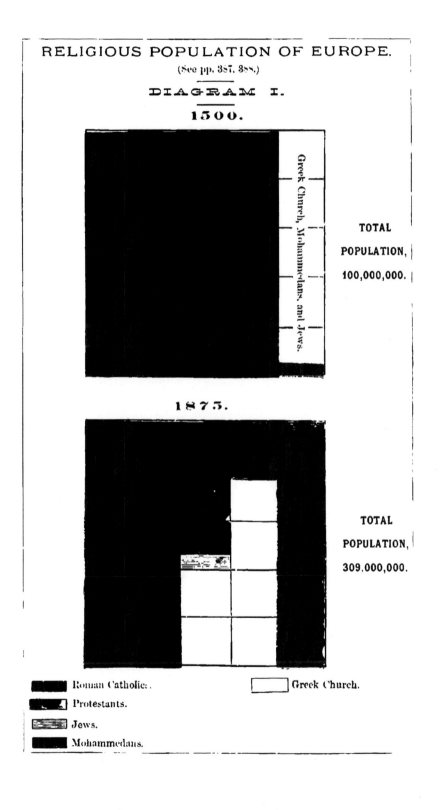

RELIGIOUS POPULATION OF EUROPE.

(See pp. 387, 388.)

DIAGRAM I.

1500.

Greek Church, Mohammedans, and Jews.

TOTAL
POPULATION,
100,000,000.

1875.

TOTAL
POPULATION,
309,000,000.

Roman Catholics.

Greek Church.

Protestants.

Jews.

Mohammedans.

back! How great is the change in the position and influence of the Pope in Italy, shorn of his temporal power, and with Protestant churches under the very shadow of St. Peter's!

Protestantism has numerous missions among the papal population of Roman Catholic countries.

In Ireland eight Protestant missionary societies are operating; in France, eight societies; in Italy, Sicily, and Malta, seventeen societies; in Spain, Gibraltar, Portugal, and Madeira, nineteen societies; in Canada, nine societies; in Mexico, Central America, and South America, twenty-three societies, making, in all, eighty-four distinct Protestant missionary movements among Papal populations, operating on more than 1,546 stations and sub-stations, and sustaining 1,499 ministers and 2,146 lay agents. Thirty of the eighty-four societies, several years ago, reported 95,920 mission communicants. All these missions are continually enlarging, and many others being established. Roman Catholic countries are invaded on every side, and the foundations are laid for vast future movements.

It is a frequent remark that Romanism is smitten with decay all over Europe. The populations of Roman Catholic countries have had meager growths. Spain and Italy, leading populations of the continent in the year 1500, are now among the smaller, the increase of both, with their large territories, in three hundred and eighty years, being only about two thirds of the increase of England and Wales, with their small areas, in the same period. Comparing three Papal with three non-Papal countries, we have—Austria, in fifty-nine years, (1792–1851,) increased 13,014,397; France, in eighty-nine years, (1762–1851,) increased 14,014,170; Spain, in one hundred and eleven years, (1723–1834,) increased 5,607,194; total, 32,635,761, in an aggregate of two hundred and fifty-nine years: but Great Britain, in fifty years, (1801–1851,) increased 11,675,271; Prussia, in sixty-three years, (1786–1849,) increased 10,331,187; and Russia, in sixty-seven years, (1783–1850,) increased 34,688,000; total, 56,694,458, in an aggregate of one hundred and eighty years, or twenty-four millions more, in seventy-nine less years, than the increase of the three Papal nations. The increase, *per annum*,* was:

In the Papal Countries.	In the non-Papal Countries.
Austria, .94 of one per cent.	Great Britain, 1.48 per cent.
France, .72 " " "	Prussia, 2.73 " "
Spain, .66 " " "	Russia, 1.89 " "

The tendency of Rome is to dwarf the mind, to beggar the nations, and repress progress—the opposites of the tendencies of Protestantism. "Throughout Christendom, whatever advance has been made in knowledge, in freedom, in wealth, and in the arts of life, *has been made in spite of her*, (Rome,) and has every-where been in inverse proportion to her power.

* See "Compendium of United States' Census," 1850, p. 131.

The loveliest and most fertile provinces of Europe have, under her rule, *been sunk in poverty*, in political servitude, and in intellectual torpor, while Protestant countries, once proverbial for sterility and barbarism, have been turned by skill and industry into flourishing gardens, and can boast of a long list of heroes and statesmen, philosophers and poets." *

When the " Invincible Armada" threatened to overthrow Protestant England, Spain could boast of forty-three millions of subjects. Now she has only sixteen millions. England, Wales, and Scotland then numbered only about four millions; but they now have more than twenty-seven millions, besides colonial subjects all over the world, swelling the number to three hundred millions, and their wealth has centupled, while Spain has become impoverished.

The old Concordat, in Spain, is repudiated, and toleration is allowed. In Italy, under the very eyes of the Pontiff, the old foundations are sliding away; and, as Garibaldi said in a letter not long ago, " There is no place on earth where the Pope is less regarded than in Rome." For sixty years Italy has been reviving, for the first thirty years slowly, and the last thirty very rapidly. " The 'States of the Church,' after one thousand years of dark pre-eminence, no longer appear on the map of the world. In 1870 the various States and Provinces were

* Lord Macaulay.

united under one crown, and Rome became, once more, the capital of united Italy. The present government affords as much freedom for Protestant worship as any other in Europe. A new enlightenment is becoming apparent. Priestly influences, long hostile to education, have given way to new forces. The Italian government energetically introduced the work of public instruction, made a parliamentary grant of one million sterling for school purposes, and added to it the greater portion of the vast revenues of 2,400 monastic establishments it had confiscated. Education, self-government, telegraphs, and railroads are working an elevation. From the windows in the Vatican the Pope beholds the flag of the reprobate king who rules in his stead, and a depository of Bibles with its eager seekers after the word of life."

The religious results in Italy are beginning to assume tangible numerical forms. In 1877 Father Gavazzi said : " Fifteen years ago there were only 5 Protestant congregations and 400 communicants in all Italy, while there are now 8,000 communicants and about 41,000 hearers." These figures do not include the Waldensians in Northern Italy. In 1879, at the Evangelical Alliance, in Basel, Professor Comba furnished definite data of these Christian heroes who bear " the scars of thirty persecutions." The Waldensians number, in all Italy, 56 churches, 32 mission stations, about 15,000 communicants, a theological school, 55 pastors, 50 teachers, and 4,400 Sunday-school scholars. The Free Church, founded in 1848, has 8 congregations and 30 stations. The Free Italian Church, beginning in 1865, has * 36 churches, 35 missionary stations, 15 pastors, 15 lay-preachers, 1,800 communicants, 800 Sunday-school scholars, 2,085 children in day-schools, under 21 teachers, and 17 students in a theological seminary. The Wesleyan Church, formed in 1861, has 22 pastors, 6 helpers, 6 evangelists, 1,350 communicants, and 704 Sunday-school scholars. The Baptist Church, established in 1855, has 9 pastors, 155 members, and 5 Sunday-schools. The Methodist Episcopal Church, begun in 1873, now numbers 6 pastors, 9 evangelists, 1 colporteur, 5 Bible readers, and 709 communicants. Seven Protestant denominations, with 53 Protestant schools, are represented in the City of Seven Hills. The "Alphabetical Guide of the Protestant Churches of Italy," recently published in Naples, says there are 138 organized Protestant Italian Churches, besides churches where divine service is conducted in English, French, and German.

Crossing the Alps into Switzerland we find Romanism declining. It has decreased to two fifths of the population. But, while 1,500,000 of the 2,500,000 inhabitants are Protestants, within the last twenty-five years important changes for the worse

* Statistics given by Father Gavazzi, November 28, 1880.

have taken place in Swiss theology. It has become decidedly rationalistic, the Churches are sparsely attended, the communion service is sadly neglected, and divorces are painfully numerous. The Methodists and Baptists are penetrating the country and gaining a respectable footing among the State Churches. The new leaven is a good omen.

In France, the hope of the Papacy after the loss of the temporal power in Italy, it has declined, lost the countenance of the government, and each successive election reduces its influence in the Cabinet and in the Assembly. France is becoming one of the fairest, ripest, and richest fields for Protestant missions in the world. In the Republic there are 650,000 Protestants. They have had to contend with great embarrassments, but have made considerable progress during this century. In 1806 there were only 171 Protestant pastors, and the Protestant Church had no schools. To-day it has 850 pastors, Alsace and Lorraine not included, 1,250 Protestant schools, and 30 religious journals. The Reformed Church has a membership of 560,000 ; the Church of the Augsburg Confession, 80,000 ; the English Free Church, 43 church edifices and 5,000 members ; the Wesleyan Methodist Church, 28 pastors, 18 evangelists, a theological seminary, and 175 preaching places ; the Baptist Church, 12 native preachers, 8 Churches, and 706 members. Rev. Mr. Réveiland has become an apostle of religious prog-

ress. A new work has been inaugurated in Paris,
under Mr. and Mrs. M'All, extending into some outside localities, which is one of the brightest omens
of the times. During the year 1878 not less than
85,000 people attended the services of these evangelists, and their Sunday-schools number 42,000
scholars. The movement is under the protection
of the government, as a means of promoting morality among the laboring classes.

In Bavaria, until recently the strongest German
center of Popery, it has been snubbed by the civil
authorities, and Protestantism has come to number
nearly one third of the population. In Austria the
influence of Rome is less absolute, and Protestant
worship is more generally allowed; but within three
years Bohemia has been stained with the blood of
martyrs. In Belgium alone does Romanism show
much vigor.

The following table * will show the religious
statistics of Austria, Hungary, Bavaria, and Belgium :

Countries.	Popula- tion.	Roman Catholics.	Protest- ants.	Greek Church.	Jews.	Other Churches.
Austria	21,565,435	15,766,000	351,000	2,303,000	683,000	500,000
Hungary........	15,564,533	7,502,000	3,133,000	1,588,000	552,000	2,641,000
Bavaria	5,022,390	3,573,742	1,392,120	......	51,335	5,793
Belgium.........	5,336,185	5,321,685	13,000	......	1,500	......

In Germany the Papacy has suffered a kind of
self-defeat, in consequence of its Jesuitical attempts
to interfere with the imperial policy, and the grow-

* Collected from the "Statesman's Year-Book." 1881. London.

ing Protestant population is leaving behind the
Roman Catholic.

	Protestant Population.	Papal Population.
1867	24,921,000	14,564,000
1875	26,718,823	15,371,227

These figures show a Protestant increase of
1,797,823 to a Roman Catholic increase of 807,227
in eight years.

PROPORTION TO 1,000 INHABITANTS.

	Protestants.	Roman Catholics.
1867	621	363
1875	625	360

But there are dark shadows resting on the religious prospects of Germany. Skepticism reigns supreme in some classes; the thinking of large masses
is unchristian, Socialism is working harm to evangelical religion, and the skeptics welcome the Roman Catholics as a means of helping on a general
disintegration. But there are also hopeful indications. The unity of Protestantism is greater than
ever before, the evangelical sentiment is gaining in
the universities, and the Baptists and Methodists
are multiplying their Churches there, promoting
spirituality and new life. They have been looked
upon with distrust by the older communions, as
threatening evil to the State Churches; but they
are coming to be favorably recognized on account
of the good work they are doing. In the chair of
the Basle session of the Evangelical Alliance, in
1879, Count Bismarck-Bohlem said, that "if men

from abroad come into Germany and preach a pure Gospel, and the people are attracted toward it, they are worthy of all confidence," and that, " if the State Churches lose their power, God will put it into other hands."

Roman Catholicism was predominant, a hundred years ago, in all the frontier provinces acquired by Prussia in the days of Frederick the Great; but since the German immigrants have widely propagated the Protestant faith in these districts, the condition is changed.

The facts of religious progress in Prussia since 1849 show that Protestantism has steadily gained upon Romanism. The statistical bureau of Berlin has recently published comparative statistics of Romanism and Protestantism in Prussia, conclusively showing, from the official censuses, that in every province in Prussia Protestantism is increasing more rapidly than Roman Catholicism. The same is reported from the Grand Duchy of Baden.

The " Statesman's Year-Book" * (London, 1881) says of Prussia: " Nearly two thirds of the population are Protestants, and one third Roman Catholics. At the last census, taken December 1, 1875, the Protestants numbered 16,636,990, being 64·65 per cent. of the total population of the kingdom, and the Roman Catholics 8,625,840, or 33.51 per

* Pp. 117, 118.

cent.   The number of Jews was 339,790, or 1·82 per cent. of the population, at the date of the census. In the provinces of Prussia, Pomerania, Branden- burg, and Saxony, the great majority are Prot- estants; while in Posen, Silesia, Westphalia, and Rhenish Prussia, the Roman Catholics predominate. In the new provinces annexed to the kingdom in 1866, the Protestants form the mass of the popula- tion.   There are a few members of the Greek Church, mostly emigrants from Russia.   Jews are to be found in all the provinces, but especially at Posen. At the census of December 3, 1864, there were in the kingdom as then constituted, 11,736,734 Prot- estants, being 60.23 per cent. of the total popula- tion, and 7,201,911 Roman Catholics, equal to 36·81 per cent., besides 262,001 Jews, and about 52,000 adherents of other creeds.   The annexation of the new provinces, after the war of 1866, altered the proportion in favor of the Protestant ascend- ency. . . . Protestantism is otherwise gradually spreading among the population, and Roman Ca- tholicism decreasing."

Passing to Ireland, we discover a great change in its population, from 8,175,124 in 1841 to 5,411,416 in 1871, occasioned chiefly by emigration.   Eight ninths of the emigration has been shown to be Ro- man Catholic.   Instead of four and one third Ro- man Catholics to every Protestant, as in 1841, there are now only three and one fourth for every Protestant. The proportion of Papists and Protestants to the whole population has stood as follows:

	1834.	1861.	1871.
Roman Catholics.............	80.9	77.9	76.7
Church of England...........	10.7	11.8	12.7
Other Protestant Churches	8.4	10.3	10.7
Total.................	100.	100.	100,

Relatively Romanism has lost and Protestantism has gained 4.2 per cent., though it still holds an immense preponderance.*

But Roman Catholics console themselves for their loss on the Continent and in Ireland by strong assertions of the prosperity of their cause in England;† and the Pope, in his Allocution, while acknowledging decline in other lands, has referred to Protestant England as a field of victory.

What, then, are the relative prospects of Romanism and Protestantism in England?

In England the Roman Catholic Church has made some progress; but not so great as would sometimes seem from the reports in the newspapers. Her gain has been chiefly from the transference of her population thither from Ireland. The two countries, then, must be considered together, in order to determine whether or not Romanism has gained.

* For fuller statistics of Romanism in Ireland, see Tables XIX to XXIII in the Appendix.

† The "Catholic World," January, 1870, said: "We have certainly gained ground in Protestant nations, but probably not much more than we have lost in old Catholic nations."

We omit Scotland from the calculation, because we have no definite statement of the Roman Catholic population of that country.

	1851.	1871.
Population of England and Wales......	17,905,831	22,712,266
Population of Ireland.................	6,574,278	5,411,416
Total of England, Wales, and Ireland	24,480,109	28,123,682
Roman Catholics in Ireland..........	5,378,949	4,141,933
Roman Catholics in England and Wales	758,800	1,000,000
Total R. C. in Engl'd, Wales, and Irel'd	6,137,749	5,141,933
Deduct, leaving non-Catholics.......	18,342,360	22,981,749

In the above table* the statistics of the Roman Catholics in England and Wales may appear to some too small, as they did at first to ourselves; but we can only say that they have been taken from the highest English authorities, namely, the "Statesman's Year-Book," and "Whitaker's Almanac," both for 1880, and the edition of the "Encyclopædia Britannica," now in course of publication, all of which agree. The latter work says the Catholics in England and Wales in 1877 are "barely one million;" but we have allowed that number in 1871. According to the above figures, in 1851 the Roman Catholics were twenty-five per cent. of the whole population of England, Wales, and Ireland; in 1871 they were nineteen per cent. In the three countries the actual increase of the non-papal population was nearly five millions, and the

* See also Table XXIII in Appendix.

actual decrease of the papal population was one million.

The statistics for England, Scotland, and Wales, show that the Roman Catholic churches and chapels increased from 647 in 1850 to* 1,543 in 1880, with a corresponding increase of priests, and even larger increase of convents and monasteries. But Protestant churches have increased more relatively; and it has been clearly demonstrated that there is now a less per centage of Papists in the British population than there was at the beginning of the century. The question has been sifted by English statisticians,† and Robenstein's "Denominational Statistics" (1875) gives the following:

"There are now nearly a million Roman Catholics in England and Wales, and these are divided according to their nationality thus: English Roman Catholics, 179,000; foreigners, 52,000; Irish, 742,560. This is one side of the subject; now look at the other. In 1801 the population of Great Britain and Ireland was about fifteen millions and three quarters, of whom four millions and a quarter were Roman Catholics, or twenty-seven per cent. of the whole population. *Now* the population is nearly thirty-one millions and a half, of whom little more than five and a half are Roman Catholics, or only eighteen per cent. of the whole population. In other words, while the Roman Catholics have

---

* See Table XX in Appendix. † See Table XXIII in Appendix.

increased at the rate of twenty-eight per cent.,
the Protestants have increased at the rate of one
hundred and twenty per cent. Protestantism has
therefore been advancing nearly five times faster
than Romanism since the beginning of the present
century."

The new "Encyclopædia Britannica"* gives a
more extended and thorough statement of Roman
Catholic progress in England, with similar results.

"It is stated by Hallam, that in the reign of Queen
Elizabeth the Roman Catholics numbered one third
of the entire population; but the effect of the many
repressive laws enacted against them was, that at
the end of the seventeenth century, when the already
referred to religious census of 1699 was taken, the
total number was only 27,696, being barely one half
per cent. of the population. It was estimated that
the number of Roman Catholics in England had increased to 68,000 in 1767, being about one per cent.
of the population, and that it stood at 69,400 in
1780, being less than one per cent. On the basis
of the marriage returns of the Registrar General,
the estimated number of Roman Catholics in England and Wales was 284,300 in 1845, or 1.70 per
cent. of the population; but within the next six
years, when there was a large immigration of Irish,
the numbers rapidly rose, and at the end of 1851
the total number of Roman Catholics was calculated

* Article, England.

at 758,800, being 4.22 per cent. of the population. The numbers kept rising till 1854, when there were estimated to be 916,600 Roman Catholics in England and Wales, being 4.94 per cent. of the population; but there was a fall after this year, if not in numbers yet in percentage. The calculated number was 927,500, or 4.61 per cent., in 1861, and 982,000, or 4.62 per cent., in 1866.* It is estimated that in the middle of 1877 the number of Roman Catholics in England and Wales had barely reached one million, being a less percentage than in 1866, and about one half the number comprised natives of Ireland with their families. It would thus seem that Roman Catholicism has not been progressive in England for about a quarter of a century. However, the wealth of the body increased very greatly, owing mainly to the secession of many rich persons of both sexes to the Church, which led to a vast increase of Roman Catholic places of worship. They numbered 616 in 1853, and had risen to 1,095 in 1877, with a clergy of 1,892."

The progress of Romanism in England has been from Irish immigrants and a few of the higher classes of English society. The Tractarian movement, from which Rome has reaped a small harvest, confined to a class of scholarly mystical men, represented no reaction toward Popery among the English people, though it unquestionably made a

* See Table XXII, Appendix.

great impression upon the leading ecclesiastics in
Italy, who thought they saw in it the vanguard of
a vast national movement.   The most chimerical
notions prevailed in the Vatican, in whose eyes the
whole English nation was only waiting for some
timely word to call them once more to the spiritual jurisdiction of Rome.   Unfortunate at home, a
fugitive from his own city, and restored only by
the force of French arms, not seeing far into the
various phases of human thought and character,
the Pope flattered himself that Heaven was about
to make up for the domestic disasters of his reign
by making him the instrument of the reclamation
of England to the Papal faith.

Little significance did the Pope see, if he saw the
fact at all, in the fact that at least five sixths of all
the Catholics in England were Irish by birth or extraction.   The gains among the higher classes, and
in political influence, by no means constituted any
loss to genuine Protestantism.   The religious denominations, earnestly Protestant — the Independents, Baptists, Methodists, Presbyterians, etc.—no
more suffered from secessions to Rome than the
same denominations in the United States.   Only
the Church of England felt alarm from the inroads
of Rome, and even that Church was only relieved
of a few nobles and clergymen, whose Romeward
tendencies compromised and embarrassed her.
Upon the Protestant character of England the

movement exerted a beneficial influence. While
the privileged classes of England were drawing
nearer to the most conservative and backward-
looking power in Europe, the masses in England,
as in Italy, Spain, Austria, and, indeed, in almost
every civilized country in the world, were moving
forward in a contrary direction, and causing to the
Church of Rome losses a hundred fold greater than
her gains in England.

The alarm which some have expressed, in consequence of the concession of some of the English
nobility and a few Ritualistic clergymen to Popery,
is without just foundation. "In many instances
the family histories would show some ancestral
mental tendency or aberration, adequately explain-
ing the phenomena." Such eccentricities are abnormal and sporadic, not affecting the great middle
classes, upon whom the character and destiny of
the nation depend, nor the laws of population, of
opinion, and of progress, before which Romanism
is doomed the world over. "No thinkers are more
humbugged than those who suppose that because
of an occasional local movement of Popery, like
that in England, the civilization of the age is about
to give way, and the world roll backward. The
aberrations of the very planets are compensated
and rectified at last by the general laws of the
mécanique celeste."

In Papal America.

But Roman Catholics have confidently asserted that in America they are retrieving their waning fortunes. The most clamorous and preposterous statements of Protestant declension and Papal growth have been made by Papists and various classes of skeptics. The recent utterances of Mr. Froude, in the "North American Review," have been not the least remarkable, but are characteristically inaccurate, borrowed largely from his imagination rather than from facts.

Looking, first, at the whole American field, North and South, we notice the familiar fact that one hundred years ago, and even until within about fifty years, all South America was Roman Catholic. Not a single Protestant Church existed on that vast continent, unless, perhaps, in Guiana. But in 1872 sixteen Protestant missionary societies occupied 37 stations, and sustained 84 clerical and lay laborers there. Since that time the number has been increased, and within three years that redoubtable apostolic missionary, Rev. William Taylor, has projected a line of missions all along the western coast, and in Brazil, with favorable indications.

Less than a generation ago the Roman Catholic Church in Mexico was the richest ecclesiastical establishment in the world, with landed property, mortgages, and rents, worth $150,000,000, besides untold millions invested in cathedrals, Church edifices of the costliest construction, gold and silver vessels, etc. 108 church edifices in the city of Mexico alone were worth $50,000,000. The revenues of the clergy were large, the annual income of the archbishop being at one time $130,000, and of eight bishops $400,000. The Roman Catholics of Mexico repeatedly contributed * of their ample means to aid the struggling Catholics of the United States in establishing their Churches among us. But this vast and powerful establishment has received a stunning blow, from which it can never recover. The Inquisition, with its horrors, existed until within a quarter of a century. The orders of friars, nuns, sisters of charity, and the Jesuits have all been disbanded and abolished in Mexico, and the magnificent churches and convent buildings formerly occupied by those orders have been offered for sale by the general government. Since 1861 six distinct Protestant missions have been established, numbering now 23 principal stations, 88 sub-stations, 53 ordained missionaries, 98 lay-helpers, about 8,700 communicants, and 16 Bible and Tract depositories, all protected by the government. †

* "History of Catholic Church in the United States," pp. 355, 356. By De Courcy.

† At the Conference of Foreign Missions in London, in 1878,

Passing to the North, we find the vast region of the two Canadas, as late as the time of the English Conquest, wholly Roman Catholic, and about a fifth part of the population of the more easterly maritime provinces of the present British dominion was also of the same faith:

	Popula- tion.	Roman Catholic.	Protest- ant.
In 1765, The Canadas	69,810	69,810	....
In 1767, Nova Scotia	11,779	1,718	9,961*
" New Brunswick and P. Ed. Isle	1,196	152	1,024†
" Cape Breton	519	276	243
Total	83,304	71,956	11,228

Here are six and a half Roman Catholics to one Protestant.

In 1820, according to Mackenzie's "Messenger," the proportion of the Roman Catholics to the Protestants was as 19 to 7. In 1851 the religious census of New Brunswick was not taken; but for the remaining provinces of the present British dominion the figures were, Roman Catholics, 983,680; Protestants, 1,065,728; not given, 69,652; Jews, 354; Mormons, 259, or ten Protestants to nine Roman Catholics. In 1861 the statistics for all the provinces were, 1,680,790; Roman Catholics, 1,372,923; Jews, 1,195; Mormons, 111; not given,

Senora Liva said there were 61 Protestant congregations and 7,000 converts to Protestantism in Mexico.—Report of said Conference, p. 89.

* Not given, 100.   † Not given, 20.

35,542; or 16 Protestants to 13 Catholics. In 1871 there were 1,967,532 Protestants, 1,492,033 Roman Catholics, 1,015 Jews, 534 Mormons, and 22,630 not given, or 19 Protestants to 14 Roman Catholics.

The relative progress may be stated as follows:

In 1765–67 there was 1 Protestant for $6\frac{1}{4}$ Roman Catholics.
In 1820   "   1   "   " $2\frac{5}{7}$ "
In 1851   " $1\frac{1}{12}$ "   " 1   Roman Catholic.
In 1861   " $1\frac{3}{10}$ "   " 1   "
In 1871   " $1\frac{1}{3}$ "   " 1   "

PROPORTION OF THE WHOLE POPULATION.*

	Protestants.	Roman Catholics.
In 1765–67	14 per cent.	86 per cent.
In 1820...................	27 "	73 "
In 1851...................	50.29 "	46.41 "
In 1861..................	54.38 "	44.42 "
In 1871..................	56.45 "	42.80 "

Here are decided indications of the relative progress of Protestantism and the relative decline of Romanism, in the whole territory of the British Dominion. Instead of only 10 Protestants for 65 Romanists, as in 1765–67, there are $86\frac{2}{3}$ Protestants for 65 Romanists. Protestantism has gained 42.45 per cent. on the whole population, and Romanism has lost 43.20 per cent. on the whole population.

Examining the leading provinces singly, we find Romanism greatly preponderant, and even relatively gaining a little upon Protestantism, in Lower Canada.

* See Table XXIV, in Appendix.

PROPORTION OF THE WHOLE POPULATION.

	Protestants.	Roman Catholics.
In 1851.......	15.4 per cent.	83.8 per cent.
In 1871.......	14.2 "	85.6 "

Here is a relative loss of 1.2 per cent. by Protestantism, and a relative gain of 1.8 per cent. by Romanism. The actual gain by Romanism was 272,796 inhabitants, and by Protestantism 31,308 inhabitants.

In Upper Canada the situation and prospect are very different. Protestantism is vastly in the ascendency, and is growing more rapidly than Romanism.

PROPORTION OF THE WHOLE POPULATION.

	Protestants.	Roman Catholics.
1851....	741,422, or 77.8 per cent.	167,695, or 17.6 per cent.
1871....	1,325,053, or 81.7 "	274,166, or 16.9 "

In twenty years Protestantism actually gained 583,631, or 3.9 per cent. on the whole population ; and Romanism actually gained 106,471, but lost relatively seven tenths of 1 per cent. on the whole population.

In Nova Scotia the numerical strength of Protestantism is nearly three times as great as Romanism ; and its relative gain on the whole population, from 1851 to 1871, was a little greater than that of Romanism.

PROPORTION TO THE WHOLE POPULATION.

	Protestants.	Roman Catholics.
1851....	186,383, or 67.3 per cent.	69,131, or 24.8 per cent.
1871....	284,299, or 73.3 "	102,001, or 26.8 "

Protestantism gained, actually, 97,916, and, relatively, 6 per cent. on the whole population. Romanism gained, actually, 32,870, and, relatively, 1.5 per cent. on the whole population.

The religious census of New Brunswick was not taken in 1851. The comparison, therefore, for that province, will be made between the years 1861 and 1871, when it was as follows:

PROPORTION TO THE WHOLE POPULATION.

	Protestants.	Roman Catholics.
1861....	166,264, or 65.9 per cent.	85,238, or 33.8 per cent.
1871....	188,948, or 66.1 "	96,016, or 33.6 "

The actual gain of Protestantism was 22,684, and its relative gain on the population was only two tenths of 1 per cent. The actual gain of Romanism was 10,778, and it lost, relatively, two tenths of 1 per cent. on the population.

The numerical exhibit of the religious denominations in the British Dominion in 1871 was as follows:*

Denomination.	Upper Canada.	Lower Canada.	New Brunswick.	Nova Scotia.	Total.
Roman Catholics...	274,166	1,019,850	96,016	102,001	1,492,033
Baptists............	86,630	8,686	70,597	73,430	239,343
Congregationalists..	12,856	5,252	1,193	2,538	21,841
Church of England.	331,484	62,636	45,481	55,143	494,744
Jews..............	518	549	48	....	1,115
Lutherans.....	32,399	496	82	4,958	37,935
Methodists	462,264	34,100	29,856	40,871	567,091
Mormons..........	460	....	59	15	534
Presbyterians.......	356,449	46,165	38,852	103,539	545,005
Quakers...........	7,106	116	26	96	7,345
Other denominations	35,863	11,780	2,861	3,724	54,228
Without creed......	4,908	420	131	116	5,575
Not given..........	13,849	1,461	392	1,353	17,055

* See Table XXIV, in Appendix.

Within the present territorial area of the United States there are large sections once wholly under the control of the Roman Catholic Church. The only religious occupancy was exclusively Roman Catholic. Rome had the opportunity of shaping the religious life, and possessing it wholly. It is a fair inquiry, What is the relative strength of Romanism and Protestantism in these regions? Statistics show that Protestantism has invaded this territory, once exclusively occupied by the papacy, and has far outrun it in the race of progress.

Florida, Texas, New Mexico, and California were occupied by papal missions before Protestantism gained its first permanent foothold within the original United States, (and they long continued under the religious sway of the papacy.) In Florida and Texas no Protestant Churches were planted until within the present century, and not many until within fifty or sixty years; in California, not until within a generation; and in New Mexico not until fifteen years ago. In the gulf region, ancient Louisiana, (comprising the whole region west and north-west of the Mississippi,) Illinois, Wisconsin, and Michigan, the Roman Catholic Church was the only religious force. The Indian missions were numerous, and the French-Indian trading-posts and forts were extensive. Cahokia, Kaskaskia, the Wabash region, and Detroit, had considerable populations, some of the settlements dating back as far as the founding of Philadelphia. Rome pre-empted this large field. No Protestant Churches were founded in Illinois until about 1800; in Louisiana, Missouri, Alabama, Mississippi, and Michigan, until some years later; in Wisconsin and Arkansas, until more than thirty years later; in Detroit, until 1815; and in St. Louis, until 1818. The first Protestant Churches, in many localities, encountered strong papal prejudices and even persecution. Maryland, as an original papal colony, belongs in this list. Such was the beginning.

What progress have Protestantism and Romanism made in these large regions? The impartial statistics of the United States census shall tell the story:

CHURCH EDIFICES IN 1870.

States.	Methodist.*	Baptist.†	Other Evang'l Protestant.	Total Protestant.	Roman Catholic.
Maryland ..	757	78	397	1,232	103
Michigan...	469	232	481	1,182	148
Illinois.....	1,124	571	1,166	2,861	249
Missouri...	626	518	508	1,652	166
Wisconsin..	396	141	590	1,127	304
Arkansas ..	485	397	144	1,026	11
Louisiana..	202	208	80	490	102
Mississippi.	776	652	302	1,730	27
Alabama...	892	772	240	1,904	19
Florida	215	123	48	386	9
California ..	155	44	136	335	144
New Mexico	1	1	3	5	149
Texas......	244	211	137	592	36
Total..	6,342	3,948	4,232	14,522	1,187

* All branches of Methodism.   † All kinds of Baptists.

In these originally papal regions Protestantism had, in 1870, 14,522 church edifices, and Romanism 1,187, or less than one twelfth as many. The Methodists had 6,342 Churches, or 5½ times as many as Romanism ; and the Baptists 3,948, or 3⅓ times as many as the Roman Catholics.

CHAPTER III.

RELIGIOUS PROGRESS AND STATUS IN THE UNITED STATES.

DIFFICULTIES OF THE SITUATION.

I. THE ACTUAL PROGRESS.

The Evangelical Churches.
The Liberal Churches.
The Roman Catholic Church.

II. THE RELATIVE PROGRESS.

The Churches Compared with the Population.
The Evangelical, Liberal, and Catholic Churches Compared with each other.
The Churches and Higher Education.
Modern and Early Christian Progress.
Encouraging Conclusion.

CHAPTER III.

RELIGIOUS PROGRESS AND STATUS IN THE UNITED STATES.

THE boast of Romanists of their great growth in this country; the frequently expressed fears that the Papacy will gain the ascendency here; the oft-repeated assertions of skeptics that Christianity is being outgrown by the population, and is destined to be left behind in the march of progress; the impressions of some that the "Liberal" Churches are relatively advancing more than the "Evangelical" Churches; the misapprehensions and despondency of some good people in regard to the condition of the Churches of the United States; the fact that here Christianity exists under conditions unknown (purely voluntary) for long centuries, awakening much interest and inquiry among European divines and statesmen, now pressed with the question of Disestablishment; and the great intrinsic importance of the question of religious progress in this country, in the estimation of those who believe that our nation and its Churches sustain an intimate relation to the best progress and welfare of the world,—these are reasons which

27

prompt to a closer analysis and a more extended examination of the growth and status of religion in the United States. Nearer access to the necessary data favors our task, and enables us to do what we could not do in our sketches of religious progress in Europe.

But we shall fail to appreciate the growth and present position of American Christianity, unless we first briefly consider some of the *local difficulties and competing forces* with which it has had to contend during this century.

Consider the vast extent of the field which Christianity in the United States has been called to fill and provide for, religiously, during the last eighty years.

The immense region from the Alleghanies to the Pacific has been opened and largely occupied almost entirely since the year 1800. At that time there were probably less than 200 Church organizations in this vast area, of about 2,500,000 square miles, exclusive of Alaska, equal to about twelve times the area of France. Five eighths of the States and Territories of our nation have been organized in this region, and Christianity has been called upon to furnish to these numerous communities religious institutions and watchcare, and all the appointments of a Christian civilization. In the year 1870 there were in this trans-Alleghany territory 37,855 Protestant Church organizations, with 30,687 church edifices, valued at $97,183,492, besides 47,637 Evangelical Protestant Sunday-schools, and several hundred colleges, universities, theological seminaries, and academies, founded and sustained by the Churches, and numerous other institutions and societies incidentally connected with them and dependent upon them. To prepare this great work has severely tested the pecuniary resources, the benevolence, and the zeal of the American Churches.

Consider the unparalleled increase of the population of the United States.

In 1800 our population numbered five and a third millions, in 1880 a little more than fifty millions, a nine and a third fold increase in eighty years, probably greater than in any other country in ancient or modern times. The "Compendium of the United States Census for 1850," p. 131, contains a table which shows the growth of leading European nations in population through long terms of years. Those increasing the least rapidly gained at the rate of about three fourths of one per cent. annually, and the nation gaining most rapidly increased at the rate of little more than two and a half per cent. (2.73) annually; but the United States, from 1800 to 1850, gained eight and seventeen one hundredths (8.17) per cent. annually in her population. An increase of 45,000,000 of people in eighty years has devolved great responsibilities upon the American Churches. To religiously care for these rapidly multiplying millions has seriously taxed the activity and zeal of the religious bodies.

Consider the character of the new populations added to our original stock.

If these new additions were homogeneous the case would be much more favorable, for then they could be more easily molded and saved by the American Churches.

To go no farther back than 1850, in the last thirty years about eight millions of foreigners have been added to our population. Their immediate offspring are at least four millions more. Twelve millions of persons, foreign in character, ideas, and sympathies, have thus been incorporated into our national life in these years. During this period the total population of the United States increased about twenty-seven millions, of which twelve millions, or four ninths, almost one half, was essentially foreign. Of these twelve millions not less than three fifths were originally Roman Catholic. Going back to the beginning of our history, the editor of the "Irish World" (July 25, 1874) calculated that the original Catholic stock entering this country, and their descendants, if all had remained true to Romanism, would make (in 1874) a Roman Catholic population of about twenty-four millions. At the present time they would number twenty-six millions. Besides these there have been other adverse elements—communists, nihilists, rationalists, and skeptics of various grades, convicts, and paupers.

A goodly number of exceptions to these classes have been received, from the British Provinces in North America, from Great Britain and Ireland, and from the European Continent, who have come shoulder to shoulder with our best moral, religious, and philanthropic forces, in all good labors. All honor to such. But the major portion have been very different. Large numbers have come from the prisons and pauper houses of Europe to fill up the ranks of our social outcasts. From a late report of the Howard Society, of London, it appears that " seventy-four per cent. of the Irish discharged convicts have found their way to the United States." This large influx of foreign criminals, added to our own dangerous classes, has militated severely against the public weal.

The major part of these new-comers have been not merely heterogeneous, but positively antagonizing forces—largely anti-Protestant, anti-Sabbath, anti-Bible, and anti-temperance—and have assailed this young Republic in the experimental period of its existence. The infusion of such large adverse elements into our national life has occasioned a severe strain upon public virtue, and enhanced the labors and responsibilities of the Protestant Churches.

Such have been some of the disadvantages under

which the Protestant Churches of the United States have prosecuted their work. What has been the progress?

The question of progress will be considered in a twofold form : *actual* and *relative*. The Evangelical Protestant Churches will be selected first, because they historically and numerically constitute the leading religious force of the country ;* next, the Churches commonly designated as Liberal; and then the Roman Catholic. The actual progress of each will be first considered ; then their relative progress, as compared with the population, with each other, and with the progress of higher education.

I.—THE ACTUAL PROGRESS.

Since the year 1800 the most remarkable progress has been made by the Protestant Churches of the United States, far exceeding any thing ever seen elsewhere, even in the apostolic era. The exhibit of this progress is truly wonderful. In preparing and stating it, great care and research have been exercised, that it may be worthy of the fullest confidence. In making the comparisons, periods have been selected furnishing the most full and reliable data, and abnormal periods have been excluded.

* This classification is made for this additional reason, that the Evangelical, the Liberal, and the Roman Catholic Churches stand before the public as competing forces ; and the public mind has long been accustomed to make comparisons between them.

"EVANGELICAL" DENOMINATIONS.*

Church Organizations.

In the year 1775, according to Rev. Robert Baird, D.D.,† there were 1,918 Church organizations of this class. The United States census for 1870 gives 64,914 ‡ of this kind—an increase of 62,996 since 1775. In Tables II to V (Appendix of this volume) we have the following statistics of Churches, organizations, and congregations. In some instances congregations are given, as the Lutherans; in others, parishes, as the Episcopalians; but in most instances the Church organizations, which perhaps themselves are somewhat variable bodies. They comprise what may generally be called societies.

In 1800...........	3,030	In 1870...........	70,148
In 1850...........	43,072	In 1880...........	97,090

These figures, being made up on the same basis for each period, answer very well in representing the remarkable progress of the Churches—a thirty-two fold increase in eighty years, and an increase of 26,942 in the last ten years, largely in the new communities of the great trans-Mississippi territories, and as yet small and feeble, but like all similar beginnings.

* For a list of these denominations, see Tables I–V, in Appendix.
† "Religion in America," p. 210. Harper & Brothers.
‡ See Table XIII, in Appendix.

Church Edifices.

No statistics of this item, in the United States census, antedate 1850. Nor are the data for 1880 yet available to the public. The Church edifices* of the Evangelical Protestant bodies were as follows: In 1850, 34,537; in 1860, 48,037; in 1870, 56,154.

Inasmuch as the statistics of the number of sittings and the valuation are largely estimates, and have been topics of frequent comment, we will not introduce them here.

Ministers.

By referring to Tables I–V the following statistics of the number of ordained ministers of the evangelical Churches will be found:

In 1775	1,435	In 1870	47,609
In 1800	2,651	In 1880	69,870
In 1850	25,555		

In addition to these there are between 30,000 and 40,000 local preachers, licentiates, etc. An increase of 44,315 ordained ministers in thirty years, and 22,261 in the last ten years, is a vast augmentation of the evangelical forces of the country.

Sunday-Schools.

This great religious agency, one of the most active, conspicuous, and important in our times, is wholly the product of a century. Founded in En-

* See Table XIII, in Appendix.

gland in its distinctive character, 1780–84, a few organizations only were effected in the United States prior to 1800; so that, in this country, it may be said to be the work of the past eighty years. The statistics for the United States, in 1880, as prepared by Mr. E. Payson Porter, Statistical Secretary of the International Sunday-School Convention for the United States and the British American Provinces, are as follows: Sunday-schools,* 82,261; teachers, 886,328; scholars, 6,623,124; total, 7,509,452.

In 1830 the number of Sunday-school scholars in the United States† was 570,000. The increase in fifty years has been over 6,000,000. In 1830 there was 1 Sunday-school scholar for 22 inhabitants. In 1880 there was 1 Sunday-school scholar for $7\frac{1}{2}$ inhabitants—a threefold increase, relatively.

Communicants.

The United States census has never included the ecclesiastical communicants. The only recourse, therefore, is to the "Year-Books" and published "Minutes" of the Churches. From these sources we have collated and prepared, with great research and care, tables (Appendix, II–V) which furnish the following summaries:

* These are statistics of the Sunday-schools of the "Evangelical" Churches. No others are thoroughly tabulated. See Table VII, in Appendix.

† See "American Quarterly Register," 1830.

	Communicants.	Increase.
In 1800..............	364,872	....
In 1850............ ...	3,529,988	3,165,116
In 1870..............	6,673,396	3,143,408
In 1880..............	10,065,963	3,392,567

Gain from 1800 to 1880................. 9,701,091

These are remarkable gains.   It will be noticed that the increase from 1870 to 1880 was a little more than in the next previous twenty years, (1850-1870,) and more than in the first fifty years, (1800-1850.)   And the gain of 9,701,091 enrolled communicants, in the last eighty years, is a stupendous record of religious progress, without a parallel in any former times.

The receipts * of three leading benevolent agencies of the Evangelical Churches—the Foreign and Home Mission Boards and the Religious Publication Houses — afford impressive exhibits :

From 1800 to 1860.......................’...... $76,876,338
From 1860 to 1880 162,512,844

Total from 1800 to 1880.............. $239,389,182

THE " LIBERAL " CHURCHES.

Church Organizations.

The United States census gives the following in 1870 : New Jerusalem, 90 ; Spiritualist, 95 ; Unita-

* See Tables XV, XVI, XVII, in Appendix, for a full view of these offerings.

rian, 331; Universalist, 719; making a total* of 1,135.

The "Year-Books" of these denominations furnish the following statistics of parishes : †

	1840.	1850.	1860.	1870.	1880.
Unitarian.........	230	246	254	328	335
Universalist.......	853	1,069	1,264	917	956
New Jerusalem....	20	....	38	....	93
Christians ‡.......	1,500	....	1,500	....	1,200
	2,603	....	3,056	....	2,584

Many persons connected with these four bodies are, doubtless, Evangelical Christians, but it is impossible for us to discriminate in these statistics. As denominations they are distinct from the evangelical Churches. Great pains have been taken to obtain the above data, and every thing has been collated from official sources.§   The footings show an increase of 453 parishes from 1840 to 1860, but a decrease of 472 parishes since 1860, leaving now 19 less than in 1840. The Unitarians and the New Church have gained 136 parishes since 1860; but the Universalists and the Christians have lost, the former 308, and the latter 300.

* The census reports comprise the Christians with the Disciples, so that they cannot be tabulated.   They are quite different bodies.

† In the United States.

‡ Official estimates.   Those for 1840 are from Rev. David Millard ; for 1880, from the Christian Publishing Agent, Dayton, Ohio. All agree in acknowledging a decline since 1840.

§ See Tables VIII and X, in Appendix.

"Liberal" Church Edifices.

The United States census gives the following summaries:

	1850.	1860.	1870.
Unitarian	245	264	310
Universalist	530	664	602
New Jerusalem	21	58	61
Spiritualist	..	17	22
Total *	796	1,003	995

Here is a decrease of 8 church edifices from 1860 to 1870. While the others have had small gains, the Universalists have lost 62.

Communicants.

The figures for this item in 1880, given by a leading official of the Christian denomination, are 100,000, which he says is "an estimate, but carefully made." In 1844 Rev. David Millard estimated their members at 325,000. They suffered very much from the Advent excitement, and have since declined. In 1870 they were estimated in their Minutes at "a little short of 150,000."

The Swedenborgians report 3,994 communicants, fifteen of their Churches not reporting. The Universalists report 37,646 communicants in the United States. They have given this last item only since 1872.

---

* The Christians, being combined with the Disciples in the United States census, cannot therefore be tabulated here.

THE ROMAN CATHOLIC CHURCH.

The question of Roman Catholic growth in the United States is one of interest the world over. Conceding heavy losses in the old countries, it has been the habit of Romanists to boast of their large gains in this country, sufficient to compensate for their losses elsewhere.

Has the Roman Catholic Church realized a large actual increase in the United States? And has it relatively increased? Yes: no.

It has made large accessions to its numbers, multiplied its adherents manifold, increased its churches, priests, schools, convents, etc., and appointed high ecclesiastics in the main centers of the population. It has organized about eighty brotherhoods and sisterhoods here, whose monasteries and convents are nearly a thousand, and who number their working members by tens of thousands. Its parochial schools are more than two thousand, and the pupils nearly half a million. It exerts a very large, and, in some localities, a controlling, influence in politics. Its magnificent cathedrals, its artistic music, its subtle logic, and its political patronage, have captivated and led away some of our Protestant population. It was never plotting more deeply and desperately than now, and some fear it will yet severely test the safety of our free institutions. There will be need of vigilance and hard work; but it will not triumph.

. *Roman Catholic Church Edifices.*

According to the Census the church edifices were: in 1850, 1,222; in 1860, 2,550; 1870, 3,806. An increase of 2,584, or twofold. The value of this church property in 1870 was $60,985,506—a very considerable increase—over fifty millions of dollars in thirty years.

The statistics of Roman Catholic churches, chapels,* and stations, as given in their Year-Books, are as follows:

In 1850.......... 1,830		In 1870.......... 5,392
In 1860.......... 3,797		In 1880.......... 8,540

These figures also indicate a large increase, as do also those in their Year-Books, which give the number of the

Priests. †

In 1850.......... 1,302		In 1870.......... 3,966
In 1860.......... 2,316		In 1880.......... 6,402

Other Roman Catholic Statistics

show great growth in the past thirty years:

	1850.	1880.
Dioceses	29	69
Ecclesiastical Students...........	322	1,170
Male Religious Houses...........	35	176
Female Religious Houses	65	673
Educational Institutions for Young Men and Young Ladies........	123	618
Parochial Schools	No report.	2,389
Pupils in Parochial Schools.......	" "	423,383
Hospitals, Asylums, etc.	108	386

* See Table XII in Appendix.   † Ibid.

Roman Catholic Population.

Without any definite statistics of their population, and dependent upon conjectural estimates, it is not strange that the most diverse and even amusing statements of their numerical strength should be made. Taking only those of the Roman Catholics themselves, and going no farther back than the famous letter of Bishop England, in 1837, we present the following contradictory, but instructive, estimates, and the authority for each:

ROMAN CATHOLIC POPULATION OF THE UNITED STATES.

Year.	Estimates.	Catholic Authorities.
1800.	**100,000.**	REV. I. T. HECKER, "Catholic World," 1879, generally accepted.
1837.	1,000,000. to 1,200,000.	Bishop England, of South Carolina, in letter to the Propaganda, at Lyons, said : "It is doubtful whether the number of Catholics rises above a million, but it may amount to 1,200,000."
1840.	1,300,000.	"Metropolitan Catholic Almanac," 1841.
"	1,500,000.	Rev. I. T. Hecker, "Catholic World," 1879.
1845.	1,071,800.	"Metropolitan Catholic Almanac," for 1846. Fourteen dioceses, estimated by the Bishops, gave 811,800. Eight dioceses, estimated by the editor, 260,000 more. The editor says, this number "cannot fall short of the truth," though "less than for several years past."
1850.	**1,614,000.**	"METROPOLITAN CATH. ALMANAC," 1851.
"	2,000,000.	"Annals" of the Lyons Propaganda.
"	3,000,000.	Archbishop Hughes.
"	3,500,000.	Rev. I. T. Hecker, in "Catholic World," 1879.
1852.	1,930,000.	"Metropolitan Catholic Almanac." Also indorsed by Rev. Dr. Mullens, of Ireland.
"	3,500,000.	Archbishop Hughes.
1853.	4,000,000.	Bishop O'Connor, of Pittsburgh.
1860.	4,500,000.	Rev. I. T. Hecker, in "Catholic World," 1879.

ROMAN CATHOLIC POPULATION OF THE U. S. (Continued.)

Year.	Estimates.	Catholic Authorities.
1865.	4,400,000.	" The Catholic World."
1866.	5,000,000.	" *Civita Catholica*," Papal organ, Rome.
1868.	5,000,000.	" The Catholic World."
"	9,000,000 to 10,000,000.	Hon. J. F. Maguire, member of Parliament, from Cork, in his book, " The Irish in America," p. 539, says : " I am inclined to agree with those who regard from nine to ten millions of Catholics as a fair and moderate estimate."
1869.	3,354,000.	" German Catholic Year-Book," by Rev. E. A. Reitter, a Jesuit priest, Buffalo, N. Y. In the preface, pp. 6, 7, the editor says : " After the nearest possible account of the German Catholics in the United States, that is, of such as have their children baptized, their number is 1,044,000. The number of Catholics of all other nations is 2,310,000, making the whole number 3,354,000, which is less than is commonly thought. . . . If to these are added the incredibly large number of those who, after their arrival in this country, have only too soon thrown over their Catholic faith, we may with good reason, as the judgment of those who know, and my experience of fifteen years has taught me, add one half to the number above, which would bring it to 5,031,000. Yet such cannot now or ever be taken into account ; as in this country *nothing is more seldom than a backslidden Catholic ever to be reclaimed, even on their death-beds*."
"	6,000,000 to 7,000,000.	" Catholic World."
1870.	4,600,000.	" SADLIER'S CATHOLIC DIRECTORY " gives thirty-four dioceses reporting estimates amounting to 2,649,800. The remaining twenty-four dioceses comprise eight of the very largest, five quite large, and others much smaller. Supposing the twenty-four not reporting to average with those reporting, we have 4,600,000 for the total.

ROMAN CATHOLIC POPULATION OF THE U. S. (Continued.)

Year.	Estimates.	Catholic Authorities.
1870.	10,000,000.	"The St. Peter's," in reply to the "New York Times," said, "The Roman Catholics in the United States are ten millions strong."
"	5,000,000.	"The Catholic Telegraph," Cincinnati, said the estimate of "The St. Peter's" would be correct had Romanism kept all its children received by immigration, but it had lost half of them.
1872.	8,000,000.	"Catholic World," June, 1872, "We number 8,000,000 souls."
1875.	6,000,000.	Kehoe, manager of the Catholic Publication Society, New York.
1876.	9,000,000.	Father Sack; estimated on the basis of three masses to each priest, and each priest representing a congregation of 2,000 devout, indifferent, children, etc.
"	6,500,000.	"History of the Catholic Church in the United States," by J. O'Kane Murray, p. 577.
"	6,240,000.	"Sadlier's Catholic Directory;" five dioceses not reporting that year, supplied from estimates given in other years.
"	Over 6,000,000.	"Catholic Family Almanac," 1876.
1877.	6,304,950.	"Sadlier's Catholic Directory;" eight dioceses not reporting that year, supplied from estimates given in other years.
1878.	Over 7,000,000.	Mr. Kehoe's Report to Bureau of Statistics, Washington, D. C.
"	7,000,000.	Rev. I. T. Hecker, in "Catholic World," 1879.
"	9,000,000.	A priest in Indiana, estimating like Father Sack.
"	6,375,630.	"Sadlier's Catholic Directory," 1879, all dioceses reported.
1879.	6,143,222.	"Sadlier's Catholic Directory," 1880, all dioceses reported.
1880.	6,367,330.	"SADLIER'S CATHOLIC DIRECTORY," 1881. All but three very small dioceses reported.

The striking variations of the foregoing estimates, even those of high Roman Catholic officials, show the necessity of careful discrimination in order to arrive at satisfactory numbers of the Roman Catholic population. We notice five estimates, between 1868 and 1876, which exceed almost all made since 1876. And the estimates given by the Catholic Directories and Almanacs, all the way through, contrast with the random figures of others. These official estimates are all made up on the basis of reports from the Bishops of the different dioceses, each one estimating the Catholic population of his diocese. Some years the Bishops neglect to estimate their populations, and the editor supplies the vacancy by some information at his command, or from the estimates of other years.

Our statistics of the communicants of the Protestant Churches are made up for the years 1800, 1850, 1870, and 1880. In order to future comparisons it is necessary, therefore, to select the most reliable estimates of the Catholic population for these years. For 1800, Protestants and Romanists are agreed upon the number 100,000. For the three remaining periods we take the estimates given from the Catholic Year-Books, and thus have bases for comparison made by uniform processes:

ROMAN CATHOLIC POPULATION.

1800.............	100,000	1870.................	4,600,000
1850.................	1,614,000	1880.................	6,367,330

These figures show a large Roman Catholic increase. From 1800 to 1850 it averaged 302,800 each decade ; from 1850–1880, 1,584,443 each decade.

We have before noticed that the number of immigrants landed on our shores, from 1850 to January 1, 1880, was about eight millions. Of these, at least three fifths, or 4,800,000, were Roman Catholics, which is 46,670 more than the total increase of the Roman Catholic population in the same period, as given in their Year-Books. Full seven eighths of all the immigrants from Ireland have been Papists. The Roman Catholic immigrants, from all countries, and their offspring, during the past thirty years, must have amounted to seven millions, making no account of those here prior to 1850, and their descendants. But their Year-Book for 1881 gives the total Catholic population 6,367,330, which is 632,670 less than the Catholic immigration during the last thirty years, and their natural increase, not to mention the natural increase of those already here in 1850.

That Romanism has grown here, and very largely, too, is unquestionable. And it is likely to grow still more. Every thing grows in the United States. But its gains have been almost wholly by immigration, and its losses have been heavy, immensely more than its gains. By its own acknowledgment, it has lost millions. " This country is the biggest grave for Popery ever dug on earth." Under strongly predominant Protestant influences, her children have been extensively alienated and lost to the Church. Papists know this well, and hence their hostility to our common-school system.

A TABULATED VIEW OF ROMAN CATHOLIC LOSSES IN THE UNITED STATES, AS ACKNOWLEDGED BY ROMANISTS.

Year.	Estimated Losses.	Catholic Authorities, Remarks, etc.
1837.	2,800,000 to 3,000,000.	Bishop England, of South Carolina, in a letter to Lyons Propaganda, said : "If there had been no losses, the number of Catholics would have amounted to 4,000,000." Deducting his estimate (1,000,000 to 1,200,000) of Catholics then living in the United States, we have the annexed figures.
1852.	2,000,000.	Rev. Robert Mullen, D.D., based upon an elaborate statistical calculation, ("Christian Union," August, 1852, p. 251.) He said:
	One third of all the Irish immigrants.	"Of the number of Irish Catholics emigrating to the United States one third at least are lost to the Roman Catholic Church." He also said that Rev. Bishop Reynolds, of Charleston, S. C., told him, "You will save religion by proceeding, on your return to Ireland, from parish to parish, telling the people not to lose their immortal souls by coming to America ;" and that Archbishop Hughes said to him :
	Thousands lost in cities; more in the country.	"The people at home (Ireland) do not fully understand the position of the emigrants — thousands being lost in the large cities, while in the country the faith has died out of multitudes."
	Typical cases of loss of descendants.	In the "Freeman's Journal," June 5, 1852, a correspondent said: "We know of a Catholic couple, who settled in an adjoining county some seventy or eighty years ago; their de-

A Tabulated View of Roman Catholic Losses, (Continued.)

Year.	Estimated Losses.	Catholic Authorities, Remarks, etc.
		scendants are very numerous, but there is not a Catholic now among them! In another county an old Irish couple are still living, and still preferring the Catholic faith, whose children, grandchildren, and great-grandchildren number something over one hundred souls, yet there are but two or three Catholics at present among them."
1855.	Sixty per cent. of the children.	The editor of the "Celt," lecturing in Ireland, advised his countrymen to "stay at home, because the Roman Catholic Church loses sixty per cent. of the children of Roman Catholic parents in the United States."
1862.	3,000,000 to 4,000,000.	Bishop of Toronto.
1864.	Five hundred lost to Popery to one convert from Protestantism.	"The Tablet," New York city, said: "Few insurance companies, we venture to assert, would take a risk on the national life of a creed which puts five hundred daily into the grave for one it wins over to its communion; and yet this is what the Catholic Church is doing, in these States, while we write."
1869.	"1,700,000 in 15 years."	German Catholic "Year-Book."
1875.	Thousands upon thousands.	An archbishop in Ireland, after visiting the United States, told his people in Ireland, "It is far better for you to live here in poverty, and die in the faith, and be sure of saving your immortal souls, and going to heaven, than to go to a country where thousands upon thousands of our race, our Irish race, deny the faith."
1876.	Loss greater than the gain.	"Life of Archbishop Spaulding." Speaking of the period "in which the hierarchy has been in existence, (1790–1876,)" the biographer says: "We have lost in numbers by far

A TABULATED VIEW OF ROMAN CATHOLIC LOSSES, (Continued.)

Year.	Estimated Losses.	Catholic Authorities, Remarks, etc.
1876.		more than we have gained, if I may express an opinion, beyond all doubt."
	More fallen away than now living.	Mr. J. O'Kane Murray, "History of Catholic Church in United States," p. 583, says: "It may be safely said that more Catholics have fallen away from the faith in this country during the last two centuries and a half than are to-day living in it."
	18,000,000.	J. O'Kane Murray, "History of Roman Catholic Church in the United States," pp. 610, 611. The following is Mr. Murray's full statement, and the basis on which it is predicated : "Two points frequently discussed are, 1. What are the relative proportions of the Celtic and the Anglo-Saxon or English element in the population of the United States? 2. How many members has the Catholic Church probably lost in this country? In regard to the first question, there can be no doubt that the Celtic element far exceeds that of the Anglo-Saxon. This is a settled fact. A careful analysis of our statistics proves it. Just a quarter of a century ago the Hon. William E. Robinson, in a remarkable speech at Hamilton College, Clinton, N. Y., said: 'I think it would be quite good-natured in me to allow that about *one eighth* of this country is English, or what is called Anglo-Saxon.' By means of statistics he then clearly demonstrated the correctness of this opinion. (See 'New York Tribune,' July 30, 1851.) Rev. Stephen Byrne, O.S.D., in his 'Irish Emigration to the United States,' 1873, puts the Celtic element at *one half* of our present population, the Anglo-Saxon at *one fourth*. The New York 'Irish World,' whose editor, Mr. Ford,

A TABULATED VIEW OF ROMAN CATHOLIC LOSSES, (Continued.)

Year.	Estimated Losses.	Catholic Authorities, Remarks, etc.
1876.		is well known as a diligent student of statistics, holds that *two thirds* of our people are Celts by birth or descent, and only about *one ninth* are Anglo-Saxon.

"As to the Church's loss in the United States, it is no easy problem to solve. Neither higher algebra nor calculus can help us to grapple with it. The geologists say that *past time is long.* As to its *exact* length, they hesitate to put it into figures, or when they do, scarcely two are alike. It is the same with the American loss to the Faith. The earnest student of our history is obliged to confess that *it was large ;* but how large it may have been is an unsettled question. The 'Irish World' of July 25, 1874, *maintained that* 18,000,000 *have been lost to Catholicity in this Republic.* It backed up this assertion with the following table, which, I believe, is, in the main, reliable :

"*Table Showing the Relative Proportions of the Constituent Elements of the Population of the United States in* 1870, *in which is Indicated the Number of Catholics that should be in the Country now,* (1874.)

 I. Total white population of the thirteen colonies at the close of the Revolutionary War ..   3,172,000

 II. Relative proportions of the constituent elements in colonial population

A TABULATED VIEW OF ROMAN CATHOLIC LOSSES, (Continued.)

Year.	Estimated Losses.	Catholic Authorities, Remarks, etc.
1876.		—Celtic (Irish, Scotch, Welsh, French, etc.).. 1,903,200
		(Irish separately) 1,141,920
		Anglo-Saxon ... 841.800
		Dutch and Scandinavians 427,000
		III. Product, in 1870, of the population of 1790 .... 9,496.000
		IV. Product, in 1870, of the separate elements of the population of 1790:
		Celtic 5,697,000
		(Irish separately) 3,418,200
		Anglo-Saxon ... 2,504,000
		Dutch and Scandinavians 1,295,000
		V. Product, in 1870, of population gained by acquisition of new territory since 1790 1,500,000
		VI. Product, in 1870, of Irish and French immigration from Canada 2,000,000
		VII. Total strength of Colored element in 1870 4,504,000
		VIII. Total immigration to U. S., 1790 to 1870 . 8,199,000

A TABULATED VIEW OF ROMAN CATHOLIC LOSSES, (Continued.)

Year.	Estimated Losses.	Catholic Authorities, Remarks, etc.
1876.		Irish immigration from 1790 to 1870 ...... 3,248,000 Anglo-Saxon immigration, from 1790 to 1870.. 796,000 Immigration of all other elements .... 4,155,000 IX. Product of total immigration to U. S., from 1790 to 1870........... 23,000,000 Product of Irish immigration (from 1790)... 9,750,000 Product of Anglo-Saxon immigration(from 1790)........ 2,000,000 Product of all other immigration(from 1790) 11,250,000 X. Total population of U. S. in 1870 .... 38,500,000 XI. Joint product, in 1870, of Irish Colonial element and subsequent Irish immigration (including that from Canada). 14,325,000 Joint product, in 1870, of Anglo-Saxon Colonial

A TABULATED VIEW OF ROMAN CATHOLIC LOSSES, (Continued.)

Year.	Estimated Losses.	Catholic Authorities, Remarks, etc.
1876.		element and subsequent Anglo-Saxon immigration . . . . 4,522,000 Joint product, in 1870, of all other Colonial elements and all subsequent immigiation (including Colored population) . . . . 19,653,000 Total joint product 38,500,000
		XII. Total Celtic element (*Irish, Scotch, French, Spanish, Italian*) in United States in 1870 . . . . 24,000,000 Total Irish element in U. S. in 1870 . . . . 14,325,000 Total Anglo-Saxon element in U. S. in 1870 . . . . 4,522,000 Total of all other elements (not Celtic nor Anglo-Saxon) in U. S. in 1870 . . 9,978,000
		"Almost the entire Celtic element (24,000,000) might be safely regarded as the descendants of men who were Catholics on settling in America."

Is it asked, Has not Romanism, in spite of these losses, relatively gained? We answer, Yes: no.

In our plan of investigation we shall soon be ready to enter upon this question. We next consider,

II. The Relative Progress.

1. What has been the progress of the three religious forces under consideration—the "Evangelical" Protestant, the "Liberal," and the Roman Catholic—relatively to the whole population of the United States.

The Evangelical Denominations.

In 1775 there was one *Church organization* of this class for 1,376 inhabitants; in 1870, one for 612 inhabitants. Taking the societies, (before explained as including in some instances parishes and congregations,) there were, in 1800, one for 1,740 inhabitants; in 1850, one for 895; in 1880, one for 520 inhabitants.

The *ministers* were, in 1775, one for 1,811 inhabitants; in 1800, one for 2,000 inhabitants; in 1850, one for 907 inhabitants; in 1880, one for 717 inhabitants.

How is it with the *evangelical communicants?*

An impression prevails in some quarters that, while the number of Church members in this country is constantly on the increase, the growth does not keep pace with the increase of the population. Some have contended that they are irrecoverably falling behind. This question is one of general interest; and it can be determined only upon a well-prepared basis of facts, covering a considerable term of years.

Twenty years ago a writer in the "Southern Observer" showed that, in 1750, the proportion of members of evangelical Churches to the entire population was one to thirteen; in 1775, one to sixteen; in 1792, one to eighteen; in 1825, one to fourteen; in 1855, one to six and three eighths; in 1860, one to five and a half. We have not at hand the statistics upon which these conclusions are based; and we very much doubt whether definite data for the first three periods ever were or ever can be obtained. But we have no doubt of the substantial accuracy of the conclusions, from what is well known of the religious tendencies of those times, as already sketched in previous chapters of this volume. For the periods within the present century we have statistics which we believe to be as accurate as such masses of statistics can well be, a great amount of care, research, and correspondence having been devoted to the work, for the last ten years.

In a previous paragraph, we have given the summaries showing the actual increase of the communicants. Compared with the population at the different periods, we find the following results: In 1800 there was one evangelical communicant in 14.50 inhabitants in the whole country. In 1850 there was one in 6.57 inhabitants. In 1870 there was one in 5.78 inhabitants. In 1880 there was one in 5 inhabitants.

These figures indicate a very large relative gain

upon the population—three communicants in the same number of inhabitants where there was one in 1800. While the population from 1800 to 1880 increased without a parallel in ancient or modern times, devolving upon the Protestant Churches the responsibility of meeting the religious needs of these rapidly multiplying millions, it is creditable to them, and an occasion of gratitude to God, that they have so far met these extraordinary demands, and achieved the brightest triumphs known in their whole history.* While the population since 1800

* Some have thought that it cannot be true that one in every five persons in the whole population is a communicant in the Evangelical Churches. To this we reply, that many rural communities can be found where the average is one in two or three inhabitants, as we know from persnoal examination. A single city in Massachusetts, of sixteen thousand inhabitants, has one Evangelical communicant in five inhabitants. Within a radius of ten miles, which includes Boston, Mass., there are about one in nine inhabitants, notwithstanding from twenty-seven to thirty-eight per cent. are foreign born. The colored communicants are relatively more numerous in proportion to their whole population, than the white communicants to the white population. The following are the totals of colored communicants :

African Methodist Episcopal Church	387,566
" " " Zion Church	300,000
Colored Methodist Episcopal Church	112,938
Methodist Episcopal Church.	189,395
Baptist Church	661,358
American Missionary Association	4,961
Presbyterian Freedmen's Unions	11,108
Methodist Episcopal Church, South	1,245
Several other denominations	20,000
Total	1,688,571

The colored population of the United States in 1880 was 6,577,151. The communicants of the colored Churches, therefore, were one for three and nine tenths of the whole colored population.

has increased 9.46 fold, the communicants of these Churches increased 27.58 fold, or almost three times as fast relatively.

The period since 1850 has been one of severe strain upon American Protestantism, on account of the great activity of modern rationalism, materialism, and spiritualism, and the large immigration. Because of these things, it has been claimed that, whatever increase the Evangelical Churches have had, they have, nevertheless, fallen behind the growth of the population during the last thirty years. But the statistics already noticed prove the contrary. Even during this trying period, while the population increased 116 per cent., the communicants of these Churches increased 185 per cent., or a half faster relatively than the population. And during the severe strain of the depression in the last decade, while the population increased 30 per cent., the communicants increased 50 per cent. The total increase of the communicants from 1850 to 1880 was 6,535,985, or more than twice as large as the increase in the fifty years from 1800 to 1850. The last thirty years, then, has been the period of the grandest progress, both actually and relatively.

THE LIBERAL CHURCHES AND THE POPULATION.

Combining the Unitarian, Universalist, New Jerusalem, and the Christian denominations, as in the table on a previous page of this chapter, we have,

SOCIETIES.

In 1840, 2,603, or one society for 6,557 inhabitants.
In 1860, 3,056,   "   " 10,256   "
In 1880, 2,584,   "   " 19,427   "

In 1880 these societies were only one third as many, in proportion to the whole population, as in 1840. They have steadily decreased relatively.

Making separate comparisons of two of these denominations, we have

UNITARIAN SOCIETIES.

In 1840, 230, or one society for 74,215 inhabitants.
In 1860, 254,   "   " 123,792   "
In 1880, 335,   "   " 149,851   "

In 1880 the Unitarian societies were only one half as many in the same population as in 1840. A steady relative decrease.

UNIVERSALIST SOCIETIES.

In 1840, 853, or one society for 20,011 inhabitants.
In 1860, 1,264,   "   " 24,875   "
In 1880, 956,   "   " 52,510   "

In 1880 the Universalist societies were two and a half times less relatively to the whole population than in 1840.

Each of the above calculations clearly shows that Liberal Christianity, as it has been pleased to style itself, is signally failing to maintain itself in organized forms. The organizing element characteristic of all life has been wanting, their attitude from the beginning having been one of criticism toward the generally accepted theology, and consequently negative rather than positive.

PROGRESS OF THE ROMAN CATHOLIC CHURCH COMPARED WITH THE POPULATION.

This denomination has made a large advance, relatively, upon the population. Three forms of comparison will show this fact clearly.

According to the United States census the *church edifices* of this body were :

> In 1850, 1,222, or one church for 18,977 inhabitants.
> In 1870, 3,806, "   "   " 10,130   "

According to the Roman Catholic "Year-Books' their *priests* were:

> In 1850, 1,302, or one priest for 17,812 inhabitants.
> In 1870, 3,966,   "   "   "   9,725   "
> In 1880, 6,402,   "   "   "   7,844   "

The Roman Catholic *population*, as *estimated* in their "Year-Books," was :

> In 1850, 1,614,000, or one Roman Catholic for 14.37 inhabitants.
> In 1870, 4,600,000,   "   "   " 8.38   "
> In 1880, 6,367,330,   "   "   " 7.88   "

At every point we discover evidences of a large gain, relatively, upon the whole population of the country. But the greatest gain was from 1850 to 1870. Since 1870 their relative gain has been very small.

2. *What has been the progress of the Evangelical, Liberal, and Roman Catholic denominations, as compared with each other?*

The immense disparity of the Evangelical and the Liberal Churches makes a comparison almost unnecessary; but we will take a single point furnished by an impartial source—the United States census—the *church edifices:*

	Evangelical.*	Liberal.†
1850	34,537	796
1860	48,037	1,003
1870	56,154	995

From 1850 to 1870 the Evangelical church edifices increased 21,617, and the Liberal 199; from 1860 to 1870 the Evangelical increased 8,117, and the Liberal decreased 8. We have already shown ‡ that the "Year-Books" of the Liberal Churches indicate the same fact.

The Evangelical Protestant and the Roman Catholic churches require a more extended comparison. Taking the church edifices we have :

	Evangelical.	Roman Catholic.
1850	34,537	1,222
1870	56,154	3,806
Increase	21,617	2,584

An increase of 2,584 Roman Catholic churches in twenty years is small to the increase of 21,617 Evangelical churches.

* See Table XII, in Appendix.
† In a previous paragraph in this chapter.　　　‡ Ibid.

29

Comparing the Evangelical ministers and the Roman Catholic priests, we have the following :

	Evangelical Ministers.	Roman Catholic Priests.
1850......................	25,555	1,302
1880......................	69,870	6,402
Increase............	44,315	5,100

The percentage of the increase of the Roman Catholic priests is much greater than that of the Evangelical ministers, but the actual increase of 5,100 priests is a small offset to an increase of 44,315 Evangelical ministers.

We next compare the communicants of the Evangelical Churches with the Roman Catholic population :

	Communicants.	R. C. Population.
1850...................	3,529,988	1,614,000
1870...................	6,673,396	4,600,000
1880...................	10,065,963	6,367,330
Increase, 1850–1870..	3,143,408	2,986,000
" 1870–1880..	3,392,567	1,767,330
" 1850–1880..	6,535,985	4,753,330

It appears that in the period of the largest Roman Catholic immigration, from 1850 to 1870, the increase of the enrolled communicants of the Evangelical Churches was 157,408 larger than the increase of the whole Roman Catholic population. In the last ten years it was 1,625,237 greater ; and in the whole thirty years (1850–1880) it was 1,782,655 greater.

While the Roman Catholic Church, largely aided by immigration, has relatively gained upon the population, it has, nevertheless, not gained upon Protestantism. The Evangelical Protestant Churches, with only small accessions from abroad, have far outstripped her. The increase of single classes of Protestant Churches has far exceeded the whole increase of Romanism. While the church edifices of the Roman Catholic Church, from 1850 to 1870, increased 2,584, those of the several bodies bearing the name Baptist increased 4,399; and of the various bodies bearing the name Methodist, 9,035. The " Year-Books " of the Churches show that while the Roman Catholic priests, from 1850 to 1880, increased 5,100, the ordained ministers of the various Presbyterian bodies increased 4,276; of the Baptist bodies, 11,428; of the Methodist bodies, 15,430—the Baptist alone more than twice as much, and the Methodist alone three times as much. The ordained ministers of the Methodist Episcopal Church (North) alone, and also of the Baptist Church (North and South) alone, not to include other bodies bearing the names Methodist and Baptist, are twice as numerous as the Roman Catholic priests. Taking the communicants of four classes of Churches, those bearing the name Baptist, Methodist, Lutheran, and United Brethren, leaving out of the account all the Presbyterian, Congregational, Episcopal, and about a dozen other Evangelical denominations, increased more, from 1850 to 1880, than the whole Roman Catholic population, as estimated in their " Year-Books."

There is another view of this matter which must not be overlooked. In all our comparisons, hitherto, we have given Romanism every possible advantage. We have compared the registered communicants of the Evangelical Churches with the Roman Catholic estimates, based upon conjectures or only meager data ; and we have also compared these duly en- rolled and yearly revised lists of communicants, seven eighths of whom are above eighteen years of age, with the whole Roman Catholic population. Their estimates (we have it on the authority of those who have assisted the Bishops in making them) include whole households, all baptized chil- dren as well as adults. The bases for comparison, therefore, are very unlike, and unfair to evangelical Protestantism.

In order to make the comparison equitable, the whole population of the Evangelical Churches should be compared with the Roman Catholic population. This may be done by multiplying the communicants of these Churches by $3\frac{1}{2}$, (the usual number is 4, but we prefer to not seem to overrate any thing.) There must be at least two and a half additional persons for every communicant who is an adherent of the Evangelical Churches. Calculating thus, we have the following results :

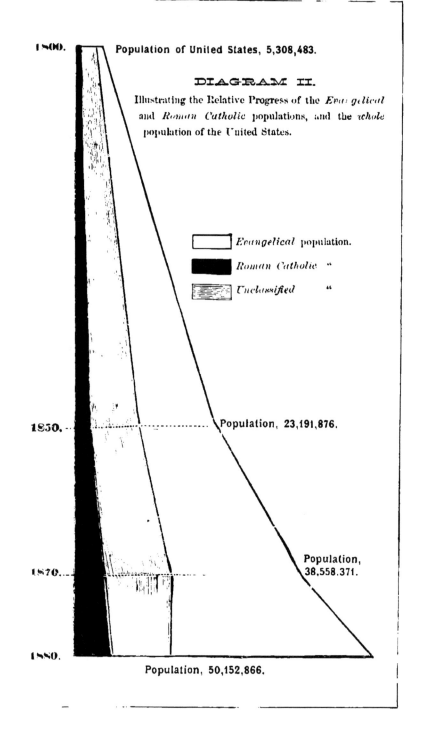

1800.

Population of United States, 5,308,483.

DIAGRAM II.

Illustrating the Relative Progress of the *Evangelical*
and *Roman Catholic* populations, and the *whole*
population of the United States.

☐ *Evangelical* population.

■ *Roman Catholic* "

▦ *Unclassified* "

1850. Population, 23,191,876.

Population,
38,558.371.

1870.

1880.

Population, 50,152,866.

	Population of the Evangelical Churches.	Roman Catholic Population.
In 1800	1,277,052	100,000
In 1850	12,354,958	1,614,000
In 1870	23,356,886	4,600,000
In 1880	35,230,870	6,367,330

These figures show the relative position and growth of these two religious classes during the century. The increase has been:

	Evangelical Pop.	R. C. Population.
1800–1880	33,953,818	6,267,330
1850–1880	22,875,912	4,753,330
1870–1880	11,873,984	1,767,330

From 1800 to 1880 the Evangelical population increased 5.42 times more than the whole Roman Catholic population; from 1850 to 1880, 4.80 times more; and from 1870 to 1880, 6.72 times more. The last ten years has been, relatively, the best for Evangelical progress.

What percentage of the whole population has been Evangelical Protestant, and what percentage Roman Catholic, in these different periods, is an interesting inquiry. The following is the statement, and the *diagram* on the opposite page, with measurements carefully calculated, will illustrate the relative progress.

The Evangelical population was:

In 1800, 24.06 per cent. of the whole population.
In 1850, 53.22 " " " "
In 1870, 60.57 " " " "
In 1880, 70.003 " " " "

The Roman Catholics were,

In 1800,   .02 per cent. of the whole population.
In 1850,   .07   "   "   "
In 1870, 11.93   "   "   "
In 1880, 12.68   "   "   "

From the foregoing it will appear that the proportion of the population of the United States, not included as adherents of the Evangelical Churches, in the different periods, was as follows :

In 1800, 75.94 per cent.   In 1870, 39.43 per cent.
In 1850, 46.78   "   In 1880, 30   "

These last per centages include the Roman Catholics, the adherents of the Liberal Churches, and the masses who wholly stand aloof from all the Churches. In the past eighty years this part of the population has been reduced from 75.94 to 30 per cent. of the whole inhabitants.

It is unnecessary to pursue these comparisons further. Romanism has made large gains, even upon the population, but chiefly from immigration, and evangelical Protestantism has gained relatively much more than Romanism. During the last ten years the gain of Romanism has been less than in the two preceding decades, while the Evangelical Churches have gained more than ever before. Present indications justify the prediction that *Romanism has passed the period of her most rapid increase in the United States, and must henceforth relatively decline.*

An intelligent Roman Catholic layman in Boston, not many years ago, said: "*We shall hold our ground for awhile; but we understand that in the fight of a hundred years we shall be whipped.*"

There is another aspect of the question of religious progress, which, in an age when educational culture is one of the chief factors of the world's progress, must not be overlooked—the relation of the Christian Churches to the higher forms of education. We ask attention, therefore, to

3. *The Churches in their Relation to the Higher Educational Institutions.*

The influence of the Churches upon scholarship, and the share of the Churches in institutions for advanced culture are signs of true progress.

It has been freely asserted, of late, that the Churches are losing their hold upon the intellect of the age; that few young men in the colleges are Christians, in the usual acceptation of the term ; that denominational colleges are relatively declining, and are destined to be superseded.

What are the facts?

Availing ourselves of General Eaton's very able reports, as Commissioner of Education, the Year-Books of the Churches, and consultations with men occupying high positions in connection with collegiate education, we have prepared an exhibit (Table XIV, in Appendix) of the denominational and

non-denominational colleges in the United States.
In so doing we have discarded the terms "sectarian" and "non-sectarian," sometimes used, because not truly expressing the character and relations of these institutions.   They use no ecclesiastical tests in admitting students, or in any subsequent requirements in regard to attendance upon
religious worship, or otherwise, unless some of the
Roman Catholic colleges do it.   Harvard College,
reported as "non-sectarian," is no more so than
over two hundred others reported as sustaining denominational relations; for Harvard, during more
than half a century, has been under the direction
of a "Board of Fellows," all of whom have been
Unitarians, except one elected within two or three
years; and, besides, the Theological School of Harvard College is uniformly mentioned in the Unitarian "Year-Book," as a Unitarian institution, of
which Charles W. Eliot, LL.D., is president.
Furthermore, Harvard College had a purely religious origin, and was supported for generations by
the religious life of New England.   Yale, Princeton,
and Columbia Colleges, also reported in General
Eaton's late reports as "non-sectarian," only two
or three years ago were reported as Congregational, Presbyterian, and Episcopal colleges.   But
they have neither changed nor annulled their ecclesiastical relations, and are now as truly the colleges of those denominations as ever, and yet it is

also true that they are, in the legitimate sense of the offensive phrase, non-sectarian, for they employ no ecclesiastical tests.

Changing the phraseology, therefore, and using the terms *denominational* and *non-denominational*, and we have, on the one hand, the colleges of the Churches, comprising those closely related to the Churches in origin, sympathy, and support, some of which are organically held by ecclesiastical bodies ; and, on the other hand, those which sustain no particular denominational relations. This classification fairly covers the question at issue, What are the Churches doing for collegiate education, or how far are they identified with advanced intellectual culture? In carrying out this classification, the advantage of any doubt, in regard to institutions not clearly designated, has been given to the non-denominational list.

Of the sixty-four colleges classified * as non-denominational, twenty-three are State institutions, some of them founded before the disruption of the union between the Churches and the States; four city institutions, three military, two agricultural, one a deaf-mute institution, and the remaining thirty-one are not very clearly designated as to their character. Nearly half of the latter, however, are under the presidency of evangelical divines. Eight of the State and city institutions have clergy-

* See Table XIV, in Appendix.

men for presidents, and many of the professors and
students are active evangelical communicants.

The number of the colleges in 1878 * was as
follows:

Date of Founding.	Denomina-tional.	Non-denomi-national.	Total.
Prior to 1800	12	8	20
1800–1850.............	87	15	102
1850–1878.............	213	41	254
Total.............	312	64	376

The organization of 56 non-denominational and
300 denominational colleges, or five and a half
times as many of the latter as of the former since
1800, and 41 non-denominational and 213 denominational colleges, or more than five times as many
of the latter as of the former since 1850, does not
indicate that the Churches have been negligent in
the work of providing for the collegiate education
of their people, nor that they are losing their hold
upon advanced culture.

The property of the above institutions was as
follows:

Colleges.	Buildings, Grounds, Productive Funds.
Denominational........................	$68,824,853
Non-denominational....................	21,301,934
Total.......................	$90,126,787

The property of the denominational colleges is
more than three times as large as that of the
others, notwithstanding that one half of the latter

* See Table XIV, in Appendix.

are either city, state, military, or agricultural institutions, favored with donations from public treasuries.

It will not be regarded as a fact of slight significance that the Churches of the United States have accumulated and set into operation more than $68,000,000 for the promotion of the highest form of education, and that more than two thirds of this sum has been accumulated within the last thirty years.

But the question of students is the most important.   The whole number of students in the higher collegiate course for the degree of A.B. was 30,359 ;* of which number 5,883, or less than one fourth, were in non-denominational colleges, and 24,476, or about four fifths, were in denominational colleges.

Of the whole number of college students 65 per cent. are in the colleges of the Evangelical Churches. Of the whole number in the denominational colleges 81 per cent. are in the colleges of the Evangelical Churches :

Baptists (all kinds)............................ 4,011 students.
Congregationalists.............................. 2,428   "
Congregational and Presbyterian................ 311   "
Christians and Disciples....................... 2,026   "
Evangelical Association........................   39   "

---

* On page lxxxviii of the Report for 1878 Gen. Eaton gives 57,987 students in universities and colleges ; but these numbers include students in preparatory departments.   The true figures are from Table IX, pp. 526, etc., column 17, amounting to 30,368.   Slightly revising the statistics by the aid of some ecclesiastical "Year-Books," we have the above-mentioned number, 30,359.

See Table XIV, in Appendix, for fuller details.

Episcopalians.................................... 827 students.
Friends....................................... 261   "
Lutherans (all kinds) 1,152   "
Methodists (all kinds)........................ 4,496   "
Presbyterians (all kinds)...................... 3,459   "
Roman Catholics............................. 3,564   "
Reformed Churches (Dutch and German) 521   "
Swedenborgians 17   "
Seventh-day Advent........................... 39   "
United Brethren 286   "
Universalists 226   "
Unitarians 813   "

A comparison, covering a period of forty-eight years, upon good and satisfactory bases, at each extreme, will help to a fuller solution of the question under consideration. The "American Quarterly Register" for May, 1831, gives the statistics of the American colleges for 1830, prepared by Revs. Elias Cornelius and B. B. Edwards, D.D. The 48 colleges in that list had 4,021 undergraduates. Eighteen of these institutions were non-denominational, with 1,360 students, and 30 were denominational colleges, with 2,661 students. Comparing these with the statistics for 1878, we see very marked progress in the colleges of the Churches:

Number of Colleges.	1830.	1878.	Increase in 48 yrs.
Denominational.................	30	312	282
Non-denominational..........	18	64	46
Total *colleges*	48	376	328

Number of Students.			
In denominational colleges	2,661	24,476	21,815
In non-denominational colleges.	1,360	5,883	4,523
Total *students*............	4,021	30,359	26,338

Here is evidence of very great educational progress. While the population of the country increased
a little more than three and a half fold the colleges increased nearly eight fold, and the students
seven and a half fold, or more than twice as much,
relatively, as the population. The table shows
that for this extraordinary educational progress
the country is indebted chiefly to the Churches,
the denominational colleges increasing more than
tenfold and their students ninefold, while the non-
denominational colleges increased only three and a
half fold, and their students fourfold. In 1830 the
non-denominational colleges had 30 per cent. of
the whole number of the students, and the denominational colleges 70 per cent. In 1878 the students in the non-denominational colleges had fallen
to 17 per cent., and in the denominational colleges
they had risen to 83 per cent. of the whole number.

We are unable to make any comparisons testing,
in an exact form, the educational progress of the
Roman Catholic Church, but the progress has been
very great. Four of its colleges were founded prior
to 1830, but the number of students was not then
reported. In 1878, according to Gen. Eaton's re
port, there were 52 colleges of this denomination ;
but the Catholic " Year-Book " for 1880 reported
78 colleges, and for 1881 there were 79. Probably
the number given by Gen. Eaton comprises the
better class of their colleges, many of which are

very young, and have not yet emerged from the rank of preparatory institutions. These 52 institutions had 3,564 students. Probably no denomination in the country has made greater progress in education, although the quality of education given in all their institutions of learning is inferior to that furnished in other American institutions. But single Protestant denominations still far outrank the Roman Catholics in the number of college students. The Baptists (all kinds) have 4,011 ; the Methodists, (all kinds,) 4,496 ; and all the colleges of the Baptists and Methodists, except Brown University, have been founded within the same recent period in which the Catholics have founded theirs.

The theological seminaries also indicate great educational progress in the Churches, as will appear from the following table :

	1830.*		1878.†	
	No of Schools.	No. of Students.	No. of Schools.	No. of Students.
Schools of Evangelical Churches...	17	631	103	3,297
" Unitarian Churches....	1	78	2	39
" Universalist Churches	....	....	2	49
" New Church........... ..	....	....	1	3
Total Protestant............	18	709	108	3,388
Roman Catholic........... ..	....	....	17	932
Aggregate................	18	709	125	4,320

The students of the Protestant schools of theology are 3.6 times as many as those of the Roman Cath-

* See "American Quarterly Register," May, 1831.
† Report of Gen. Eaton, Commissioner of Education, 1878.

olic, but we have no data for the comparison of the latter with any former period. In 1830 the Protestant theological students were one for 18,146 inhabitants ; in 1878 they were one for 13,127 inhabitants. In 1874 the Protestant students were above 4,500, or one for 9,500 inhabitants. The financial embarrassments from 1873 to 1878 diminished the number somewhat.

The female colleges for the superior instruction of women have also greatly multiplied, and they are very largely under the supervision of the Churches. Of 225 institutions of this class in 1878, reported by Gen. Eaton, only 9 existed prior to 1830. The relations of 7 not specified ; 71 are non-denominational ; 18, Roman Catholic ; and 129 belong to Protestant denominations. But the list is yet imperfect.

Religious Students.

The statistics gathered by societies of Religious Inquiry show that the proportion of college students professedly religious and connected with Evangelical Churches, has relatively increased since 1830. In that year, out of 2,633 students in 28 colleges, 693, or 26 per cent., were " professedly pious." Returns were obtained in 1850 from 30 colleges, with 4,533 students, of which 1,727, or 38 per cent., were religious ; in 1865, from 38 colleges, with 7,351 students, of which 3,380, or 46 per cent., were religious ; in 1872, in a smaller list of 12 colleges, with 1,891 students, 50 per cent. were professors of religion.   In 1880,* out of 12.063 students in 65 colleges, 6,081, or 50 per cent., were professors of religion.   From these incomplete returns it appears that the number of religious young men in the colleges is relatively twice as great as in 1830. Fuller returns might not be quite as favorable, but would, doubtless, show great progress.   The principles of Evangelical Christianity are evidently extending their influence over the educated young men of the land.

In the "Sunday Afternoon," for September, 1878, Mr. C. F. Thwing furnished a careful article upon the question of Religion and the American Colleges, upon which the following editorial appeared, soon after, in the "Boston Journal:"

As we very often hear opinions to the effect that the colleges are degenerating, both as regards morality and religion, and that skepticism and worldliness are taking the place of the old-time piety, it is particularly satisfactory to find that the facts and statistics, so far from sustaining such opinions, directly disprove them.   While it is true that there has been an abatement in sectarianism and in the rigidity of discipline, as compared with the earlier days; and while it is doubtless also true, though upon this point Mr. Thwing's statistics do not guide us, that the proportion of students who are fitting themselves for the ministry is smaller now than formerly, these facts do not make against the conclusions which Mr. Thwing reaches.   An abatement in sectarianism is not, of necessity, accompanied with

---

* "Year-Book" of the Young Men's Christian Association, New York, 1880, pp. 92–95.

a diminution of piety; and the smaller proportion of theological students simply indicates that the necessity of introducing the Christian leaven into other professions and occupations is more keenly felt than formerly.

It is a well-known fact that religion was both the motive and the basis of the establishment of the older colleges in the East, as well as of the newer institutions in the West and South. Harvard was founded because of the dread of "leaving an illiterate ministry to the Churches," and Yale was established for the nurture of a more rigid orthodoxy than that prevailing at Harvard, and for the education of a ministry for the New Haven Colony. So of Princeton, Dartmouth, Bowdoin, Amherst, and others, the religious idea was dominant and fundamental in their establishment. The Western colleges are, in a large number of cases, the direct outgrowth of missionary movements, and had for their first purpose the propagation of religious truth. Iowa College was founded by the famous "Andover Band," and has always been an active agent in evangelization. At Oberlin, in its early years, a banner waved from the flag-staff, bearing the inscription, "Holiness to the Lord," and a spirit of aggressive piety has marked the institution in all stages of its growth down to the present day. At Harvard, in the early days, the rules compelled the regular reading of the Scriptures twice daily by each student; the repeating of sermons in public when required; the rendering of the Old and New Testaments from the originals into the Latin; and many other religious studies and observances, now obsolete.

But while the colleges have ceased to be distinctively religious institutions, the religious element has still, in a vast majority of cases, Mr. Thwing asserts, a very important influence in the daily life and on the character of the students. A large majority of the members of our college faculties are members of the Church, and what President Seelye writes of Amherst is largely true of other institutions, that, although no religious test is made the condition of holding an office of instruction, "we should no more think of appointing to a post of instruction here an irreligious than we should an immoral man, or one ig-

30

norant of the topics he would have to teach." Of the twenty
thousand students who are now pursuing regular college courses
in this country, almost one half are Christians. The lowest
extreme is at Harvard, where the proportion of Christians to
those not Christians is one to five. At Amherst, Williams,
Wesleyan, Middlebury, Iowa, and Berea, on the other hand,
four out of every five of the students are Christians. There
has been a very marked increase in the proportion of Christian
collegians during the last twenty-five years. In 1853, at Harvard, only one man in ten was a professor of religion; at
Brown, only one in five; at Yale, Dartmouth, and Bowdoin,
one in four; at Williams, one in two; at Amherst, five in eight.
At Harvard, as already stated, the proportion is now one to
five; at Brown, three in five; at Yale, two in five; at Dartmouth and Bowdoin, one in three; and at Williams and Amherst, four in five. If the comparison is made with a still earlier
date the progress is even more marked. At Harvard and Yale,
at the beginning of this century, the number of Christian students was smaller than at any other period in their history,
owing to the influence of English and French infidelity. In
the first eight classes at Bowdoin there was only one Christian,
and at Williams, at about the same time, there was but a single
Church member among the students..

Another interesting fact is stated by Mr. Thwing, namely,
that revivals are of more frequent occurrence, of longer continuance, of greater pervasiveness, and of a calmer, more intellectual character among college men than in any other class
of the community. Although at Yale, Harvard, Brown, and a
few other colleges, revivals have been infrequent of late years,
in most colleges a class rarely completes its course without
passing through a revival. At Princeton each of the last
twenty-five classes, with one or two exceptions, has experienced a season of revival, and three years ago over a hundred
students were converted in a single term. So at Amherst,
Williams, Dartmouth, and other Eastern colleges, and at Oberlin and other Western colleges, revivals are frequent and powerful. In some of these colleges nearly one half of the students

became Christians during their course.. The thoughtfulness
engendered by study, the influence of Christian professors, and
the close intimacy of non-Christian with Christian students,
combine to bring about a condition very favorable to religious
awakenings. Yale has had no less than thirty-six revivals, resulting in at least twelve hundred conversions; Dartmouth
nine, resulting in two hundred and fifty conversions; and Middlebury and Amherst at least twelve each, resulting, in the
case of the latter, in three hundred and fifty conversions.
These and similar facts which Mr. Thwing presents should
check the pessimism of those who maintain that, religiously
and morally, the colleges are going to the bad. Much of the
religious history of these institutions remains, of necessity,
unwritten, and the matter is one with regard to which it is not
easy to procure statistics, but the facts which Mr. Thwing has
ascertained justify a very hopeful feeling concerning the religious future of our colleges.

The foregoing statistics demonstrate the strong
and enduring progress of Protestantism; that it is
fully identified with the highest educational culture
of the age; and that the denominational institutions
are not likely to be superseded, as some have confidently predicted. These facts augur well for its
future.

One more aspect of the question of relative progress remains to be briefly considered.

4. The Progress of Evangelical Christianity in the United States, in the Present Century, compared with its Progress in
the First Centuries of the Christian Era.

It is very common to look back to the first Christian centuries as a period of the greatest growth of

Christianity; but those who do so do not act intelligently. The last one hundred and fifty years has been a period of greater Christian progress in the whole world than any previous period. This will appear in the last chapter of this volume. But in the United States alone, in the last eighty years, the progress of the first Christian centuries has been greatly exceeded.

The progress of Christianity in the first centuries of the Christian era has been usually estimated as follows:

	Christians.
Close of the 1st Century	500,000
" " 2d "	2,000,000
" " 3d "	5,000,000
" " 4th "	10,000,000
" " 5th "	15,000,000
" " 6th "	20,000,000
" " 7th "	25,000,000
" " 8th "	30,000,000

In the United States the enrolled communicants increased in eighty years (1800–1880) 9,701,091, which is nearly equal to the total increase of Christianity in the first four centuries of the Christian era. But much of the latter increase was only nominal, under the military conquests of Constantine, etc. Taking, therefore, the entire evangelical population of the United States, as we have already figured it, numbering, in 1880, 35,230,870, and we see that this growth here in eighty years exceeded the growth of Christianity in the first eight

centuries after Christ, by an excess of more than
five millions.

It would seem that no mind could fail to be impressed with these wonderful facts of American
Protestantism, so transcending in magnitude and
significance any thing ever before seen in the history of Christianity. But those who have written
the heavy indictments quoted in the opening chapter of this volume must be either wholly ignorant
of these statistical facts, or have not duly studied
them, or are accustomed to flippantly ignore them,
as only mathematics, which can have no relation to
religious matters. But such persons overlook the
almost universal application of figures to all departments of science, of political, moral, and social life.
We summarize moral tendencies and crime in statistical tables, analyze them, and deduce conclusions. Figures represent the speed and momentum
of material bodies, the weight and power of steam,
the measure of gas and heat, the forces of electricity,
etc. As, therefore, the mathematical *formulæ* of
chemistry represent the combinations and operations of material elements, and those of astronomy
the position and movements of the heavenly bodies,
so the numerical exhibits of ecclesiastical bodies,
carefully analyzed and combined, represent the existence and operation of spiritual forces; but each
in the light of its own peculiar sphere. The statistics which we have given are those of religious phe-

nomena. On the principles of exact science they are as legitimate and indubitable, in their sphere, and as worthy of classification, as any other phenomena.

Is it said that there are certain questions of religious vitality and spirituality, of Christian character and life, which are not indicated by figures; that the type of piety is manifestly declining; that the average morality of the communicants of these Churches and of the public has seriously deteriorated; and that radical changes and modifications have taken place in the theology of these denominations, so that the statistics of to-day do not stand as exponents of the same ideas, even in the same religious bodies, that they did fifty, or seventy-five, or a hundred years ago?

This plausible objection has been anticipated and considered in the preceding chapters on Faith, Morals, and Spiritual Vitality, in which it has been demonstrated that, whatever imperfection exists in these respects, an intelligent analysis of modern progress shows a great advance in the better elements of piety and morals. The existence of an unabated force, operating even more powerfully and aggressively during the last two or three decades than at any previous period, so strikingly exhibited by the statistics since 1850, is a fact of too great significance to be lightly discarded or ignored by any candid, discriminating mind.

CHAPTER IV.

FOREIGN MISSIONS.

Inception.
Papal and Protestant Mission Fields.
Foreign Missions of the United States.
Foreign Missions of Christendom.
Papal and Protestant Missions.
Missions Vindicated by Testimony.
Results.

CHAPTER IV.

FOREIGN MISSIONS.

THE pessimistic complaint includes foreign missions in its indictment, and talks loudly of their failure. "Why such tardy results from such vast expenditures of men and means?" The inquiry contains the fallacious assumption that the results are meager—begs the question; and too many missionary discourses make admissions, seriously compromising the cause and embarrassing the support of the laborers.

Tested by ordinary *criteria*, Christian missions do not suffer by comparison with moral and secular enterprises. Like the progress of mechanical science, political knowledge, and æsthetic culture, the missions of Protestantism have advanced with rapid strides, and are so securely planted in many heathen countries, that, if all support were withdrawn, they would be sustained by the native ministry and membership alone. A considerable number are already self-sustaining.

Protestant foreign missions are yet in their infancy—almost wholly the work of the present century. The few feeble efforts antedating the year

1800 may be briefly outlined in a single paragraph: the Swedish movements among the Lap-
landers, under the patronage of Gustavus Vasa I., in
the early days of Protestantism ; the arbitrary efforts
of the Dutch, at the beginning of the seventeenth
century, to convert the natives of Ceylon to Christianity ; the more spiritual, but only temporarily
successful, labors of Robert Junius, beginning in
1634, on the island of Formosa ; the Indian missions
in New England and other American colonies, commencing in 1646 under Rev. John Eliot, followed
by the Mayhews, Edwards, Brainerd, Wheelock,
the Moravians, the agents of the " Scottish Society
for the Promotion of Christian Knowledge," etc. ;
the movements of the London "Society for the
Propagation of the Gospel in Foreign Parts," organized in .1701, chiefly for English colonists ; the
missions of the Danes,* in 1705, in Southern India,†
subsequently extending to Ceylon, and comprising,
in 1775, 13 missionaries, 50 native assistants, 633
scholars, and 1,000 communicants ; the wonderful missions of the Moravians, beginning in 1732,
in the West Indies, and soon after in Greenland ;
and the Wesleyan foreign missions, from 1760
onward, chiefly under the management of Rev.

---

* These missionaries completed a translation of the New Testament into the Tamil language in 1715, and of the Old Testament
in 1726.

† Schwartz's more than forty years of heroic missionary labors
were performed in these missions.

Thomas Coke, LL.D., but more formally organized in 1813. So meager was the exhibit of the foreign missions of Protestantism in the first two and three fourths centuries of its existence.

It is no exaggeration to say that the period preceding the full inauguration of modern missions was one of the darkest in the history of the Christian Church, and the darkest in the history of Protestantism. The Protestantism of the Reformation had spent its force. Turned back, at first, by the great Papal reaction, in which the famous Roman Catholic missions, in the sixteenth and seventeenth centuries, under the Franciscans, the Dominicans, and the new missionary brotherhood of the Jesuits, were begun, it wasted itself in internal conflicts, lost its independence by alliance with the State, and even entered into truce with its inveterate foes. In Great Britain the Wesleyan movement was yet in its infancy, and in America the feeble Christian life was sorely taxed in a struggle for self-preservation. About one hundred years ago the aggressive power of Protestantism was reduced to its minimum.

The science, the philosophy, and the culture of that age were almost wholly against evangelical Christianity. Never before nor since has infidelity combined relatively so much wealth, culture, and power. Hume's acute logic, Gibbon's historic learning and skill, Paine's nameless blasphemies,

Voltaire's brilliant wit and amazing industry, and the French Revolution, with its mighty sweep of radical revolt, combined to subvert the popular belief in Christianity, and brand the Church as a creature of superstition and falsehood. This revolt did not wholly spend its force in the eighteenth century, but struggled hard in the first quarter of the nineteenth century, against the new incoming tides of spiritual life and the reviving faith in the Churches. After 1817, in the course of a few years, 5,768,900 volumes of the works of Voltaire, Rousseau, and other infidel writers, besides countless tracts, were circulated on the continent of Europe.

The new mechanical inventions and mighty forces, since subsidized by the Churches in the interests of Christ's kingdom, were then unknown. No steamship plowed any ocean or river; magnetic telegraphs, cylinder presses, and railroads were unborn; and the commerce of nations was carried over mountains and deserts on the backs of mules and dromedaries, or over oceans in vessels dependent upon the wind and tide. But exploration, invention, ambition, avarice, commerce, and the sword—strangely providential factors of progress— have wrought out changes preparing the way, and furnishing new means and opportunities for the spread of the Gospel.

In 1790 only three foreign missionary societies

existed in Europe, and none in America; but new life was pulsating. In 1792 the English Baptist Missionary Society was formed; in 1795 the London Missionary Society, in 1796 the Scottish and the Glasgow Societies, in 1797 the Netherlands' Society, and in 1799 the Church Missionary Society. These societies at first encountered great unbelief and opposition from many in the Churches and ridicule from the world. Ecclesiastical bodies in Scotland denounced the scheme of foreign missions as "illusive," "visionary," and "dangerous," and decreed that it was absurd to think of propagating the Gospel abroad, "so long as there remained a single individual at home without the means of religious knowledge."

After the year 1800 foreign missions received a new impulse, both in Europe and America, though they still encountered opposition and ridicule. Between 1800 and 1830 sixteen foreign missionary societies were organized, between 1830 and 1850 thirty-three more, and, at the present time, Protestantism numbers over seventy* foreign boards, besides numerous subsidiary organizations. Sixteen woman's foreign missionary boards have been organized in the United States since 1861, and all but one since 1868.

*Some have united.

PAPAL AND PROTESTANT MISSION FUNDS.

The Roman Catholic Church, also, since its missionary revival, after the discoveries of Columbus and the birth of Protestantism, has developed organizations for the spread of the Papal faith : First, in connection with the rise of the Jesuits and their early and more distinctively missionary labors, through organized movements in France, large sums of money were raised to aid the Jesuit missions in New France, as Canada was then called. The motives were partly religious, but chiefly prompted by wild conceptions of the illimitable extension of French dominion in the vast territories of the New World, for which the Jesuits were continually scheming.

The Propaganda at Rome, founded in 1662 for the training of men for the missionary priesthood ; the famous Propaganda at Lyons, organized in 1822 ; the Leopold Propaganda at Venice, formed in 1829; and the " Society of the Holy Childhood," with special reference to heathen orphans, formed soon after the next preceding, comprise the missionary organizations of the Roman Catholic Church. In recent years the annual receipts of the latter have been about $200,000, and of the Leopold Society $50,000. The Lyons Society received, in 1852, $891,025 ; in 1872, $1,129,529; in 1879, $1,206,325. Total receipts of the latter since its foundation, (1822–1879,) $36,943,935, collected from all parts of the world, from a nominal Catholic population twice as great as that of Protestantism. The Roman Catholics of the British Isles contributed for foreign missions, in 1879, $40,560,* and those of the United States about $15,000.

What sums have been raised by the Protestant foreign missionary societies? Professor Christlieb† has estimated that, in 1800, the *total sum* annually contributed in all Christendom for Protestant missions hardly amounted to $250,000. In 1850 the income of these boards in Europe and America was $2,959,541 16.‡ In 1872 the amount had increased to $7,874,155,§ or seven times as much as the receipts of the Lyons Propaganda for that year.

From 1852 to 1872 the receipts of the Lyons Propaganda advanced 25 per cent., and of the Protestant boards 162 per cent. The actual increase of the Protestant boards during that time was nearly $5,000,000, while that of the Lyons Propaganda was about $230,000. The aggregate receipts of the Protestant foreign missionary societies of Europe and America, from their origin to

---

* See "Kalendar of the English Church," for 1881, p. 265.

† Recent volume on "Protestant Foreign Missions," Randolph & Co., New York, 1880, p. 18.

‡ "Christian Retrospect and Register," App., Rev. R. Baird, D.D.

§ "Statistics of Protestant Missions," by Rev. W. B. Boyce. London, 1874. See also article on Missions in M'Clintock & Strong's Cyclopedia.

the present time, calculated on a basis of numerous data at hand, cannot be less than $270,000,000, of which nearly or quite $200,000,000 have probably been raised within the last thirty years.

For the British Isles and the United States we have more exact data.

The " Kalendar of the English Church," for 1881, pp. 258–265, gives the following summary of British contributions for Protestant foreign missions for 1879, compiled by Rev. W. A. Scott-Robertson:

Twenty Church of England societies........	£449,886
Eleven undenominational "	156,985
Fifteen English Nonconformist "	297,382
Seventeen Scottish . " "	162,643
Five Irish Presbyterian "	11,670
Total for 1879	£1,078,566

Contributions of above societies for nine years (1871–79,) £9,064,298, or $45,321,490. Combining these figures with those of our own land, we have,

The British Isles in one year (1879).........	$5,392,830
The United States in one year (1879–80)	2,623,618*
Total........................	$8,016,448†
The British Isles in nine years	$45,321,490
The United States in nine years............	22,209,354
Total........................	$67,530,844

* Professor Christlieb, in his address to the Evangelical Alliance at Basel, 1879, estimated these receipts less than $2,000,000, and the total receipts, in a single year, of the Foreign Missionary Societies of all Christendom at $5,762,000, which is evidently far too small.

† The receipts of the societies on the Continent of Europe would swell this amount considerably more.

THE FOREIGN MISSIONS OF THE PROTESTANT CHURCHES OF THE UNITED STATES.

In this country about twenty foreign missionary boards, besides sixteen woman's missionary societies, are engaged in the work of raising funds and sending out missionaries into various foreign fields. The statistics of the pecuniary receipts are most inspiring. The following table * will impressively exhibit the aggregate amount received from sixteen denominational societies and fourteen woman's boards from the origin of each:

Years.	Amount.	Average yearly.
1810–1819.............	$206,210	$20,621
1820–1829.............	745,718	74,571
1830–1839.............	2,885,839	288,583
1840–1849.............	5,078,922	507,892
1850–1859.....	8,427,284	842,728
1860–1869.............	13,074,129	1,307,412
1870–1880 (11 years)....	24,861,482	2,260,143
Not reported by decades.	2,349,362	
Total 1810–1880......	$57,628,946	

From 1870–1880, $24,861,482 were received, which is two and a half times more than was received in the forty years from 1810 to 1850. Eighty-three per cent. of the aggregate for seventy years (1810–1880) has been received in the last thirty years. This money was raised exclusively for foreign missions.

* See Table XV, in Appendix.

31

What results can the foreign mission societies of the *United States* show for this remarkable expenditure ?

By the aid of Tables XXXIV and XXXV, (Appendix,) the exhibit is easily made :

	1850.	1880.	Increase.
Missions	77	129 [4]	52
Principal stations.....................	196	758 [34]	562
Sub-stations........................	.... [1]	3,925 [10]	....
Ordained ministers, foreign and native.	438	1,792	1,354
Lay assistants, foreign and native	829 [30]	4,167 [11]	3,338
Total laborers	1,267 [31]	5,959 [21]	4,692
Communicants	47,266 [10]	205,132 [13]	157,866
Day-schools	883 [10]	1,392 [62]	509
Day-school pupils	29,210 [11]	65,825 [55]	36,615

The small figures above the others indicate the number of missions not reporting the given item.

The above tabular exhibit is sufficiently clear and convincing without extended comments. The Churches of the United States are sustaining, directly or indirectly, 5,959 laborers in more than 4,683 principal and sub-stations in foreign lands, and have in their missions more than 205,132 enrolled communicants—an increase in the latter of more than 300 per cent. in 30 years.

Turning from this narrower view, we ask attention to a broader survey of this field :

TOTAL PROTESTANT FOREIGN MISSIONS OF EUROPE AND AMERICA.

By the aid of Tables XXXVI, XXXVII, and XXXVIII, (Appendix,) a clear exhibit can be made, covering fifty years:

	1830.	1850.	1880.	Increase.	
				1830–80.	1850–80.
Missions	122	178	504	382	326
Principal stations	502	700	52 5,765	5,263	5,065
Sub-stations	....	....	273 12,209	....	....
Ordained ministers......	656	1,672	51 6,696	6,040	5,024
Lay helpers............	1,236	4,056	136 33,856	32,620	29,800
Total laborers.........	1,892	5,728	187 40,552	38,660	34,824
Hearers, or adherents....	....	....	310 1,813,596	....	....
Communicants...... ...	70,289	210,957	148 857,332	787,043	646,375
Day-schools...........	....	2,739	271 9,316	....	6,577
Scholars..............	80,656	147,930	247 447,602	366,946	299,663

The small figures above the others in column 1880 indicate missions not reporting the given item.

Probably more than 20,000 stations are occupied. More than 40,000 mission laborers, lay and clerical, are in the foreign fields, 136 missions not reporting the former, and 51 not reporting the latter item— probably 45,000 at least of these laborers. From 356 of the 504 missions we have 857,332 communicants reported. Returns from the remaining 148 would doubtless swell the aggregate to over

1,000,000. These figures do not include nominal converts from heathenism, but enrolled Church members. The increase from 70,289 mission communicants, in 1830, to 210,957 in 1850, and 857,332 in 1880, is a marvelous reduplication. The scholars in the *day*-schools of the missions increased from 80,656 in 1830, to 447,602 in 1880, almost one half of the missions not reporting this item. Probably at least three quarters of a million of youth are being instructed in the mission schools. The nominal adherents or hearers reported in about two fifths of the missions are 1,813,596—probably from three to three and a half millions in all.

The reader can make further comparisons of the progress in different sections of the world by referring to the tables in the Appendix.

How vast the extent of Protestant missions! On the continent of North America, in Mexico, Central America, Greenland, Labrador, the Hudson Bay region, among the aborigines in British America and the United States, and the Chinese in California ; on the continent of South America, in New Granada, Brazil, Peru, Chili, Uruguay, the Argentine Republic, Guiana, the contiguous Falkland Islands, and Terra del Fuego ; on the continent of Europe, among the rationalistic, Papal, Jewish, and Mohammedan populations in Scandinavia, Germany, Austria, Bohemia, Hungary, Croatia, Sclavonia, Holland, Belgium, Switzerland, France, Italy, Spain, Portu-

gal, Turkey, Greece, Roumania, and Bulgaria ; on
the continent of Africa, in Egypt, Tunis, Algiers,
Abyssinia, Zanzibar ; in 368 stations and 1,112
sub-stations all over South Africa ; in 135 stations
and 454 sub-stations in Central and Western Africa ; on the continent of Asia, in Turkey, Syria,
Palestine, Persia, in 46 principal and more than 383
sub-stations ; in India, in 418 principal and 1,032
sub-stations ; in China, in Thibet, Japan, Burmah,
Siam, " the Straits' Settlements," and the Indian
Archipelago ; on the islands of the Atlantic, the
Bahamas, the Bermudas, and the West Indies ; in
Madagascar and Mauritius ; on 300 islands in Polynesia ; and all over the mighty world of Australasia,
45,000 Christian workers are toiling, and great multitudes are rising up as witnesses for Christ.

ROMAN CATHOLIC AND PROTESTANT MISSIONS.

In the mission fields long occupied by Romanism,
Protestant missions, starting much later, are gaining
rapidly upon the Roman Catholic ; while in the
newer, simultaneously opened to both, the Papal
missions are making slow progress. A few facts in
regard to two of the older and two of the later fields,
will show the relative progress and work of Papal
and Protestant missions.

China, one of the oldest Roman Catholic, and one
of the latest Protestant mission grounds, has been
sometimes referred to, by the English press and by

travelers, in terms of disparagement to Protestant-ism. They point to the 400,000 Roman Catholic,* and the small number of Protestant converts, over-looking the fact that Roman Catholic missions be-gan in China in 1589, when Protestantism was in its infancy, eighteen years before the first permanent settlement in the United States, and two hundred and fifty years before the first Protestant mission in China. In this long period of nearly three hun-dred years the Roman Catholic missions, though sometimes persecuted, were generally favored by the imperial government, from which they have received grants of land, buildings, etc. By a quasi recognition of Chinese idolatry and customs they have conciliated the civil power, but have weakened their religious influence, and failed to truly Chris-tianize and elevate the people.

Protestantism gained its first, but only tentative, footholds in China only a half century ago, and was restricted to five specific ports until the treaty of 1858–60. Prior to that time we could only think of Protestant missions "as dotted here and there

---

* Rev. Dr. Legge said: "Possibly the adherents of the Roman Catholic missions in China amount to nearly half a million, though, according to the 'Bulletin des Missions Catholiques' for 1876, they were then only 404,550, and a priest in Chinan, capital of Shan-tung told me, in 1873, that their annual increase all over China was only about 2,000." "Give us three hundred years to work in, and the adherents of Protestant missions will far transcend the present number of Romish Christians."

along the coast," hardly anywhere penetrating fifty
or a hundred miles into the interior. In 1872 there
were 26 Protestant missions, with 337 principal
and sub-stations and about 9,000 communicants in
China. During the past few years these missions
have greatly increased, and the statistics for 1880
(not quite complete) show 32 missions, 173 principal stations, 487 sub-stations, 326 ordained ministers, foreign and native, 1,145 lay assistants, native
and foreign, 19,767 communicants, and 4,962 pupils
in 164 schools. There are 21 theological schools,
in which more than 200 students are preparing for
the ministry. In 1876 there were also reported 16
mission hospitals, with 3,730 in-patients and 87,505
out-patients. There were 24 mission dispensaries,
which ministered to 41,281 cases in the same year.
Said Dr. Legge,[*] in 1878: "The converts have
multiplied in thirty-five years two thousand fold,
the rate of increase being greater year after year.
Suppose it to continue the same for other thirty-
five years, and in A. D. 1913 there will be in China
26,000,000 of communicants, and a professedly
Christian population of 100,000,000."

As to the Chinese converts, Rev. Dr. Legge, who
will be accepted as the very best authority, said:[†]
"It has been asked, in deprecation or depreciation

* "Proceedings of General Conference of Foreign Missions,"
1879, p. 177. London: John F. Shaw & Co., publishers.
   † Ibid., p. 173.

of my statements, 'But what is the character of these thirteen thousand communicants? Can they be accepted as real Christians—as true converts?' It would take long to explain how it has come about that a bad report of the constituency of mission Churches has gone widely abroad; but I do not hesitate to declare that it is wantonly untrue and unjust. When administering the communion to a Church of English-speaking members that were under my charge in Hong-Kong, I often spoke to them to this effect, 'In the afternoon your places before me will be occupied by the members of the Chinese Church. I have confidence in you as Christian men and women, but I shall not have less confidence in our Chinese brethren and sisters.' . . . There are fallings away among the Chinese Christians. They have, also, some peculiar weaknesses and inconsistencies. But these things cannot be said of them more than of the members of the Churches among ourselves. . . . Yes, the converts are real. Your missionaries, in receiving them, and watching over them, are careful and strict. If they err, it is in being overscrupulous, rather than in being lax."

Insisting upon a considerable acquaintance with the doctrines of Christianity, a renunciation of every form of idolatry, and good evidence of a moral change, as conditions of baptism, Protestant progress means moral reformation and elevation, as well as intellectual enlightenment. Many social changes and modifications of life also follow.

A recent traveler* in China, in his observations upon the Papal missions in that country, said: "They manifest no intelligent zeal for the enlightenment and elevation of the people. Few, if any, of the priests possess that noble ambition which characterized their predecessors, Ricci, Schaal, Verbiest, and others. I have never observed any indications among them of men grappling with the language, and girding themselves with ardor to overthrow the mighty evils which are stalking abroad among the natives. As a rule, they content themselves with superintending native priests and catechists, and other purely official duties. They never preach, nor publish any books. . . . We are thus left in a great measure dependent upon Protestant missions for the advancement of knowledge, civilization, and true progress among the people. This department has not failed us."

Protestant missionaries "have given their days and nights to the study of the Chinese language, day by day have preached to the people, thus spreading light in all directions, arousing generous impulses, and training up converts to be well-informed, truth-seeking men and women. 'To such men,' says the 'Supreme Court and Consular Gazette,' (Nov. 14, 1868,) 'are we indebted for

* Alexander Williamson's " Journeys in North China."

more than nine tenths of our knowledge of China and the Chinese.'" They have thus opened the inner life of the nation to the world.

Not to speak of the long, patient studies and elaborate productions of Morrison, Milne, Medhurst, and Legge, of the translations of the Scriptures and other religious books into Chinese, of the dictionaries and grammars now in common use, of the " lesson books," the schools, and weekly periodicals, all the work of Protestant missionaries, numerous works of science also have been translated into Chinese by these devoted laborers. Dr. Hobson has given them works on physiology, surgery, medicine, chemistry, and natural philosophy ; Mr. Wylie, Euclid, algebra, arithmetic, geometry, calculus, Herschel's large Astronomy and Newton's Principia ; Mr. Edkins, Whewell's Mechanics and works on Western literature ; Mr. Muirhead, English history and universal geography; Dr. Bridgeman, an illustrated history of the United States ; Dr. Martin, Wheaton's International Law, and illustrated volumes on chemistry, natural philosophy, etc. More even may be said. Many of these works have been reprinted verbatim, by native gentlemen, attesting their literary accuracy ; and some of them have been reproduced in Japan by the Japanese. This has been done mainly since 1850. Romanism shows no such results, after a three hundred years' occupancy of China. It is plain that, with this preparatory work, so directly affecting the best thought of the nation, the future of China must belong to Protestantism.

Roman Catholic missions in *India* date back almost to the discovery of America, to the conquest of Goa, by the Portuguese, in 1510, and were at first conducted by the Franciscans and the Dominicans. The arrival of St. Francis Xavier, in 1542, gave them a new impulse. "Vicarate Apostolics," or inchoate dioceses, were established in Verapoli, in 1659; in Bombay and Poona, in 1660; in Further India, in 1624; in Southern Burmah, in 1722, etc. After 370 years of mission work, Romanism reports,[*] in all India, Ceylon, Burmah, Siam, and "the Malabar coasts:"

Bishops and archbishops....................	19
Priests.............................	1,009
Catholic schools...........................	1,192
Scholars............................	51,781
Roman Catholic population (estimated).......	1,046,932

Protestantism, within the same limits, after 180 years since a few Danish missionaries began their labors in South India, and, for the most part, after less than ninety years of labor, reported: [†]

	Statistics in 1880.	Mis'ns not reporting.
Missions (in India, Burmah, Siam, and Ceylon)	74	..
Principal stations	562	3
Sub-stations........................	1,642	41
Ordained ministers, foreign and native..	1,137	6

[*] Sadlier's Catholic Almanac and Directory, 1879, Part ii, p. 135.
[†] See Table XXXVIII in Appendix.

	Statistics in 1880.	Mis'ns not reporting.
Lay assistants, foreign and native	7,093	11
Total workers	8,230	17
Communicants	126,409	4
Hearers	246,018	28
Day-schools	3,741	18
Day-school pupils..................	181,945	14

These statistics show that the Protestant missions are rapidly outgrowing the Roman Catholic. Protestant ministers already outnumber the Roman Catholic; and the day-school pupils of Protestantism are three and a half times as many as theirs. The following figures * will indicate the progress:

Year.	Christian Population.†	Communicants of Mission Churches.
1830................	27,000	....
1851................	127,000	22,400
1861................	213,370	49,688
1871................	318,363	78,494
1880................	500,000	126,409

Turning from these older to two of the later mission fields, Australia and New Zealand—really one field, and, for the sake of conciseness, combined un-

* Partly from reports to the English House of Commons, ordered to be printed April 23, 1873, and partly from the "Proceedings of the General Conference of Foreign Missions," held in London, October, 1878, pp. 119–121.

† The "Statesman's Year-Book," 1881, gives the following religious statistics of India:

Hindus.......................	139,248,568
Mohammedans.................	40,882,537
Buddhists....................	2,832,851
Sikhs	1,174,436
Christians...................	897,216
Other creeds.................	5,102,823
Not known...................	1,977,400
Total................	192,511,831

der one term, Australasia—we see very clearly the feebleness of modern Roman Catholic missions.

In Australia, ninety years ago, there was not a single civilized man where there are now nearly two millions. All the vast world of Australasia was in a similar condition.

In 1879 the Roman Catholic Church had in all Australasia 285 priests, 135 schools, and 12,379 scholars, 3 dioceses not reporting the last item. In 1880 Protestantism had,

	Statistics for 1880.	Missions not reporting.
Missions	17	..
Principal stations..................	1,251	2
Sub-stations	891	12
Ordained ministers, native and for'gn	429	..
Lay assistants, native and foreign...	1,785	11
Total laborers.....................	2,214	11
Communicants	33,143	2
Hearers	229,955	6
Day-schools.......................	26	14
Pupils.............................	3,658	11

Besides the above, we have the reports of the English census of 1871 for Australia and New Zealand, as follows: " Roman Catholics, 412,802 ; Protestants, 1,317,310 ; Jews, Chinese, natives, etc., 138,802."

Other recently occupied fields show a similar numerical superiority of Protestantism. Only in fields occupied several hundred years ago by Romanism, and less than a century by Protestantism, has Romanism any preponderance. In respect to moral renovation, enlightenment, and social elevation, Protestant mission communities are incomparably superior to those of the Papal Church.

MISSIONS VINDICATED BY TESTIMONY.

Testimonies of the highest authority have attested the genuine worth, high character, and real progress of Christian missions. A few brief extracts from an official statement in the English " Parliamentary Blue Book," in 1873, ought not to be omitted:

The mission presses in India are twenty-five in number. During the years between 1852 and 1862 they issued 1,634,940 copies of the Scriptures, chiefly single books; and 8,604,033 tracts, school-books, and books for general circulation. During the ten years between 1862 and 1872 they issued 3,410 new works, in thirty languages; and circulated 1,315,503 copies of books of Scripture, 2,375,040 school-books, and 8,750,129 Christian books and tracts. . . . A very large number of Christian communities scattered over India are small, especially in the country towns: and they contain fewer than a hundred communicants, and three hundred converts of all ages. At the same time some of these small congregations consist of educated men, have considerable resources, and are able to provide for themselves. From them have sprung a large number of native clergy and ministers in different Churches, who have received a high education in English institutions, and who are now taking a prominent place in the instruction and management of our indigenous Christian Church. . . .

Taking them together, these rural and aboriginal populations of India, which have received a large share of the attention of the missionary societies, now contain among them *a quarter of a million* native Christian converts. The principles they profess, the standard of morals at which they aim, the education and training which they receive, make them no unimportant element in the empire which the government of India has under its control. These populations must greatly influence the communities of which they form a part; they are thoroughly loyal to the British crown; and the experience through which many have passed has proved that they are governed by solid principle in the conduct they pursue. . . .

Insensibly a higher standard of moral conduct is becoming familiar to the people, especially to the young, which has been set before them, not merely by public teaching, but by the millions of printed books and tracts scattered widely through the country. . . . And they augur well of the future moral progress of the native population of India, from these signs of solid advance already exhibited on every hand, and gained within the brief period of two generations. This view of the general influence of their teaching, and of the greatness of the revolution which it is silently producing, is not taken by missionaries only; it has been accepted by many distinguished residents in India and experienced officers of the government, and has been emphatically indorsed by Sir Bartle Frere.

The following is Sir Bartle Frere's testimony:

I assure you that, whatever you may be told to the contrary, the teaching of Christianity among the one hundred and sixty millions of civilized industrious Hindus and Mohammedans in India, is effecting changes, moral, social, and political, which, for extent and rapidity of effect, are far more extraordinary than any thing you or your fathers have witnessed in modern Europe.

Lord Lawrence, Viceroy and Governor-General of India, said:

I believe, notwithstanding all that the English people have done to benefit India, the missionaries have done more than all other agencies combined.

"The Friend of India and Statesman," Calcutta,
April 25, 1879, contains a remarkable lecture delivered by Baboo Keshub Chunder Sen, the leading
man in the Church of Brhum, in which this high
official bears the following generous testimony in
favor of Christian missions:

Is not a new and aggressive civilization winning its way day
after day, and year after year, into the very heart and soul of the
people?   Are not Christian ideas and institutions taking their
root, on all sides, in the soil of India?   Has not a Christian
government taken possession of its cities, its provinces, its villages; with its hills and plains, its rivers and seas, its homes
and hearths, its teeming millions of men and women and children?   Yes! the advancing surges of a mighty revolution are
encompassing the land; and, in the name of Christ, strange innovations and reforms are penetrating the very core of India's
heart.   Well may our fatherland sincerely, earnestly, ask,
"Who is this Christ?"

Who rules India?   What power is that that sways the destinies of India at the present moment?   You are mistaken if
you think that it is Lord Lytton in the cabinet, or the military
genius of Sir Frederick Haines in the field, that rules India.   It
is not politics, it is not diplomacy, that has laid a firm hold of
the Indian heart.   It is not the glittering bayonet, nor the fiery
cannon that influences us. . . . Armies never conquered the
heart of the nation.   No!   If you wish to secure the attachment and allegiance of India, it must be by exercising spiritual
and moral influence.   And such, indeed, has been the case in
India.   You cannot deny that our hearts have been touched,
conquered, and subjugated by a superior power.   That power
is Christ!   Christ rules British India, and not the British Government.   England has sent us a tremendous moral force in
the life and character of that mighty Prophet to conquer and
hold this vast empire.   None but Jesus, none but Jesus, none

but Jesus ever deserved this bright, this precious diadem—India; and Christ shall have it.

India is unconsciously imbibing this new civilization, succumbing to its irresistible influence. It is not the British army, I say again, that deserves honor for holding India. If to any army appertains that honor, that army is the army of Christian missionaries, headed by their invincible Captain, Jesus Christ. Their devotion, their self-abnegation, their philanthropy, their love of God, their attachment and allegiance to the truth, all these have found, and will continue to find, a deep place in the gratitude of our countrymen. It is needless for me to bestow eulogium upon such tried friends and benefactors of our country.

Mr. Robert Mackenzie has said: *

The greatest of all fields of missionary labor is India. . . . For fifty years Hindu youth in increasing numbers have received an English education. A revolution of extraordinary magnitude has been silently in progress during those years, and even now points decisively to the ultimate, although still remote, overthrow of Hindu beliefs and usages. A vast body of educated and influential natives acknowledge that their ancient faith is a mass of incredibilities. A public opinion has been created, by whose help such practices as infanticide and the burning of widows have been easily suppressed. . . . Through the open gateway of the English language English knowledge and ideas and principles are being poured into India. . . . The Hindu mind is awakening from its sleep of ages. . . . A higher moral tone is becoming familiar to the people. . . .

England has undertaken to rescue from the debasement of ages that enormous multitude of human beings. No enterprise of equal greatness was ever engaged in by any people. Generations will pass away while it is still in progress, but its

* The "Nineteenth Century." Franklin Square Library, pp. 39. 45.

final success cannot be frustrated. We who watch it in its
early stages see mainly imperfections. Posterity will look
only upon the majestic picture of a vast and utterly barbaric
population, numbering well nigh one fourth of the human
family, subdued, governed, educated, Christianized, and led up
to the dignity of a free, self-governing nation by a handful of
strangers, who came from an inconsiderable island 15,000
miles away.

Mr. Mackenzie says of the missions of South Africa: *

Southern Africa was the home of the Bechuanas, a fierce,
warlike race, cruel, treacherous, delighting in blood. No traveler could go among them with safety; they refused even to
trade with strangers. They had no trace of a religion, no
belief in any being greater than themselves, no idea of a future
life. . . . Christianity is now almost universal among the Bechuanas. Education is rapidly extending; natives are being
trained in adequate numbers for teachers and preachers;
Christianity is spreading out among the neighboring tribes.
The Bechuanas have been changed by Christian missions into
an orderly, industrious people, who cultivate their fields in
peace, and maintain with foreigners a mutually beneficial
traffic.

Rev. S. J. Whitmee, missionary at Samoa, said: †

At the present time we have in Polynesia nearly two hundred ordained native ministers doing, in some respects, more
than the English and American missionaries. I have had the
honor of placing some of these men, as pioneer missionaries,
on heathen islands, among the native savages. Then I have
afterward seen what God has done by their agency. Whole

* The "Nineteenth Century." Franklin Square Library, p. 19.
† Volume of "London Conference of Foreign Missions," 1878,
p. 200.

populations of islands and groups of islands have been brought out of idolatry, and have received Christianity and civilization, and all through the agency, not of Englishmen, but of native missionaries. They are Polynesians, who have received the Gospel themselves, whose hearts the grace of God has touched, who have been trained in native colleges, and who have then gone as missionaries to preach the unsearchable riches of Christ to their heathen fellow-islanders.

Again,*

Christianity has, also, become a power for good, in most of our older missions, over the people generally. Public morality has been benefited by it. The political, social, and domestic life of the people has, to a greater or less extent, received a more healthy moral tone. . . . The Sabbath is usually strictly observed. Nearly all the people make a practice of attending public worship at least once on the Lord's day.

It has been said that, under the influence of pagan superstitions, men evince an inanity and a torpor, from which no stimulus has proved powerful enough to arouse them but the new ideas and principles imparted by Christianity. If not already proved, but little time longer will be needed to demonstrate the fact, that Protestant missions are the most effective means ever brought to operate upon the social, civil, commercial, moral, or spiritual interests of mankind. Commencing at a time when the larger pagan nations (China, Japan, etc.) were inaccessible, Polynesia and Australasia were

* Volume of "London Conference of Foreign Missions," 1878, p. 269.

providentially opened as the trial-ground on which
the great problem of foreign missions was to be
tested and wrought out.   In these dark moral
wastes the densest ignorance has been enlightened,
the fiercest cannibalism confronted, the lowest conditions of humanity elevated, the most abominable
idolatries overthrown, and the pure worship of the
Prince of Peace substituted.   Well-organized civil
institutions have been established, a literature has
been created and learned, new ideals of life produced, and new types of society developed.

Many of the results of modern missions cannot
be definitely expressed.   No array of figures, nor
terms, nor illustrations, will adequately set them
before us.   Who can measure the preparatory
work, the learning of the imperfect languages, in
some cases, almost creating them ; the translating
of the Bible into such crude tongues, without
words to express the higher forms of thought ; the
development of a religious literature, sometimes
among people without any literature ; the removal
of prejudices seated in the lowest passions ; and
the establishment of confidence.   Mountains and
hills have been made plains, valleys exalted, chasms
bridged, the far off brought nigh, and foundations
laid.   The centrifugal aversions of paganism are
giving way to the centripetal attractions of Christianity ; the habitations of cruelty are becoming safe,
peaceful abodes ; and the dark vapors and clouds

of superstition are vanishing before the brightening light of Gospel day.

The translation and diffusion of the holy Scriptures, at once one of the factors and one of the achievements of this world-wide evangelization, deserve particular mention.

Reaching, as we have, the semi-millennial anniversary of the first complete translation of the Bible into the English language, we joyfully recognize that grand consummation as one of the great way-marks of the Church's progress.

Seven great events mark distinct epochs in the history of the Bible: The giving of the Law on Mount Sinai, B. C. 1491; the compilation of the Hebrew Bible by Ezra, B. C. 450; the Septuagint version, B. C. 287; the Vulgate version, about A. D. 400; Wycliffe's version, A. D. 1380; King James' version, 1611; and the newly-revised English version, completed probably the present year.

Each of these dates has marked an era of more rapid and widely-extended progress of God's kingdom. The Pentateuch, for nearly fifteen hundred years, was the basis of the national life and order of a people, who, though numerically small, acted a leading part in the earlier religious movements of the world. The work of Ezra brought into consistent unity and permanence the fragmentary revelations of a long dispensation, for the benefit of after

ages.   The Septuagint invested the Hebrew Scriptures in a language the most perfect and beautiful
ever written or spoken, and introduced them into
the widely-extended realm of letters during the
great centuries of ancient classical culture.   The
Vulgate, appearing simultaneously with the conquest of the old world by Christianity, conveyed
the sacred volume to the numerous rising nations
of northern, western, and southern Europe, among
whom for centuries the Latin tongue was the current medium of communication.   Wycliffe's version
introduced the divine word into the vernacular of a
young nation just coming into prominence, and destined to act a leading part in the most active era
of progress the world has ever seen.   In King
James' version, completed near the close of a
period of extended Papal colonization, and at the
opening of the period of Protestant colonization in
the new world, the Bible has become the corner-
stone of numerous new Christian States, in both
hemispheres, the impulse and purifier of our civilization, and the inspiration of the great world-wide
evangelizing movements, which are the crowning
glory of our age.   And may we not confidently
anticipate for the revised version, now nearly completed, in this age of steamships, railroads, telegraphs, telephones, and electric light, a glorious
providential mission, in connection with the advancement of the divine kingdom, demonstrating

anew the wonderful possibilities of the word of God; that it can live and work with increasing power in all the languages of the successive ages; that it not only satisfies the advancing necessities of the world, but also leads the column of progress; that each new verbal investiture, notwithstanding outward diversities, is both a symbol and a factor of an increasing spiritual unity, bringing the common heart of Christendom nearer to the core of truth, a fresh illustration of the two eternal facts, that God's kingdom is unchanged amid changes, and is capable of perpetual rejuvenescence.

One hundred and twenty years ago, in a room in Geneva, Voltaire boastingly said, " Before the beginning of the nineteenth century Christianity will have disappeared from the earth." Since that time the very room where these vain words were uttered has been used as a Bible Depository, and Christianity has won the greatest, the widest, and the most glorious triumphs of her whole history. Of all the periods of religious history, the most wonderful is that included in the last seventy-six years, since the organization of the British and Foreign Bible Society in 1804—sometimes called the era of Bible Societies—but, more comprehensively, the era of evangelizing agencies. Numerous data, collected at the opening of this century, show that large portions of professedly Protestant countries were without copies of the sacred Scriptures, and that they could be obtained only with great difficulty and at great cost. On the continent of Europe, in Lithuania, among 32,800 families, not a Bible could be found; in Holland one half of the population was destitute; in Poland a Bible could scarcely be obtained at any price; in the district of Dorpat, in a population of 106,000, not 200 New Testaments could be found, and there were Christian pastors who did not possess the Bible in the dialects in which they preached; in Iceland, in a population of 50,000, almost all of whom could read, not more than forty or fifty copies of the Bible existed; in the United States no Bible was published until the close of the Revolution ; the pagan world was wholly destitute, and in papal countries it did not exist in the dialects of the people.

There are libraries in which are to be found copies of every edition of the Bible ever printed, and it is probable that in 1804 there were much less than 5,000,000 of Bibles in all the world, a far greater number, probably, than were in the hands of mankind during the thirty centuries from Moses to Luther. But since 1804 over 160,000,000 * copies, in whole or in part, of the word of God have been scattered abroad in three quarters of a century, more than thirty times as many as existed in all the previous thirty-three centuries since the law was given on Mount Sinai.

* See Report of American Bible Society, 1880, pp. 182, 3.

At the beginning of this century, the Bible existed, in some fifty translations, in the languages of one fourth of the earth's population; now it exists in the languages of over four fifths of the inhabitants of the world—in 250 * languages and dialects, thirty-nine of which had no written form †
until Protestant missionaries created it. Such has been the accelerated progress in our time, in supplying the unevangelized world with scriptural knowledge.

Many of the results of modern missions are magnificent. Some of the largest local Churches in the world are mission Churches on some of the islands of the Pacific, not sixty years removed from utter barbarism, and now sending out missionaries to other Pacific islands. On the Fiji Islands, whose inhabitants, less than fifty years ago, feasted on human flesh, more than one hundred thousand hearers assemble for Christian worship, and twenty-five thousand are enrolled communicants. In 1820 there was not a native Christian on the Friendly Islands; now twenty thousand assemble for Sabbath worship, and nearly eight thousand are enrolled as communicants of the Wesleyan Societies. In 1860, forty years after the first mission began on Madagascar, there were only a few hundred scattered,

---

* Some say over 300.

† Within seventy years, sixty or seventy languages have been made to possess a literary history.

persecuted converts. Now the Queen and her prime minister, with 253,000 of their subjects, are adherents of Christianity; over seventy thousand are enrolled communicants; and forty-eight thousand pupils are in schools. In 1877, the last vestige of slavery was abolished on that island. Western Africa numbers over thirty-two thousand communicants, and over ninety thousand Christian hearers. Over two thousand miles of coast have been reclaimed from the slave-trade, and churches and schools have taken the place of slave-pens.

One hundred years ago Polynesia,* with its 12,000 islands, was, for the first time, clearly made known to Europeans by the discoveries of Captain Cook. Its population was entirely heathen, of the lowest degree, grossly and savagely heathen, their hideous vices sadly contrasting with the wonderful natural beauty of their island groups. Now, by far the greater portion of Polynesia has become, in a good degree, Christianized. Heathenism is mainly con-

---

* Rev. S. J. Whitmee, at the London Foreign Mission Conference, in 1878, (see volume, p. 268,) gave the following statistics of the Polynesian Missions :

		Members of the Churches.
1. *Malayo-Polynesian* area—		
London Missionary Society.........................	17,025	
Wesleyan Missionary Society.....................	10,315	
Hawaiian Association..............................	8,739————36,079	
2. *Micronesian* area, (approximate).............................	1,500	
3. *Melanesian* area—		
Wesleyan Missionary Society.....................	26,634	
London Missionary Society.	3,105	
Presbyterian Missionary Society.................	783————30,522	
Total Church members.........	68,101	

fined to the islands in the western portion, upon which the missionary societies are now concentrating. The London Missionary Society has undertaken the work in New Guinea; the Melanesian Mission, in the Banks' and Solomon Islands; the Presbyterians, in the New Hebrides; the Wesleyans, in New Britain and New Ireland; and the American Board, in connection with the Hawaiian Churches, are widening their labors in Micronesia.

More than 60,000 converts were gathered into the Protestant Mission Churches of the world in 1878 —a number nearly equal to the whole number of members of the Mission Churches fifty-five years ago. Marvelous harvests were reaped in India, Burmah, and Siam. Over 18,000 souls, at once, joined the Anglicans in Tinnevelly, subsequently increased by 6,000 more in the same presidency. About 6,000 converts were added to the Arcot Mission of the Reformed Dutch Church. In the American Baptist Mission, among the Telugus, there was a similar immense ingathering of 10,537 converts in one year.

"Seventy years from the first promulgation of Christianity," said a religious journal, discussing the success of missions, "it is probable that there were not more avowed Christians in the world than there are now in India and Burmah." The nominal Christian population of the world, at the close of the second century, has been quite uniformly estimated at two millions. But the Christian hearers reported on three fifths of the foreign Protestant missions, in 1880, at the close of ninety years since the great English foreign missionary societies were organized, was 1,813,596. Complete returns would probably give more than three millions at the present time; and the enrolled communicants quite one million. And yet, in the face of these unparalleled results in the widely extended field of the world, and an increase of 9,679,619 communicants in the Evangelical Churches of the United States during the past eighty years, a writer in the "Catholic World" not long ago had the hardihood to declare, "All historians agree that the triumphs of Protestantism closed with the first fifty years of its existence."

The eyes of India, China, and Japan are turning more and more to Christian lands as the sources whence are to be obtained the blessings of knowledge and culture. Young men from these three countries, now numbered by hundreds, are enrolled as pupils in our schools and colleges, taking prizes at our universities, and fitting for the Christian ministry at our theological seminaries. Japanese princesses, also, have come to join their dusky brothers in Christian halls of science, fulfilling the Scriptures: "The Gentiles shall come to thy light;" "thy sons shall come from far, and thy daughters shall be nursed by thy side."

CHAPTER V.

THE WORLD-WIDE VIEW.

Christian Populations.
Christian Governments.
Papal and Protestant Governments.
Papal and Protestant Areas.
The English-speaking Population.
Civil Supremacy of Protestantism.
The Ascending Sun.

CHAPTER V.

THE WORLD-WIDE VIEW.

THE progress of Christianity during the past one hundred years is one of the most palpable of all the phases of the world's history. The following table,* published as a conjectural, but probable, estimate of the progressive increase of the number of Christians in the world, in the successive centuries, intelligently made up from carefully collated data, has been generally accepted. For the period more especially under consideration— the time since the birth of Protestantism—the following are the figures :

| 1500,† | 100,000,000 Christians. | 1700, | 155,000,000 Christians. |
| 1600, | 125,000,000 " | 1800, | 200,000,000 " |

Before 1847 Rev. Sharon Turner said : ‡ " In this nineteenth century the real number of the

---

* See Ferussac, " Bull. Univ. Geog.," January, 1827, page 4.

† The statistics of the earlier periods are as follows :

	Christians.			Christians.
First century	500,000	Eighth century		30,000,000
Second "	2,000,000	Ninth "		40,000,000
Third "	5,000,000	Tenth "		50,000,000
Fourth "	10,000,000	Eleventh "		70,000,000
Fifth "	15,000,000	Twelfth "		80,000,000
Sixth "	20,000,000	Thirteenth "		75,000,000
Seventh "	25,000,000	Fourteenth "		80,000,000

See Mr. Turner's " History of the Anglo-Saxons."

‡ " History of the Anglo-Saxons," sixth edit., vol. iii, p. 484, note.

Christian population of the world is nearer to *three hundred millions,* and is visibly much increasing from the missionary spirit and exertions which are now distinguishing the chief Protestant nations of the world."

The latest estimates are as follows :

Year.	Christians.	Authorities.
1830..............	228,000,000	Malté Brun.
1840..............	300,000,000	Rev. Sharon Turner, D.D.
1850..............	342,000,000	Rev. Robert Baird, D.D.
1876..............	394,000,000	Prof. Schem, LL.D.
1880..............	410,900,000	Prof. Schem, LL.D.

The above are probably the most reliable representations of the later progress of Christianity in the whole world, showing its wonderful growth in later years, far exceeding its previous progress. In fifteen hundred years it gained one hundred millions ; then, in three hundred years, it gained one hundred millions more ; then, in seventy-nine years, it gained two hundred and ten millions more. In the last seventy-nine years it gained as much as in the eighteen centuries previous to 1800. During the nearly ten centuries of almost exclusive papal dominion, Christianity gained only about eighty-five millions. Since the birth of Protestantism, a period about one third as long, it has gained nearly four times as much. And since the great religious quickening of Protestantism under the Wesleys and Whitefield, in the middle of the last century, it has gained two hundred and thirty-five millions.

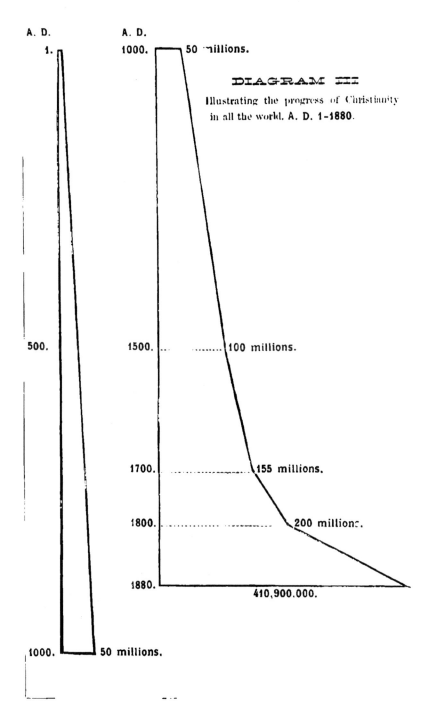

A. D.
1.

A. D.
1000.   50 millions.

DIAGRAM III

Illustrating the progress of Christianity
in all the world. A. D. 1-1880.

500.   1500. ...   . 100 millions.

1700. .... 155 millions.

1800. .... 200 millions.

1880.

410,900,000.

1000.   50 millions.

But the portion of the earth's population under Christian governments has increased even more rapidly than the number of Christians, as will be seen by the following well-established figures:

UNDER CHRISTIAN GOVERNMENTS.

Year.	Population.	Authorities.
1500	100,000,000	Rev. Sharon Turner, D.D.
1700	155,000,000	Rev. Sharon Turner, D.D.
1830	387,788,000	Adrian Balbi.
1876	685,459,411	Prof. Schem, LL.D.

These figures show the wonderful growth of the Christian nations, the enlargement of their national domains, and the increase of their populations. They demonstrate the rapid extension of Christian influences and the Christian subjugation of the world. Nearly seven times the number of people are under the control of Christian nations as at the opening of the sixteenth century, when Protestantism arose. The increase in the one hundred and forty years since Wesleyanism arose in England has been five hundred millions, equal to more than one third of the population of the globe.

But has this wonderful increase been in the Greek, or the Roman Catholic, or the Protestant form of Christianity? Let us see. The following table, based upon statistics furnished in Seaman's "Progress of Nations," will show the relative strength of these forms of Christianity in the world in the year 1700:

33

Countries.	Pop'n under Roman Catholic Governments.	Pop'n under Greek Church Governments.	Pop'n under Protestant Governments.
Italy and islands..........	18,000,000	.....	.....
Spain and Portugal........	13,500,000	.....	.....
France and colonies.......	20,700,000	.....	.....
Great Britain and colonies..	.....	.....	9,000,000
Ireland...................	2,400,000	.....	.....
Holland and colonies......	.....	.....	1,800,000
Belgium..................	1,400,000	.....	.....
Prussia...................	.....	.....	7,500,000
Denmark and colonies.....	.....	.....	1,300,000
Sweden and Norway.......	.....	.....	2,400,000
Germany..................	.....	.....	8,500,000
Switzerland	.....	.....	1,500,000
Austria and Hungary... ..	18,000,000	.....	.....
Poland...................	3,000,000	.....	.....
Spanish and Portuguese Am.	13,000,000	.....	.....
Russia	.....	17,000,000	.....
Greece and isles..........	.....	12,000,000	.....
Africa, etc...............	.....	4,000,000	.....
Total..............	90,000,000	33,000,000	32,000,000

In the year 1500 about 80,000,000 of people were
under Roman Catholic governments, and not far
from 20,000,000 under the Greek Church governments. The following estimates by Adrian Balbi,
for 1830, and by Prof. Schem, for 1876, will serve
our purpose :

Year.	Pop'n under Roman Catholic Governments.	Pop'n under Greek Church Governments.	Pop'n under Protestant Governments.	Total.
1500...	80,000,000	20,000,000	....	100,000,000
1700...	90,000,000	33,000,000	32,000,000	155,000,000
1830...	134,164,000	60,000,000	193,624,000	387.788,000
1876 *.	180,787,905	96,101,894	408,569,612	685,459,411

* See Table XXXIX, in Appendix, for a fuller exhibit of the statistics for 1876.

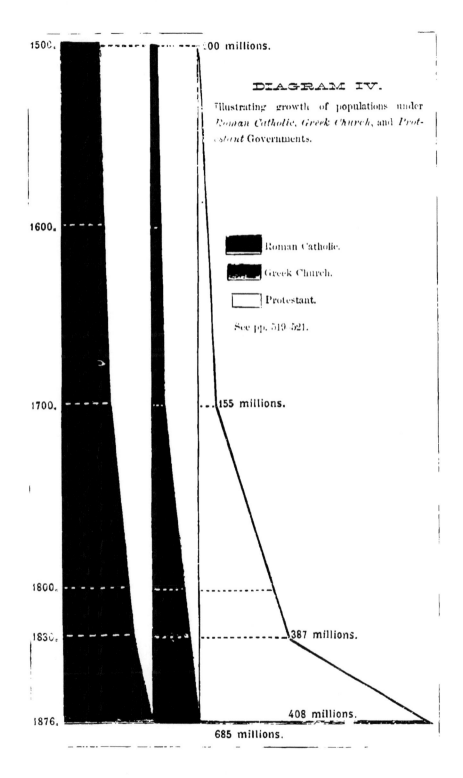

1500. — — — — — — — — — 00 millions.

DIAGRAM IV.

Illustrating growth of populations under *Roman Catholic, Greek Church*, and *Protestant* Governments.

1600.

Roman Catholic.

Greek Church.

Protestant.

See pp. 519–521.

1700. ... 155 millions.

1800.

1830. 387 millions.

408 millions.

1876.

685 millions.

One hundred and eighty years ago only 155,000,000 of the earth's population were under Christian governments. Then the Grand Seignior, the Sophi, and the Great Mogul were the most potent arbiters of the destinies of the race. Nearly all Asia and Africa were under pagan and Mohammedan sway. The mighty worlds of Australasia, Polynesia, and the Indian Archipelago lay in the undisturbed slumbers of savagery and superstition. Scarcely four hundred thousand Protestant colonists occupied both American continents; all the remainder was pagan or Catholic. All the religious missions of the world, excepting a few among the aborigines in the American colonies, were papal, and the only religion not disseminating itself and gaining ground was the Protestant. Great Britain and her colonies did not number ten million of people. Now she comprises a population of more than three hundred million * under her civil sway.

The population under Roman Catholic governments, in the year 1700, as we have seen, was 90,000,000. This has increased to 180,787,905 in 1876, simply doubling. The population under the Greek Church governments, in 1700, was 33,000,000. This increased to 96,101,894, nearly trebling. The population under Protestant governments, in 1700,

* According to the census for 1872 the inhabitants of India were 237,552,958, of whom 191,300,000 were directly governed by British rulers, and 46,250,000 by native governments dependent upon the British.

was 32,000,000.   This increased to 408,569,612 in
1876, a more than twelve fold increase.   While Romanism brought 90,787,905 more people under her
sway, Protestantism extended her dominion over
376,569,612 more people—an actual gain more than
four times as great as that of Romanism in the
same period.   Since 1830, while Romanism added
about 46,000,000 of people to her civil sway, Protestantism added 215,000.000 to hers.   In these
calculations Italy, France, and Mexico, rapidly
passing out from under the civil control of the Papacy, are reckoned with Romanism.   In twenty
years more they will probably be transferred to the
other side, and much of South America also.

The Roman Catholic and the Protestant populations of the world, which were not long ago supposed to be nearly equal, the transitions from the
one to the other nearly balancing, have relatively
changed very greatly during the last thirty years,
the preponderance being now very largely in favor
of Protestant nations.   The losses and gains of Romanism and Protestantism are now far from balancing each other, the preponderance of the gains being
immensely in favor of Protestantism.   The signs of
the times clearly indicate that the future will bring
still greater relative gains to Protestantism.   In
Spain, Italy, France, Mexico, Chili, and in almost
every Catholic country of the globe, Protestantism
is gaining more rapidly and substantially than

Romanism is gaining in any country wholly or predominantly Protestant. Under the spread of toleration, other papal lands are opening to the introduction of Protestantism, and Rome is losing her exclusive hold upon other long-occupied seats of power.

While Rome is thus losing to a great extent the control of the great nations hitherto nominally connected with her, it must be admitted that she is making some gains in the aristocracy of some Protestant countries. The number of Roman Catholic peers in Great Britain, in one hundred years, increased from nine to more than thirty. In Germany the facts are similar. The Marquis of Bute and the Count of Schönburg are examples. The explanation of this fact is not difficult. The aristocracy of those countries is no less opposed to the liberalizing tendencies of modern civilization than Rome, and is thus drawn into natural alliance with Rome. She may still continue to make such gains, and increase her wealth; but among the masses of the people the effect can only be favorable to Protestantism. The opposition to the principles of progress and liberty is more and more centering in the Roman Catholic Church; and the plainer this becomes the sooner will society emancipate itself from her influence, for the irreversible drift of the world is in the direction of popular freedom.

Looking at the territorial area of the earth, we notice similar progress. The latest computations fix the total area at 52,062,470 square miles, of which Christian nations have under their civil control 32,419,915 square miles; and the pagan and Mohammedan, 19,624,555—three fifths Christian and two fifths pagan and Mohammedan. Dividing the Christian nations, we find under the civil dominion of Protestant governments, 14,337,187 square miles; under Roman Catholic, 9,304,605 square miles; and under Greek Church governments, 8,778,123 square miles.

"The acquisition of foreign territory by Great Britain is without a parallel in the history of the human family. She bears rule over one third of the surface of the globe, and one fourth of its population. Her possessions abroad are in area sixty times larger than the parent State. She owns three millions and a half of square miles in America, one million each in Africa and Asia, and two and a half millions in Australia. These enormous acquisitions have been gained chiefly within the last hundred years. There are thirty-eight separate colonies, or groups of colonies, varying in area from Gibraltar with its two miles, to Canada, with three million and a half. Their population aggregates eleven millions, and steadily continues to increase." *

Great changes are also taking place in the prevailing language of the world, the English coming more than ever to be the means of intercommuni-

* "The Ninteenth Century," p. 45.

cation among the great nations. Baron Kolb, the German statistician, after extensive research, has given the following statement of the prevalence of leading languages. The German is spoken by fifty to sixty millions of people; the French and Spanish, by forty millions each; the Russian by fifty-five millions; and the English, by eighty millions. "Whitaker's Almanac" for 1881 (p. 157) puts the latter at eighty-one millions. These the same authority divides as follows:

Episcopalians	18,000,000
Methodists	14,250,000
Presbyterians	10,250,000
Baptists	8,000,000
Congregationalists	6,000,000
Unitarians	1,000,000
Minor sects	1,500,000
Total Protestants	59,000,000
Roman Catholics	13,500,000
Of no particular religion	8,500,000
Aggregate	81,000,000

In the year 1800 the English-speaking population of the globe did not exceed twenty-four millions, of which five millions and a half were Roman Catholics; four millions and a half were of no particular religion; and fourteen millions were Protestants. According to this analysis, the English-speaking population has increased two hundred and thirty-seven per cent.; the Roman Catholic population among English-speaking people, one hundred and forty-five per cent.; the non-religious English-

speaking population about one hundred per cent.;
and the Protestant English-speaking population,
three hundred and twenty-one per cent.

The Bible, in the year 1800 existing in the languages of only one fifth of the earth's population,
has now been translated into the languages of nine
tenths of the inhabitants of the world.

The institution of Sunday-schools, which one
hundred years ago was just coming into being, at
the end of the first half century of its existence, in
1830,* had less than two millions of teachers and
scholars. Now it has a world-wide existence, and
over fourteen millions of members.

	Officers and Teachers.	Scholars.	Total.
Europe	550,001	5,332,813	5,882,814
Asia	1,772	38,000	39,772
Africa	300	15,000	15,300
North America	931,740	6,974,454	7,906,194
South America	3,000	150,000	153,000
Oceanica	17,800	170,000	187,800
Total † in world	1,504,613	12,680,267	14,184,880

In the Middle Ages the Roman Catholic Church
exerted the controlling influence in civil legislation
and administration all over Europe. It claimed the
sole right of dictating legislation, exempted its
priests and monks from civil jurisdiction, and ac-

* See "American Quarterly Register" for 1830.

† This table takes in only the Sunday-schools of Evangelical Protestant Churches, and the figures are probably incomplete. See
Table XXX, in Appendix.

cumulated within its hands a very large portion of the wealth of the nations.

The Reformation was a movement in the direction of freedom. It sought to break this exclusive control of the Church over the State, and to make all citizens equal before the law. Immense advances have every-where been made toward the realization of this reform. "Although the Catholic Church has still a larger membership than all the Reformed Churches combined, the power and commanding influence upon the destinies of mankind are more and more passing into the hands of States and governments which are separated from Rome. In the New World, the ascendency of the United States and British America, in both of which Protestantism prevails, over the States of Spanish and Portuguese America, is not disputed even by Catholics. In Europe, England has become the greatest world power, and, in its wide dominions, new great Protestant countries are springing into existence, especially in Australia and South Africa. In Germany, the supreme power has passed from the declining Catholic house of Hapsburg to the Protestant house of Hohenzollern, and the new Protestant German Empire marks an addition of the greatest importance to the aggregate power of the Protestant world. The combined influence of the three great Teutonic peoples, the United States, Great Britain, and Germany, continues to be cast in a steadily increasing ratio, for the defense of that freedom from the dictation of Rome which was first won by the Reformation. That freedom is now not only fully secured against any possible combination of Catholic States, but the Parliaments of most of the latter, as France, Austria, Italy, Portugal, are as eager in the defense of this principle as the Protestant States. Thus it may be said that, after an existence of about three hundred and fifty years, *the Reformation has totally annihilated the influence of Rome upon the laws and the government of the civilized world.*" [*]

"Once the slightest whispers of the Roman pontiff upon political affairs caused every throne of Europe to nod;" but now his utterances are of " little more account than the ghosts of Tam O'Shanter." How greatly has the area of liberty extended since the days of Louis XV. and George II. Thirty years ago an able writer said, "We do not despair of yet hearing a Protestant sermon within the gates of the Eternal City." It is now more than an accomplished fact, for Protestant Churches, Sunday-schools, and Bibles are penetrating all Italy, and are established under the very shadow of St. Peter's. Protestantism has steadily gained power, and widely extended the blessings of a higher civilization. The Anglo-Saxon race, now in the ascendant, that has stretched its power over Amer-

---

[*] M'Clintock & Strong's "Cyclopædia," art., Reformation.

ica, India, and Australia, has "a history and a temperament that will never allow it to become the craven minion of Rome."

How marvelous the changes that have taken place in China within thirty years. This exclusive, circumvallated people have admitted innovation after innovation, and are accepting the Christian civilization, as a thing no longer to be resisted. Japan is putting on the new civilization as a garment, effecting changes in her political constitution and social habits, the like of which no other State ever accomplished in a century.

Very early one morning several hundred eager tourists, in scanty apparel, stood shivering on one of the Alpine summits, waiting the rising of the sun. So long was his approach delayed, that it seemed as though somewhere in the far East unexpected events had detained him. Soon deep shadows began to lift and retire, and purple streaks gleamed athwart the eastern horizon. Clearer and louder notes from an Alpine horn roused the weary waiters to the tiptoe of expectation; and on the cloudless blue there soon formed a band of gold, swiftly growing in brilliancy, until the full-orbed sun blazed, and blinded all eyes with its brightness.*

Long ago the purple streaks and dispersing shadows of the world's great day-dawn and the fillet of its earliest rays appeared. Christianity is

* Rev. W. H. Withrow, D.D.

now far beyond its dawn.   We see something more
than the purple tints of Christ's kingly presence
in the affairs of men.   Though dark shadows,
hideous specters and poisonous malaria still lin-
ger in deep vales, yet we behold his rising glory,
diffusing light and warmth, purifying and sweet-
ening the world.   Higher and higher is Christ's
scepter lifted.   Willing nations, rejoicing in the
day of his power,

> "To Him all majesty ascribe,
> And crown him Lord of all."

In the last moments of the Convention that
framed the Constitution of the United States, while
the members were affixing their signatures to the
document, Benjamin Franklin arose in his seat, and
pointing to a painting of the rising sun on the wall
behind the President, said: "Painters, in their
art, have found it difficult to distinguish between
a rising and a setting sun.   I have often, in the
course of the session of this convention, in the vi-
cissitudes of hope and fear as to its issue, looked
at that picture, without being able to tell whether
it was rising or setting.   But now, at length, I have
the happiness to know that it is a rising and not a
setting sun."

There have been periods, since the conquest of
the old Roman world by Christianity, when some
friends have entertained grave doubts whether it
would not soon go down in darkness and wholly

disappear. Many times have its enemies confidently predicted such disaster.

But, at the present time, no intelligent person, standing in the light of the last four centuries, and beholding the great religious movements of this age, can doubt whether Protestant Christianity is a setting or a rising sun. Every year it is robing itself in fuller effulgence, and pouring its blessed illumination upon new millions of earth's benighted children.

How marvelous the advances of Christ's kingdom in our days! What a privilege to be witnesses and sharers in the great movements! That devout commentator, Rev. Albert Barnes, deeply interested in the kingdom of God, rejoicing in its advances, and the clear indications of still greater strides of progress soon to come, was accustomed often to say that he would like to live a hundred years longer than the allotted term of human life, that he might participate in the glories of the grand advancing era.

Much yet remains to be done. Heavy duties and arduous toils are before us. Stern battles are to be fought. All along the vast lines of Christ's militant hosts the conflict rages. Skepticism and worldliness are rallying their forces. Subtle and specious forms of evil are seeking to undermine and destroy. But over the storm of battle hangs the bright bow of promise; and tidings, from afar

and near, of mighty conquests cheer us.   Even in
the tomb, where some think faith is being buried,
we see the angels of resurrection standing.   The
rapidly accumulating treasures of humanity are
being joyfully laid at the feet of the Son of God.
The utilities of art, invention, and enterprise; the
sublimest discoveries of science and exploration;
the broadest researches of history, ethnography,
and philology; the beautiful charities of the good;
the best thought of the wise; the cultured ameni-
ties of the rich and the loving gratitude of the poor,
unite in a common homage, and chant hymns of
praise to the great Redeemer.

" *The continual and steady growth of Christianity,
its vigorous life in spite of various seasons of una-
voidable ebb, and notwithstanding the presence of
many sources of corruption, and its continual rejuvenescence, are no ordinary proof of its divine origin,
as well as of its superior fitness for the position in
the world which it claims to occupy.*" *

* " Encyclopædia Britannica," ninth edition, art. " Christianity."

APPENDIX.

ECCLESIASTICAL STATISTICS.

APPENDIX.

ECCLESIASTICAL STATISTICS.

UNITED STATES.

TABLES I TO XVII.

TABLE I.[1]

CHURCHES AND MINISTERS IN 1775.

DENOMINATIONS.	Churches.	Ministers.
Congregational	700	575
Episcopalian, Protestant	300	250
Baptist	380	350
Presbyterian	300	140
Lutheran	60	25
German Reformed	60	25
Dutch Reformed	60	25
Associate Reformed	20	13
Moravian	8	12
Methodist[2]	30	20
Total	1,918	1,435

[1] All this table, except the item in regard to the Methodist Church, then not organized as a national body, was taken from Rev. Dr. Baird's "Religion in America," p. 210. Harper & Brothers, 1856. There were 52 Roman Catholic Churches and 26 priests not included in this table.

[2] The "Minutes" for 1775 give 20 preachers, 10 circuits, and 3,418 members. Each circuit comprised several societies, or Church organizations.

34

TABLE II.

CHURCHES, MINISTERS, AND COMMUNICANTS, 1800.

DENOMINATIONS.	Church Organizations or Congregations.[1]	Ministers.	Communicants.
Baptists, Regular [2]......................	1,500	1,200	100,000
Baptists, Free-will [3]......................	....	...	3,000
Congregational [4].......................	810	600	75,000
Friend [5]	....	....	50,000
Methodist Episcopal Church [6]...........	....	287	64,894
Presbyterian [7]..........................	500	300	40,000
Protestant Episcopal [8].................	320	264	[9] 11,978
SMALLER BODIES.			
Lutheran, Dutch, and German Reformed, Seventh-day Baptist, Six-Principle Baptist, Mennonite, Moravian, etc., estim'd.	....	....	20,000
Total....................................	3,030	2,651	364,872

[1] In some cases the congregations are given.

[2] "Christian Retrospect and Register," by Rev. Dr. Baird, p. 220; also articles on the "History of the Baptists,"by Rev. Rufus Babcock, D.D., in "American Quarterly Register," 1841–42.

[3] Appleton's old "Encyclopedia," article, Free-will Baptists.

[4] "Historical Sketches of Congregationalism," by Rev. Joseph S. Clark, D.D., and Dr. Baird's "Christian Retrospect and Register," p. 220.

[5] Estimated.

[6] "General Minutes of Methodist Episcopal Church."

[7] Rev. Robert Baird, D.D.

[8] "Episcopal Record," 1860.

[9] Dr. Baird, in "Report to Evangelical Alliance," 1850, set the number of communicants at 16,000, in 1800.

TABLE III.

CHURCHES, MINISTERS, AND COMMUNICANTS, 1850.

DENOMINATIONS.	Church Organizations or Congregations.[1]	Ministers.[2]	Communicants.[3]
Baptist,[4] Regular, North [5]..............	3,557	2,665	296,614
" " South [5].............	4,849	2,477	390,193
Total.......................	8,406	5,142	686,807

TABLE III, (Continued.)

DENOMINATIONS.	Church Organizations or Congregations.[1]	Ministers.[2]	Communicants.[3]
Baptist, Free-will [6]	1,126	867	50,223
" Seventh-day [7]	71	58	6,351
" Seventh-day German [4]	....	4	400
" Six-Principle [4]	21	25	3,586
" Anti-mission [4]	2,035	907	67,845
Total *Baptist*	11,659	7,003	815,212
Congregational [8]	1,971	1,687	197,197
Disciple, or Campbellite [4]	1,898	848	118,618
Dutch Reformed [9]	286	299	33,780
Dunker [4]	152	160	7,849
Episcopal, Protestant [10]	1,350	1,595	89,359
Evangelical Association [11]	200	195	[12]21,374
Friend (Evangelical) (est'd by Friends)..	....	....	70,000
German Reformed [6]	600	260	70,000
Lutheran [8]	1,603	1,400	163,000
Mennonite [8]	400	240	25,000
Moravian [8]	31	27	3,027
Methodist Episcopal Church, North [13] ..	....	4,129	[14]693,811
"　　　"　　　" South[15]...	....	1,556	[14]514,299
"　　　"　　　" African [16].	...	127	[14]22,127
"　　　"　　　" " Zion [15]	....	71	[14]4,817
" Protestant [15].................	....	807	[14]65,815
" Wesleyan [16]	....	400	[14]21,400
" Primitive [15]...	....	12	[14]1,112
" Reformed [15]	....	50	[14]2,050
" Stillwellite [15]...............	....	....	200
Total *Methodist*	[16]17,000	[17]7,152	[14]1,325,631
Presbyterian, Old School [18]	2,595	1,926	207,754
" New School [19]	1,568	1,473	139,797
" Reformed General Synod of, in North America [20]..	63	43	6,800
" Ref'd Synod of, in N. Am.[20]	50	33	6,000
" Associate [15]	214	120	18,000
" Associate Reformed [15]	332	219	26,340
" Cumberland [21]	500	450	75,000
" Other small bodies (est'd).	....	....	8,000
Total *Presbyterian*.............	5,322	4,264	487,691

TABLE III, (Continued.)

DENOMINATIONS.	Church Organizations or Congregations.[1]	Ministers.[2]	Communicants.[3]
Second Advent [22]	....	....	40,000
Schwenkfelder [15]	....	....	800
United Brethren [23]...................	500	450	[14]50,450
Several small bodies (estimated)........	100	75	11,000
Aggregate	43,072	25,655	3,529,988

[1] In some cases, probably, congregations are reported instead of Church organizations.

[2] Local preachers and licentiates not included.

[3] Some Churches include baptized children, but not many.

[4] "Baptist Almanac," 1851.

[5] Divided on the basis of the two General Conventions, which, since the schism in 1845, have not affiliated, as is also the case with the Methodist Episcopal Churches, North and South, and the Presbyterian.

[6] Free-will Baptist "Register," for 1851.

[7] Seventh-day Baptist "Manual," for 1852.

[8] "Christian Almanac," 1850, and Dr. Baird's "Christian Retrospect and Register."

[9] "Christian Retrospect and Register," by Dr. Baird.

[10] "Church Almanac."

[11] Official document, number of churches estimated.

[12] Ministers added with members to make the total communicants, as with the Methodist bodies, because of peculiarities of Church polity. See "Methodist."

[13] "Minutes of the Methodist Episcopal Church," 1850.

[14] According to the polity of the Methodist Churches, it is necessary to add the number of preachers to the number of members, in order to get the total communicants, because they are not reckoned into the number of communicants in the local Churches, as with other denominations.

[15] Fox and Hoyt's "Ecclesiastical Register."

[16] The Methodist Minutes do not report the number of Church organizations. The United States Census for 1850 gave 14,861 church edifices, (all kinds of Methodists.) The organizations or societies considerably exceed the edifices; hence the above number is partly estimated.

[17] Besides 10,599 local preachers.

[18] "Minutes of General Assembly," Old School, 1850.

[19] "Minutes of General Assembly," New School, 1850.

[20] Rev. R. Baird, D.D., in "American and Foreign Christian Union," vol. ii, pp. 77, 78.

[21] "Christian Retrospect and Register," by Rev. Robert Baird, D.D.

[22] Estimated by Revs. J. Litch and J. V. Hines.

[23] Official sources. Number of churches estimated.

TABLE IV.

CHURCHES, MINISTERS, AND COMMUNICANTS, 1870.

DENOMINATIONS.	Church Organizations.[1]	Ministers.[1]	Communicants.[1]
Baptist,[2] Regular, North[3].............	5,857	4,112	495,099
" " South[3].............	10,777	6,331	790,252
" " Colored[3]..........	811	375	125,142
Total *Regular Baptist*.....	[14]17,445	10,818	1,410,493
" Free-will[4].................	1,355	1,116	65,605
" " " Minor bodies[4].....	174	....	8,549
" Seventh-day[5].............	78	86	7,609
" " " German[6].......	20	....	2,000
" Six-Principle[6].............	22	20	3,000
Total *Baptist*............	[15]19,094	12,040	1,497,256
Congregational[7]....................	3,121	3,194	306,518
Disciple, or Campbellite[8].............	[16]2,478	2,200	450,000
Dunker[6]............................	300	250	40,000
Episcopal, Protestant[9]...............	[16]2,752	2,803	207,762
Evangelical Association[5].............	[12]815	587	[13]73,566
Friend,[10] Evangelical................	392	....	57,405
Lutheran,[11] General Synod...........	[16]997	591	91,720
" " Council............	998	527	129,516
" " Synod of N. Amer.	214	121	16,662
" Other Synods............	1,183	686	150,640
Total *Lutheran*...........	[16]3,392	1,925	[17]388,538
Mennonite[18].......................	270	325	39,100
Moravian[19]........................	72	66	7,634
Methodist Episcopal Church[20]........	.....	9,193	[13]1,376,327
" " " South[20]...	.....	2,922	[13]598,350
" " " African[21]..	.....	560	[13]200,560
" " " " Zion[21]	.....	694	[13]164,694
" Protestant[21]...............	.....	423	[13]72,423
" Wesleyan[21].................	.....	250	[13]20,250
" Free[20].....................	.....	128	[13]7,866
" Primitive[21].................	.....	20	[13]2,020
" Welsh Calvinistic[22].........	.....	20	2,000
" Reformed[6]..................	.....	....	3,000
" Congregational[23]............	.....	100	6,000
"The Methodist Church"[24]...........	.....	766	[13]54,562
Total *Methodist*...........	[12]25,278	15,076	[13]2,499,052

TABLE IV, (Continued.)

DENOMINATIONS.	Church Organiz- ations.[1]	Minis- ters.[1]	Communi- cants.[1]
Presbyterian, General Assembly[25]	4,526	4,238	446,561
" " " South[25]..	1,469	840	82,014
" United of North America.[25]..	729	553	69,805
" Reformed, Synod[26]..........	87	86	8,577
" " " General[26]..	60	....	6,000
" " Ass. Syn. of South[26]	.....	....	4,500
" Cumberland[25]..............	1,600	1,116	80,000
" Free Synod[25]..............	.....	60	6,000
" Minor bodies[6]	.....	....	10,000
Total *Presbyterian*........	8,471	6,893	713,457
Reformed Church, (late Dutch)[27]	464	493	61,444
" " (late German)[27].....	1,179	526	96,728
Second Advent[28].................	225	....	56,000
" " Seventh-day[28]........	.....	....	10,000
United Brethren[5]...............	[12]1,445	881	[13]118,936
Winebrennarian, or Church of God[2] ...	400	350	30,000
MINOR BODIES NOT WELL KNOWN.			
Bible Christian, Schwenkfelder, German Evangelical Ch. Union, River Breth- ren, Bible Union[6]............. ...	......	......	20,000
Aggregate.....................	70,148	47,609	6,673,396

[1] See References (1, 2, 3) under previous Table.   [2] " Baptist Year-Book," 1871.
[3] For the division, see Explanation under Table V, Reference 6.
[4] Free-will Baptist " Register," 1871.   [5] Official statement to the author.
[6] Estimated.   [7] "Congregational Quarterly," 1871.
[8] Estimate of leading officials.   Number of Churches from " U. S. Census," 1870.
[9] Church Almanac, 1871.   [10] " Friends' Review," 1871.
[11] "N. Y. Observer Year-Book," 1871.   [12] " United States Census," 1870.
[13] Ministers added with members, to make the full number of communicants. See Explanation under Tables III and V.
[14] In 1870 the " United States Census" reported 3,061 less Church organizations of the Regular Baptists than their " Year-book" gave. See "Compendium of Census," 1870, p. 517, note.
[15] " United States Census" gave 15,829 Baptist Churches of all kinds.
[16] Congregations, or Parishes.   [17] Includes baptized children in some synods.
[18] Prof. Schem, 1867.   [19] Official Statement.   [20] " Annual Minutes," 1870.
[21] " Methodist Almanac," 1871.   [22] Appleton's "Annual Cyclopedia," 1870.
[23] " N. Y. Observer Year-Book," 1871.   [24] " Minutes" of said Church, 1871.
[25] " Official Minutes," 1870.   [26] For 1866.
[27] " New York Observer Year-Book," 1871.
[28] Estimated by Revs. J. Litch and J. V. Hines.

TABLE V.
CHURCHES, MINISTERS, AND COMMUNICANTS, 1880.[1]

EVANGELICAL DENOMINATIONS.	Church Organizations or Congregations.[2]	Ministers.[3]	Members or Communicants.[4]
Baptist,[5] Regular, North[6]...............	6,782	5,280	608,556
" " South[6]..............	13,827	8,227	1,026,413
" " Colored[6]............	5,451	3,089	661,358
Total.......................	26,060	16,596	2,296,327
Baptist, Free-will[7]	1,432	1,213	78,012
" " " Minor bodies[8]......	....	....	25,000
" Anti-mission[5]	900	400	40,000
" Seventh-day[9].................	94	110	8,539
" " " German (estimated)	25	....	3,000
" Six-Principle[5]................	20	12	2,000
Total *Baptist*	[10]28,531	18,331	2,452,878
Congregational (Orthodox)[11]...........	3,743	3,654	384,332
Disciple[12]...........................	5,100	3,782	591,821
Dunker[13]............................	250	200	60,000
Episcopal, Protestant[14]..............	[15]3,000	3,432	338,333
" Reformed[16]	....	100	9,448
Evangelical Association[17]............	1,477	893	112,197
Friend, Evangelical (partly estimated)..	392	200	60,000
Lutheran,[18] General Council..........	1,151	624	184,974
" General Synod, South......	214	122	18,223
" " " North	1,285	841	123,813
" Independent.............	913	369	69,353
" Synodical Conference......	1,990	1,176	554,505
Total *Lutheran*	[19]5,553	3,132	[20]950,868
Methodist Episcopal[21]....	....	12,096	[22]1,755,018
" " South[23].........	....	3,887	832,189
" " African[24]........	....	1,738	387,566
" " " Zion[25] ...	....	1,800	300,000
" " Colored[26]	....	638	112,938
" Congregational[27]...........	....	225	13,750
" Free[25].....................	....	260	12,318
" Primitive[28]	....	52	3,369
" Protestant[27]	....	1,385	135,000
" Reformed (estimated).......	....	....	3,000
" Union American[26]..........	....	101	2,250
" Wesleyan in United States[29].	....	400	17,087
Total *Methodist*	[30]29,278	22,582	[22]3,574,485

TABLE V, (Continued.)

EVANGELICAL DENOMINATIONS.	Church Organizations or Congregations.[2]	Ministers.[3]	Members or Communicants.[4]
Mennonite (estimated)................	300	350	50,000
Moravian [28].........................	84	94	9,491
Presbyterian, General Assembly [31]......	5,489	5,044	578,671
" " " South [31]	1,928	1,060	120,028
" United, of North America [31]	813	684	82,119
" Cumberland [31]...........	2,457	1,386	111,863
" Synod of Reformed [31].....	117	111	10,473
" Gen. Synod of Reformed [32]	50	32	6,800
" Welsh Calvinistic [33]	137	100	11,000
" Associate Synod of South [31]	112	121	6,686
" Other bodies (estimated)..	....	....	10,000
Total *Presbyterian*.............	11,103	8,538	937,640
Reformed Church (late Dutch) [31].......	510	544	80,208
" " (late German) [34]	1,405	748	155,857
Second Advent [35]....................	800	600	70,000
" " Seventh-day [31]	[36]640	144	15,570
United Brethren [37]	4,524	2,196	157,835
Winebrennarian, or Church of God [5] ...	400	350	30,000
German Evang'l Ch. Union, Bible Christians, Schwenkfelders, Bible Union, River Brethren, little known (estimat'd)	....	....	25,000
Aggregate	97,090	69,870	10,065,963

[1] The "Year-Books" for 1881 contain the statistics for 1880; but some of the "Annual Minutes" of the Churches give the statistics for the given year.

[2] In some cases the congregations are reported; in others, only the organized Churches.   [3] Local preachers and licentiates not included.

[4] A few denominations reckon baptized children as members, but by far the smaller part.   [5] "Baptist Year-Book," for 1881.

[6] Divided on the basis of the two General Conventions, North and South, which are as separate as the Methodist and the Presbyterian Churches, North and South. The colored associations are also independent of the others.

[7] Free-will Baptist "Register," for 1881.   [8] Ibid., 1880.

[9] "Minutes of Seventh-day Baptist Convention," for 1880.

[10] Probably to some extent congregations. See references 14 and 15, under previous table.

[11] Official Statistics, furnished by Rev. A. H. Quint, D.D., 1881.

[12] Furnished by Rev. F. W. Green, Corresponding Secretary of the Missionary Society of the Disciples.   [13] Official returns for 1877.

14 " Church Almanac, for 1881." Another Almanac, a few more. 16 Parishes.
16 Statistics published after late Convention. 17 "Almanac Evang. Ass'n, 1881.
18 " Lutheran Church Almanac," 1881. 19 Congregations.
20 Including baptized children in some Synods. 21 To December, 1880.
22 Including ministers, because not reckoned elsewhere as communicants, and also probationers. See explanation under Table III.
23 " Almanac of Methodist Episcopal Church, South," for 1881.
24 " Official Report," for 1880.
26 Furnished by Rev. R. G. Dyson, a prominent minister of said Church.
26 " Methodist Almanac," 1881. 27 Furnished for 1880 by a leading minister.
28 " Minutes," for 1880. 29 Minutes of said Church, for 1879.
30 Church organizations of the Methodist Churches are not published in the " Minutes," and therefore cannot be accurately gathered. The " United States Census" reported 25,278 for all Methodist bodies in 1870. It is a moderate estimate to suppose that they have since increased 4,000. One branch of Methodism has increased its church edifices 3,700 since 1870.
31 " Official Minutes," 1880. 32 Furnished by Rev. David Steele, D.D., Phila.
33 Report of the Second Council of the Presbyterian Alliance, p. 963.
34 " Almanac of Ref'd Ch.," 1881. 35 Estimated by leading Advent officials.
36 Congregations. 37 " Almanac of United Brethren," for 1881.

TABLE VI.

RECAPITULATION.

Year.	Churches or Congregations.	Ordained Ministers.	Communicants.
1775	1,918	1,435	. . . .
1800	3,030	2,651	364,872
1850	43,072	25,555	3,529,988
1870	70,148	47,609	6,673,396
1880	97,090	69,870	10,065,963

POPULATION OF THE UNITED STATES.

1775	2,640,000	1870	38,558,371
1800	5,305,925	1880	50,152,866
1850	23,191,876		

RATIO OF COMMUNICANTS TO THE POPULATION.

1800, one in 14.50 inhabitants. | 1870, one in 5.78 inhabitants.
1850, one in 6.57 " | 1880, one in 5 "

From 1800 to 1880 the population increased 9.46 fold ; the communicants 27.52 fold.

From 1850 to 1880 the population increased 116 per cent. ; the communicants 184 per cent.

ACTUAL INCREASE OF COMMUNICANTS.

1800–1850...3,165,116 in 50 yrs. | 1870–1880...3,392,567 in 10 yrs.
1850–1870...3,143,408 in 20 yrs. | 1800–1880...9,701,091 in 80 yrs.

TABLE VII.

SUNDAY-SCHOOL STATISTICS.[1]

Collected by Mr. E. PAYSON PORTER.[2]

UNITED STATES.	Sunday-schools.	Teachers.	Scholars.	Total.
Alabama..............	1,000	6,300	77,000	83,300
Alaska Territory........	3	10	500	510
Arizona Territory	9	50	303	353
Arkansas..............	505	4,542	33,312	37,854
California	800	3,648	45,600	49,248
Colorado	67	700	5,200	5,900
Connecticut	1,031	17,578	139,797	148,375
Dakota Territory........	73	517	2,873	3,390
Delaware	200	3,000	22,003	25,003
District of Columbia.....	60	1,150	10,350	11,500
Florida...............	500	2,500	21,000	23,500
Georgia	2,547	22,808	167,254	190,062
Idaho Territory.........	7	42	455	497
Illinois	6,535	65,806	502,898	568,704
Indian Territory	98	319	2,400	2,719
Indiana..............	3,915	38,785	324,110	362,895
Iowa	4,200	45,000	245,000	290,000
Kansas	2,792	30,712	125,472	156,184
Kentucky	2,501	29,436	214,121	243,557
Louisiana	1,377	13,220	96,843	110,063
Maine	1,200	11,500	78,500	90,000
Maryland	2,003	19,495	205,525	225,020
Massachusetts	1,337	24,095	207,917	232,012
Michigan	2,258	19,998	255,182	275,180
Minnesota	887	8,115	55,953	64,068
Mississippi	1,583	14,244	104,452	118,696
Missouri	2,833	24,247	179,840	204,087
Montana Territory	28	169	1,243	1,412
Nebraska	1,231	8,864	62,329	71,193
Nevada...............	67	411	2,928	3,339
New Hampshire	600	4,585	52,277	56,862
New Jersey............	1,899	29,586	188,631	218,217
New Mexico Territory...	38	224	1,646	1,870
New York.............	5,936	98,992	806,427	905,419
North Carolina	1,985	17,867	131,026	148,893
Ohio	6,770	85,982	590,038	676,020
Oregon...............	180	1,136	11,286	12,422
Pennsylvania	7,798	105,870	754,420	860,290
Rhode Island..........	401	5,998	43,994	49,992
South Carolina	1,412	12,704	93,164	105,868
Tennessee	2,451	22,055	161,736	183,791
Texas................	2,500	10,000	70,000	80,000
Utah Territory..........	30	171	2,199	2,370

TABLE VII, (Continued.)

UNITED STATES.	Sunday-schools.	Teachers.	Scholars.	Total.
Vermont	650	6,855	60,145	67,000
Virginia	3,911	35,904	229,213	265,117
Washington Territory	87	471	3,977	4,448
West Virginia	1,500	12,500	75,000	87,500
Wisconsin	2,454	18,094	165,925	184,019
Wyoming Territory	12	73	660	733
Totals for United States	82,264	886,328	6,623,124	7,509,452

[1] Of the "Evangelical" Churches. Some were collected in 1875, and others in 1878–79. For 1880 the figures would be larger.

[2] For explanations see Mr. Porter's "Report to the Robert Raikes' Centennial Convention," London, England, June 28–July 3, 1880.

TABLE VIII.
UNITARIAN SOCIETIES.

STATES AND SECTIONS.	1830.	1840.	1850.	1860.	1870.	1880.
Maine	12	15	15	14	20	19
New Hampshire	11	19	13	15	18	23
Vermont	3	..	.5	3	6	5
Massachusetts	147	150	165	163	176	176
Rhode Island	2	} 10	{ 3	2	4	4
Connecticut	2		{ 5	2	2	2
Total New England	177	194	206	199	226	229
Western States	2	17	17	26	62	76
Middle "	12	} 19	{ 18	26	37	27
Southern "	2		{ 5	3	3	3
Out of New England	16	36	40	55	102	106
Total in United States.	193	230	246	254	328	335

The Unitarians have two Theological Schools, at Meadville, Pa., and Cambridge, Mass., with 40 students.

The receipts of the American Unitarian Association, from all sources, from 1825 to 1880, amount to $1,883,529 03, of which sum $33,768 91 has been appropriated to its single foreign mission in India, an average of $3,083 42 yearly since it was founded in 1855.

The average annual sales of books, tracts, etc., during the past ten years has been $8,697 29.

TABLE IX.

UNIVERSALIST MINISTERS IN THE UNITED STATES. [1]

STATES.	1835.	1840.	1851.	1860.	1870.	1880.
Maine................	29	69	60	46	40	49
New Hampshire.......	32	33	24	27	15	23
Vermont.............	25	40	40	41	34	41
Massachusetts........	67	109	142	126	107	133
Rhode Island........	2	8	4	5	3	8
Connecticut..........	14	10	16	15	17	18
Total in New England	169	269	286	260	216	272
Out of New England...	139	243	356	425	409	457
Total in United States	308	512	642	685	625	729

[1] Each "Year-Book" gives the statistics of the previous year.

NOTE. This denomination has 4 colleges, with 279 students, and 2 theological seminaries, with 42 students. They also have a publishing house in Boston, whose sales amount to about $50,000 annually.

TABLE X.

UNIVERSALIST PARISHES IN THE UNITED STATES.

STATES.	1835.	1840.	1851.	1860.	1870.	1880.
Maine................	101	100	130	139	89	91
New Hampshire.......	72	81	70	78	29	35
Vermont.............	80	92	108	82	60	64
Massachusetts........	90	131	150	168	· 105	115
Rhode Island........	5	7	10	12	5	8
Connecticut..........	45	27	33	27	16	18
Total in New England	393	438	501	506	304	331
Out of New England...	260	415	568	758	613	625
Total in United States	653	853	1,069	1,264	917	956

TABLE XI.

THE NEW JERUSALEM CHURCH.

YEAR.	Societies.	Ministers.	Communicants.
1850..................	4	42	....
1860[1]..............	57	54	1,960
1880[2]..............	93	89	3,994

[1] From Professor Schem's " Ecclesiastical Year-Book " for 1880.

[2] From the Minutes of the General Convention for 1880. This denomination has a General Convention, organized in 1820, one collegiate and one theological institution.

TABLE XII.
THE ROMAN CATHOLIC CHURCH.

	1775	1800.	1830.	1845.	1850.	1860.	1870.	1880. [1]
Dioceses, Vicar Apostolics....	..	1	9	22	29	48	58	69
Churches, etc..	52	......	......	675	1,245	2,519	3,912	6,817
Chapels, stat'ns	..	......	......	592	585	1,278	1,480	1,723
Priests........	26	50	232	707	1,302	2,316	3,966	6,402
Ecc'l students.	..	......	......	220	322	499	1,015	1,170
Male relig. ho.[3]	..	......	......	....	35	100	115	[2] 176
Female do.[4]...	..	......	......	28	65	173	297	[3] 673
Educ'l institu's								618
for young men and ladies....	..	4	......	89	123	....	467	2,389
Parochial sch's	..	......	......	....	....	660	1,214	
Pupils in Parochial schools..	..	......	......	....	....	57,611	257,600	423,383
Hosp'ls, asyl's.	..	......	......	94	108	....	295	386
Est. Cath. Pop.	..	100,000	500,000	1,071,800	1,614,000	2,789,000	4,600,000	6,367,330

NOTE. The above statistics from 1830 to 1880 have been collated from the
"Metropolitan Catholic Almanac" and Sadlier's "Catholic Directory." They
do not entirely agree with Father Hecker's table in the "Catholic World," June,
1879. We prefer to rely upon the "Year-Books" of the Church.

[1] From Sadlier's "Catholic Directory" for 1881, giving the statistics collected
in 1880. This rule has been observed throughout this table.

[2] Not tabulated in the "Year-Book," but collated from the reports of the dioceses. It is difficult sometimes to distinguish between the convents and the academies.　　　　[3] Monasteries.　　　　[4] That is, convents.

TABLE XIII.
CHURCH EDIFICES AND ORGANIZATIONS.
(From the U. S. Census for 1870.)

DENOMINATIONS.	EDIFICES.			ORGANIZATIONS.[1]
	1850.	1860.	1870.	1870.
"Evangelical" Bodies.				
Methodist (all kinds)	13,302	19,883	21,337	25,278
Baptist　　"	9,563	12,150	13,962	15,829
Presbyterian　"	4,858	6,406	7,071	7,824
Congregationalist.............	1,725	2,234	2,715	2,887
Lutheran	1,231	2,128	2,776	3,032
Episcopalian	1,459	2,145	2,601	2,835
Reformed Church (late Dutch) .	335	440	468	471
" 　　　(late German)	341	676	1,145	1,256
United Brethren.............	14	....	937	1,445
Evangelical Association.......	39	....	641	815
Disciple	600	1,200	1,772	2,478
Friends	726	726	662	692
Moravian..................	344	49	67	72
Total Evangelical.........	34,537	48,037	56,154	64,914

TABLE XIII, (Continued.)

DENOMINATIONS.	EDIFICES.			ORGANI-ZATIONS.
	1850.	1860.	1870.	1870.
"Non-Orthodox" Bodies.				
Unitarian	245	264	310	331
Universalist	530	664	602	719
All others — Christians, Jews, New Jerusalem, etc.........	1,527	2,494	2,210	2,368
Total "Non-Orthodox"	2,302	3,422	3,122	3,418
Roman Catholic	1,222	2,550	3,806	4,127
Aggregate...............	38,061	54,009	63,082	72,459

NOTE.—The above table has been so arranged for convenience in comparisons, which are sometimes desired.

[1] Ecclesiastical organizations, variously called "Societies," "Parishes," "Churches." Reported in the U. S. Census for the first time, in 1870.

TABLE XIV.

THE COLLEGES AND THE CHURCHES.[1]

DENOMINATIONAL RELATIONS.[2]	Number of Colleges.	Founded prior to 1800.	Founded from 1800 to 1850.	Founded from 1850 to 1877.	Students in the Course for A. B.[3]	Total College Property.[6]
Baptists, Regular, North and South ..	40	1	14	25	3,560	$9,630,765
" Free-will................	4	..	..	4	250	515,000
" Seventh-day...............	2	..	..	2	201	222,251
Total *Baptist*	46	1	14	31	4,011	10,368,016
Christian and Disciple[4]....	23	..	1	22	2,026	3,112,200
Congregational	28	3	8	17	2,428	9,704,595
Congregational and Presbyterian	4	..	4	..	311	1,216,000
Episcopal, Protestant	12	2	4	6	827	8,759,715
Friend.........	6	..	1	5	261	1,255,000
Evangelical Association.............	1	..	..	1	39	147,000
Lutheran......................	17	..	3	14	1,152	1,388,000
Methodist Episcopal, North.........	38	..	13	25	3,107	8,859,600
" " South...........	14	..	6	8	1,220	1,863,700
" Protestant	4	..	..	4	150	265,000
" African	1	..	..	1	19	62,300
Total *Methodist*................ ...	57	..	19	38	4,496	11,050,600

TABLE XIV, (Continued.)

DENOMINATIONAL RELATIONS.[2]	Number of Colleges.	Founded prior to 1800.	Founded from 1800 to 1850.	Founded from 1850 to 1877.	Students in the Course for A.B.[3]	Total College Property.[6]
Presbyterian, North and South.......	26	3	8	15	2,695	6,306,447
" United................	6	..	2	4	256	246,000
" Reformed and Associate	3	..	2	1	114	202,500
" Cumberland	6	..	..	4	394	319,000
Total *Presbyterian*.......	41	3	14	24	3,459	7,073,947
Refor'd Churches (Dutch and German)	8	1	1	6	521	1,456,107
Swedenborgian or New Church.......	1	..	..	1	17	42,000
Seventh-day Advent.................	1	..	..	1	39	147,000
United Brethren	7	..	1	6	286	515,782
Universalist	5	..	..	5	226	1,621,100
Unitarian	1	1	..	..	813	5,657,491
Total *Protestant*	258	11	70	177	20,912	63,514,553
Roman Catholic [5]...................	52	1	17	34	3,564	5,250,300
Mormon............................	1	..	..	1	....	....
Jewish	1	..	..	1	....	60,000
Total *Non-Protestant*	54	1	17	36	3,564	5,310,300
Total, with denominational relations	312	12	87	213	24,476	68,824,853
Non-denominational [2]...............	64	8	15	41	5,883	21,301,934
Aggregate	376	20	102	254	30,359	$90,126,787

[1] A great amount of research, review, and care has been expended upon the above table. The author cannot claim for it completeness or entire accuracy; but it is a close approximation, the best that conscientious care and extensive inquiry can make. The data are chiefly for 1878, and have been gathered from the report on Education by General Eaton, the omissions of that year being supplied from his previous reports, and from the Year-Books of the Churches. Consultations have also been had with prominent educators.

[2] Under this term is comprised the colleges which are closely associated, by origin, sympathy, and support, with particular Churches. The non-denominational are those designated in General Eaton's reports as "non-sectarian," or not specified at all. Some, however, of those thus designated in his reports, as Yale, Princeton, Harvard, and Columbia, but really Congregational, Presbyterian, Unitarian, and Episcopal, have been included in the list of denominational colleges, because they are such in all their relations. None of the denominational colleges have any sectarian tests, and the distinction, sectarian and non-sectarian, is often unfair and offensive. (See discussion, pp. 459–466.)

[3] Students in the regular course for the degree of A.B.

[4] Chiefly belonging to the Disciples or Campbellites.

[5] The Roman Catholic Church "Year-Book," for 1881, gives 79 colleges, but some are not yet fully developed.

[6] Comprising grounds, buildings, and productive funds.

TABLE XV.

RECEIPTS OF THE FOREIGN MISSIONARY SOCIETIES OF THE UNITED STATES FROM THE ORIGIN OF EACH.[1]

SOCIETIES.	1810 to 1819.	1820 to 1829.	1830 to 1839.	1840 to 1849.	1850 to 1859.	1860 to 1869.	1870 to 1880.[2]	Total 1810 to 1880.
American B. C. F. M.	$162,430	$664,247	$1,684,751	$2,550,277	$3,140,811	$4,519,112	$5,243,137	$17,964,765
" Baptist Miss. Union	43,780	81,471	591,230	769,265	1,061,608	1,429,149	2,753,977	6,730,480
Methodist Episcopal[3]	....	....	195,403	330,213	785,357	1,505,550	3,773,887	6,590,410
Protestant Episcopal	....	....	227,816	309,026	559,435	709,200	1,270,731	3,076,208
Presbyterian Board[4]	....	....	186,639	784,750	1,772,873	2,372,552	4,885,241	10,002,055
Southern Baptist	....	....	....	65,886	276,263	238,365	404,428	984,942
American For. Ch. Union (chiefly foreign)[5]	....	....	....	246,505	608,424	829,164	518,613	2,274,706
Reformed Ch. (Dutch) with A. B. C. F. M. until 1857	....	....	....	....	41,111	568,424	701,576	1,311,111
Evangelical Lutheran[6]	....	....	....	20,000	35,000	80,000	165,000	300,000
" Association	....	....	....	12,000	30,000	62,000	145,000	249,000
United Brethren	....	....	....	....	44,402	161,101	345,150	550,653
" Presbyterian	....	....	....	....	....	400,331	609,298	1,009,629
Southern "	....	....	....	....	....	54,767	483,174	537,941
Reformed "	....	....	....	....	....	....	92,732	92,732
Disciples[6]	....	....	....	....	....	....	33,177	33,177
Free-will Baptist[6]	....	....	....	....	....	....	....	340,362
Methodist Episcopal, South (estimated)	....	....	....	....	....	....	....	2,000,000
Total, exclusive of Woman's Boards	$206,210	$745,718	$2,885,839	$5,087,922	$8,427,284	$12,929,715	$21,425,121	$54,048,171

Woman's Boards.[7]

Woman's Union Society............	....	....	....	....	....	119,827	473,221	593,048
" Congregational, East......	....	....	....	....	....	20,495	688,134	708,629
" Interior........	....	....	....	....	....	4,092	169,364	173,456
Methodist Episcopal......	....	....	....	....	....	....	595,246	595,246
Presbyterian, Philadelphia......	....	....	....	....	....	....	567,394	567,394
" New York......	....	....	....	....	....	....	166,194	166,194
" North-west......	....	....	.:.	....	....	....	207,560	207,560
" Albany and Troy....	....	....	....	....	....	....	45,341	45,341
Baptist, East........	....	....	....	....	....	....	281,100	281,100
" West.........	....	....	....	....	....	....	104,841	104,841
Protestant Episcopal......	....	....	....	....	....	....	67,278	67,278
Reformed Church (Dutch)....	..:	....	....	....	....	....	35,369	35,369
United Brethren Church......	....	....	....	....	....	....	15,000	15,000
Meth. Epis. Church, South	....	..:	....	....	....	....	20,319	20,319
Total Woman's Boards ...	....	....	....	....	....	$144,414	$3,436,361	$3,580,775
Aggregate[7]	$206,210	$745,718	$2,885,839	$5,087,922	$8,427,284	$13,074,129	$24,861,482	$57,628,946

1 In a few cases the earlier receipts have not been ascertained.

2 This period comprises eleven years.

3 For foreign missions only, commencing with African mission.

4 For many years the N. S. Presbyterians contributed to the A. B. C. F. M., but not since 1870.

5 Formerly more largely foreign than of late years.

6 Estimated by a leading official of that denomination.

7 In some instances the receipts of the Woman's Boards are embraced in the statistics of the large denominational Boards; but there are some amounts of foreign mission funds which we have been unable to collect and tabulate, quite enough to justify the adding the receipts of all the Woman's Boards in the grand aggregate.

35

TABLE XVI.

RECEIPTS OF THE HOME MISSIONARY SOCIETIES OF THE UNITED STATES FROM THE ORIGIN OF EACH.[1]

Societies.	1820 to 1829.	1830 to 1839.	1840 to 1849.	1850 to 1859.	1860 to 1869.	1870 to 1880.[2]	Total, 1820 to 1880.
Presbyterian, O. S., Board	$105,643	$860,599	$394,482	$1,012,281	$1,190,657	} [3]$4,314,327	$9,668,664
" N. S. "	.....	.....	.....	612,658	1,178,017	}	
American Home Missionary Soc..	65,173	724,231	1,107,852	1,746,963	1,975,878	3,119,584	8,739,681
Methodist Episcopal Domestic[4]..	63,010	390,806	660,426	1,576,714	3,011,100	2,907,635	8,609,691
Protestant Episcopal "	.....	108,184	320,613	463,204	754,507	1,827,724	3,474,232
Am. Church Missionary Society..	.....	.....	.....	.....	453,097	517,690	970,787
Reformed Church (Dutch).......	.....	31,661	64,297	139,490	202,534	308,516	746,498
American Baptist Home Mission.	.....	134,534	243,444	441,762	1,149,161	2,330,585	4,299,486
Seamen's Friend Society[5]	.....	94,697	172,128	254,914	430,766	689,796	1,642,301
Am. Missionary Association[6]	.....	.....	51,112	421,249	1,829,624	3,743,113	6,045,098
Evangelical Association[6]........	.....	.....	48,000	120,000	248,000	580,000	996,000
United Brethren............	.....	.....	.....	88,804	322,201	693,291	1,104,296
Southern Baptist Domestic......	.....	.....	.....	266,356	495,020	258,279	1,019,655
Young Men's Chris'n Associations	.....	.....	.....	908,000	[7]7,384,218	6,773,082	[8]15,065,300
Disciples...................	.....	.....	.....	27,714	84,410	650,078	762,202
United Presbyterian Church.....	.....	.....	.....	.....	186,801	369,661	556,462
Southern Presbyterian Board.....	.....	.....	.....	.....	117,728	457,633	575,361
Cumberland Presbyt'n (last 9 yrs.)	.....	.....	.....	.....	.....	209,287	209,287
Free-Will Baptist.............	.....	.....	.....	.....	.....	.....	269,927
Meth. E. Ch., South (estimated)..	.....	.....	.....	.....	.....	.....	3,000,000

Lutheran [9]						
Seventh-day Baptist [9]						
Reformed Church (German) [9]						
Reformed Presbyterian [9]						
Protestant Methodist [9]	....	....	....	....	....	3,000,000
Wesleyan Methodist [9]						
Free Methodist [9]						
African Methodist [9]						
Moravian, etc., etc. [9]						
Freedmen's Aid Societies: [10]						
Methodist Episcopal (in 13 years)	....	....	....	...	893,918	893,918
Presbyterian (in 11 years)	....	....	....	...	503,671	503,671
United Presbyterian (in 14 years)	....	....	....	...	124,284	124,284
Aggregate..........	$233,826	$2,342,712	$3,062,354	$8,080,109	$21,015,719	$31,272,154	$72,276,801

[1] The earlier receipts of some Boards have not been ascertained.
[2] This period includes eleven years.
[3] United in 1870.
[4] Divided on the basis of domestic appropriations.
[5] Chiefly domestic.
[6] Estimated by a leading official of that denomination on partial data.
[7] Including the expenditures of the Christian Commission, organized by the Young Men's Christian Association.
[8] These figures are official.
[9] Partially estimated.
[10] This work is Home Mission. The Freedmen's work of some denominations is included in the reports of the Home Mission Societies.

TABLE XVII.

RECEIPTS OF THE RELIGIOUS PUBLICATION HOUSES OF THE EVANGELICAL CHURCHES OF THE UNITED STATES, FROM ALL SOURCES, FROM THE ORIGIN OF EACH.

PUBLICATION HOUSES.	1790 to 1829.	1830 to 1839.	1840 to 1849.	1850 to 1859.	1860 to 1869.	1870[1] to 1880.	Total, to 1880.
Methodist Book Concerns, 1790[2]	$1,200,000	$1,300,000	$1,731,741	$4,608,677	$10,309,766	$15,672,138	$34,822,322
American Bible Society, 1809	687,023	972,106	1,670,058	3,598,480	5,696,205	6,666,407	19,290,279
Mass. Bible Society, 1806	57,107	23,036	22,014	178,676	283,717	358,830	923,380
Am. Tract Society, Boston, 1814	85,379	187,343	349,335	653,289	1,259,535	177,933	2,712,814
Am. Tract Society, N. Y., 1824	145,860	844,088	1,472,822	3,777,213	3,956,338	5,318,634	15,514,955
Am. Sunday-School Union, 1824	199,558	900,817	1,004,879	2,268,855	2,798,626	1,942,913	9,115,648
Baptist Publishing Board, 1824	10,235	67,216	170,328	496,271	1,461,566	4,192,563	6,398,179
Presbyterian, O. S., 1832[3]	......	......	......	951,957	1,196,535	2,423,965	5,266,225
Presbyterian, N. S., 1852[3]	......	......	......	332,292	361,476		
Congregational Board, 1832	......	94,490	225,920	378,554	1,073,686	1,274,318	3,046,968
Am. and Foreign Bible Soc, 1836	......	150,000	500,000	418,402	320,714	141,779	1,530,895
Evangelical Association, 1842	......	......	40,306	107,369	389,608	1,546,750	2,084,033
United Brethren, 1850	......	......	......	326,974	558,099	1,002,770	1,887,843
American Bible Union, 1850	......	......	......	285,308	347,158	358,512	990,978
Southern Presbyterian, 1865	......	......	......	......	106,566	359,062	465,628
Free-Will Baptist, 1826[4]	......	......	......	......	......	......	900,000
Reformed Church (Dutch)[5]	......	......	......	......	......	237,456	237,456
United Presbyterian[6]	......	......	......	......	......	156,338	156,338
Cumberland Presbyterian[7]	......	......	......	......	......	339,495	339,495

Methodist Episcopal, South..						
Lutheran..						
Reformed Church (German)..						
Moravian..						
Seventh-Day Baptist..	......	......	......	......	......	$3,800,000
Wesleyan Methodist..						
Protestant Methodist..						
African Methodist..						
Disciples..						
Aggregate..........	$2,385,162.	$4,539,096.	$7,187,403	$16,382,317	$30,119,595	$42,169,863 $109,483,436

NOTE.—All of the above denominational houses comprise Sunday-school and Tract departments, and most of them do much home missionary work.

[1] This period includes eleven years.
[2] Receipts of Methodist Book Concerns from 1790 to 1843, estimated on partial data; but since the latter date exactly reported.
[3] Cannot obtain figures prior to 1850.
[4] Estimated by a leading Free-Will Baptist official.
[5] Cannot obtain figures prior to 1870.
[6] For last six years only.
[7] For last nine years only.
[8] Have been unable to obtain data. Estimated.

THE BRITISH ISLANDS.

TABLES XVIII to XXIII.

THE BRITISH ISLANDS.

TABLE XVIII.

THE PROTESTANT CHURCHES.

DENOMINATIONS.	Archbishops.	Bishops.	Clergy.	Churches, Parishes, or Congregations.	Communicants.
Church of England :[1]					
in England and Wales	2	29	23,000	....	....
in Scotland....................	..	7	232	226	....
in Ireland....................	2	10	1,800	....	....
in the Colonies...............	..	61	2,700	....	....
Total *Church of England*...	4	107	27,732	226	....
Free Church of England[1]	..	...	....	40	....
Baptist :[2] England	..	...	1,360	1,893	203,304
" Wales.	..	...	344	534	67,859
" Scotland.................	..	...	79	88	9,234
" Ireland	..	...	17	30	1,251
Total *Baptist*...............	..	...	1,800	2,545	281,648
Congregational :[3] England and Wales	..	...	2,572	[4]3,277	
" Scotland.........	..	...	121	106	}[5]360,000
" Ireland..........	..	...	20	30	
Total *Congregational*	..	...	2,713	3,413	[5]360,000
Catholic Apostolic (Irvingites)[1]....	..	...	....	19	....
Countess of Huntingdon Connection[1]	..	...	....	37	....
Friends (England and Wales)[1].....	..	...	265	327	14,500
Moravians[1]......................	..	...	....	38	5,604
New Jerusalem[1]...................	..	...	....	64	4,987
Unitarians[1]......................	..	...	357	370	....
Presbyterian :[6]					
Established Church of Scotland	..	...	1,530	1,420	[9]515,786
Free Church of Scotland	..	...	1,060	1,043	300,000
United (Scotl'd, Engl'd, Irel'd) .	..	...	600	593	183,221

TABLE XVIII, (Continued.)

DENOMINATIONS.	Archbishops.	Bishops.	Clergy.	Churches, Parishes, or Congregations.	Communicants.
Presbyterian,[6] (continued :)					
Church in Ireland............	..	...	632	674	104,769
Church in England...........	..	...	258	276	54,135
Reformed Synod in Ireland....	..	...	31	40	4,438
Synod of Reformed Ch. in Scot'd	..	...	8	13	1,197
United "Original Seceders"...	..	...	32	40	5,450
Total *Presbyterian*[6]........	..	...	4,151	4,099	1,168,996

BODIES OF METHODISTS.[1]

	Chapels.[7]	Ministers.[8]	Local Preachers.[8]	Members.[8]	Probationers.[8]	Sunday-school Scholars.[7]
Wesleyans.	6,859	2,158	15,100	401,141	26,547	787,143
New Connection	437	170	1,135	20,950	3,696	76,457
Primitive..........	4,302	1,142	14,507	182,691	....	372,570
United Free Churches	1,238	370	3,165	64,712	6,580	181,218
Reform Union	2,256	18	605	7,360	368	10,078
Bible Christians.....	577	182	1,453	20,043	394	35,357
Irish Conference	....	244	1,800	25,186	....	....
Calvinistic..........	1,319	920	....	118,251	....	155,159
Total *Methodist*	16,988	5,204	37,765	840,334	37,585	1,617,982

[1] From "Whitaker's Almanac," (London,) 1881.

[2] From "American Baptist Year-Book," for 1881.

[3] From "English Congregational Year-Book," for 1880.

[4] Churches, Branch Churches, and Stations.

[5] Rev. H. M. Dexter, D.D., estimates 376,074.

[6] From the "Report of Second General Council of the Pan-Presbyterian Alliance," September, 1880, pp. 961, 962.

[7] For Great Britain only.   [8] For the United Kingdom.

[9] For nine hundred and twenty Churches.

TABLE XIX.

DISSENTERS IN ENGLAND AND WALES.[1]

In 1699 ...... 214,000, or 4.18 per cent. of the population.
" 1845 ...... 1,315,000, or 8.08 " "
" 1851 ...... 1,958,000,[2] or 10.89 " "
" 1861 ...... 3,090,000,[2] or 15.36 " "
" 1866 ..... 3,686,000,[2] or 17.38 " "
" 1876 ...... 4,500,000,[2] or 20.00 " "

"In 1876, in Wales, the dissenters constituted the majority of the population; in six counties they were one third of the whole population; in London one tenth."

According to the above figures the increase of the whole population, from 1851 to 1876, was 35 per cent.; but the dissenting population increased 130 per cent.

---

[1] "Encyclopædia Britannica," ninth edition, vol. viii, pp. 246, 247.
[2] The above statistics are not altogether satisfactory. When the religious census of Great Britain was taken, in 1851, the returns showed 3,773,474 in attendance upon public worship in the Church of England congregations, to 3,487,558 in the Dissenting Chapels, and the Church of England places of worship were 14,077 to 20,390 of the Dissenters. In the last thirty years, according to all accounts, the Dissenters have gained more than the Established Church.

TABLE XX.

ROMANISM IN THE BRITISH ISLES.

	England and Wales.			Scotland.			Ireland.			Total British Isles.		
	1850.[1]	1870.[2]	1880.[3]	1850.[1]	1870.[2]	1880.[3]	1850.[1]	1870.[2]	1880.[3]	1850.	1870.	1880.
Dioceses	..	13	14	..	3	6	28	28	28	28	44	48
Archbishops and Bishops........	..	14	16	..	3	6	28	29	29	28	46	51
Priests..........	833	1,528	1,942	..	199	276	2,552	3,334	3,450	3,385	5,061	5,668
Churches, chapels, and stat'ns.	560	1,151	1,264	87	203	279	2,205	2,341	2,371	2,852	3,695	3,914
Communities of men	12	69	87	..	..	11	41	164	176	53	233	274
Communities of women........	38	216	285	..	17	24	160	209	256	198	442	565

[1] "Metropolitan Catholic Almanac." Baltimore, 1850.
[2] Sadlier's "Catholic Almanac and Directory." New York, 1871.
[3] Ibid., 1881.

TABLE XXI.

ROMANISM, PROTESTANTISM, AND THE POPULATION IN IRELAND.[1]

RELIGIOUS BODIES.	1834.		1861.		1871.	
	Religious Population.	Per ct. of the whole Population.	Religious Population.	Percent. of the whole Population.	Religious Population.	Percent. of the whole Population.
Roman Catholics	6,436,066	80.9	4,505,265	77.9	4,141,933	76.7
Established Church	853,106	10.7	693,357	11.8	683,295	12.6
Other Protestant Churches.	664,880	8.4	600,245	10.3	577,531	10.7
Total	7,954,100	100.0	5,798,867	100.0	5,402,759	100.0

[1] English official sources.

TABLE XXII.

ROMANISM AND THE POPULATION IN ENGLAND AND WALES.

YEARS.	Number of Roman Catholics.	Per cent. of the whole Population.
1558–1603..........................	....	33.33
1699........................	27,696	0.50
1767...............................	68,000	1.00
1780...............................	69,400	0.90
1845...............................	284,300	1.70
1851...............................	[1]758,800	4.22
1854...............................	916,600	4.94
1861...............................	927,500	4.61
1866............................	982,000	4.62
1877...............................	[2]1,000,000	[3]4.07

NOTE.—The above data have been taken chiefly from the "Encyclopædia Britannica," ninth edition, vol. viii, pp. 246, 247.

[1] This increase followed the Potato Famine in Ireland of 1846-47.
[2] "Whitaker's Almanac," London, (1880,) says there are two millions in England, Wales, and Scotland.
[3] Calculated on the basis of population for that year adopted by the Registrar-General.

TABLE XXIII.

ROMAN CATHOLICS IN ENGLAND, WALES, AND IRELAND.

YEARS.	Roman Catholic Population.	Per cent. of the whole Population.
1841	6,958,737	28.8
1851	6,137,749	25.1
1871	5,141,933	18.2
Decrease from 1841 to 1871........	1,816,804	10.9

THE BRITISH DOMINION IN NORTH AMERICA.

TABLE XXIV.

TABLE XXIV.

RELIGIOUS STATISTICS OF THE BRITISH DOMINION IN NORTH AMERICA.

(From the Canadian Census Reports, 1851, 1861, 1871.)

1851.	Roman Catholic.	Baptists.	Ch'ch of Engl'nd.	Congregationalists.	Jews.	Lutherans.	Methodists.	Mormons.	Presbyterians.	Quakers.	Other denom's.	No Creed.	Not given.	Total population.
U'r Canada.	167,695	53,583	223,190	7,747	106	12,089	213,365	247	204,148	7,465	19,835	....	42,538	952,004
L'r Canada.	746,854	4,943	44,682	3,927	248	20	21,199	12	33,470	163	29,419	...	5,774	890,261
N. Brunswick.	....	...	...	...	..	..	....	..	....	...	....	...	...	193,800
Nova Scotia.	69,131	42,643	36,115	2,639	..	4,087	23,593	..	72,924	188	4,194	...	21,340	276,854
Total.....	983,680	101,169	303,987	14,313	354	16,196	258,057	259	310,542	7,816	53,448	....	69,652	2,312,919
1861.														
U'r Canada.	258,151	70,524	311,559	9,357	614	24,299	350,373	74	303,374	7,383	34,889	17,373	8,121	1,396,091
L'r Canada.	943,253	7,751	63,487	4,927	572	857	30,844	3	43,735	121	8,811	1,477	5,728	1,111,566
N. Brunswick	85,238	57,730	42,776	1,290	9	113	25,637	7	36,632	38	2,048	12	517	252,047
Nova Scotia	86,281	62,941	47,744	2,183	..	4,382	34,167	27	88,755	158	1,905	...	2,314	330,857
Total.....	1,372,923	198,946	465,566	17,757	1,195	29,651	441,021	111	472,496	7,700	47,653	18,862	16,680	3,090,561
1871.														
U'r Canada.	274,166	86,630	331,484	12,858	518	32,399	462,264	460	356,449	7,106	35,863	4,908	13,849	1,620,851
L'r Canada..	1,019,850	8,686	62,636	5,252	549	406	34,100	..	46,165	116	11,780	420	1,461	1,191,516
N. Brunswick	96,016	70,597	45,481	1,193	48	82	29,856	59	38,852	26	2,861	131	392	255,594
Nova Scotia	102,001	73,430	55,143	2,538	..	4,958	40,871	15	103,539	96	3,724	116	1,353	387,800
Total.....	1,492,033	239,343	494,744	21,841	1,115	37,935	567,091	534	545,005	7,345	54,228	5,575	17,055	3,485,761

Additional: Greeks, 18; Mohammedans, 13; pagans, 1,886.

ECUMENICAL STATISTICS.

TABLES XXV to XXXIX.

ECUMENICAL STATISTICS.

TABLE XXV.

THE ANGLICAN COMMUNION [1] IN THE WHOLE WORLD.

COUNTRIES.	1860. Archb'p and Bishops.	1860. Clergy.	1880. Archb'p and Bishops.	1880. Clergy.
EUROPE:				
England and Wales	28	17,000	34	23,000
Scotland	7	158	7	232
Ireland	12	1,456	12	1,800
Gibraltar, etc...........	1	....	1	60
Continental chaplaincies of the Prot. Epis. Ch. of U. S.	1	....	1	6
Total *Europe*........	49	18,614	55	25,098
AMERICA:				
United States...........	43	2,073	64	3,400
British North America....	10	873	17	829
West Indies and other isles	3		6	220
Mexico.................	..	....	1	4
South America	1	1	2	66
Total *America*.......	57	2,947	90	4,519
ASIA..................	1	52	14	659
AFRICA	1	11	15	300
AUSTRALASIA AND POLYNESIA	..	..	20	680
Aggregate	[2]108	[2]21,624	195	31,256

[1] Including the Protestant Episcopal Church in the United States and its missions. Impossible to obtain the statistics of the communicants except of the latter Church. The above statistics for 1880 have been gathered from the " Kalendar of the English Church," for 1881, the "Church Almanac," United States, for 1881, and from " Whitaker's (London) Almanac," for 1881. Those for 1860 were taken from Professor Schem's " American Ecclesiastical Year-Book," for 1860.   [2] Incomplete.

TABLE XXVI.

BAPTISTS[1] IN THE WHOLE WORLD.

COUNTRIES.	1860.[2] Communicants.	1880.[3] Church's.	1880.[3] Ministers.	1880.[3] Communicants.
AMERICA:				
United States............	1,135,868	28,531	18,331	2,452,878
British North America....	35,618	880	523	76,541
West Indies, Bahamas, etc.	36,250	157	91	28,352
Mexico	....	8	3	150
South America...........	....	3	2	214
Total *America*.......	1,207,736	29,579	18,950	2,558,135
EUROPE:				
British Islands..........	200,000	2,545	1,800	281,648
France and Holland.....	938	9	12	1,191
Germany and Switzerland.	5,944	91	85	15,827
Sweden, Norway, Denmark	4,655	332	172	21,581
Spain..............	....	4	3	140
Italy	....	20	16	420
Austria, Greece, Turkey ..	20	3	3	310
Russia, Poland, Finland...	....	16	13	5,833
Total *Europe*.......	211,557	3,020	2,104	326,950
ASIA:				
India, Farth. India, Ceylon.	16,858	497	246	40,169
China	30	21	30	1,822
Japan	....	2	12	76
Total *Asia*	16,888	520	288	42,067
AFRICA	1,384	60	44	3,603
AUSTRALASIA	6,000	143	95	7,918
Aggregate............	1,443,565	33,322	21,481	2,938,673

[1] All bodies bearing the name Baptist.

[2] The statistics for 1860 are chiefly from the " American Ecclesiastical Year-Book " of Professor Schem, for 1860.

[3] The statistics for 1880 are chiefly from the " Baptist Year-Book," for 1881, adding the Free-Will Baptists in the British Provinces, and a few other additions.

TABLE XXVII.

CONGREGATIONALISTS [1] IN THE WHOLE WORLD.

COUNTRIES.	1880.		
	Churches.	Ministers.	Communi-cants.
AMERICA:			
United States [2]	3,743	3,654	384,332
British Provinces [3]	110	88	6,676
Mexico [4]	1	1	173
Jamaica and British Guiana......	40	26	3,673
Total *America*	3,894	3,769	394,854
EUROPE:			
British Islands [5]	3,219	2,718	[6] 376,074
France and Belgium [3]	97	101	....
Spain and Portugal [4]...........	3	2	190
Italy and Switzerland [3].........	118	130	....
Austria and Turkey [4]...........	4	15	237
Total *Europe*	3,441	2,966	376,501
ASIA:			
Western Asia [4]..................	91	104	6,383
India and Ceylon [4][7]...........	170	141	9,182
China [4][7]......................	65	50	3,696
Japan [4]........................	16	14	514
Total *Asia*..............	342	309	19,775
AFRICA:			
Continent [4][8][10]	[11] 17	55	5,212
Madagascar [7]..................	[11]	86	70,125
Total *Africa*...........	17	141	75,337
POLYNESIA [8][4][7]................	[11] 96	340	[10] 30,275
AUSTRALASIA	206	[9]145	....
Aggregate	7,996	7,670	896,742

[1] Orthodox.
[2] Congregational "Year-Book," 1881.
[3] Congregational "Quarterly," 1877, pp. 64, 65.
[4] "Missionary Herald," January, 1881.
[5] English Congregational "Year-Book," 1880.
[6] Estimate by Rev. Henry M. Dexter, D.D.
[7] Report of the London Missionary Society, for 1880.
[8] Report of American Missionary Association, 1880.
[9] Statistics of Foreign Missions, by Rev. William B. Boyce. London, 1873.
[10] In part from Report of London Missionary Society, for 1879. The statistics of the Sandwich Islands are for 1878.
[11] The Churches of the London Missionary Society not given in their Report.

TABLE XXVIII.

METHODISTS[1] IN THE WHOLE WORLD.

COUNTRIES.	1860.[2]			1880.		
	Ministers	Local Preachers.	Communi-cants.	Ministers.	Local Preachers.	Communi-cants.
AMERICA:						
United States	12,843	....	[2]1,930,714	25,373	26,875	[3]3,775,753
British N. America ..	688	....	89,726	1,682	4,323	173,361
W. Ind., Bahamas, etc	....	....	40,260	108	....	51,905
Mexico..............	....	....	....	27	17	1,087
Central America.....	....	....	500	5	....	1,086
South America	1	....	4,067	25	9	4,958
Total *America*.	13,532	....	2,065,267	27,220	31,224	4,008,150
EUROPE:						
British Isles	3,377	....	[3]698,111	5,080	[4]44,153	[3][5]881,137
France	31	....	1,551	37	92	2,041
Spain, Portugal	....	....	63	10	....	398
Germany, Switzerland	13	....	1,279	98	94	21,276
Scandinavia	4	....	44	96	99	13,150
Italy, Malta.........	....	....	....	48	2	2,586
Bulgaria	3	....	....	6	....	44
Total *Europe*.	3,460	....	701,048	5,375	44,440	920,632
ASIA:						
India and Ceylon....	6	....	1,173	164	105	10,005
China	6	....	72	143	46	2,884
Japan.	....	....	....	8	5	628
Total *Asia* .	12	....	1,245	315	156	13,517
AFRICA..............	21	....	17,726	177	52	51,657
AUSTRALASIA AND POL-YNESIA	175	....	33,128	435	3,771	75,153
Aggregate........	17,200	35,000	2,818,414	33,522	79,643	5,069,109

[1] All bodies bearing the name Methodist, the Evangelical Association, and the United Brethren, both of which Churches are Methodistic in origin, polity, and doctrine.

[2] "Christian Advocate," January 26, 1860, and "Ecclesiastical Year-Book," for 1860, by Professor Schem.

[3] Exclusive of members in mission fields, who are reckoned in countries where they live.

[4] Including six or seven thousand who should be reckoned in mission fields, but we are unable to distribute them for lack of sufficient data.

[5] "Whitaker's London Almanac," 1881.

TABLE XXIX.

MORAVIANS IN THE WHOLE WORLD,[1] 1880.

COUNTRIES.	Congregations.	Ministers.	Communicants.
AMERICA:			
United States......................	59	75	9,491
Greenland and Labrador..............	12	62	1,245
North American Indians..............	4	9	124
West Indies, Barbadoes..............	41	89	14,576
Central America.....................	6	16	242
South America......................	16	72	5,619
Total *America*	138	323	31,297
EUROPE:			
British Isles	38	57	3,361
Bohemia	4	2	153
German Provinces...................	26	}	5,878
Diaspora and other Home Agents. { Germany, Prussia	28	} 162	} 115
Scandinavia	7		
Russia, Baltic, Poland	14		
Switzerland...................	6		
Total *Europe*	123	221	9,507
AFRICA	15	64	2,588
ASIA..............................	3	7	15
AUSTRALASIA........................	2	6	30
Missionaries and their families...........	...	....	317
Aggregate	281	621	43,754

[1] Moravian Year-Book, 1881.

TABLE XXX.

PRESBYTERIANS[1] IN THE WHOLE WORLD, 1880.

COUNTRIES.	Churches.[2]	Ministers.	Communicants.
AMERICA:			
United States	[1]11,613	[1]9,082	[1]1,017,848
British Provinces	[2]2,303	704	125,000
Mexico...........................	[3]22	4	4,207
West Indies......................	[2]54	27	7,228
South America	[2]20	19	1,189
Total *America*	14,012	9,836	1,155,472

TABLE XXX, (Continued.)

COUNTRIES.	Churches.[2]	Ministers.	Communi-cants.
EUROPE :			
England......................	[3] 276	[3] 258	[3] 54,135
Scotland	3,109	3,230	1,005,654
Ireland......................	714	663	109,207
Total *British Isles*...........	4,099	4,151	1,168,996
Belgium........................	28	18	....
Holland......................	[2] 1,651	1,885	....
Switzerland	....	[3] 382	[3] 6,437
Austria........................	[2] 3,405	2,123	[3] 72,628
France	....	[3] 51	[3] 3,700
Spain	....	5	224
Italy and Piedmont.............	[2] 141	83	16,571
Total *Europe*	9,324	8,698	1,268,556
ASIA :			
Western Asia....................	....	50	2,251
India and Ceylon...............	[3] 110	139	5,696
China.........................	....	64	4,837
Japan.........................	....	25	1,189
East Indies	....	[3] 31	[4] 85,500
Total *Asia*....................	110	309	99,473
AFRICA........................	....	[3] 108	[3] 32,234
AUSTRALASIA	[3] 577	[3] 631	[3] 22,100
POLYNESIA	....	[3] 51	[3] 872
Aggregate	[3] 24,023	[3] 19,633	[3] 2,578,707

NOTE.—The data for the above table have been collected from Annual Minutes of the various Presbyterian bodies in the United States, from the Annual Reports of their Foreign Missionary Societies, and from the just-published Reports of the late Pan-Presbyterian Council, (held in Philadelphia, in September, 1880.) See pp. 611 and 959-964 of the latter volume.

[1] Including the (Dutch) Reformed Church, because essentially Presbyterian, and all bodies having the name Presbyterian.

[2] In some instances congregations are included with Churches.

[3] These items are incomplete, because only partially reported.

[4] Probably includes baptized children.

TABLE XXXI.

NEW JERUSALEM (Swedenborg) CHURCH IN THE WHOLE WORLD.

COUNTRIES.	1860.[1]			1880.[2]		
	Soci-eties.	Minis-ters.	Commu-nicants.	Soci-eties.	Minis-ters.	Commu-nicants.
United States..........	57	54	1,960	93	89	3,994
Canada	...	...	....	5	2	....
England and Scotland ..	[4]69	...	....	[3]70	[3]34	....
Germany[5].............	...	...	....	12	1	....
Austria[5]...............	...	...	....	2	1	....
Switzerland[5]...........	...	...	....	6	...	....
France[5]................	...	...	....	3	...	....
Norway[5]..............	...	...	....	2	...	....
Sweden[5]	...	...	....	9	1	....
Denmark[5].............	...	...	....	3	...	....
Italy[5].................	...	...	....	3	1	....
West Indies[5]	...	...	....	1	...	....
South Africa[5]..........	...	...	....	1	...	....
Mauritius[5].............	...	...	....	1	...	....
Australasia[5]	...	...	....	11	3	....
Total..........	126	54	1,960	222	132	3,994

[1] From Professor Schem's " American Ecclesiastical Year-Book," 1860.
[2] From the " Journal of the General Convention of the New Jerusalem Church in the United States for 1880."
[3] " Manual and Year-Book of the London Association of the New Church," '81.
[4] Including twenty-one not in connection with the General Association.
[5] After diligent search we are unable to fill any of the above blanks.

TABLE XXXII.

UNITARIAN SOCIETIES[1] IN THE WHOLE WORLD.

COUNTRIES.	1840.	1860.	1880.
United States[2]......................	230	254	335
British Possessions in North America[2]..	1	2	2
England................................	242[3]	235[4]	
Scotland...............................	6[3]	6[4]	
South Wales...........................	25[3]	30[4]	370[5]
Ireland	36[3]	42[4]	
European Continent[6]..................	...	...	...
Asia[7]................................	...	1	1
Aggregate	540	567	708

[1] We can get no other statistics.
[2] From the Year-Books of the American Unitarians.
[3] From " Unitarianism Exhibited," London, 1846.
[4] From article on " Unitarianism," Appleton's " Cyclopedia," first edition.
[5] " Whitaker's Almanac," London, 1880, which gives 290 chapels and 80 stations.
[6] No statistics. The Unitarian population in Transylvania has been reported
at 120,000.
[7] One Unitarian mission in Calcutta.

TABLE XXXIII.

SUNDAY-SCHOOLS IN THE WHOLE WORLD.

By E. Payson Porter,[1] Philadelphia.

COUNTRIES.	Sunday-Schools.	Teachers.	Scholars.	Total.
EUROPE :	.			
England and Wales.........	....	422,222	3,800,000	4,222,222
Scotland...................	....	47,972	494,533	542,505
Ireland....................	....	30,175	320,920	351,095
Total Great Britain	....	500,369	4,615,453	5,115,822
Norway....................	....	5,600	65,000	70,600
Sweden...................	100	15,000	150,000	165,000
Denmark..................	....	4,000	45,000	49,000
Germany	2,000	10,000	200,000	210,000
City of Berlin............	....	....	22,000	....
Holland...................	1,000	3,000	100,000	103,000
City of Amsterdam........	80	....	9,500	....
City of Rotterdam........	70	....	8,000	....
Belgium	50	112	1,100	1,212
France	1,080	4,500	45,000	49,500
City of Paris.............	90	818	8,414	....
Switzerland	776	5,320	76,260	81,580
French Switzerland.......	601	3,128	36,260	....
German Switzerland.......	175	2,192	40,000	....
Italy.....................	150	600	10,000	10,600
Spain.....................	100	400	8,000	8,400
Portugal	30	100	2,000	2,100
Not enumerated above.......	....	1,000	15,000	16,000
ASIA :				
Persia....................	68	272	3,000	3,272
Other portions of Asia.......	....	1,500	35,000	36,500
AFRICA...................	....	300	15,000	15,300
NORTH AMERICA :				
United States.............	82,261	886,328	6,623,124	7,509,452
British American Provinces...	5,640	42,912	326,330	369,242
Other portions of N. America.	600	2,500	25,000	27,500
SOUTH AMERICA.............	....	3,000	150,000	153,000

TABLE XXXIII, (Continued.)

COUNTRIES.	Sunday-Schools.	Teach-ers.	Scholars.	Total.
OCEANICA:				
Australia..................	1,300	12,000	100,000	112,000
City of Melbourne........	70	1,300	14,000	....
Tasmania.................	....	1,200	11,800	....
New Zealand..............	300	3,000	30,000	33,000
Reported in (London) Union	121	1,130	10,527	....
Hawaiian Islands...........	....	1,300	15,000	16,300
Other portions of Polynesia ..	....	1,500	25,000	25,600

RECAPITULATION.

COUNTRIES.	Teachers.	Scholars.	Total.
Europe......................	550,001	5,332,813	5,882,814
Asia........................	1,772	38,000	39,772
Africa......................	300	15,000	15,300
North America..............	931,740	6,974,454	7,906,194
South America..............	3,000	150,000	153,000
Oceanica	17,800	170,000	187,800
World..................	1,504,613	12,680,267	14,184,880

[1] The above statistics were reported by Mr. Porter to the Robert Raikes' Centennial Convention, in London, England, June 28 to July 3, 1880. They comprise those of the Evangelical denominations. They are incomplete; full returns would swell all the aggregates.

TABLE XXXIV.
FOREIGN MISSIONS OF THE UNITED STATES.—1850.

Countries.	Missions.	Principal Stations.	Working Forces. Ord. Mission's, For'n and Nat.	Assistants.	Native Assistants.	Total Laborers.	Communicants.	Day-schools.	Scholars.
EUROPE:									
Greece	2	3	3	5	3	11	10	3	510
Missions not reporting....	..	..	..	..	1	1	....	..	....
Turkey in Europe..........	1	3	7	8	10	25	105	..	....
Missions not reporting....	..	..	..	..	..	....	..	1	1
Germany..................	1	40	40	..	80	120	5,000	..	....
Missions not reporting....	..	..	..	1	..	1	....	1	1
France	2	13	14	..	..	14	300	..	....
Missions not reporting....	..	..	..	2	2	4	....	2	2
Total *Europe*...........	6	59	64	13	93	170	5,415	3	510
Missions not reporting..	..	..	..	3	3	6	....	4	4
ASIA:									
Western...................	4	16	32	39	32	103	463	62	1,107
Missions not reporting....	..	..	..	..	1	1	1	..	1
India	5	12	60	52	100	212	575	111	4,950
Missions not reporting....	..	..	..	..	1	1	2	..	....
China	8	13	41	35	16	92	50	16	340
Missions not reporting....	.	..	..	2	5	7	2	2	2
Siam, Burmah.............	3	10	29	32	124	185	7,492	82	2,143
Ceylon	1	4	11	16	22	49	345	102	4,373
Total *Asia*..............	21	55	173	174	294	641	8,925	373	12,913
Missions not reporting..	..	..	..	2	7	9	5	2	3
AFRICA:									
Western..................	7	10	40	40	12	92	1,333	45	1,591
Missions not reporting....	..	..	1	..	4	5	1	..	....
Southern	1	12	12	20	..	32	78	8	185
Missions not reporting....	..	..	..	..	1	1	....	..	....
Total *Africa*	8	22	52	60	12	124	1,411	53	1,776
Missions not reporting..	..	..	1	..	5	6	1	..	....
AMERICA:									
Indians in U. S.............	37	50	110	117	22	249	8,220	54	1,749
Missions not reporting....	..	..	..	2	2	4	2	2	2
South America	1	1	1	..	..	1	51	..	...
Missions not reporting....	..	..	..	1	1	2	....	1	1
West Indies	2	2	15	..	..	15	42	6	250
Missions not reporting....	..	..	..	1	2	3	1	..	....
Total *America*...........	40	53	126	117	22	265	8,313	63	1,999
Missions not reporting..	..	..	..	4	5	9	3	3	3
OCEANICA[1]...................	2	7	23	39	5	67	23,102	393	12,012
Missions not reporting....	..	..	..	..	1	1	1	1	1
Aggregate...............	77	196	438	403	426	1,267	47,266	883	29,210
Missions not reporting..	..	..	1	9	21	31	10	10	11

NOTE.—The above table has been collated and arranged from data collected by Rev. R. Baird, D.D., ("Christian Retrospect and Register,") with a few corrections and additions.

[1] Confined to Polynesia.

TABLE XXXV.
FOREIGN MISSIONS OF THE UNITED STATES, 1880.[1]

COUNTRIES.	Missions.	Stations.		Working Forces.			Communicants.	Day-schools.	Scholars.
		Principal Stations.	Sub-stations.	Ord. Missionaries, For'n and Native.	Lay Helpers.	Total Laborers.			
EUROPE:									
Scandinavia........	5	204	475	293	104	397	32,051	....	....
Missions not repor'g	..	1	....	1	2	3	....	5	5
Germany and Switzerland............	4	126	1,493	123	161	284	44,988	....	....
Missions not repor'g	..	1	1	1	1	2	....	4	4
France............	2	8	26	1	14	15	773	....	....
Missions not repor'g	..	..	1	1	1	2	....	2	2
Spain and Portugal..	2	5	9	5	11	16	280	....	....
Missions not repor'g	..	..	....	....	....	....	....	2	2
Italy	3	12	15	26	6	32	772	....	....
Missions not repor'g	..	..	2	1	1	2	1	3	3
Austria	1	2	3	3	10	13	....	....	....
Missions not repor'g	..	..	....	....	....	....	1	1	1
Greece.............	3	5	....	4	15	19	9	....	700
Missions not repor'g	..	..	3	1	....	1	2	3	2
Bulgaria and Turkey in Europe........	3	6	18	18	44	62	45	....	....
Missions not repor'g	..	..	1	....	....	...	1	3	3
Total *Europe*......	23	368	2,039	473	365	838	78,918	....	700
Missions not repor'g	..	2	8	5	5	10	5	23	22
ASIA :									
Western Asia	6	23	380	334	517	851	9,077	292	15,751
Missions not repor'g	..	..	1	....	1	1	1	2	1
India	15	86	336	249	1,176	1,425	34,687	531	21,045
Missions not repor'g	..	..	3	1	....	1	1	2	2
Ceylon	1	7	15	13	54	67	922	130	7,688
Burmah and Siam...	2	15	440	90	450	540	21,594	173	5,233
Missions not repor'g	..	..	1	....	....	....	....	....	....
China	17	88	232	186	606	792	7,968	83	2,697
Missions not repor'g	..	..	1	....	....	....	1	6	....
Japan..............	7	20	57	82	183	265	2,222	13	1,102
Missions not repor'g	..	..	2	....	...	...	1	3	1
Total *Asia*	48	239	1,460	954	2,986	3,940	76,470	1,222	53,516
Missions not repor'g	..	..	8	1	1	2	4	13	4
AFRICA :									
Western Africa......	8	25	63	57	137	194	3,408	24	1,406
Missions not repor'g	..	..	3	....	....	....	2	3	2
Southern Africa.....	1	8	11	10	71	81	630	29	937
Egypt	1	6	42	14	147	161	985	44	2,218
Total *Africa*	10	39	116	81	355	436	5,023	97	4,561
Missions not repor'g	..	..	3	....	....	....	2	3	2
NORTH AMERICA :									
Chinese in California.	4	4	..	7	38	45	413	20	1,841
Missions not repor'g	..	1	4	1	....	1	1	....	....
Indians	26	55	152	152	211	363	15,207	17	1,152
Missions not repor'g	..	1	3	1	2	3	1	4	10
Mexico	6	23	78	53	98	151	8,919	16	1,551
Missions not repor'g	..	..	3	1	....	1	....	3	2

TABLE XXXV, (Continued.)

COUNTRIES.	Missions.	Stations. Principal Stations.	Sub-stations.	Working Forces. Ordained Missionaries, Foreign and Native.	Lay Helpers.	Total Laborers.	Communicants.	Day-schools.	Scholars.
SOUTH AMERICA :									
Brazil, Guiana	5	15	9	16	38	54	1,339	4	605
Missions not repor'g	..	..	3	....	3	3	....	4	3
Columbia...........	1	1	....	....	1	1	23	1	29
Missions not repor'g	..	..	1	1	....	1	....	....	....
Argentine Republic..	1	3	12	6	9	15	462	3	100
Chili	1	4	....	6	7	13	92	4	65
Missions not repor'g	..	..	1	....	....	....	....	....	....
WEST INDIES	1	3	10	11	19	30	362	6	160
Total *America*	45	108	261	251	421	672	26,817	71	5,503
Missions not repor'g	..	2	15	4	5	9	2	11	15
POLYNESIA	3	4	45	33	40	73	17,904	2	1,545
Missions not repor'g	..	..	....	....	....	....	....	12	12
Aggregate.........	129	758	3,925	1,792	4,167	5,959	205,132	1,392	65,825
Missions not repor'g	..	4	34	10	11	21	13	62	55

[1] Collected from reports for 1880.

TABLE XXXVI.

FOREIGN MISSIONS OF EUROPE AND AMERICA, 1830.

COUNTRIES.	Missions.	Principal Stations.	Working Forces. Ordained Missionaries, Foreign and Native.	Assistants.	Native Assistants.	Total Laborers.	Communicants.	Scholars in Day-schools.
EUROPE :								
Greece, Malta, Smyrna, etc.	4	4	10	15	..	25	...	...
ASIA :								
Western Asia..................	3	4	14	10	..	24	..	...
Siberia......................	1	3	5	2	..	7	...	...
China........................	3	3	8	7	..	15	2	...
India	10	111	100	101	292	495	1,967	27,922
Burmah, Siam.................	3	6	15	16	9	40	100	671
Ceylon.......................	4	20	26	33	91	150	1,000	9,900
Indian Archipelago...........	3	14	17	58	3	78	...	4,279
Total *Asia*..................	27	161	185	227	397	809	3,069	41,872

TABLE XXXVI, (Continued.)

COUNTRIES.	Missions.	Principal Stations.	Working Forces.				Communicants.	Scholars in Day-school.
			Ordained Missionaries, Foreign and Native.	Assistants.	Native Assistants.	Total Laborers.		
AFRICA:								
Western Africa	9	26	21	19	10	50	1,117	1,800
South "	6	43	65	50	..	115	1,486	2,128
Egypt, Abyssinia	2	2	5	..	..	5	...	63
Madagascar, Mauritius	2	2	5	6	..	11	...	3,429
Total *Africa*	19	73	96	10	10	181	2,603	7,420
AMERICA:								
North American Indians	26	145	200	317	..	517	7,124	3,000
South America, Guiana	5	8	13	..	8	21	2,167	1,000
West Indies	31	70	118	90	7	215	52,876	9,000
Total *America*	62	223	331	407	15	753	62,167	13,000
OCEANICA:								
Australasia	3	5	7	22	..	29	...	199
Polynesia	7	36	27	30	38	95	2,450	18,165
Total *Oceanica*	10	41	34	52	38	124	2,450	18,364
Aggregate	122	502	656	776	460	1,892	70,289	80,656

NOTE.—The above table has been collated and arranged from data furnished, by a very able survey of the religious condition of the world, in the "American Quarterly Register," August, 1830, pp. 25–60, from the pen of that eminent scholar, Rev. B. B. Edwards, D.D. It is not presumed to be absolutely accurate at every point, nor is it complete, there being numerous omissions of important items, which could not be supplied; but it is a close approximate to a full exhibit, and the best that can now be obtained for that period. It is an understatement, as are also the tables for later periods. This will appear more clearly on examination of the table for 1880, where the number of missions not reporting given items is carefully specified.

TABLE XXXVII.

FOREIGN MISSIONS OF EUROPE AND AMERICA, 1850.

COUNTRIES.	Missions.	Principal Stations.	Working Forces.				Communicants.	Day-schools.	Scholars.
			Ordained Missionaries, For. and Nat.	Assistants.	Native Assistants.	Total Laborers.			
EUROPE:									
Germany..............	1	40	40	...	80	120	5,000	....	....
France................	2	13	14	...	...	14	300	....	....
Greece...............	2	3	1	1	9	11	14	5	462
Turkey in Europe	3	6	10	14	7	31	115	1	510
Total *Europe*........	8	62	65	15	96	176	5,429	6	972
ASIA:									
Western...............	5	20	44	51	41	136	467	61	2,305
India.................	18	133	359	97	1,591	2,047	24,878	1,111	47,897
China................	12	23	63	41	18	122	67	20	269
Siam, Burmah..........	3	8	30	38	125	193	7,493	83	2,303
Ceylon...............	5	27	53	16	324	393	2,651	345	11,914
Indian Archipelago......	3	6	6	...	5	11	24	3	390
Total *Asia*..........	46	217	555	243	2,104	2,902	35,580	1,623	65,078
AFRICA:									
Western...............	12	28	93	170	75	338	9,625	152	13,631
Southern	11	130	214	155	8	377	12,016	60	20,102
Eastern	3	5	8	1	4	13	18	3	178
Total *Africa*........	26	163	315	326	87	728	21,659	215	33,911
NORTH AMERICA:									
Indians...............	40	62	235	119	70	424	24,703	89	2,886
Greenland and Labrador .	2	10	53	...	....	53	1,082	....	3,057
SOUTH AMERICA..........	4	15	15	6	5	26	1,521	15	1,153
West Indies	40	84	266	20	344	630	71,984	135	9,869
Total *America*......	86	171	569	145	419	1,133	99,290	239	16,965
OCEANICA:									
Australasia.............	8	15	100	10	515	625	13,751	214	13,694
Polynesia..............	4	72	68	44	52	164	35,248	442	17,319
Total *Oceanica*	12	87	168	54	567	789	48,999	656	31,013
Aggregate...........	178	700	1,672	783	3,293	5,728	210,957	2,739	147,939

NOTE.—The above table has been prepared from data furnished by Rev. Robert Baird, D.D., ("Christian Retrospect and Register," Appendix,) with a few corrections, and some omissions supplied. It is not presumed to be absolutely correct, some items being frequently omitted in the reports of some of the Missionary Societies, and some having methods of making up their statistics very different from others. The aggregates are believed to be short of the full numbers. But the table is worthy of confidence, as a close approximation to the true facts, and the best that can be obtained for that period.

TABLE XXXVIII.

Foreign Missions of Europe and America, 1880.

Countries.	Missions.	Principal Stations.	Sub-stations.	Working Forces.			Communicants.	Hearers or Adherents.	Number of Day-schools.	Pupils.
				Ordain'd Mins. Nat. and For.	Lay Assistants.	Total.				
NORTH AMERICA:										
Greenland, 1880 ..	1	6	....	23	61	84	783	1,533	....	....
Miss. not repor'g	..	..	1	..	....	...	....	....	1	1
Addi'l (Dan.) 1873	1	10	....	8	57	65	....	9,000	....	....
Miss. not repor'g	..	..	1	..	....	...	1	....	1	1
Labrador, 1880....	1	6	....	39	48	87	462	1,260	....	....
Miss. not repor'g	..	..	1	..	....	...	....	....	1	1
Brit. Domin'n, 1880	3	244	402	680	71	751	55,598	90,134	20	836
Miss. not repor'g	..	1	2	..	2	2	....	1	2	2
Additional, 1873..	10	318	137	299	1,363	1,662	20,657	46,849	....	....
Miss. not repor'g	..	2	8	1	5	6	6	8	10	10
Indians, 1880	27	59	152	161	223	384	15,331	....	17	1,470
Miss. not repor'g	..	1	4	1	2	3	1	27	5	10
Chinese, 1880.....	4	4	....	7	38	45	413	....	20	1,841
Miss. not repor'g	..	1	4	1	....	1	1	4	....	1
Mexico, 1830......	6	23	78	53	98	151	8,919	....	16	1,551
Miss. not repor'g	..	..	3	1	....	1	....	6	3	2
Cen. America, 1880	2	7	18	20	58	78	1,328	4,030	10	817
Miss. not repor'g	..	..	1	..	....	....	....	....	1	1
West Indies, 1880.	25	261	418	295	1,295	1,590	105,030	179,248	285	29,499
Miss. not repor'g	..	4	5	..	2	2	2	9	11	9
Additional, 1873..	3	13	9	17	16	33	3,312	....	18	1,335
Miss. not repor'g	..	..	2	..	2	2	1	3	1	1
Total *N. America*	83	951	1,214	1,602	3,328	4,930	211,833	332,054	386	37,349
Miss. not repor'g	..	9	32	4	13	17	12	58	36	38
SOUTH AMERICA:										
Guiana, 1880	4	31	65	89	503	592	11,065	47,585	41	4,657
Miss. not repor'g	..	..	3	1	1	2	....	....	2	2
Brazil, 1880.......	5	15	9	16	38	54	1,339	....	4	605
Miss. not repor'g	..	..	3	..	3	3	....	5	4	3
Columbia, 1880 ...	1	1	....	..	1	1	23	....	1	29
Miss. not repor'g	..	..	1	1	....	1	....	1	....	....
Argentine Rep. '80	1	3	12	(	9	15	462	....	3	100
Miss. not repor'g	..	..	..	..	....	....	....	1	..	..
Chili, 1880........	1	4	....	(	7	13	92	....	4	65
Miss. not repor'g	..	..	1	..	....	....	....	1	....	....
Total *S. America*.	12	54	86	117	558	675	12,981	47,585	53	5,456
Miss. not repor'g	..	..	....	2	4	6	....	8	6	5
Total *America* ..	95	1,005	1,300	1,719	3,886	5,605	224,814	379,639	439	42,805
Miss. not repor'g	..	9	40	6	17	23	12	66	42	43
EUROPE:										
Ireland, (Pap.,) '80	1	29	370	34	51	85	4,076	9,179	22	1,076
Additional 1873..	5	70	....	90	336	426	623	....	313	6,593
Miss. not repor'g	..	1	5	..	1	1	4	5	2	4
Engl'd, (Jews,) '80	1	4	....	8	20	28	....	....	..	....
Miss. not repor'g	..	.	1	..	....	....	1	1	1	1

TABLE XXXVIII, (Continued.)

COUNTRIES.	Missions.	Principal Stations.	Sub-stations.	Working Forces.			Communicants.	Hearers or Adherents.	Number of Day Schools.	Pupils.
				Ordain'd Mins. Nat. and For.	Lay Assistants.	Total.				
EUROPE :										
Denmark, Sweden, Norway, 1880...	6	205	493	300	110	410	32,696	....	....	300
Miss. not repor'g.	..	1	....	1	2	3	....	6	6	5
Germany, Austria, Switzerl'd, 1880.	7	176	1,699	169	348	517	47,155	9,506	3	210
Miss. not repor'g.	..	1	2	1	1	2	2	6	6	6
France, 1880......	6	35	218	41	169	210	2,957	12,300	13	512
Miss. not repor'g.	..	..	2	1	2	3	2	2	3	3
Additional, 1873 .	1	2	....	2	....	2	79	115	....	....
Miss. not repor'g.	..	..	1	....	1	1	....	....	1	1
Spain and Portugal, 1880.........	4	10	20	19	58	77	902	2,250	24	2,359
Miss. not repor'g.	..	..	1	....	1	1	....	3	3	2
Additional, 1873 .	8	19	12	26	32	58	812	6,000	3	199
Miss. not repor'g.	..	..	5	....	4	4	6	5	7	7
Italy, Naples, and Malta, 1880.....	10	110	103	59	65	124	4,658	2,688	11	780
Miss. not repor'g.	..	..	5	3	5	8	2	7	7	7
Greece, 1880......	4	6	....	4	15	19	9	....	....	700
Miss. not repor'g.	..	..	4	1	1	2	3	4	4	3
Bulgaria and Turkey in Europe,'80	5	9	19	24	62	86	69	38	5	628
Miss. not repor'g.	..	..	2	....	....	....	2	4	3	3
Additional, 1873 .	5	7	....	9	19	28	....	....	....	....
Miss. not repor'g.	..	..	5	....	....	....	5	5	5	5
Total *Europe*...	63	682	2,934	785	1,285	2,070	94,036	42,076	394	13,366
Miss. not repor'g.	..	3	33	7	18	25	27	48	48	47
AFRICA :										
South Africa, 1880	26	217	1,100	319	2,020	2,339	45,308	152,677	392	20,191
Miss. not repor'g.	..	2	12	....	3	3	....	5	12	11
Additional, 1873 .	24	151	112	148	177	325	13,888	18,795	23	5,893
Miss. not repor'g.	..	2	17	7	12	19	11	19	23	18
Middle and Western Africa, 1880.	24	116	454	177	1,114	1,291	25,846	79,564	263	15,246
Miss. not repor'g.	..	..	7	....	2	2	6	15	7	6
Additional, 1873 .	7	19	....	69	174	243	7,118	10,400	37	3,031
Miss. not repor'g.	..	1	7	....	4	4	1	5	4	5
North-east. Africa	5	16	45	20	188	208	1,320	....	52	3,388
Miss. not repor'g.	..	..	2	....	1	1	2	4	1	1
Additional, 1873 .	11	25	62	35	36	71	17	....	17	1,121
Miss. not repor'g.	..	2	9	2	2	4	10	11	7	5
Madagascar, 1880.	2	29	1,152	97	7,345	7,442	70,187	253,402	882	48,050
Miss. not repor'g.	..	..	1	....	....	....	...	....	1	1
Additional, 1873 .	1	5	9	19	4	23	288	158	9	704
Mauritius, 1880 ...	2	8	....	10	36	46	456	2,169	21	757
Miss. not repor'g.	..	..	2	....	....	....	....	....	1	....
St. Helena, 1880..	1	3	....	3	....	3	273	910	....	....
Miss. not repor'g.	..	..	1	....	1	1	....	....	1	1
Total *Africa*...	103	589	3,934	897	11,094	1,991	164,701	518,075	1,696	98,381
Miss. not repor'g.	..	7	58	9	25	34	30	59	57	48

TABLE XXXVIII, (Continued.)

COUNTRIES.	Missions.	Principal Stations.	Sub-stations.	Ordain'd Mins. Nat. and For.	Lay Assistants.	Total.	Communicants.	Hearers or Adherents.	Number of Day Schools.	Pupils.
				Working Forces.						
ASIA:										
Western Asia. 1880	13	33	383	348	581	929	10,380	1,781	303	17,390
Miss. not repor'g.	..	..	5	....	2	2	4	9	4	3
Additional. 1873	10	13	...?	17	152	160	....	....	....	220
Miss. not repor'g.	..	3	10	2	6	8	10	10	10	9
India, 1880	44	342	1,002	764	5,313	6,077	80,975	209,966	2,721	135,054
Miss. not repor'g.	..	3	20	3	5	8	8	12	11	5
Additional, 1873 .	22	7?	30	158	325	483	16,562	21,764	180	6,250
Miss. not repor'g.	..	..	18	3	6	9	6	12	6	8
Burmah, Siam, '80	2	15	440	90	450	540	21,594	....	173	5,233
Miss. not repor'g.	..	..	1	....	....	....	....	2	....	....
China, 1880.......	29	158	465	302	1,088	1,390	19,434	9,436	161	4,926
Miss. not repor'g.	..	..	7	....	3	3	2	25	12	5
Additional, 1873 .	3	15	22	24	57	81	333	....	3	36
Miss. not repor'g.	..	..	1	....	1	1	1	3	1	2
Japan, 1880.......	11	29?	58	97	201	298	2,436	297	22	1,248
Miss. not repor'g.	..	..	5	....	1	1	1	9	6	4
Ceylon, 1880......	6	129	170	125	1,005	1,130	7,278	14,288	667	35,408
Miss. not repor'g.	..	..	2	....	....	....	....	2	1	1
East Indies, 1880 .	14	56	....	48	17	65	85,814	63,754	13	11,518
Miss. not repor'g.	..	11	14	7	....	7	10	....	10	11
Additional, 1873 .	21	36	....	60	77	137	879	20,400	22	575
Miss. not repor'g.	..	11	21	10	16	26	19	20	16	18
Total *Asia*.....	175	902	2,570	2,033	9,266	11,299	245,685	341,686	4,265	217,858
Miss. not repor'g.	..	28	104	25	40	65	61	104	77	66
OCEANICA:										
Australasia, 1880..	17	1,251	891	429	1,785	2,214	33,143	229,955	26	3,658
Miss. not repor'g.	..	2	12	....	11	11	2	6	14	11
Additional, 1873 .	25	293	133	374	341	715	19,214	80,474	....	859
Miss. not repor'g.	..	3	19	2	18	20	11	18	25	23
Polynesia, 1880 ...	24	1,032	414	422	6,105	6,527	75,006	218,691	2,425	68,675
Miss. not repor'g.	..	..	6	2	....	6	8	4	8	8
Additional, 1873 .	2	11	33	37	94	131	733	3,000	71	2,000
Miss. not repor'g.	..	..	1	....	1	1	1	1	....	1
Total *Oceanica*.	68	2,587	1,471	1,262	8,325	9,587	128,096	532,120	2,522	75,192
Miss. not repor'g.	..	5	38	4	36	40	18	33	47	43
Aggregate....	504	5,765	12,209	6,696	33,856	40,552	857,332	1,813,596	9,316	447,602
Miss. not repor'g.	..	52	273	51	136	187	148	310	271	247

NOTE.—The above table is not quite complete. The author, not having many of the reports of the Missionary Societies of the European Continent, for 1880, has supplied this lack with the *additional* for 1873 (see above) from a semi-official source. The statistics of the British and American Societies for 1880 are nearly complete. The reader is referred to the chapter on Foreign Missions. The full fruitage of Protestant foreign missions should strictly take in all the religious life of Canada, Australia, West Indies, etc.

TABLE XXXIX.

INDEPENDENT STATES UNDER CHRISTIAN GOVERNMENTS,[1] 1876.

States, inclusive of Colonies and Dependencies.	Sqr. Miles.	Inhabitants.
PROTESTANT STATES.		
British Empire	8,755,159	283,604,841
German Empire	208,729	41,060,864
United States.......................	3,611,844	38,555,983
Netherlands	674,100	26,569,000
Sweden and Norway	294,030	6,063,800
Madagascar........................	228,600	5,000,000
Switzerland	15,992	2,669,147
Denmark...........................	54,308	1,988,000
Liberia	9,567	718,000
Transvaal Republic	114,000	300,000
Orange Free State	42,479	57,000
Sandwich Islands....................	7,629	56,877
Australian Isles, exclusive of European possessions.........................	320,750	1,926,100
Total *Protestant*.................	14,337,187	408,569,612
ROMAN CATHOLIC STATES.		
France	577,195	41,736,000
Austro-Hungary.....................	240,954	35,904,435
Italy	114,409	26,801,154
Spain	316,075	25,196,100
Brazil	3,288,100	10,296,238
Mexico............................	741,823	9,158,247
Portugal...........................	741,625	8,028,500
Belgium	11,373	5,253,821
Colombia...........................	320,738	2,894,992
Peru...............................	503,468	2,500,000
Chili...............................	126,034	2,074,000
Bolivia	500,880	2,000,000
Argentine Confederation..............	838,605	1,812,500
Venezuela	403,272	1,784,194
Ecuador	248,300	1,308,000
Guatemala..........................	40,778	1,194,000
San Salvador	7,335	600,000
Hayti	9,233	572,000
Honduras...........................	47,092	350,000
Uruguay	69,800	300,000
Nicaragua	58,169	250,000
Paraguay	56,714	221,079
Luxemburg	999	197,528

TABLE XXXIX, (Continued.)

States, inclusive of Colonies and Dependencies.	Sqr. Miles.	Inhabitants.
Costa Rica	21,433	185,000
San Domingo	19,959	136,500
Andorra	144	12,000
Lichtenstein	68	8,060
San Marino	24	7,816
Monaco	6	5,741
Total *Roman Catholic States*	9,304,605	180,787,905
EASTERN CHURCH STATES.		
Russian Empire	8,535,142	85,686,000
Roumania	46,710	4,500,000
Abyssinia	158,400	3,000,000
Greece	19,353	1,457,894
Servia	16,817	1,338,000
Montenegro	1,701	120,000
Total *Eastern Church States*	8,778,123	96,101,894
Aggregate under Christian govern'ts.	32,419,915	685,459,411

[1] These statistics were prepared in 1875. See "Methodist Quarterly," January, 1876. Professor Schem is the authority. Italy, France, and Mexico can hardly be said to be now under Papal governments, but they have been allowed to the Papists in this calculation. These governments are, however, not distinctively of this class. Transposing them to the class of Protestant States, which they are rapidly becoming, and we have the following exhibit:

	Area.	Inhabitants.
Protestant States	15,770,610	486,265,013
Roman Catholic States	7,871,178	103,093,504
Greek Church States	8,778,183	96,101,894

INDEX.

38